The Mystery Is History

A Hebraic Commentary and Historical Evaluation of the Apocalypse

Adam Drissel

FOREWORD

Consider what the believing world would be like without the most influential Biblical book in history – The Revelation, or Apocalypse. I reckon the fear of 'great tribulations,' propaganda about world-wide catastrophes and rumors of coming dragons, beasts and hideous giants, would not be nearly so prevalent – fueled as they are today by social media, loud preachers and fanatics. The Revelation *does* exist and portrays such events; there is no putting it back or away now. Every false interpretation imaginable has been brought forth and believed, even in this skeptical world.

What if Revelation was interpreted in its classical context? What if a proper reading indicated that such cataclysms had been fulfilled nineteen hundred, forty-seven years ago? What if such could be proven?

Decades ago, I taught a Futurist interpretation of The Revelation (I was actually rehashing prophecy "experts" from the TV). Coincidentally, I was also skimming Josephus' work entitled "The Jewish War." I discovered incidents in The Jewish War that were reminiscent of, even identical to those in The Revelation. I began marking these passages – and soon there were *many*. I began to see that the mystery of the Apocalypse was history written in purloined fashion. My soul began to rejoice in the holy spirit for revealing my liberty.

Skip to 2014: I became acquainted with a young Bible teacher: Adam Drissel of North Carolina. In short order, I discovered Adam is to "Bible mysteries" what a terrier is to rats. We talked of The Revelation. He expressed his Futurist views. I said to Adam, "The Mystery is History. Revelation has been fulfilled." He seemed disturbed and perplexed, and I was too – because he couldn't see it *my way!* So, we scheduled a friendly, online debate: Futurist v. Partial Preterist. Adam caught the scent. I felt certain then that he wouldn't lose it until he mastered his prey.

The present: Adam unveils his "secret book." He titles it, "The Mystery is History," *and here it is in your hands.* Prepare yourself! If you are a Revelation Futurist and full of apprehension and fear of the future, this could be the antidote to your antichrist. Treat the text as consecrated to and anointed by the Father. Don't miss reading a page or even a word. Keep your Bible and a copy of The Jewish War at hand; check and recheck Adam's conclusions; tell others – your family, your friends, your church – for you will be instilled with an anointing to set yourself and your world free of the vile threats of dragons, beasts and the end of the world. Receive your anointing, then do the work of an evangelist!

Rev. Dr. Jackson H. Snyder II
Editor, *The Nazarene Acts of the Apostles*

CONTENTS

PREFACE

Denial, anger, bargaining, depression and acceptance are generally known as the five stages of grief. Interestingly enough, however, those are the very same stages a diligent student of the scriptures will go through when faced with a belief or doctrine that goes against everything they've previously held dear. When I first heard the phrase, "The Mystery is History," my defenses were raised to high alert. There were aspects of the overall message that couldn't be denied as truth of course, even by the staunchest of Futurists. However, I refused to believe I had once again been deceived by the nameless, faceless masses declaring what truth is.

In realizing that I had blindly allowed deceit to take hold in this area of my walk of faith I was infuriated. My reaction to statements and facts presented to me was to attack the messenger. My blows were like boxing in the dark, though. I had no defense for my stance beyond "I just can't believe what you're saying to be true." Eventually I settled into the fact that denying facets of what I had been told was no longer possible. The evidence was right there before my eyes. However, I wasn't ready to let it all go. My bargaining consisted of me trying to squeeze the new truths I'd accepted into my nice doctrinal box. Then it would all make sense, right? No.

As more undeniable facts continued to present themselves before me I began to wonder if this was something that could ever truly be figured out. Would the rabbit hole ever end? Would I ever reach a place in my research where I could place my feet firmly on solid ground? It was at that point that a systematic review of the Apocalypse against the historical record became more than just a passing desire. It became a necessity. I *had* to understand what was going on here. There *had* to be something other than endless generations of cloudy and mystical speculations about the meaning and interpretation of the Apocalypse.

It was at that point that I accepted and embraced the fact that I was wrong in my previous understanding. That acceptance produced exactly what it had every other time I went through the five stages of ~~grief~~ "realizing the truth." It produced an elucidation of many of the scriptures that had just never made sense or were until then shrouded in mystery or biased and blindly accepted doctrine.

It is my hope that through this work many other students of the scriptures who have had their minds and spirits pricked on this topic will find here what is necessary to put all the pieces of the puzzle together. I am confident that the outcome will not only result in a deeper knowledge of the truth and more action-oriented faith, but also in a glorification of our heavenly Father Yahweh, through His son Yeshua the Messiah.

WORKS CITED
and
Abbreviations

Apollonius. Philostratus. *The Life of Apollonius of Tyana*. Trans. F. C. Conybeare, M.A. New York: The Macmillan Co., 1912. Print.

Beatus. Beatus of Liébana. *Sancti Beati Presbyteri Hispani Libanensis Ac Plurimas Utrisque Foederis Pagnias Commentria*. Work and Study by R. P. Doct. Henrici Florez. Madrid: Catholicae Majestatis Typographum, 1770. Print.

Bourgel. Bourgel, Jonathan. "The Jewish Christians' Move from Jerusalem as a Pragmatic Choice", in Dan Jaffé (ed). *Studies in Rabbinic Judaism and Early Christianity*, (AJEC 74; Leyden: Brill, 2010), p. 107-138.
<https://www.academia.edu/4909339/THE_JEWISH_CHRISTIANS_MOVE_FROM_JERUSALEM_AS_A_PRAGMATIC_CHOICE>

Campbell. Campbell, Duncan B. "Dating the Siege of Masada." *Zeitschrift Für Papyrologie Und Epigraphik*, vol. 73, 1988, pp. 156–158. Web. 14 July 2017. *JSTOR*, <www.jstor.org/stable/20186870>

Chilton. Chilton, David. *Days of Vengeance: An Exposition of the Book of Revelation*. Texas: Dominion Press, 1987. Print.

Clarke. Clarke, Adam. *The New Testament of our Lord and Saviour Jesus Christ with a Commentary and Critical Notes*. Volume I. New York: G. Lane & C. B. Tippett, 1846. Print.

Cotton. Cotton, Hannah M. "The Date of the Fall of Masada: The Evidence of the Masada Papyri." *Zeitschrift Für Papyrologie Und Epigraphik*, vol. 78, 1989, pp. 157–162. Web. 14 July 2017. *JSTOR*, <www.jstor.org/stable/20187128>

Desperez. Desperez, B. D., Rev. P. S. *Apocalypse Fulfilled in the Consummation of the Mosaic Economy and the Coming of the Son of Man.* London: Longman, Brown, Green and Longmans, 1855. Print.

Dio. Dio, Cassius. *Roman History by Cassius Dio.* Bill Thayer, n.d. Web. 27 June 2017. <http://penelope.uchicago.edu/Thayer/E/Roman/Texts/Cassius_Dio/home.html>

Edersheim. Edersheim, Alfred. *The Temple: Its Ministry and Services as they were at the time of Jesus Christ.* Boston: Ira Bradley & Co., 1881. Print.

Epiphanius, On Weights and Measures. Epiphanius. "Epiphanius of Salamis, On Weights and Measures." N.p., n.d. Web. 16 July 2017. <http://www.tertullian.org/fathers/epiphanius_weights_03_text.htm>

Epiphanius, Panarion. Epiphanius. *Panarion of Epiphanius of Salamis.* Trans. Frank Williams. Book I: Boston: Brill, 2009. Print. Books II & III: Boston: Brill, 2013. Print.

Eusebius. Eusebius. *Eusebius' Ecclesiastical History: Complete and Unabridged.* Trans. C. F. Cruse. Peabody, MA: Hendrickson, 2004. Print.

Farrar. Farrar, F.W. *The Early Days of Christianity.* Volume II. New York, London, and Paris: Casser, Petter, Galpin & Co., 1882. Print.

Felker. Felker, Stewart James. "First Century Coin of Nero Found in Jerusalem - the "Mark of the Beast"?" *Atheology.* N.p., 16 Sept. 2016. Web. 19 July 2017. <http://www.patheos.com/blogs/atheology/2016/09/first-century-coin-of-nero-found-in-jerusalem-the-mark-of-the-beast/>

Finegan. Finegan, Jack. *Handbook of Biblical Chronology.* Revised Ed. Peabody, MA: Hendrickson, 1998. Print.

Gesenius. Gesenius, Wilhelm. *Gesenius' Hebrew and Chaldee Lexicon to the Old Testament: Thesaurus and Other Works.* Trans. Samuel Prideaux Tregelles. London: S. Bagster, 1846. Print.

Gittin. *Babylonian Talmud: Tractate Gittin.* Trans. Maurice Simon. Ed. Rabbi Dr. Isidore Epstein. N.p., n.d. Web. 28 July 2017. <http://halakhah.com/gittin/index.html>

Irenaeus. Irenaeus. *Ante-Nicene Christian Library: Translations of the Writings of the Fathers Down to 325 A.D.* Ed. Rev. Alexander Roberts, D.D. and James Donaldson, L.L.D. Vol. 5. Edinburgh: T & T Clark, 1868. Print.

Jones. Jones, Floyd Nolen. *The Chronology of the Old Testament.* 16th Ed. Green Forest: New Leaf Publishing Group, 2007. Print.

Josephus, Antiquities. Josephus, Flavius. *The Works of Josephus: Complete and Unabridged.* Trans. William Whiston. Peabody, MA: Hendrickson, 1987. Print.

Josephus, Wars. Josephus, Flavius. *The Works of Josephus: Complete and Unabridged.* Trans. William Whiston. Peabody, MA: Hendrickson, 1987. Print.

Justin, Dialogue. Martyr, Justin. *Justin Martyr: The Dialogue With Trypho.* Trans. A. Lukyn Williams, D.D. New York: The Macmillan Co., 1930. Print.

Masterman. Masterman, E. W. G. "The Water Supply of Jerusalem, Ancient and Modern." *The Biblical World*, vol. 19, no. 2, 1902, pp. 87–112. *JSTOR*, <www.jstor.org/stable/3137039>

Muratorian. The Muratorian Fragment (about A.D. 170). *The Muratorian Fragment.* Ed. Hans Lietzmann. N.p., n.d. Web. 23 Aug. 2017. <http://www.bible-researcher.com/muratorian.html>

Newton. Newton, Isaac. *Observations on the Prophecies of Daniel and the Apocalypse of St. John: In Two Parts.* London: J. Darby, 1733. Print.

Origen, Celsus. Origen. *Ante-Nicene Christian Library: Translations of the Writings of the Fathers Down to 325 A.D.* Ed. Rev. Alexander Roberts, D.D. and James Donaldson, L.L.D. Vol. 10. Edinburgh: T & T Clark, 1869. Print.

Origen, Matthew. Origen. *Ante-Nicene Christian Library: Translations of the Writings of the Fathers Down to 325 A.D.* Ed. Rev. Alexander Roberts, D.D. and James Donaldson, L.L.D. Vol. 9. New York: Charles Scribner's Sons, 1906. Print.

Parker & Dubberstein. Parker, Richard A., Waldo H. Dubberstein. *Babylonian Chronology 626 B.C. – A.D. 75.* Eugene, OR: Wipf & Stock, 2007. Print.

Parkinson. Parkinson, James. *Manuscript Evidence and the English New Testament.* Web. 8 August 2017. <http://heraldmag.org/olb/Contents/reference/mscript1.pdf>

Recognitions, Latin. Clement of Alexandria. *Ante-Nicene Christian Library: Translations of the Writings of the Fathers Down to 325 A.D.* Ed. Rev. Alexander Roberts, D.D. and James Donaldson, L.L.D. Vol. 3. Edinburgh: T & T Clark, 1867. Print.

Recognitions, Syriac. Gebhardt, Joseph Glen. *The Syriac Clementine Recognitions and Homilies: The First Complete Translation of the Text.* Trans. Joseph Glen Gebhardt. Nashville: Grave Distractions Publications, 2014. Print.

Russell. Russell, James Stuart. *The Parousia: A Critical Inquiry into the New Testament Doctrine of our Lord's Second Coming.* London: Daldy, Isbister & Co., 1878. Print.

Severus. Severus, Sulpitius. *A Select Library of Nicene and Post-Nicene Fathers of the Christian Church.* Ed. Philip Schaff and Henry Wallace. Vol. 11. New York: Christian Literature, 1894. Print. Ser. 2.

Smith. William Smith, LLD. William Wayte. *A Dictionary of Greek and Roman Antiquities*. G. E. Marindin. Albemarle Street, London. John Murray. 1845. Print.

Strabo. Strabo. *The Geography of Strabo with an English Translation by Horace Leonard Jones, PH.D. LL. D.* Volume 8. Cambridge, MA: Harvard University Press, 1949. Print.

Suetonius. Tranquillus, C. Suetonius. *The Lives of the Twelve Caesars*. Trans. Alexander Thomson. Ed. J. E. Reed. Philadelphia: Gebbie, 1889. Print.

Tacitus, Annals. Tacitus, Cornelius. *The Annals*. Trans. William Jackson Brodribb and Alfred John Church. London: Macmillan, 1876. Print.

Tacitus, Histories. Tacitus, Cornelius. *The Histories*. Trans. Clifford H. Moore and John Jackson. Cambridge, MA: Harvard University Press, 1876. Print.

Thayer. Thayer, Joseph Henry, Carl Ludwig Wilibald Grimm, and Christian Gottlob Wilke. *A Greek-English Lexicon of the New Testament: Being Grimm's Wilke's Clavis Novi Testamenti*. New York: American Book, 1889. Print.

Victorinus. Victorinus Of Poetovio. "St Victorinus of Poetovio: Commentary on the Apocalypse." Translated by Kevin Edgecomb, Web. 4 August 2017. <earlychurchrevival.files.wordpress.com/2013/11/st-victorinus-of-poetovio-translated-by-kevin-edgecomb.pdf>

Webster. Webster, Noah. *An American Dictionary of the English Language*. San Francisco: Foundation for American Christian Education, 2002. Print.

Whiston. Whiston, William. *Primitive Christianity Revived: An Essay on the Apostolical Constitutions*. Vol. 3. London, 1711. Print.

INTRODUCTION

The Goal of This Work

Many have endeavored to publish a comprehensive commentary on the Apocalypse. Authors such as James Stuart Russell, David Chilton, Kenneth Gentry, and Moses Stuart have gone to great lengths to do just that. Their works have no doubt served as extremely valuable resources in unbiased inquiries into the proper interpretation and understanding of the Apocalypse. That, however, is not the goal of the present work. We do not plan to exhaust every possible facet of either the scriptures or the historical record in our search for the truth. Rather, in the end, we believe we would have presented such a preponderance of evidence that the conclusion and the true interpretation of the messages in the Apocalypse will be apparent and undeniable.

Our goal is to go beyond where the authors above have as it relates to the correspondence of the apocalyptic and prophetic imagery to real historical events. Ultimately, John's purpose in writing the message of Yahweh through Yeshua was to convey to his audience what they should expect to see occur around them in their very near future. He consistently uses terminology and imagery that his recipients would have readily recognized as references to the prophetic utterances in the scriptures that they were all too familiar with. Any potential uneducated interceptor of this clandestine correspondence would be none the wiser to its underlying message. Only those with "eyes to see and ears to hear" would truly be able to see through the imagery.

The Apocalypse, however, is a work above all others in its genre. If the historical record is scoured and studied in detail, then compared with the signs and symbols written by John, one can find real events that mirror them with such accuracy that the divine origin of the message can hardly be questioned. Where the other authors' commentaries have failed in their historical research is in their unnecessary and clumsy breaking of what is otherwise a flawless timeline. If, for instance, a record in a work of Josephus is referenced as it relates to a particular judgment or plague, it is often done so at a place where the timeline of the Apocalypse is already well past it. We plan to show that this is an unnecessary and confusing blunder that has caused many willing students of the scriptures to be blinded to the truth of the Apocalypse's historical fulfillment.

Anti-Dispensationalist

In addition to the above-stated goal, this work is built off of a different foundation and takes a different stance than any others we are aware of. Most, if not all other authors are what is known today as "dispensationalists." Simply put, they believe that the destruction of Jerusalem and the temple therein placed a permanent and official end to the "Mosaic Economy/Covenant," being widely defined as the end of Torah-observance. While various aspects of this are indeed true, the overall conclusion of the other authors leads inevitably to antinomianism, covenant-breaking, and in general a gross deviation from the teachings and examples of our Messiah, Yeshua of Nazareth. We intend to show within the text of the commentary itself or in various appendices that it was never the intent of our Creator Elohim, Yahweh Almighty, to give freedom to His chosen ones to break the aspects of his Torah[1] that were given as perpetual statues.

---

[1] Most commonly referred to as the "Law" or the "Mosaic Law." This is a misnomer as the Hebrew word תּוֹרָה, torah, comes from the word יָרָה, yarah,

In general, we believe that this colossal mistake is made because of an incorrect understanding of what the scriptures refer to as a "covenant." The phrase "make a covenant," though very common in the scriptures[2], is literally rendered "cut a covenant." This is due to the fact that a covenant made between two men involved the dividing of an animal asunder and the two parties walking between the animal with the understanding that the party that breaks the covenant will become as the animal. We even see this in covenants made between man and Elohim.

Genesis 15:8b-18a
(8) O Master Yahweh, whereby shall I know that I shall inherit it?
(9) And he said unto him, Take me a heifer three years old, and a she-goat three years old, and a ram three years old, and a turtle-dove, and a young pigeon.
(10) And he took him all these, and **divided them in the midst,** and laid each half over against the other: but the birds divided he not.
(11) And the birds of prey came down upon the carcasses, and Abram drove them away.
(12) And when the sun was going down, a deep sleep fell upon Abram; and, lo, a horror of great darkness fell upon him.
(13) And he said unto Abram, Know of a surety that your seed shall be sojourners in a land that is not theirs, and shall serve them; and they shall afflict them four hundred years;
(14) and also that nation, whom they shall serve, will I judge: and afterward shall they come out with great substance.
(15) But you shall go to your fathers in peace; you shall be buried in a good old age.
(16) And in the fourth generation they shall come here again: for the iniquity of the Amorite is not yet full.
(17) And it came to pass, that, when the sun went down, and it was dark, behold, **a smoking furnace, and a flaming torch that**

---

meaning "to teach, instruct," and is more correctly translated as "Teaching." See Gesenius. Entry #4 under the Hiphil stem for יָרָה. Page 366.
[2] Genesis 26:28; Exodus 34:10; Joshua 9:7; Jeremiah 31:31; et al.

passed between these pieces.
(18) In that day Yahweh made a covenant with Abram.

Yahweh, represented by a smoking furnace and flaming torch in Abraham's dream, passed through the divided animals sealing His covenant with him. The slaying of animals in sacrifice and sprinkling of blood in covenants such as that with Noah[3] and Israel[4] are no different.

The mistake made by most authors arises because they equate "covenant" with "Torah" (or "Law"). This is inaccurate in all regards. Webster defines "covenant" as follows.

> "A mutual consent or agreement of two or more persons [*parties*], to do or to forbear some act or thing."[5]

As it relates to the Torah, or the "Mosaic Law" as it is more commonly known, the covenant is the *agreement* between the people and Yahweh that they will keep the Torah. Let's restate that more concisely. The covenant is the *agreement* to keep the Torah, *not* the Torah itself. A breaking of the agreement doesn't break or nullify the Torah. Because understanding this truth is so essential to proper exegesis and interpretation of scripture we will provide the reader with an example that should help illustrate the point.

When a couple chooses to unite themselves in marriage they make a covenant, an agreement with one another to perform the general duties involved in a marriage – to love, honor, respect, and in all ways devote themselves whole-heartedly to the other. Some marriage duties are specific to one party[6]. This covenant is witnessed by many and is

---

[3] Genesis 8:20-22.
[4] Exodus 24:3-8.
[5] Webster. Entry #1 for "COVENANT."
[6] Such as the husband being required to provide for the basic needs of his wife as it relates to food, clothing, and sexual relations.

typically sealed with a document of some sort, whether civil, ecclesiastical, or both. The marriage is intended to be a life-long commitment, never to be forsaken[7]. Once the covenant is sealed, it is permanent. However, as we know all too well, this doesn't always happen. Adultery is an all too common infringement of the marriage covenant. Though committing adultery breaks the covenant of the marriage, the agreement and promise between the husband and wife, it does not nullify the duties of a marriage. The death of one of the parties is also a breaking of the covenant, though not an unlawful one. If a covenant is broken in a marriage due to the death of one of the parties, the duties of a marriage in general remain. If the living chooses to marry another, those duties are again agreed upon via a different covenant, though specific duties may be fulfilled by the appropriate party's actions.

Apply the above example to the covenant between Yahweh and His bride, Israel. The Torah contains all of Yahweh's marriage duties, general and party-specific. His specific duties consist of His promises to bless Israel in all ways[8] if she was faithful to the covenant. In a very real way, Yahweh proposed to His bride-to-be by presenting her with His promises and the duties on both sides, which she had to either accept or reject. The covenant was accepted by her agreeing to keep all the duties of the marriage declaring "All the words which Yahweh has spoken will we do."[9] Israel soon after committed spiritual adultery by worshipping an idol thereby breaking her covenant with Yahweh. The duties of the marriage, however, contained in the commands of the Torah, remained. Yahweh, being a gracious husband, welcomed his bride back, but the duties remained the same.

Time passed and Israel continued to break her covenant with Yahweh by numerous adulteries. Through the prophet Jeremiah, He promised that a new covenant would be made, one different than that which was made at Mount Sinai.

---

[7] Matthew 19:4-6.
[8] Deuteronomy 28:1-14.
[9] Exodus 24:3.

Jeremiah 31:31-34
(31) Behold, the days come, says Yahweh, that I will make a new
covenant with the house of Israel, and with the house of Judah:
(32) not according to the covenant that I made with their
fathers in the day that I took them by the hand to bring them
out of the land of Egypt; which my covenant they broke,
although I was a husband unto them, says Yahweh.
(33) But this is the covenant that I will make with the house of
Israel after those days, says Yahweh: I will put my Torah in their
inward parts, and in their heart will I write it; and I will be their
Elohim, and they shall be my people.
(34) And they shall teach no more every man his neighbor, and
every man his brother, saying, Know Yahweh; for they shall all
know me, from the least of them unto the greatest of them, says
Yahweh: for I will forgive their iniquity, and their sin will I
remember no more.

Unlike the previous covenant, which required the people to rigorously
attempt and continue to fail to observe all His commandments on their
own, He promised to help them by forgiving all their previous
adulteries and put his Torah into their hearts. This New Covenant was
enacted by the shedding of the blood of Yeshua[10], and the knowledge of
obedience to the commands was given through the indwelling of
Yahweh's holy spirit in faithful believers. Prophecies of a time well in
Israel's future, well after the death and resurrection of Yeshua, still tell
us of some of the marriage duties we are to fulfill.

Isaiah 66:17, 22-23
(17) They that sanctify themselves and purify themselves *to go*
unto the gardens, behind one in the midst, **eating swine's flesh,
and the abomination, and the mouse, they shall come to an end**
together, says Yahweh.
(22) For as the new heavens and the new earth, which I will
make, shall remain before me, says Yahweh, so shall your seed
and your name remain.
(23) And it shall come to pass, that from one new moon to

---

[10] Matthew 26:26-29.

xiv

another, and from one **Sabbath** to another, shall all flesh come to worship before me, says Yahweh.

Isaiah 56:1-8
(1) Thus says Yahweh, Keep justice, and do righteousness; for my salvation is near to come, and my righteousness to be revealed.
(2) Blessed is the man that does this, and the son of man that holds it fast; that **keeps the Sabbath from profaning it**, and keeps his hand from doing any evil.
(3) Neither let the foreigner, that has joined himself to Yahweh, speak, saying, Yahweh will surely separate me from his people; neither let the eunuch say, Behold, I am a dry tree.
(4) For thus says Yahweh of the eunuchs that **keep my Sabbaths**, and choose the things that please me, and **hold fast my covenant**:
(5) Unto them will I give in my house and within my walls a memorial and a name better than of sons and of daughters; I will give them an everlasting name, that shall not be cut off.
(6) Also the foreigners that join themselves to Yahweh, to minister unto him, and to love the name of Yahweh, to be his servants, **every one that keeps the Sabbath from profaning it**, and **holds fast my covenant**;
(7) even them will I bring to my holy mountain, and make them joyful in my house of prayer: their burnt-offerings and their sacrifices shall be accepted upon my altar; for my house shall be called a house of prayer for all peoples.
(8) The Master Yahweh, who gathers the outcasts of Israel, says, Yet will I gather *others* to him, besides his own that are gathered.

Zechariah 14:16
And it shall come to pass, that every one that is left of all the nations that came against Jerusalem shall go up from year to year to worship the King, Yahweh of hosts, and **to keep the feast of tabernacles**.

Exodus 31:16
Wherefore the children of Israel **shall keep the Sabbath**, to observe the Sabbath throughout their generations, **for a**

perpetual covenant.

Observing the Sabbath, keeping the Feast of Tabernacles, and abstaining from the eating of unclean foods are just a few of the things that are a part of the marriage duties we agreed to. We should not be surprised at this. After all, did not our Messiah teach the same thing?

Matthew 5:17-20
(17) Think not that I came to destroy the Torah or the Prophets: **I came not to destroy, but to fulfil.**
(18) For truly I say unto you, **Till heaven and earth pass away, one jot or one tittle shall in no wise pass away from the Torah**, till all things come to pass[11].
(19) Whosoever therefore shall break one of these least commandments, and shall teach men so, shall be called least in the kingdom of heaven: but whosoever shall do and teach them, he shall be called great in the kingdom of heaven.
(20) For I say unto you, that except your righteousness shall exceed *the righteousness* of the scribes and Pharisees, you shall in no wise enter into the kingdom of heaven.

Matthew 7:21-23
(21) Not everyone that says unto me, Master, Master, shall enter into the kingdom of heaven; but he that does the will of my Father who is in heaven.
(22) Many will say to me in that day, Master, Master, did we not prophesy by your name, and by your name cast out demons, and by your name do many mighty works?
(23) And then will I profess unto them, I never knew you: *depart from me, you that work **lawlessness**.*

Certain aspects of the Torah and the Prophets have indeed been fulfilled, or have "come to pass," such as Yeshua's coming at the time he was speaking. However, Yeshua's death and resurrection didn't fulfill the need for each human body to have a rest one day a week, on

---

[11] Gr. γένηται. This translation will be detailed further in chapter 22 below under the section entitled "Continued Torah Observance."

the Sabbath. It didn't fulfill the requirement to abstain from murder, adultery, theft, bestiality, envy, incest, idolatry, cannibalism, etc. What the authors of other commentaries fail to realize is that the "consummation of the Mosaic Economy"[12] would remove the requirement of obedience from all the above listed abominations. What is fulfilled, such as the sacrificing of animals for sin[13], has no continued observation as that marital duty is complete.

We believe there is a simple concept that every person desiring to faithfully serve Yeshua can readily accept. "He that says he abides in him ought himself also to walk even as he walked."[14] If we assert that Yeshua is our Master, and we his servants, it should be enough for us to be like him, not better than him. What good would our Master's example of life be for us if we were intended to disregard or forget that example after his death? If he wanted lawless servants he would have been a lawless master. The message of both the Old and New Testaments are consistent throughout on this topic. The following passages summarize this from views both before and after the death of Messiah. We will let them suffice to say that dispensationalism, the bold and presumptive effort to modify the marital duties set down by our spiritual husband, to which we agreed, is wrong at best, and blasphemous at worst.

Ecclesiastes 12:13
(13) *This is* the end of the matter; all has been heard: Fear Elohim, and keep his commandments; for this is the whole *duty* of man.

1 John 5:3
(3) For this is the love of Elohim, that we keep his commandments: and his commandments are not grievous.

---

[12] Desperez.
[13] Hebrews 9:11-28.
[14] 1 John 2:6.

Use of the American Standard Version

The American Standard Version (ASV) was and has continued to be a very trusted, literal translation of the Bible. It's pre-1911 publication date allows for modification of terms such as "God," "Jesus," and "Christ," among others, without infringing upon any copyright laws. We have made every effort to modify the text to exchange the more archaic "thee" and "thou" words with their modern equivalents. Italicized words or phrases are native to the ASV and represent either quotes from the Old Testament or words not explicitly found in the underlying text but implied by context.

Use of the Hebrew Names and Words

Throughout this work, except for quotes from sources outside of the scriptures, you will see various words that are more "Hebraic" in nature. Some of them, such as the proper names of the Father and the Son, though, are just more accurate scripturally and historically. For the name of the Father you will consistently see "Yahweh," for the name of the Son you will see "Yeshua," for the term "Christ" you will see "Messiah," for the words "God/god/gods" you will see "Elohim/elohim" and for the word "Law/law" you will see "Torah," where the underlying word or context requires it. Reading the scriptures in light of the culture and context they were written, including the use of the proper Hebrew words and names, helps greatly in properly exegeting them.

Apocalyptic Terminology

A proper understanding of any prophetic or apocalyptic work requires a fundamental knowledge of how various terms are used symbolically and what those symbols represent. While the list below may not be comprehensive, it should suffice for the present work. The reader will be referred to this list throughout the work, where applicable, for a better understanding of the text.

The interpretations or meanings provided in the table are pulled from the context of the many prophecies in the Old Testament. Reading the context of the various prophecies usually reveals the meaning of words or phrases that would otherwise seem unintelligible. A plethora of examples will be quoted in chapters 8, 9, 11, 12, 16, et al, below. Any honest inquirer of the truth will be able to discern that the messages John communicates to his audience in the Apocalypse are symbolic, not literal. A man walking around with a sword protruding from his mouth. A slain lamb taking a scroll with a hand that lambs don't have. The visible heavens being rolled up as a scroll, which would in itself destroy all life. Great stars falling from the heavens, which would have the same result, etc. Though the underlying symbols may have a literal fulfillments in history, the meaning of those symbols in prophetic and apocalyptic terminology needs to be sought out first.

Sir Isaac Newton did essentially the same thing in 1733. His work[15] has been and will continue to be valuable in the proper interpretation and understanding of apocalyptic and prophetic scriptures. Thus, we have chosen to display the most relevant words or phrases defined in his work in the table below. The reader will be directed back to this table from time to time within the work where desired or necessary.

---

[15] Newton. Chapter II, "Of the Prophetic Language." Pages 16-23.

Apocalyptic Term/Phrase	Interpretation/Meaning
Heaven and Earth	The Whole of the political world or nation, consisting of thrones and rulers.
Heavens	Thrones or dignities; people of high societal rank; contextually, the literal heavens or dwelling-place of Yahweh
Earth	Inferior people of lower societal rank; contextually, the entire globe or more specifically the land of Israel
Ascending to Heaven Or Descending to Earth	The rise and fall of a nation or nations
Shaking of the Heavens Or (Great) Earthquakes	The shaking of kingdoms so as to distract or overthrow them
Sun	The whole species or race of kings in a political body
Moon	Body of the common people, considered as the king's wife
Stars	Subordinate princes and great men such as priests or elders
The setting of the Sun, Moon, and Stars	The ceasing or desolation of a kingdom, usually proportional to the darkness specified
The Sun turning black or the Moon turning to blood	Same as above
Fire or stars falling from heaven burning anything	The consuming of the thing by war
Fire consuming anything, or something being thrown into a lake of fire	The complete consumption of the thing by war

Apocalyptic Term/Phrase	Interpretation/Meaning
The ascending of smoke of burning thing forever and ever	The continuation of a conquered people under the misery of subjection and slavery
The sun scorching anything	Wars, persecutions, and troubles inflicted by the conquering king
A storm of thunder, lightning, hail, and overflowing rain	A tempest of war descending from the heavens to the political world or nation
A sea, river, or flood	People of several regions, nations, or dominions
The embittering of waters	Great affliction of the people by war and persecution
The making of waters to blood	The death and dissolution of political bodies local or national
Mountains and islands	Cities of the political earth and seas
Houses and ships	Families, assemblies, and towns in the political earth and seas
Trees	People of a high societal rank
Grass	People of a low societal rank
A Beast	A kingdom against Yahweh or His people
The head(s) of a Beast	The great men who rule or govern the kingdom
The tail of a Beast	The inferior people who are governed
The horns of a Beast	The number of dominions or kingdoms supporting the Beast
Adultery, harlotry, or fornication	Idolatry, civil or ecclesiastical
The giving of a white stone	Absolution
The giving of a new name	The bestowal of a new dignity

Time Indicators

There are several words or phrases in the scriptures that are used by various people to emphasize the either the nearness or distance of certain events. Three of these phrases are found in the Apocalypse, which we need to investigate in the context of their scriptural usage.

"At Hand"

> 1:3 Blessed is he that reads, and they that hear the words of the prophecy, and keep the things that are written therein: for the time is **at hand**.

> 22:10 And he says unto me, Seal not up the words of the prophecy of this book; for the time is **at hand**.

The phrase "at hand" literally book-ends the Apocalypse. It is as if the giver of the message himself, Yeshua, wanted to ensure that the hearers knew to listen with the "ears" of urgency and at the end remind them of the same. The Greek phrase translated "at hand" is ὁ καιρὸς γὰρ ἐγγύς ἐστιν, *ho kairos gar engus estin*. A little time needs to be spent dedicated to the definition and usage of καιρὸς.

The clearest and most accurate definition of καιρὸς, as will be shown below, is a "set/fixed time." It is used over 250 times in the Septuagint (LXX), the Greek version of the Old Testament dated to the 3rd century BCE. More importantly for this work, however, is that it is used in the New Testament over 80 times. Joseph Thayer compares this word to the Hebrew words עֵת, *ath* ("a fit/proper time")[16] and מוֹעֵד, *moed* ("a set/appointed time")[17], the latter of which is used for the appointed feasts and festivals of Yahweh in the Torah. Each of those feasts had specific days of each year as their appointed time of observation and celebration. When speaking specifically of the phrase ὁ καιρὸς in his

---

[16] Gesenius. Entry for עֵת, Pages 661-662.
[17] Gesenius. Entry for מוֹעֵד, Page 457.

Lexicon, Thayer states the following:

> "ὁ καιρὸς alone, the time when things are brought to a crisis, the decisive epoch waited for: so of the time when the Messiah will visibly return from heaven; Mk. xiii 33."[18]

Just a little later in the same lexical entry he references the two passages in the Apocalypse we quoted above.

It is here admitted that the phrase "at hand" does convey a sort of mixed message in the Old Testament scriptures. In certain instances, the phrase is used to refer to a distance in time beyond the prophet's lifetime. A perfect example of this is found in Isaiah 13:6, 17 concerning Babylon:

> (6) Wail you; for the day of Yahweh is at hand; as destruction from the Almighty shall it come...
> (17) Behold, I will stir up the Medes against them, who shall not regard silver, and as for gold, they shall not delight in it.

The conquering of Babylon by the Medo-Persian empire didn't take place until around 539 BCE when Cyrus the Great invaded. Isaiah likely prophesied about Babylon's demise sometime at the end of the eighth century BCE. But then we have a different example that conveys a much more contemporary meaning in Deuteronomy 15:9:

> Beware that there be not a base thought in your heart, saying, The seventh year, the year of release, is at hand; and your eye be evil against your poor brother, and you give him nothing; and he cry unto Yahweh against you, and it be sin unto you.

Other examples of each can be provided, but these two should suffice for the sake of this discussion. How, it may be asked, can we solve this apparent conundrum? The answer is simple – context! The examples we really need to focus on, those in the New Testament, provide much

---

[18] Thayer. Entry for καιρὸς. Page 318.

more of this context.

Matthew 3:2
Repent you; for the kingdom of heaven is **at hand**.

Matthew 4:17
From that time began Yeshua to preach, and to say, Repent you; for the kingdom of heaven is **at hand**.

Matthew 10:7
And as you go, preach, saying, The kingdom of heaven is **at hand**.

Mark 1:14-15
(14) Now after John was delivered up, Yeshua came into Galilee, preaching the gospel of Elohim,
(15) and saying, The time is fulfilled, and the kingdom of Elohim is **at hand**: repent you, and believe in the gospel.

Each of these passages speak of the kingdom of heaven being "at hand." Yeshua had much to say about this kingdom and those teachings will provide the necessary context to aid in our interpretation. One parable is found in the book of Luke:

Luke 19:11-27
(11) And as they heard these things, he added and spoke a parable, because he was near to Jerusalem, and because they supposed that the **kingdom of Elohim** was immediately to appear.
(12) He said therefore, A certain nobleman went into a far country, to receive for himself a kingdom, and to return.
(13) And he called ten servants of his, and gave them ten pounds, and said unto them, Trade with this till I come.
(14) But his citizens hated him, and sent an ambassador after him, saying, We will not that this man reign over us.
(15) And it came to pass, when he was come back again, having received the kingdom, that he commanded **these servants, unto whom he had given the money,** to be called to him, that he might

know what they had gained by trading.

(16) And the first came before him, saying, Master, your pound has made ten pounds more.

(17) And he said unto him, Well done, you good servant: because you were found faithful in a very little, have you authority over ten cities.

(18) And the second came, saying, Your pound, Master, has made five pounds.

(19) And he said unto him also, Be you also over five cities.

(20) And another came, saying, Master, behold, here is your pound, which I kept laid up in a napkin:

(21) for I feared you, because you are an austere man: you take up that which you laid not down, and reap that which you did not sow.

(22) He says unto him, Out of your own mouth will I judge you, you wicked servant. You knew that I am an austere man, taking up that which I laid not down, and reaping that which I did not sow;

(23) then wherefore gave you not my money into the bank, and I at my coming should have required it with interest?

(24) And he said unto them that stood by, Take away from him the pound, and give it unto him that has the ten pounds.

(25) And they said unto him, Master, he has ten pounds.

(26) I say unto you, that unto every one that has shall be given; but from him that has not, even that which he has shall be taken away from him.

(27) But these my enemies, that would not that I should reign over them, bring here, and slay them before me.

Yeshua was speaking to the crowds around him after telling Zacchaeus to come down from the tree. There are some important messages in this parable that are often missed. First, Yeshua is quelling the people's belief that the kingdom of Elohim was to come *immediately*. The contemporary belief regarding the Messiah was one of immediate reign over Israel and restoration of the world to universal worship of Yahweh. However, that was not the initial goal of the Messiah as he was to suffer and die first and begin his reign later.

Yeshua proceeded to convey this message to them through the parable above. Notice how the servants who the nobleman entrusted the pounds with were to be the same ones he returned to later. We do not read that the nobleman was to leave to receive his kingdom to return to some later generation consisting of the children of those servants, or their children's children, etc. The king was to return to try the servants he had entrusted those pounds with.

The parable was speaking of Yeshua leaving this world to receive his kingdom in heaven, to return later to those with whom he entrusted the message of the good news. The king was to return in his kingdom during the lifetimes of the servants. We read something strikingly similar when Yeshua was on trial before the high priest:

Matthew 26:63-64
(63) But Yeshua held his peace. And the high priest said unto him, I adjure you by the living Elohim, that you tell us whether you are the Messiah, the Son of Elohim.
(64) Yeshua says unto him, You have said: nevertheless I say unto you, Henceforth **you** shall see the Son of man sitting at the right hand of Power, and coming on the clouds of heaven.

Yeshua, answering Caiaphas the high priest, says to him and the crowd listening in, you (plural) will see the Son of Man coming on the clouds of heaven. Yeshua's coming was to be seen by Caiaphas himself and the others present. If that were not true, and, as Futurists would like to assert, it applied to the "Jews" of any generation, Yeshua's statement would have meant nothing to Caiaphas and the others.

Another parable of Yeshua, relevant to the kingdom of heaven, is found in Matthew:

Matthew 22:1-14
(1) And Yeshua answered and spoke again in parables unto them, saying,
(2) The **kingdom of heaven** is likened unto a certain king, who made a marriage feast for his son,
(3) and sent forth his servants to call them that were bidden to

the marriage feast: and they would not come.

(4) Again he sent forth other servants, saying, Tell them that are bidden, Behold, I have made ready my dinner; my oxen and my fatlings are killed, and all things are ready: come to the marriage feast.

(5) But they made light of it, and went their ways, one to his own farm, another to his merchandise;

(6) and the rest laid hold on his servants, and treated them shamefully, and killed them.

(7) But the king was enraged; and he sent his armies, and destroyed those murderers, and burned their city.

(8) Then says he to his servants, The wedding is ready, but they that were bidden were not worthy.

(9) Go you therefore unto the partings of the highways, and as many as you shall find, bid to the marriage feast.

(10) And those servants went out into the highways, and gathered together all as many as they found, both bad and good: and the wedding was filled with guests.

(11) But when the king came in to behold the guests, he saw there a man who had not on a wedding-garment:

(12) and he says unto him, Friend, how did you come in here not having a wedding-garment? And he was speechless.

(13) Then the king said to the servants, Bind him hand and foot, and cast him out into the outer darkness; there shall be the weeping and the gnashing of teeth.

(14) For many are called, but few chosen.

The king here is, of course, Yahweh; the son is Yeshua; the marriage feast is the kingdom of heaven; the "bidding" or invitation to the feast is the presentation of the good news; and the servants are the apostles and disciples of Yeshua. The invitation to the feast was sent by the servants to those that were bidden, the Jews, and they neglected it and didn't take it seriously. Those same Jews that were bidden were guilty of persecuting and killing the apostles and disciples of Yeshua. Because of their murders, Yahweh became enraged and sent armies to destroy them and burn their city to the ground. The bidden ones, having rejected the invitation to the wedding feast, resulted in the invitation going out to all peoples and nations.

Some would ask, "Why can't this parable apply to all generations after the initial rejection of Yeshua by the Jews?" The answer is within the text itself. The invitation to the "bad and good" of the nations wasn't sent out until the city was burned. Are we to believe that the good news isn't to be preached until the final destruction of those who oppose Yahweh and his Messiah? Of course not! The historical truth is that the preaching of the good news was focused on the Jews until the temple and entire Jewish commonwealth were destroyed in 70 CE.

The one found attempting to enter the wedding feast without a wedding garment is linked to Revelation 19:8:

> And it was given unto her that she should array herself in fine linen, bright and pure: for the fine linen is **the righteous acts of the saints**.

Yeshua said the same thing:

> Matthew 7:21-23
> (21) Not every one that says unto me, Master, Master, shall enter into the kingdom of heaven; but **he that does the will of my Father who is in heaven**.
> (22) Many will say to me in that day, Master, Master, did we not prophesy by your name, and by your name cast out demons, and by your name do many mighty works?
> (23) And then will I profess unto them, I never knew you: depart from me, you that work lawlessness.

To be a part of the glorious wedding feast of the son of the King requires that one clothe themselves with righteous acts. Those who think they can just call Yeshua "Master" and that be sufficient to allow entrance into the kingdom are mistaken and will be cast out into outer darkness.

Before moving on to other time indicators, it is important to note how the passage in Mark 1:14-15 above is worded. According to that gospel, the time that was "fulfilled" was that which was *prior* to the kingdom of heaven. Could it have been fulfilled then but not realized until over two millennia later? Would that be an actual fulfillment?

"This Generation"

In many places Yeshua says that his prophecies were to take place in "this generation," referring to the one in which he and his audience were living.

Matthew 23:34-36
(34) Therefore, behold, I send unto you prophets, and wise men, and scribes: some of them shall you kill and crucify; and some of them shall you scourge in your synagogues, and persecute from city to city:
(35) that upon you may come all the righteous blood shed on the earth, from the blood of Abel the righteous unto the blood of Zachariah son of Barachiah, whom you slew between the sanctuary and the altar.
(36) Truly I say unto you, All these things shall come upon **this generation.**

The punishment for the rejection, persecution, and killing of the prophets, wise men, and scribes sent by Yeshua was to be inflicted upon that generation.

Luke 21:29-33
(29) And he spoke to them a parable: Behold the fig tree, and all the trees:
(30) when they now shoot forth, you see it and know of your own selves that the summer is now near.
(31) Even so you also, when you see these things coming to pass, know you that the kingdom of Elohim is near.
(32) Truly I say unto you, **This generation** shall not pass away, till all things be accomplished.
(33) Heaven and earth shall pass away: but my words shall not pass away.

What "things" was Yeshua referring to here that were to take place before the passing away of the generation of the audience? Verses 7 through 28 answer that question. Wars, false prophets, famines, pestilences, persecutions, the surrounding of Jerusalem by armies, signs in the sun, moon and stars, the coming of the Son of Man in great power and glory, etc. Each of those were to come to pass and be accomplished before that generation passed away. The parallel passages in Matthew[19] and Mark[20] confirm the same.

The Survival of Some Apostles

Matthew 16:27-28
(27) For the Son of man shall come in the glory of his Father with his angels; and *then shall he render unto every man according to his deeds.*
(28) Truly I say unto you, There are some of them that stand here, who shall in no wise taste of death, till they see the Son of man **coming** in his kingdom.

John 21:21-23
(21) Peter therefore seeing him says to Yeshua, Master, and what shall this man do?
(22) Yeshua says unto him, If I will that he tarry till I come, what *is that* to you? follow you me.
(23) This saying therefore went forth among the brethren, that that disciple should not die: yet Yeshua said not unto him, that he should not die; but, If I will that he tarry till I come, what *is that* to you?

The passage in Matthew above also has parallels in Mark[21] and Luke[22]. Some have said that the account of the Transfiguration in the passages following each of these is the fulfillment of Yeshua "coming in his kingdom." However, Yeshua says that when he comes it will be with the glory of the Father and the holy angels *in his kingdom.* A vision of a glorified Yeshua cannot be equated to him actually coming *in his*

---

[19] Matthew 24:3-35.
[20] Mark 13:5-31.
[21] Mark 9:1.
[22] Luke 9:26-27.

kingdom.

John, the same author of the Apocalypse, tells us of a hypothetical question Yeshua posed to Peter. Could this have been yet another saying of Yeshua foreshadowing the timing of his coming (i.e. before the death of John)?

The Kingdom of Elohim Present Already?

John 18:33-37
(33) Pilate therefore entered again into the Praetorium, and called Yeshua, and said unto him, Art you the King of the Jews?
(34) Yeshua answered, Say you this of yourself, or did others tell it you concerning me?
(35) Pilate answered, Am I a Jew? Your own nation and the chief priests delivered you unto me: what have you done?
(36) Yeshua answered, **My kingdom is not of this world**: if my kingdom were of this world, then would my servants fight, that I should not be delivered to the Jews: but now is my kingdom not from here.
(37) Pilate therefore said unto him, Art you a king then? Yeshua answered, You say that **I am a king. To this end have I been born, and to this end am I come into the world, that I should bear witness unto the truth.** Every one that is of the truth hears my voice.

Matthew 12:22-28
(22) Then was brought unto him one possessed with a demon, blind and dumb: and he healed him, insomuch that the dumb man spoke and saw.
(23) And all the multitudes were amazed, and said, Can this be the son of David?
(24) But when the Pharisees heard it, they said, This man does not cast out demons, but by Beelzebub the prince of the demons.
(25) And knowing their thoughts he said unto them, Every kingdom divided against itself is brought to desolation; and every city or house divided against itself shall not stand:
(26) and if Satan casts out Satan, he is divided against himself;

how then shall his kingdom stand?
(27) And if I by Beelzebub cast out demons, by whom do your
sons cast them out? therefore shall they be your judges.
(28) But if I by the spirit of Elohim cast out demons, **then is the
kingdom of Elohim come upon you.**

Yeshua's response to Pilate didn't contain a "no." He never denied that
he was a king. In fact, he stated that he was come to that end. He
simply clarified that his kingdom was not one of this world. It begs the
question, if he was indeed a king at that time, and his kingdom was not
of this world, could the kingdom of heaven have come already? Could
its dominance have begun at that time to soon after be consummated at
the destruction of the temple and the Jewish commonwealth?

Regarding the passage in Matthew, I don't think any true follower of
Yeshua would deny that he did indeed cast out demons by the spirit of
Elohim. If that is true, then the kingdom of Elohim, at the very least in
its beginning stages, would have already come at that time.

Luke 17:20-21
(20) And being asked by the Pharisees, when the kingdom of
Elohim comes, he answered them and said, The **kingdom of
Elohim** comes not with observation:
(21) neither shall they say, Lo, here! or, There! for lo, the
kingdom of Elohim is within you.

Though we are not in agreement with everything written or believed
by the commentator quoted below, we think his comment on Luke
17:20 above is very explanatory and sufficient:

"**Cometh not with observation** - With scrupulous observation. That
this is the proper meaning of the original, μετα παρατηρησεως,
Kypke and others have amply proved from the best Greek writers.
As if he had said: 'The kingdom of God, the glorious religion of the
Messiah, does not come in such a way as to be discerned only by
sagacious critics, or is only to be seen by those who are scrupulously
watching for it; it is not of such a nature as to be confined to one
place, so that men might say of it, Behold it is only here, or only

there: for this kingdom of God is publicly revealed; and behold it is among you; I proclaim it publicly, and work those miracles which prove the kingdom of God is come; and none of these things are done in a corner.'

Dr. Lightfoot has well observed that there are two senses especially in which the phrase 'kingdom of heaven,' is to be understood.

1.   The promulgation and establishment of the Christian religion.

2.   The total overthrow of the Jewish polity.

The Jews imagined that when the Messiah should come he would destroy the Gentiles, and reign gloriously over the Jews: the very reverse of this, our Lord intimates, should be the case. He was about to destroy the whole Jewish polity, and reign gloriously among the Gentiles. Hence, he mentions the case of the general deluge, and the destruction of Sodom and Gomorrah. As if he had said: 'The coming of this kingdom shall be as fatal to you as the deluge was to the old world, and as the fire and brimstone from heaven were to Sodom and Gomorrah.' Our Lord states that this kingdom of heaven was within them, i.e. that they themselves should be the scene of these desolations, as, through their disobedience and rebellion, they possessed the seeds of these judgments."[23]

"I Come Quickly"

Revelation 22:7
And behold, **I come quickly**. Blessed is he that keeps the words of the prophecy of this book.

Revelation 22:12
Behold, **I come quickly**; and my reward is with me, to render to each man according as his work is.

Revelation 22:20
He who testifies these things says, Yea: **I come quickly**. Amein:

---

[23] Clarke. Page 469.

come, Master Yeshua.

Three times within thirteen verses we are told that Yeshua is coming quickly. The Greek word translated "quickly" is ταχύ, *taku*, and means "*quickly, speedily (without delay)*"[24] Could the audience of the Apocalypse have, in any way, understood the word ταχύ as meaning a time period some number of centuries beyond their lifetimes? What value would the Apocalypse have had to them if that were the case?

In all the above information related to prophetic and apocalyptic time indicators, by no means comprehensive, we have a clear overall picture of what was meant. The events surrounding the coming of Yeshua, the establishment of the kingdom of heaven, and the destruction of Jerusalem, among other things, were all spoken of in such a way that the hearers and/or readers would understand that their fulfillment was to be in the very near future. For many of them, they may have understood that the events were going to transpire within their lifetimes.

It would be wise for us all to consider things from a purely practical aspect here as well. What else should we expect other than a contemporaneous fulfillment of the events in these passages given the linguistics of urgency expressed therein? If Yeshua were to have come the first time in our day, and we asked him, "When shall these things be? and what shall be the sign of your coming, and of the end of the age?,"[25] would we really expect the answer to have been anything else other than one with meaning to us and our own day? If you were Peter, James, or John, would you have asked Yeshua, "Can you tell us about the technology that will astound the world thousands of years from now?" Why would they care? What relevance would that have to them? How could that knowledge possibly affect the way they conduct their lives? Would that information change the way they walked in

---

[24] Thayer. Entry for ταχύ. Page 616.
[25] Matthew 24:3.

their obedience to Yeshua and to Yahweh? Likewise, the audience of the Apocalypse, the seven assemblies which are in Asia[26], would have been expecting the events therein to have a fulfillment in their near future. To think that every "end times" prophecy or parable that was spoken to the apostles and disciples face-to-face actually applied to some distant, unknown generation, is both naïve and ludicrous.

"A Thousand Years As One Day"

The only verse we have heard used in attempts to rebut the plain language of the immediacy of the events detailed in the Apocalypse is that found in 2 Peter 3:8:

> But forget not this one thing, beloved, that one day is with Yahweh as a thousand years, and a thousand years as one day.

However, to use the passage as Futurists do is to pull it out of its context. The author of this epistle isn't trying to set a prophetic precedent by saying that each prophecy in scripture is supposed to be read using the "day for a thousand years" principle. He is addressing an issue that existed in his day where certain "mockers" (verse 3) were questioning and doubting the return of Yeshua because of its *apparent* delay in coming. He tells his audience that those "mockers" were prophesied to come in the "last days." Since the mockers were already mocking in his day, that time was considered the "last days." The message to them is that what may seem like a "delay" to them is, in reality, the patience of Yahweh (verse 9). The author is saying, "He is not being slack, He will come right on time." No amount of time will nullify His promises. The surrounding context tells us that the audience was in eager expectation of Yeshua's return, an expectation that would have been foolish if they suddenly realized "a day" was actually meant to be interpreted as "a thousand years."

It is interesting that Futurists only seek to use this passage when it relates to the timing of the events surrounding the coming of Yeshua.

---

[26] Revelation 1:4.

The principle is not, in the vast majority of cases, taken backwards and applied to the rest of prophecy in the scriptures. To do so would, of course, be ludicrous and ridiculous.

While wresting this passage from its context, which is merely intended to emphasize the need for patience to the readers, they ignore all the other passages in the New Testament that show that the apostles and others expected his return to be imminent[27]. The context of all the scriptures must be considered. There are only three options that exist when evaluating the scriptures relating to this topic. One, John the Baptist, Yeshua, and all his apostles and disciples were so deluded and deceived that they didn't even know what they were talking about and therefore taught something false. Two, they knew exactly what the truth was, but purposefully deceived their listeners into thinking the day was near when it wasn't. Or three, they spoke the truth and Yeshua's coming was indeed very close at hand in their own day. Which would the reader choose to believe is true?

Futurism

The Futurist eschatological viewpoint should have another name – the speculative view. Futurism is, in some ways, the ideal stance. It is simultaneously undeniable and indefensible. Simply put, no one can prove it right, and no one can prove it wrong. Events or characters in the Apocalypse need only have a minute resemblance to a Futurist's theoretical equivalents. One person may interpret the hail and fire of the first angel's trumpet judgment as being one or more nuclear explosions while another considers it a meteor. One may interpret the "wormwood" of the third angel's trumpet judgment as a toxic waste spill into the oceans while another sees it as hydraulic fracturing.

What benefit is there to the Futurist belief? It is our opinion that it not only promotes fear-mongering, but actually paralyzes the followers of

---

[27] In addition to the passages already provided above, see Romans 13:11; 1 Corinthians 7:29, 10:11, 15:51; 1 Thessalonians 4:15-17; Philippians 4:5; Hebrews 9:26, 10:25; James 5:3, 7-9; 1 Peter 1:5, 20, 4:7, 17; 1 John 2:18, 28; et al.

Yeshua around the world by having them constantly focused on what *may* come to pass in the future, while ignoring what *is* needed in the present. Virtually every generation has had its own promoters of "the apocalypse." Except for the predictions of the prophets and the Messiah himself, every single prophecy about the "end" of the world has been proven false by absence. They never happened.

What does this tell us? Well, the Futurists today and of generations to come would tell us that we are still waiting and that the imagery of the Apocalypse hasn't yet revealed itself in reality. We would say that the view of the Apocalypse has become so skewed since the time it was written that its correct interpretation has almost been lost entirely. The theories and speculations of Futurists will continue to abound and morph, that much is true. Alternatively, we can choose to look to history, to the contemporaries of John and Yeshua, and to the entirety of the context of the scriptures to determine whether the grand apocalyptic event the whole world has been anticipating for generations has already come and gone. We believe the evaluation of the text contained in this work and historical background of the Apocalypse does just that and simultaneously provides the reader with all the information necessary to conclude the same. The mystery of "the Apocalypse" is indeed detailed and settled in history.

Evidence for the Early Date of Authorship

Entire volumes have been written that are dedicated solely to attempting to establish the correct time period of the authorship of the Apocalypse[28]. A full and detailed exposition of that topic is *not* the intent of this work, but we find it prudent to address it briefly here. First, let it be noted that we only provide external evidence in this section. The internal evidence is found throughout the rest of the work within the commentary, scriptures, and historical record, which we believe speaks for itself.

---

[28] See Kenneth Gentry's "Before Jerusalem Fell," James Macdonald's "Date of the Apocalypse from Internal Evidence" (Bibliotheca Sacra, Volume XXVI, January, 1869), et al.

There are two schools of thought when it comes to dating the Apocalypse. The first and more widely accepted school believes that it was written around 95-96 CE during the reign of the Roman Emperor Domitian. The second school, which we are a part of, believes that the evidence points to its authorship being around 66-68 CE during the reign of Nero. Testimony for the later date relies very heavily, if not solely upon a statement made by Irenaeus[29], which was written about a hundred years after his proposed authorship date in the reign of Domitian. Today the only extant manuscripts we have of Irenaeus' statement are in Latin. Thankfully, however, Eusebius provides us with his quote as it was in the Greek[30]:

εἰ᾽ δὲ ἔδει ἀναφανδὸν ἐν τῷ νῦν καιρῷ κηρύττεσθαι τοὔνομα αὐτοῦ, δι᾽ ἐκείνου ἂν ἐρρέθη τοῦ καὶ τὴν ἀποκάλυψιν ἑορακότος. οὐδὲ γὰρ πρὸ πολλοῦ χρόνου ἑωράθη, ἀλλὰ σχεδὸν ἐπὶ τῆς ἡμετέρας γενεᾶς, πρὸς τῷ τέλει τῆς Δομετιανοῦ ἀρχῆς.

Translated it reads as follows:

"We will not, however, incur the risk of pronouncing positively as to the name of Antichrist; for if it were necessary that his name should be distinctly revealed in this present time, it would have been announced by him who beheld the apocalyptic vision. For that was seen not a very long time since, but almost in our day, towards the end of Domitian's reign."

The translation of the quote above has been put in question by some scholars and historians. The changing of but one word can make the entire statement mean something else:

"We will not, however, incur the risk of pronouncing positively as to the name of Antichrist; for if it were necessary that his name should be distinctly revealed in this present time, it would have been announced by him who beheld the apocalyptic vision. For **he** was

[29] Irenaeus, Against Heresies. Book 5, Chapter 30, Section 3.
[30] Eusebius, Ecclesiastical History. Book 3, Chapter 18, Section 3.

seen not a very long time since, but almost in our day, towards the end of Domitian's reign."

The change, which is supported by some students and scholars of the Apocalypse, says that John, not his vision, was seen during the end of Domitian's reign. Others, however, while agreeing with the early dating, disagree with the retranslation of Irenaeus' statement. F. W. Farrar has the following insights to add to this argument:

"The chief obstacle to the acceptance of the true date of the Apocalypse, arises from the authority of Irenaeus. Speaking of the number of the Beast, and repeating those early conjectures which, as I shall show elsewhere, practically agree with what is now known to be the true solution, he remarks that he cannot give any positive decision since he believes that, if such a solution had been regarded as necessary, it would have been furnished by 'him who saw the Apocalypse. For it was not so long ago that *it* (the Apocalypse) was seen, but almost in our generation, towards the close of the reign of Domitian.' Three attempts have been made to get rid of this evidence. Guericke proposes to take '*Dometianou*' as an adjective, and to render the clause 'near the close of the Domitian rule,' *i.e.*, the rule of *Domitius Nero*. But the absence of the article on which he relies gives no support to his view, and no scholar will accept this hypothesis, though he may admit the possibility of some *confusion* between the names Domitius and Domitian. Others again make the word ἑωράθη mean '*he, i.e.*, St. John, was seen,' since no nominative is expressed. Now Irenaeus, in the same passage and elsewhere, dwells so much on the fact of the testimony given by those who had *seen* John face to face, that we cannot set aside this suggestion as impossible. It has the authority of Wetstein. Again, the Latin translator of Irenaeus renders the verb not '*vita est*,' 'the Apocalypse was seen,' but '*visum est*' the Beast (τὸ θηρίον) was seen.' The language is, unfortunately, ambiguous, and as, in uncritical times, it would naturally be understood in what appears to be the most obvious sense, it is not surprising that St. Jerome follows the supposed authority of Irenaeus in dating the Apocalypse from the later epoch. Eusebius says that St. John was banished to Patmos in the reign of Domitian, but, even if he be not misunderstanding the

THE MYSTERY IS HISTORY

meaning of Irenaeus, his evidence goes for little, since he leant to
the view that the Apocalypse was written by John the Presbyter, and
not by the Apostle. But the authority of Irenaeus was not regarded
as decisive, even if his meaning be undisputed. Tertullian places the
banishment to Patmos immediately after the deliverance from the
cauldron of boiling oil, and Jerome says that took place in the reign
of Nero. Epiphanius says that St. John was banished in the reign of
Claudius, and the earliest Apocalyptic commentators, as well as the
Syriac and Theophylact, all place the writing of the Apocalypse in
the reign of Nero. To these must be added the author of the 'Life of
Timotheus,' of which extracts are preserved by Photius. Clemens of
Alexandria and Origen only say that 'John was banished by the
tyrant,' and this on Christian lips may mean Nero much more
naturally than Domitian. Moreover, if we accept erroneous
tradition or inference from the ambiguous expressions of Irenaeus,
we are landed in insuperable difficulties. By the time that Domitian
died, St. John was, according to all testimony, so old and so infirm
that even if there were no other obstacles in the way, it is
impossible to conceive of him as writing the fiery pages of the
Apocalypse. Irenaeus may have been misinterpreted; but even if
not, he might have made a 'slip of memory,' and confused Domitian
with Nero. I myself, in talking to an eminent statesman, have heard
him make a chronological mistake of some years, even in describing
events in which he took one of the most prominent parts. We
cannot accept a dubious expression of the Bishop of Lyons as
adequate to set aside an overwhelming weight of evidence, alike
external and internal, in proof of the fact that the Apocalypse was
written, at the latest, soon after the death of Nero."[31]

To sum up his arguments, a debatable translation of Irenaeus'
statement need not be a fact for its reliability or accuracy to be
questioned. Farrar mentions a few other things in passing that we'd
like to detail further here.

Epiphanius the following states in his Panarion:

---

[31] Farrar. Pages 184-186.

"Don't you see, you people, that he means the women who are deceived by a false conception of prophecy, and will deceive many? I mean that he is speaking of Priscilla, Maximilla and Quintilla, whose imposture the Holy Spirit did not overlook. He foretold it prophetically by the mouth of St. John, who prophesied before his falling asleep, **during the time of Claudius Caesar and earlier**, when he was on the isle of Patmos."[32]

He says John prophesied during the time of Claudius Caesar, which is either Tiberius or Nero, who were both surnamed that. Both reigned before Domitian. It said he prophesied during the time of that emperor and earlier, *not* after. Eusebius himself, who maintains the full quote not extant in Irenaeus' Greek writings, doesn't think that John the Apostle was actually the one who authored the Apocalypse[33]. By calling one aspect of Irenaeus' statement into question he brings all of into question.

Many scholars and historians agree that Irenaeus' statement shouldn't be taken as the sole and decisive source as it appears to be the source of all the others' testimonies.

"It seems to us that no impartial mind can fail to see that [*the external witness*] preponderates in favor of the later date. But when we scrutinize the character and extent of this evidence, it seems equally clear that no very great stress can safely be laid upon it. For it all turns upon the single testimony of Irenaeus, who wrote according to the best authorities, about 100 years after the death of John...one clear and explicit testimony, when not opposed by other evidence, would be allowed by all fair critics to control the argument; but not so when many other considerations tend to weaken it."[34]

---

[32] Epiphanius, Panarion. Book 2, Section 4, Part 51, 33:8-9.
[33] Eusebius. Book 3, Chapter 24, Sections 17-18; Book 5, Chapter 8, Sections 5-7; and Book 7, Chapter 25, Sections 7, 8, and 14.
[34] Milton Terry, Biblical Hermeneutics.

"The clear and positive external testimony against it [*the early dating*] is not strong, being reducible (as it seems to us) to the solitary statement of Irenaeus, near the end of the second century, that the Apocalypse was seen towards the close of Domitian's reign...Irenaeus, writing a century after the fact, may easily have made the mistake of putting the name of one famous persecuting emperor instead of the other, and it is remarkable that his statement is supported by no other writer earlier than Victorious of Pettan, after a second interval of a century. Eusebius and Jerome, in the fourth century, do not strengthen what they merely repeat."[35]

"When we scrutinize the character and extent of this evidence, it seems equally clear that no very great stress can safely be laid upon it. For it all turns upon the single testimony of Irenaeus."[36]

"The testimony in respect to the matter before us is evidently successive and dependent, not coetaneous and independent...If now the number of the witnesses were the only thing which should control our judgment in relation to the question proposed, we must, so far as external evidence is concerned, yield the palm to those who fix upon the time of Domitian. But a careful examination of this matter shows, that the whole concatenation of witnesses in favour of this position hangs upon the testimony of Irenaeus, and their evidence is little more than a mere repetition of what he has said. Eusebius and Jerome most plainly depend on him; and others seem to have had in view his authority, or else that of Eusebius."[37]

The Muratorian Fragment, a document outlining the accepted canon of scripture at that time (*ca. 170 CE*), states the following:

"It is necessary for us to discuss these one by one, since the blessed apostle Paul himself, **following the example of his predecessor John,** writes by name to only seven churches in the following sequence:

---

[35] T. Randell, Revelation.
[36] Milton Terry, Biblical Hermeneutics.
[37] Moses Stuart, Apocalypse.

To the Corinthians first, to the Ephesians second, to the Philippians third, to the Colossians fourth, to the Galatians fifth, to the Thessalonians sixth, to the Romans seventh. It is true that he writes once more to the Corinthians and to the Thessalonians for the sake of admonition, yet it is clearly recognizable that there is one Church spread throughout the whole extent of the earth. For John also in the Apocalypse, though he writes to seven churches, nevertheless speaks to all."[38]

It goes without saying that the example Paul was following, that of John the apostle writing to seven assemblies, had to occur before Paul himself wrote to the seven churches listed above. How could he follow an example that hadn't yet been made? Since it is almost universally accepted that Paul was put to death in Rome between 68-69 CE, before the destruction of the temple and Jerusalem, the "example" of John writing to seven churches had to take place before then. It would be pure and unsubstantiated conjecture, devoid of any historical support, to say that John wrote seven other letters outside of those found in the Apocalypse.

The title of the Syriac version of the Apocalypse (*ca.* seventh-eighth century CE), pictured below, reads "The Revelation which was made to John the Evangelist by Elohim, in the island of Patmos, into which he was banished by Nero the Caesar."[39]

---

[38] Muratorian.
[39] Image taken from "The Apocalypse of St. John, in a Syriac Version Hitherto Unknown," edited by John Gwynn, D.D., D.C.L., 1897.

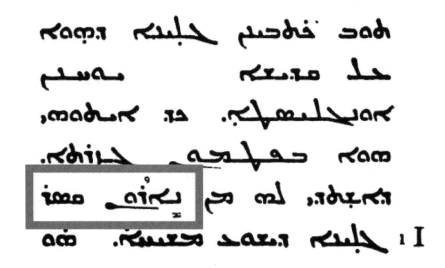

The portion outlined in grey is the phrase "Nero Caesar" in Syriac.

Several well-known and trusted scholars, such as Alfred Edersheim, also believe the evidence points conclusively to a pre-Neronic authorship date of the Apocalypse. In his work called *The Temple: Its Ministry and Services as They Were at the Time of Christ*, he states, when speaking in the context of the minutiae of Temple ministry:

> "These naturally suggest the twofold inference that the Book of Revelation and the Fourth Gospel **must have been written before the Temple services had actually ceased**, and by one who had not merely been intimately acquainted with, but probably at one time an actor in them."[40]

Robert Young, translator of the version of the Bible under his name, Young's Literal Translation, stated the following in his introduction to the book of Revelation:

> "It was written in Patmos (about A.D. 68), whither John had been

---

[40] Edersheim, Alfred. The Temple: Its Ministry and Services as They Were at the Time of Christ, Chapter 7.

banished by Domitius Nero, as stated in the title of the Syriac Version of the Book; and with this concurs the express statement of Irenaeus (A.D. 175), who says it happened in the reign of *Domitianou*, i.e. *Domitius* (Nero). Sulpicius Severus, Orosius, &c., stupidly mistaking *Domitianou* for *Domitianikos*, supposed Irenaeus to refer to Domitian, A.D. 95, and most succeeding writers have fallen into the same blunder. The internal testimony is wholly in favour of the earlier date. The temple at Jerusalem was still standing (ch. 11.1-10); the exact duration of the siege is foretold, viz., 42 months, 3 ½ years, or 1260 days; the two witnesses are to be slain in the city where our Lord was crucified; Nero was reigning at the time, for it is said of the seven kings of Rome; 'five are fallen, and one is, and the other is not yet come, and when he comes, he must continue a short space.' The five kings are Julius Caesar, Augustus, Tiberius, Caligula, Claudius. The 'one who is ' is Nero; the one who 'must continue for a short space' is Galba, who reigned only seven months. Everywhere the events are 'to come quickly,' lit. 'with haste,' or speed (ch. 1.1; 2.16; 3.11; 11.14; 22.7, 12, 20). The escape of the Christian Jews from Jerusalem to Pella is undoubtedly referred to in ch. 7.1-8, compared with Mat. 24.30."

Young actually believes that Irenaeus' account was accurate, but that he was referring to Nero and not Domitian. He also references several pieces of internal information to prove the Apocalypse's earlier date of authorship.

Rev. P. S. Desperez provides us with some other great insights that we find very worthy of quoting here.

"Here is a material difference of opinion. We have men of high classical attainments and critical acumen maintaining the Neronic date, *i.e.* that the Apocalypse was written during the reign of Nero, and consequently *before* the destruction of Jerusalem; and others of equally high reputation defending the Domitianic date, *i.e.* that it was written during the reign of Domitian, and consequently *after* the destruction of Jerusalem. Who shall decide? And yet a decision must be come to; all subsequent interpretation depends upon this question; it is a point of all others most necessary to be attained. If the Apocalypse was written in the time of Nero, *before the destruction of Jerusalem*, a consistent, reasonable, and satisfactory explanation can be given of the book: if written in the reign of Domitian, *after the destruction of Jerusalem*, that line of interpretation can only be adopted which rests on the will and caprice of the interpreter; and this opens so wide a field, and is capable of such unlimited extravagance, that it is no uncommon event for hermeneutical opponents to take contradictory views of the same symbol, or for interpreters holding the same religious tenets, to place an interval of 1000 years more or less between their several interpretations."[41]

What succinct and powerful points he makes here. Futurists are forever bond slaves to the "will and caprice" of their own interpretations with no grounding whatsoever in history or verifiable scriptural fact. Without some solid foundation to build upon how can any honest and sincere inquirer of the truth take one Futurist's view as more credible than another's when both are equally indefensible?

As a final note on the earlier dating of the Apocalypse. Some sceptics would assert that there is no historical record of persecution in Asia during the time of Nero. Well, we would contend that not only does the information above show that assertion to be false, but the following scriptures solidify it:

1 Peter 1:1, 6-7; 4:7
(1) **Peter, an apostle of Jesus Christ, to the elect** who are sojourners of the Dispersion in Pontus, Galatia, Cappadocia, **Asia**, and Bithynia...
(6) Wherein you greatly rejoice, though now for a little while, if need be, **you have been put to grief in manifold trials,**
(7) that the proof of your faith, *being* more precious than gold that perishes though it is proved by fire, may be found unto praise and glory and honor at the revelation of Yeshua Messiah...

---

[41] Desperez. Pages 2-3.

1 Peter 4:7, 12-19

(7) **But the end of all things is at hand**: be you therefore of sound mind, and be sober unto prayer...

(12) Beloved, think it not strange concerning **the fiery trial among you**, which comes upon you to prove you, as though a strange thing happened unto you:

(13) but insomuch as **you are partakers of Messiah's sufferings**, rejoice; that at the revelation of his glory also you may rejoice with exceeding joy.

(14) **If you are reproached for the name of Messiah**, blessed *are you*, because the *spirit* of glory and the spirit of Elohim rests upon you.

(15) For let none of you suffer as a murderer, or a thief, or an evil-doer, or as a meddler in other men's matters:

(16) but if *a man suffer* as a "Christian," let him not be ashamed; but let him glorify Elohim in this name.

(17) For the time *is come* for judgment to begin at the house of Elohim: and if *it begin* first at us, what *shall be* the end of them that obey not the gospel of Elohim?

(18) *And if the righteous is scarcely saved, where shall the ungodly and sinner appear?*

(19) Wherefore **let them also that suffer according to the will of Elohim** commit their souls in well-doing unto a faithful Creator.

1 Peter 5:8-9

(8) Be sober, be watchful: your adversary the devil, as a roaring lion, walks about, seeking whom he may devour,

(9) whom withstand steadfast in your faith, knowing that **the same sufferings are accomplished in your brethren who are in the world**.

(10) And the Elohim of all grace, who called you unto his eternal glory in Messiah, **after that you have suffered a little while**, shall himself perfect, establish, strengthen you.

The scriptures couldn't be any clearer. Peter's continued addressing of and encouragement for the enduring of persecution and suffering, which was also present in Asia, one of the places to which the letter was addressed, is apparent. It permeates the epistle. Peter's death was, according to all credible sources, prior to the destruction of the temple and Jerusalem, *ca.* 68 CE.

The following points are what leads us to believe that the date for the authorship of the Apocalypse was the fall or winter (September – February) of 66/67 CE:

(1) The ancient testimonies of Epiphanius, the Muratorian Fragment, and the Syriac version of the Apocalypse state explicitly that it was written prior to the death of Nero (June 9, 68 CE).

(2) The title of the Syriac version of the Apocalypse states with no uncertainty that it was written by John on the island of Patmos, to which Nero Caesar banished him.

(3) The date most commonly given for the birth of the apostle John is 6 CE, which would have made him around ninety years old at the time of his banishment to Patmos, when the later authorship date is assumed. John would have been of little use on Patmos given that the banished were sent there in order to work in the mines. If the earlier date is accepted he would have only been around sixty years old, which is much more reasonable.

(4) Persecution was in full force in Asia, the area over which John was entrusted for his ministry, making banishment a very real possibility. This persecution was likely that of the Neronic Persecution, which will be detailed in later chapters. The period of that Persecution was between late 64 CE and Nero's death on June 9, 68 CE. Since confirmation of this Asiatic persecution is found in the first epistle of Peter, which was authored before his death, the Apocalypse must have been written before then but during the Neronic persecution.

(5) The highly prophetic nature of the Apocalypse and its anchors to the historical record, the first of which is the Galilean campaign of Vespasian *ca.* February, 67 CE, requires that it be written prior to the start of that event.

(6) The testimony of several trusted scholars, translators, and theologians agree that a pre-70 CE dating is the most likely based on both external and internal evidence.

What we can conclude from all the external information above is that there is plenty of information, scripturally, historically and scholarly, that rightly casts significant doubt upon the supposed late date of 95-96 CE. As strong as the external evidence may be for the earlier dating, it is not enough to draw a definitive conclusion in and of itself. The tie-breaker must then lie in the internal evidence. We believe that all the scriptural and historical information provided below will prove that the external evidence in favor of the earlier authorship date of 66-67 CE is indeed correct and that the conclusion is therefore undeniable.

CHAPTER ONE

Prologue

(1) The Revelation of Yeshua Messiah, which Elohim gave him
to show unto his servants, *even* the things which must shortly
come to pass: and he sent and signified *it* by his angel unto his
servant John;
(2) who bore witness of the word of Elohim, and of the
testimony of Yeshua Messiah, *even* of all things that he saw.
(3) Blessed is he that reads, and they that hear the words of the
prophecy, and keep the things that are written therein: for the
time is at hand.

Several very important foundations are laid in the introduction of the
Apocalypse. First, this is not, as is commonly called, the "Revelation of
John." This is the Revelation of Yeshua, given to him by his Father and
Elohim (1:6). So, when we say something like "John said," or "John tells
us" in this work it must be understood that though John wrote it, it was
given to him by Yeshua.

Second, this book, by its very title, is *not* intended to be mysterious or
unexplainable. The Greek word for "revelation" is ἀποκάλυψις,

1

apocalupsis, and means *"an uncovering."*[42] Its root, ἀποκαλύπτω, *apocalupto*, means *"to uncover, lay open what has been veiled or covered up; to disclose, make bare."*[43] When reading or studying the Apocalypse it is essential that one knows it was given as something that could be and was supposed to be understood. Knowing who the addressees of the Apocalypse were is important for knowing where to look to for a proper interpretation and understanding. The various symbols and teachings within should be placed in their proper historical and literary context. This will be detailed more later.

Third, the things John heard and saw are said to have been "signified" to him. Different translations of the Bible mask this more accurate rendering by using words or phrases such as "communicated,"[44] "made it known,"[45] and even "made it clear."[46] We must again turn to the Greek here for a proper understanding. The Greek word translated as "signified" in the ASV is σημαίνω, *semaino*, and means *"to give a sign, signify, indicate."*[47] We are to look at the various visions contained therein as signs or symbols representing something else. For example, imagine I were to tell someone of a vision I had, saying, "I looked and I saw a great city; then I saw a great fire, in the shape of a mushroom, coming down upon the city, and upon many walls were shadows, as the shadow of a man, because of the fire." What do you think would first come to their mind? For anyone who knows anything about World War II you would likely recall the devastation unleashed upon Nagasaki and Hiroshima because of the United States dropping a nuclear bomb upon each. The "great fire" and "mushroom" signs in my vision signified the bomb itself and the mushroom-shaped cloud that results from its detonation. The "shadows" refer to the fact that the brightness of the radiation of the bombs caused shadows to form on the buildings or

---

[42] Thayer. Entry for ἀπο-κάλυψις. Page 62.
[43] Thayer. Entry for ἀπο-καλύπτω. Page 62.
[44] New American Standard Bible (NASB)
[45] International Standard Version (ISV) and English Standard Version (ESV)
[46] Bible in Basic English (BBE)
[47] Thayer. Entry for σημαίνω. Page 573.

walls behind certain people in the blast radius. Though the information pointed to historical realities, the vision was given in the form of signs and symbols.

The question may be asked – "Why?" From a scriptural perspective, these signs and symbols are given to hide things from certain people and reveal them to others. Recall the words of Yeshua, "He that has ears to hear, let him hear."[48] Yeshua, like the prophets before him, spoke and taught many things in parables.[49] For those who had understanding and sought out the deeper meaning behind things, they would get the intended message. Apocalyptic literature is, in a very real sense, a form of clandestine communication intended to prevent non-interested parties from understanding the message(s) therein. If John were trying to deliver a certain message to the followers in Asia without concern that its interception could be detrimental in some way to them, communicating in the apocalyptic would be the best way. The interceptor of the message would be none the wiser as it would all seem like fanciful gibberish to them.

Fourth, two very important time-indicating phrases are found in this passage – "shortly come to pass" and "the time is at hand." The reader should refer to the "Time Indicators" section of the Introduction for a more detailed discussion on this topic.

Fifth, the reading, hearing, and keeping of the words in the Apocalypse were intended to bring a blessing. If the Apocalypse was not written in such a way that it could be understood how could one receive the blessing that was intended? The content was to have meaning to those to whom it was addressed so as to effect actions in them resulting in blessings.

This profound prologue of the Apocalypse firmly and concretely sets the stage for correctly understanding and interpreting the entire work. Yahweh and Yeshua want the audience of the Apocalypse to

---

[48] Matthew 11:15.
[49] Matthew 13:34-35.

understand that the message given is one consisting of signs and symbols related to events set to transpire in their near future, which, if read, heard, and kept, would result in blessings for them.

Audience

(4) John to the seven churches that are in Asia: Grace to you and peace, from him who is and who was and who is to come; and from the seven spirits that are before his throne;
(5) and from Yeshua Messiah, who is the faithful witness, the firstborn of the dead, and the ruler of the kings of the earth. Unto him that loves us, and loosed us from our sins by his blood;
(6) and he made us to be a kingdom, to be priests unto his Elohim and Father; to him be the glory and the dominion forever and ever. Amein.

The contemporary audience of the Apocalypse is here identified and addressed; the seven churches that are in Asia. Interestingly enough, this passage is a very circular one. The greetings to the churches come from Elohim, the one who was, is, and is to come, and from Yeshua his son, ruler (or prince) over the kings of the earth. Then, the glory of all things, including those written in the Apocalypse itself, is to be returned to the same.

Some may ask, "If what is written in the book of Revelation related specifically to what was going to happen in Israel, why would John be addressing the churches in Asia?" First and foremost, John's area of ministry was Asia. We read the following in Eusebius' Ecclesiastical History:

"But the holy apostles and disciples of our Savior, were scattered over the whole world: Thomas, according to tradition, received Parthia as his allotted region, Andrew received Scythia, and **John, Asia**, where, after continuing for some time, he died at Ephesus."[50]

---

[50] Eusebius. Book 3, Chapter 1, Verse 1.

Each apostle was given their own area of ministry. John's addressing of the Apocalypse to those in his designated ministry locale shouldn't be surprising. The admonitions and corrections contained in the seven letters were those that related specifically to those churches. Second, though it was addressed to the churches in Asia, it is not unlikely that the message therein was disseminated to the churches in other parts of the world by word of mouth. Third, many of the things vividly detailed in the Apocalypse were taught by Yeshua himself. There is no way to tell whether each of the apostles were given a similar message to relate to their particular ministry locales. Fourth, according to Paul, the apostles James, Cephas (Peter), and John were commissioned to go unto the "circumcision" (a/k/a the Jews)[51]. We also know that the Jews throughout all of Asia heard the gospel[52].

Given the highly Hebraic nature of the content in the Apocalypse, including the constant references to the writings of the Old Testament prophets, it is highly likely that John was writing the Apocalypse to the Jewish believers in Yeshua in Asia. That being the case, the content of the Apocalypse, though referring to events taking place in Israel proper, would have had great significance to the audience. After all, Israel was their country, too. Its history was their history. Its people were their people. Why shouldn't John detail both the desolation and destruction of something of such great importance to them, as well as the blessings to come afterwards?

There are a few additional things of note that need to be pointed out in this passage of the Apocalypse. First, as a point of identification, it is Yeshua's Elohim and Father, Yahweh, who is the one sitting on the throne with the seven spirits before him. Yeshua is not the one seated on the throne in this image. Second, John here states that he *made* us (past tense) a kingdom of priests. The ruling priesthood of believers is mentioned a couple more times in the Apocalypse itself[53]. Peter also mentions it:

---

[51] Galatians 2:9.
[52] Acts 19:10, et al.
[53] Revelation 12:5, 20:4.

1 Peter 2:9-10
(9) But you are an elect race, a **royal priesthood**, a holy nation, a
people for *Elohim's* own possession, that you may show forth
the excellencies of him who called you out of darkness into his
marvelous light:
(10) who in time past were *no people,* but now are *the people of
Elohim:* who had *not obtained mercy,* but now have *obtained
mercy.*

The giving of crowns to the faithful is also found in several places in the
scriptures[54]. The use of the present and past tenses of the verbs in
these passages implies that Yeshua's followers understood and believed
they were already part of and actively working in the kingdom of
heaven.

The Sure Warning

(7) *Behold, he comes with the clouds,* and every eye shall see
him, and they that pierced him; and all the tribes of the land
shall mourn over him. Even so, Amein.
(8) I am the Alpha and the Omega, says Yahweh Elohim, who is
and who was and who is to come, the Almighty.

Coming with the clouds is a very common term used in the scriptures
when referring to a coming of Yahweh or Yeshua, in judgment or
otherwise[55]. In this instance, however, John is surely referring his
readers back to the teachings of Yeshua.

Matthew 24:29-30
(29) But immediately after the tribulation of those days *the sun
shall be darkened, and the moon shall not give her light, and the
stars shall fall* from heaven, and the powers of the heavens shall
be shaken:

---

[54] James 1:12; 1 Peter 5:4; Revelation 2:10, 3:11.
[55] Psalms 18:6-17, 104:3,; Isaiah 19:1,; Jeremiah 4:13; Ezekiel 30:3; Daniel 7:13;
Joel 2:1-2; Nahum 1:3,; Zephaniah 1:15-16; Matthew 26:64; Mark 9:7,.

(30) and then shall appear the sign of the Son of man in heaven: and then shall all the **tribes** of the land mourn, and they shall see the *Son of man coming on the clouds of heaven* with power and great glory.

The observers of this coming are the same in each – all the tribes of the land. The word translated "tribe" here is the Greek φυλή, *phule* and literally means "*a tribe*." Thayer states in his definition "in the N.T. *all the persons descended from one of the sons of the patriarch Jacob*."[56] In all verses where φυλή is used in the New Testament one of or all the twelve tribes of Israel are either specified or implied. Passages such as Revelation 5:9 and 14:6, where φυλή is used amongst many other terms (tongue, people, nation) can still refer specifically to one of or all the twelve tribes. This is, in fact, the most likely option since the people of Israel were always "set apart" from the rest. Should we not expect them to be set apart from the rest of the groups here as well? Thus, the tribes referred to here aren't generic, unnamed tribes "of the earth," but rather the known and recognized tribes "of the land [*Israel*]." Another important time-indicator is found in this passage. It is said that "they that pierced him" will see him coming with the clouds. Who were the ones who pierced him?

Matthew 27:24-26
(24) So when **Pilate** saw that he prevailed nothing, but rather that a tumult was arising, he took water, and **washed his hands before the multitude**, saying, I am **innocent** of the blood of this righteous man; see you *to it.*
(25) And all **the people** answered and said, **His blood** *be* **on us, and on our children**.
(26) Then released he unto them Barabbas; but Yeshua he scourged and delivered to be crucified.

Acts 2:22-24
(22) **You men of Israel**, hear these words: Yeshua of Nazareth, a man approved of Elohim unto you by mighty works and wonders

---

[56] Thayer. Entry for φυλή. Page 660.

and signs which Elohim did by him in the midst of you, even as you yourselves know;

(23) him, being delivered up by the determinate counsel and foreknowledge of Elohim, **you** by the hand of lawless men **did crucify and slay**:

(24) whom Elohim raised up, having loosed the pangs of death: because it was not possible that he should be held by it.

Though the Jews were required to go through the seat of their government, the Roman authorities, to inflict any capital punishment, they were ultimately responsible for Yeshua's crucifixion. They took the blood upon themselves and Peter confirmed it in his speech to the men of Israel present in Jerusalem at Pentecost.

Those who hold to a future coming of Yeshua believe that this is a generic statement referring to either Jews in general or a Roman people to live in a revived Roman Empire. To speculate the Jews living in some unknown time in the future would be the ones referred to in the above passage is a stretch, to say the least. This interpretation would remove the relevance of the passage, even the entire Apocalypse itself, from John's contemporary audience, and that within the first seven verses! The simplest interpretation of the text from an unbiased standpoint would be that John is referring to those who *actually* pierced Yeshua.

In closing this brief section, we find a declaration very similar to one commonly found throughout the Old Testament. When giving His people a guarantee that something said will come to pass He seals it with a phrase - "I am Yahweh."[57] The meaning of "I am the Alpha and Omega...who is and who was and who is to come, the Almighty," in verse 8 is giving the audience of the Apocalypse the same guarantee. The events to occur are *going* to come to pass by the hand and sure promise of Yahweh, and they are *going* to come to pass in the very near future.

---

[57] Exodus 6:8, 12:12; Leviticus 18:5, 19:3; et al.

The Great Tribulation

(9) I John, your brother and partaker with you in the tribulation
and kingdom and patience *which are* in Yeshua, was in the isle
that is called Patmos, for the word of Elohim and the testimony
of Yeshua.

John says here that he is a partaker in *the* tribulation. We often hear
the phrase "the *great* tribulation" used as a contrast to just "normal
tribulation." But, the phrase "the great tribulation" is only found once
in scripture[58]. In Matthew's account of the Olivet Discourse[59] we find
the phrase "great tribulation" without the definite article. However, in
the parallel account in the gospel of Mark[60] we only see the word
"tribulation." In Luke's account of the Discourse[61] neither version is
found, only a description of the great trials that his disciples will go
through. This is, in fact, very important to note. Throughout the
entire New Testament, the word "tribulation," the Greek θλῖψις,
thlipsis, is used to describe trials that the followers of Yeshua will
partake in[62], not the state of a nation, a people, or the world in general.
This is yet another textual clue to aid us in determining the events in
the Olivet Discourse and in the Apocalypse. We aren't looking for a
time when the *world* will be under the greatest tribulation; we are
looking for a time when the *followers of Yeshua* would be undergoing the
greatest tribulation. Based on John's use of the definite article it seems
he believed he was living at that time. We believe this time was what is
known as the "Neronic Persecution." More details on this will be
provided in the chapters below, especially chapter 13.

---

[58] Revelation 7:14.
[59] Matthew 24:21.
[60] Mark 13:19.
[61] Luke 21:10-24
[62] Matthew 24:9; John 16:33; Acts 11:19; Romans 5:3; 1 Corinthians 7:28; et al.

A Vision of Yeshua

(10) I was in the spirit on the Day of the Master[63], and I heard behind me a great voice, as of a trumpet

(11) saying, What you see, write in a book and send *it* to the seven churches: unto Ephesus, and unto Smyrna, and unto Pergamum, and unto Thyatira, and unto Sardis, and unto Philadelphia, and unto Laodicea.

(12) And I turned to see the voice that spoke with me. And having turned I saw seven golden candlesticks;

(13) and in the midst of the candlesticks one like unto a son of man, clothed with a garment down to the foot, and girt about at the breasts with a golden girdle.

(14) And his head and his hair were white as white wool, *white* as snow; and his eyes were as a flame of fire;

(15) and his feet like unto burnished brass, as if it had been refined in a furnace; and his voice as the voice of many waters.

(16) And he had in his right hand seven stars: and out of his mouth proceeded a sharp two-edged sword: and his countenance was as the sun shines in his strength.

(17) And when I saw him, I fell at his feet as one dead. And he laid his right hand upon me, saying, Fear not; I am the first and the last,

(18) and the living one; and I was dead, and behold, I am alive for evermore, and I have the keys of death and of Hades.

(19) Write therefore the things which you saw, and the things which are, and the things which shall come to pass hereafter;

(20) the mystery of the seven stars which you saw in my right hand, and the seven golden candlesticks. The seven stars are the angels of the seven churches: and the seven candlesticks are seven churches.

There are varying interpretations of what John is referring to when he writes "the Day of the Master" here. Some believe it refers to the

---

[63] Most translations read "The Lord's Day" for this phrase.

infamous phrase "the Day of Yahweh"[64]. This is unlikely, though, given that the Greek words in that phrase are τῇ κυριακῇ ἡμέρᾳ, *te kuriake emera*. If we sought the Greek version of the Old Testament[65] as our foundation for such a supposition we'd expect to see ἡ ἡμέρα κυρίου[66], *e emera kuriou*. The word κυριακός, *kuriakos*, meaning "*of or belonging to the Master,*"[67] is only found twice in the New Testament, the other being 1 Corinthians 11:20 referring to "the Master's Supper." The text would lead us to believe that the day John is seeing these visions is one specific to Yeshua, the Master. The specific day is largely irrelevant in the grand scheme of the message. What is more relevant is the fact that John says he was "in the spirit" on that day. This is John's way of telling his audience to start looking at the things he is writing through the lens of apocalyptic terminology. Unless context or specificity requires otherwise, symbolism becomes the new normal.

In verse 10 above we read that John hears a great voice, which sounded like a trumpet. The word "trumpet" here is rather deceiving given the way it is used throughout the scriptures. Verses such as Exodus 19:16, Leviticus 25:9, Joshua 6:9, Judges 7:22, et al, use the word "trumpet" when the Hebrew word is שׁוֹפָר, *shofar*, which is literally made from a ram's horn[68]. The fact that *shofar* is what is intended here is confirmed by both the Syriac Peshitta, which uses ܫܝܦܘܪܐ, *shofara*, and Franz Delitzsch's Hebrew New Testament which also uses שׁוֹפָר. The reason this is important is because of what these "trumpets" were used for in the past. The sound or blowing of a shofar was intended to demand one's undivided attention[69], to sound the charge for battle[70] and announce or pronounce events[71], whether past or future.

---

[64] "Lord" being a term used when an Old Testament passage that contained the tetragrammaton was quoted in the New Testament.

[65] The Septuagint (LXX).

[66] *C.f.* Isaiah 13:6 (LXX)

[67] Thayer. Entry for κυριακός. Page 365.

[68] Gesenius. Entry for שׁוֹפָר. Page 811.

[69] I.e. The presence of Yahweh on Mt. Sinai (Exodus 19:16).

[70] I.e. The conquering of Jericho (Joshua 6:9).

[71] I.e. The coming of the year of jubilee (Leviticus 25:9).

This "great voice, as of a trumpet" is soon after understood to be Yeshua's voice. He was demanding John's undivided attention in order to announce and proclaim to him the things that he was to record and send to the seven churches in Asia. The symbolism of trumpets will be found and continued throughout other portions of the Apocalypse. There is no need to spend too much time on the symbols found in the rest of the chapter as they are relatively clear. The seven candlesticks of verse 12 are identified as the seven churches of Asia in verse 20. The "son of man" with a "sharp, two-edged sword" coming from his mouth, clothed in royal garments, shining as the sun, who was dead and came to life to live forevermore, is Yeshua the Messiah. The seven stars of verse 16 are identified as the seven angels[72] of the seven churches of Asia in verse 20.

What is important to point out in these final verses of chapter 1 is how apparent the symbolism is. Yeshua's eyes aren't literally a flame of fire. His body, spiritual or otherwise, wasn't literally refined in a furnace. He didn't walk around the kingdom with a literal sword protruding from his mouth, and incorporeal concepts like death and Hades (the grave) don't have literal keys. Rather, Yeshua had a vision towards fiery judgment. His appearance conveyed absolute holiness and purity. His words were as a double-edged sword[73], and he had complete access to and authority over death and the grave. One cannot choose to view and apply such apparent symbolism to these verses yet interpret most other parts of the Apocalypse literally.

---

[72] "Angels" here is from the Greek ἄγγελος, *angelos*, and literally means "messenger, envoy." The word, based on the fact that symbolism is used throughout the Apocalypse, need not mean a literal angel of heaven. Rather, the leaders of the assemblies themselves may be meant here. See Thayer. Entry for ἄγγελος. Page 5.

[73] Hebrews 4:12.

CHAPTER TWO

Introduction to the Letters

Many of those who take a more "Futurist" eschatological stance tend to spiritualize the letters to the churches. This is because they need them to be able to apply to churches in the future in order for the majority, or entirety of the Apocalypse to apply to the future. Are there aspects of the seven churches in Asia that are characteristic of churches today? Of course! But, spiritualizing them to apply them to any number of churches throughout the generations since they were written is to once again remove the content therein from its chronological relevance. Hermeneutically speaking, the simplest way to read the letters is for what they are – seven letters written to seven churches that literally existed in John's day who had the literal characteristics mentioned therein.

Since the corrections, encouragements, and admonishments contained in the letters applied to churches that existed almost two millennia ago, the commentary on them will only be applicable to things relative to the present work.

Letter to Ephesus

(1) To the angel of the assembly in Ephesus write: These things says he that holds the seven stars in his right hand, he that

walks in the midst of the seven golden candlesticks:

(2) I know your works, and your toil and patience, and that you canst not bear evil men, and did try them that call themselves apostles, and they are not, and did find them false;

(3) and you have patience and did bear for my name's sake, and have not grown weary.

(4) But I have *this* against you, that you did leave your first love.

(5) Remember therefore from where you are fallen, and repent and do the first works; or else I come to you, and will move your candlestick out of its place, except you repent.

(6) But this you have, that you hates the works of the Nicolaitans, which I also hate.

(7) He that has an ear, let him hear what the spirit says to the churches. To him that overcomes, to him will I give to eat of the tree of life, which is in the Paradise of Elohim.

In this letter, we read that the removal of a candlestick out of its place corresponds to a loss of the light of Yeshua. Lack of repentance will always lead to a loss of salvation. It is through a consistently penitent life that we achieve the salvation gifted to us through the grace of Yahweh through Yeshua.

The "Paradise of Elohim" here appears to be a reference to the New Jerusalem[74], which will be dealt with in much more detail later.

Letter to Smyrna

(8) And to the angel of the assembly in Smyrna write: These things says the first and the last, who was dead, and lived *again*:

(9) I know your tribulation, and your poverty (but you are rich), and the blasphemy of them that say they are Jews, and they are not, but are a synagogue of Satan.

(10) Fear not the things which you are about to suffer: behold, the devil is about to cast some of you into prison, that you may be tried; and you shall have tribulation ten days. Be you faithful

---

[74] Revelation 22:1-2.

unto death, and I will give you the crown of life.
(11) He that has an ear, let him hear what the spirit says to the churches. He that overcomes shall not be hurt of the second death.

Smyrna is one of only two churches to which no correction is given; the other being Philadelphia. Smyrna, like the other six churches, was about to undergo trials and sufferings. This was something that they would have expected in their own time, not for some future "Smyrna-like" assembly. If this letter were intended to apply to some assembly(ies) in the future, its relevance to the believers in Smyrna is completely removed.

Letter to Pergamum

(12) And to the angel of the assembly in Pergamum write: These things says he that has the sharp two-edged sword:
(13) I know where you dwells, *even* where Satan's throne is; and you holds fast my name, and did not deny my faith, even in the days of Antipas my witness, my faithful one, who was killed among you, where Satan dwells.
(14) But I have a few things against you, because you have there some that hold the teaching of Balaam, who taught Balak to cast a stumbling block before the children of Israel, to eat things sacrificed to idols, and to commit fornication.
(15) So have you also some that hold the teaching of the Nicolaitans in like manner.
(16) Repent therefore; or else I come to you quickly, and I will make war against them with the sword of my mouth.
(17) He that has an ear, let him hear what the spirit says to the churches. To him that overcomes, to him will I give of the hidden manna, and I will give him a white stone, and upon the stone a new name written, which no one knows but he that receives it.

The "teaching of Balaam" referred to here is found in Numbers 25:1-3. The eating of foods sacrificed to idols was considered worship of those idols just as eating of the sacrifices to Yahweh were considered a necessary part of worship[75]. A first century handbook for Nazorean leaders, The Didache, says the same[76].

Yeshua "making war" with the sword of his mouth doesn't literally mean a sword was going to come forth from his mouth to slay the believers in Pergamum. Once again it means that at his word the believers would be judged and condemned if they remained impenitent.

As Sir Isaac Newton stated, and I referenced in the table of Apocalyptic terminology in the Introduction, the giving of a white stone represents absolution and the giving of a new name denotes the bestowal of a new dignity. As with the rest of the letters, Yeshua's encouragement to those who overcome proclaims judgment will be rendered in their favor and they will become new creatures.

Letter to Thyatira

(18) And to the angel of the assembly in Thyatira write: These things says the Son of Elohim, who has his eyes like a flame of fire, and his feet are like unto burnished brass:
(19) I know your works, and your love and faith and ministry and patience, and that your last works are more than the first.
(20) But I have this against you, that you suffer the woman Jezebel, who calls herself a prophetess; and she teaches and seduces my servants to commit fornication, and to eat things sacrificed to idols.
(21) And I gave her time that she should repent; and she wills not to repent of her fornication.
(22) Behold, I cast her into a bed, and them that commit adultery with her into great tribulation, except they repent of her works.

---

[75] Leviticus 10:16-20.
[76] Didache 6:3 (Kirsopp Lake's translation, 1912) – "And concerning food, bear what you can, but keep strictly from that which is offered to idols, for it is the worship of dead gods."

(23) And I will kill her children with death; and all the churches shall know that I am he that searches the reins and hearts: and I will give unto each one of you according to your works.

(24) But to you I say, to the rest that are in Thyatira, as many as have not this teaching, who know not the deep things of Satan, as they are wont to say; I cast upon you none other burden.

(25) Nevertheless that which you have, hold fast till I come.

(26) And he that overcomes, and he that keeps my works unto the end, *to him will I give authority over the nations:*

(27) *and he shall rule them with a rod of iron, as the vessels of the potter are broken to shivers;* as I also have received of my Father:

(28) and I will give him the morning star.

(29) He that has an ear, let him hear what the spirit says to the churches.

Here the one with eyes like flaming fire and feet refined in a furnace is positively identified as the Son of Elohim, Yeshua. The Jezebel mentioned is very likely an idolatress, not one who is teaching and seducing Yeshua's servants to commit physical fornication. The stories surrounding the life of Jezebel span the chapters of 1 Kings 16 through 2 Kings 9. Jezebel was one of the most idolatrous women in all of biblical history, who did much to lead her husband, Ahab, into becoming the one who "did that which was evil in the sight of Yahweh above all that were before him."[77] The believers in Thyatira, likely very familiar with the Old Testament scriptures, would have immediately associated Jezebel with idolatry and Yeshua's instruction with the requirement to immediately abandon and flee from it.

Overcomers are again given another wonderful promise. They will have authority over the nations and "rule them with a rod of iron."[78]

---

[77] 1 Kings 16:30-33.
[78] Revelation 12:5; 20:4.

CHAPTER THREE

Letter to Sardis

(1) And to the angel of the assembly in Sardis write: These things says he that has the seven spirits of Elohim, and the seven stars: I know your works, that you have a name that you lives, and you are dead.

(2) Be you watchful, and establish the things that remain, which were ready to die: for I have found no works of your perfected before my Elohim.

(3) Remember therefore how you have received and did hear; and keep *it*, and repent. If therefore you shall not watch, I will come as a thief, and you shall not know what hour I will come upon you.

(4) But you have a few names in Sardis that did not defile their garments: and they shall walk with me in white; for they are worthy.

(5) He that overcomes shall thus be arrayed in white garments; and I will in no wise blot his name out of the book of life, and I will confess his name before my Father, and before his angels.

(6) He that has an ear, let him hear what the spirit says to the churches.

In this letter, we see a new phrase – "the seven spirits of Elohim." We are told in Revelation 5:6 that these spirits are the same as the seven eyes of the Lamb. We agree with Newton above when he says that eyes in prophetic and apocalyptic language refer to understanding. In fact, we can see another representation of the seven-fold spirit of Yahweh in the following passage:

Isaiah 11:1-2
(1) And there shall come forth a shoot out of the stock of Jesse, and a branch out of his roots shall bear fruit.
(2) And the spirit of **Yahweh** shall rest upon him, the spirit of **wisdom** and **understanding**, the spirit of **counsel** and **might**, the spirit of **knowledge** and of the **fear of Yahweh**.

Yeshua, represented by the Lamb in chapter 5, is perfect in knowledge and understanding having been given all things by his Father, Yahweh, possessing the completeness of all the aspects of the seven-fold spirit written by Isaiah.

Yeshua reminds those in Sardis that they must be watchful. His usage of the phrase "come as a thief," and its implied meaning, is not new[79] and therefore would have struck a very familiar chord. The meaning of the phrase is not that Yeshua has plans of coming to plunder them of their wealth. Rather, it is to tell them that they will not know exactly when he is coming, so they need to be watching at all times.

The promise to the overcomers who are pure and holy, is that they will be clothed in white garments representing purity.

Letter to Philadelphia

(7) And to the angel of the assembly in Philadelphia write: These things says he that is holy, he that is true, he that has the key of David, he that opens and none shall shut, and that shuts and none opens:
(8) I know your works (behold, I have set before you a door opened, which none can shut), that you have a little power, and did keep my word, and did not deny my name.

---

[79] Matthew 24:43; Luke 12:39; Revelation 16:15.

(9) Behold, I give of the synagogue of Satan, of them that say they are Jews, and they are not, but do lie; behold, I will make them to come and worship before your feet, and to know that I have loved you.

(10) Because you did keep the word of my patience, I also will keep you from the hour of trial, that *hour* which is to come upon the whole world, to try them that dwell upon the earth.

(11) I come quickly: hold fast that which you have, that no one take your crown.

(12) He that overcomes, I will make him a pillar in the temple of my Elohim, and he shall go out from there no more: and I will write upon him the name of my Elohim, and the name of the city of my Elohim, the New Jerusalem, which comes down out of heaven from my Elohim, and my own new name.

(13) He that has an ear, let him hear what the spirit says to the churches.

The believers in Philadelphia are promised to be kept from the hour of trial that is coming, because of their obedience and patience. Whether this means they were to die before the very troublesome times would come, or they would be resurrected and brought to Yeshua, pulled away from those times, is unclear. Overcomers are promised to be given a permanent place in the dwelling place of the Most High, represented by a permanent structural component of the temple, a pillar.

Just as in other symbols, we don't expect these believers to be transformed into stone or some other material to become actual pillars. We also shouldn't expect the names of Elohim, the New Jerusalem, or Yeshua's name to be physically written upon them. Overcoming the trials and tribulations before them, these believers would be called a part of the family and home of the creator, Yahweh, and His son, Yeshua.

Letter to Laodicea

(14) And to the angel of the assembly in Laodicea write: These things says the Amein, the faithful and true witness, the

beginning of the creation of Elohim:

(15) I know your works, that you are neither cold nor hot: I would you were cold or hot.

(16) So because you are lukewarm, and neither hot nor cold, I will spew you out of my mouth.

(17) Because you say, I am rich, and have gotten riches, and have need of nothing; and knows not that you are the wretched one and miserable and poor and blind and naked:

(18) I counsel you to buy of me gold refined by fire, that you may become rich; and white garments, that you may clothe yourself, and *that* the shame of your nakedness be not made manifest; and eye salve to anoint your eyes, that you may see.

(19) As many as I love, I reprove and chasten: be zealous therefore, and repent.

(20) Behold, I stand at the door and knock: if any man hear my voice and open the door, I will come in to him, and will sup with him, and he with me.

(21) He that overcomes, I will give to him to sit down with me in my throne, as I also overcame, and sat down with my Father in his throne.

(22) He that has an ear, let him hear what the spirit says to the churches.

Repent; do good works; wake up; watch; clothe yourselves; all phrases used by Yeshua to admonish and correct the Laodicean believers. Overcomers are here promised a seat on the very throne of the son of Elohim. What is this throne? Heaven itself.[80] Overcomers are promised a place in the heavenly kingdom.

Final Note on the Letters

One thing that should be noted is that the phrase "let he that has an ear hear" ends each letter above. This is yet another phrase commonly used by Yeshua.[81] It is a way of asking, "Do you guys get what I'm

---

[80] Isaiah 66:1.
[81] Matthew 11:15, 13:9, 13:16; Luke 8:8.

saying here? Do you hear the message behind the words I'm speaking?" In the other instances where Yeshua used that phrase he was speaking parabolically. We should expect to see the same here. There is a message behind the words that we need to look for.

CHAPTER FOUR

A Heavenly Perspective

(1) After these things I saw, and behold, a door opened in heaven, and the first voice that I heard, a voice as of a trumpet speaking with me, one saying, Come up here, and I will show you the things which must come to pass hereafter.
(2a) Straightway I was in the spirit:

John is taken into the heavenly realm to be shown the things that are soon to come to pass. We must again remember that the visions he's seeing and the voices he's hearing are given so that he can communicate the message to his contemporary audience, the seven churches in Asia. Starting in this chapter we need to start thinking about and viewing things from a heavenly perspective.

John prefaces the things he's about to see and hear with "I was in the spirit," just as he did in 1:10 when he started seeing the fantastical vision of Yeshua. A literal interpretation of these things is not only unnecessary, but is discouraged, unless required by context or specificity. Examples of this will be noted throughout the work.

(2b) and behold, there was a throne set in heaven, and one sitting upon the throne;
(3) and he that sat *was* to look upon like a jasper stone and a sardius: and *there was* a rainbow round about the throne, like an

emerald to look upon.

(4) And round about the throne *were* four and twenty thrones: and upon the thrones *I saw* four and twenty elders sitting, arrayed in white garments; and on their heads crowns of gold.

(5) And out of the throne proceed lightnings and voices and thunders. And *there were* seven lamps of fire burning before the throne, which are the seven spirits of Elohim;

(6) and before the throne, as it were a sea of glass like unto crystal; and in the midst of the throne, and round about the throne, four living creatures full of eyes before and behind.

(7) And the first creature *was* like a lion, and the second creature like a calf, and the third creature had a face as of a man, and the fourth creature *was* like a flying eagle.

(8) And the four living creatures, having each one of them six wings, are full of eyes round about and within: and they have no rest day and night, saying, *Holy, holy, holy, is Yahweh* Elohim, the Almighty, who was and who is and who is to come.

(9) And when the living creatures shall give glory and honor and thanks to him that sits on the throne, to him that lives forever and ever,

(10) the four and twenty elders shall fall down before him that sits on the throne, and shall worship him that lives forever and ever, and shall cast their crowns before the throne, saying,

(11) Worthy are you, our Master and our Elohim, to receive the glory and the honor and the power: for you did create all things, and because of your will they were, and were created.

Being familiar with the visions of Ezekiel[82], John's audience would have immediately known who this mysterious one on the throne was. It was the Almighty Elohim, the Creator of heaven and earth, King Yahweh. To dig deeply into the type or color of each individual stone looking for some profound meaning therein is to miss the point entirely. It is not John's mission to explain the mysteries surrounding the appearance of the unseen Elohim. Rather, it is simply to have his readers understand

---

[82] Ezekiel 1, 10, 28:13.

who that being was. Lightnings and thunderings[83], the sapphire sea[84], the surrounding by living creatures and angels crying "Holy, holy, holy,"[85] and the complete submission in worship to him by all as the almighty Creator are all other indications proving the same.

The twenty-four elders surrounding the throne are unlike any other beings we see described throughout the scriptures. We are not, however, without clue as to their potential identity. Though the exact identification of these elders is not necessary to understand the fullness of John's message, we nevertheless find David Chilton's brief explanation very elucidating and sufficient.

"But the picture of the twenty-four elders is based on something much more specific than the mere notion of multiplying twelve. In the worship of the Old Covenant there were twenty-four divisions of priests (1 Chron. 24) and twenty-four divisions of singers in the Temple (1 Chron. 25). Thus, the picture of twenty-four leaders of worship was not a new idea to those who first read the Revelation: It had been a feature of the worship of God's people for over a thousand years. In fact, St. John has brought together two images that support our general conclusion: (1) The elders sit on thrones – they are *kings*; (2) The elders are twenty-four in number – they are *priests*. What St. John sees is simply the Presbytery of Heaven: the representative assembly of the Royal Priesthood, the Church."[86]

That these elders are not some select members of the angelic host itself is clear by the very use of the term "elder." That term is nowhere applied to angels in scripture but is applied repeatedly to faithful human leaders of the various assemblies, Old Testament and New[87]. Though it is admittedly mere conjecture, it would not be beyond logic

---

[83] Exodus 19:16, 20:18; Job 37:4-5.
[84] Exodus 24:9-10.
[85] Ezekiel 1; Isaiah 6:1-3.
[86] Chilton. Page 71.
[87] Exodus 12:21, 24:9-11; Numbers 11:16-17; James 5:14-15.

and reason to say that these faithful believers were a part of those raised from the dead after Yeshua's resurrection[88].

Yet another group of seven is seen in this vision, the seven lamps of fire before the throne, which are the seven spirits of Elohim. These same spirits are identified in 5:6 as the seven eyes of the lamb, which are "sent forth into all the earth." 2 Chronicles 16:9 says, "the eyes of Yahweh run to and fro throughout the whole earth." Seven, a number obviously prolific in the Apocalypse, is here applied to spirits, which are eyes. Seven is a number that very frequently represents perfection or completion in the scriptures.[89] These seven spirits before his throne represent his perfect vision. He sees all things and nothing is hidden from his sight[90]. Yeshua, as we will see in chapter 5, has been given this same vision just as he has been granted all power in heaven and on earth.[91]

The message here is clear. John said he was brought up to heaven and the creatures and imagery show the same. As we shall see in chapter 5, the purpose of this convening of the King and his heavenly council is one of judgment. The seven spirits of Elohim have finished reporting what they have seen going on throughout the land; the elders are seated on their priestly thrones; the holy angels are present. The scene is now set for the Judge's ruling to be passed down and carried out.

[88] Matthew 27:51-53.
[89] The seven days of creation (Genesis 1:1-2:3); the seven stems on the lampstand in the tabernacle (Exodus 25:37); Joshua and the Israelites marching around Jericho seven days, led by seven priests, to march on the seventh day seven times (Joshua 6:3-4); et al.
[90] Hebrews 4:13.
[91] Matthew 28:18.

CHAPTER FIVE

The Judge's Ruling

(1) And I saw in the right hand of him that sat on the throne a book written within and on the back, close sealed with seven seals.

As we saw in the previous chapter, the stage was set and the court convened to pass judgment upon the people. That this judgment to be revealed is to be complete and perfect is once again shown by the usage of the number seven. Only one appointed to open it could do so.

The Lion and the Lamb

(2) And I saw a strong angel proclaiming with a great voice, Who is worthy to open the book, and to loose the seals thereof?
(3) And no one in the heaven, or on the earth, or under the earth, was able to open the book, or to look thereon.
(4) And I wept much, because no one was found worthy to open the book, or to look thereon:
(5) and one of the elders says unto me, Weep not; behold, the Lion that is of the tribe of Judah, the Root of David, has overcome to open the book and the seven seals thereof.
(6) And I saw in the midst of the throne and of the four living creatures, and in the midst of the elders, a Lamb standing, as

though it had been slain, having seven horns, and seven eyes, which are the seven spirits of Elohim, sent forth into all the earth.

(7) And he came, and he took *it* out of the right hand of him that sat on the throne.

(8) And when he had taken the book, the four living creatures and the four and twenty elders fell down before the Lamb, having each one a harp, and golden bowls full of incense, which are the prayers of the saints.

(9) And they sing a new song, saying, Worthy are you to take the book, and to open the seals thereof: for you were slain, and did purchase unto Elohim with your blood men of every tribe, and tongue, and people, and nation,

(10) and made them *to be* unto our Elohim a kingdom and priests; and they reign upon the earth.

(11) And I saw, and I heard a voice of many angels round about the throne and the living creatures and the elders; and the number of them was ten thousand times ten thousand, and thousands of thousands;

(12) saying with a great voice, Worthy is the Lamb that has been slain to receive the power, and riches, and wisdom, and might, and honor, and glory, and blessing.

(13) And every created thing which is in the heaven, and on the earth, and under the earth, and on the sea, and all things that are in them, heard I saying, Unto him that sits on the throne, and unto the Lamb, *be* the blessing, and the honor, and the glory, and the dominion, forever and ever.

(14) And the four living creatures said, Amein. And the elders fell down and worshipped.

John heard that a lion, the king of all wild beasts, had overcome in order to be worthy to open the sealed judgment scroll. This concept of the coming Messiah being equated with a lion isn't new[92]. The Jews in

---

[92] Genesis 49:9. *Cf.* Targum Onkelos on Genesis 49:10 and Targum Pseudo-Jonathan on Genesis 49:10.

Yeshua's day were expecting their Messiah to come and immediately conquer all their enemies and put the entire world into submission to and worship of the one Elohim, Yahweh[93]. As we know, however, that was not the intent of the scriptures nor Yeshua's intent[94]. After *hearing* that an overcoming lion had come he turned and *saw* something completely different, a slain lamb. The imagery used here couldn't have been clearer to the follower of Yeshua. John was describing Yeshua the Messiah himself. Yeshua was the conquering lion of Judah, worthy to take the scroll as the king appointed by Yahweh; however, his overcoming didn't come through an immediate submission of his enemies, but through the sacrifice of himself.

Another important symbol is found in this passage. The incense offered on the heavenly altar represents the prayers of the saints. Incense was offered in the tabernacle twice daily by the priests. In the same sense the prayers of the saints are constantly ascending before the Almighty in the heavenly realm. The aroma of this incense, as we see later in the Apocalypse, spurs action from the one seated on the throne.

As noted above in chapter 1, again we see the past tense used when referring to those purchased with the blood of the Lamb. They were already *made* "a kingdom and priests;" however, in this passage an additional point is worth emphasizing. These followers of Yeshua were, in John's time, reigning upon the earth. This is significant because it tells us that John understood that the kingdom of heaven had already begun to rule over the earth. The process of the submitting of every enemy of Yeshua under his feet[95] had already begun and the saints were being placed in their positions of authority in the kingdom. Paul tells us the same thing in his letter to the Ephesians:

Ephesians 1:20-22, 2:4-6
(20) ...which he wrought in Messiah, **when he raised him from**

---

[93] Zechariah 14:9; Psalms 22:27-31; Isaiah 54:5.
[94] Psalms 22; Isaiah 53; Daniel 9:26; Zechariah 13:9; Luke 24:25-27; et al.
[95] Psalms 110:1.

the dead, and **made him to sit at his right hand in the heavenly**
***places*,**
(21) far above all rule, and authority, and power, and dominion,
and every name that is named, not only in this world, but also in
that which is to come:
(22) and he put all things in subjection under his feet, and gave
him to be head over all things to the church...
(4) ...but Elohim, being rich in mercy, for his great love
wherewith he loved us,
(5) even when **we were dead** through our trespasses, **made us
alive together with Messiah** (by grace have you been saved),
(6) and **raised us up with him,** and **made us to sit with him in the
heavenly *places*,** in Messiah Yeshua.

When Messiah was raised, he was seated in heavenly places. Paul says
that "we," referring at the very least to those he was writing to, were
made alive together with him and *made* to sit with him in the heavenly
places. Both verbs are once again in the past tense. How would the
readers have understood this? Both John's and Paul's statements would
have to have been in a future tense of some sort to be considered
prophetic of a future state of the followers of Yeshua. Paul also tells us
that our war isn't waged in the flesh or with fleshly weapons[96] and that
the armor we put on for those battles aren't fleshly things[97]. If Yeshua's
kingdom isn't of this world, our weapons aren't of this world, and we
fight battles not of this world, why would we not consider ourselves
already in positions of power in the heavenly places which are not of
this world?

Another important aspect of the Apocalypse is first presented here. We
see two phrases representing very large numbers – "ten thousand
times ten thousand" and "thousands of thousands." Ten thousand
times ten thousand is one hundred million. Are we to think that John
literally took the time to count and number 100,000,000 angels? What
about thousands of thousands? If a fixed number was already

---

[96] 2 Corinthians 10:3-4.
[97] Ephesians 6:10-20.

mentioned, why make mention of another? This is a point where understanding the numerology in the Apocalypse is important. John isn't trying to place a fixed number on the heavenly angels. The terms he uses are intended to convey the vast numbers that he saw. He looked and saw an innumerable number of angels surrounding the throne.

The judgment scroll has now been handed to the one worthy of opening it and the entirety of the heavenly host is gathered, awaiting the opening of the scroll.

CHAPTER SIX

Introduction to the Seals, Trumpets, and Bowls

Upon entering into the accounts of the seals, trumpets, and bowls the prophetic and apocalyptic link between the Apocalypse and the historical record become increasingly apparent. Here we also begin to see very intimate ties and allusions to Yeshua's Olivet Discourse[98]. Reference to this discourse will be made throughout the study on the seals, trumpets, and bowls as the link is undeniable.

From a timeline perspective, Luke's account will be primary as he is the only one who claimed to have "traced the course of all things accurately from the first" and to "write in order."[99] Where helpful information is found in the parallel accounts in Matthew and Mark they will be quoted accordingly.

It is important to stop here and emphasize one essential point. Though the historical record shows striking and extremely powerful similarities between the descriptions of the seal, trumpet, and bowl judgments, John's primary purpose is to convey the message in the apocalyptic format. Yeshua "sent and *signified*" (i.e. communicated it in signs and symbols) it to his angel to deliver to John. Mirrors of this

---

[98] Matthew 24; Mark 13; Luke 21.
[99] Luke 1:3.

format and the use of these signs and symbols are found throughout the prophets before John and will be noted where applicable.

As mentioned in the Introduction, the Apocalypse is a truly amazing work. It is unique among its kind. As will be shown in detail below, the text, both the apocalyptic and literal reading thereof, has amazing parallels with recorded history. After seeing these parallels one would be hard-pressed to not admit to the possibility and high probability that the Apocalypse had its fulfillment in the first century CE.

Sevenfold Judgments

Although John used the number seven in a symbolic fashion several times before now, "seven" takes on an entirely different meaning in the details of these judgments. Why the repeated use of "seven" as it relates to the coming judgments? There were seven seals of the judgment scroll, each representing some impending doom to come upon the people (or the cause thereof in the martyrs' prayers). Then follow seven trumpets and later seven bowls. Outside of the scriptural precedent of "seven" representing completion or perfection, John is seeking to wake up his readers and remind them of many of the promises of Yahweh.

> Leviticus 26:14-28
> (14) But if you will not hearken unto me, and will not do all these commandments;
> (15) and if you shall reject my statutes, and if your soul abhor my ordinances, so that you will not do all my commandments, but break my covenant;
> (16) I also will do this unto you: I will appoint terror over you, even consumption and fever, that shall consume the eyes, and make the soul to pine away; and you shall sow your seed in vain, for your enemies shall eat it.
> (17) And I will set my face against you, and you shall be smitten before your enemies: they that hate you shall rule over you; and you shall flee when none pursues you.
> (18) And if you will not yet for these things hearken unto me, then I will chastise you **seven times** more for your sins.

(19) And I will break the pride of your power: and I will make your heaven as iron, and your earth as brass;

(20) and your strength shall be spent in vain; for your land shall not yield its increase, neither shall the trees of the land yield their fruit.

(21) And if you walk contrary unto me, and will not hearken unto me, I will bring **seven times** more plagues upon you according to your sins.

(22) And I will send the beast of the field among you, which shall rob you of your children, and destroy your cattle, and make you few in number; and your ways shall become desolate.

(23) And if by these things you will not be reformed unto me, but will walk contrary unto me;

(24) then will I also walk contrary unto you; and I will smite you, even I, **seven times** for your sins.

(25) And I will bring a sword upon you, that shall execute the vengeance of the covenant; and you shall be gathered together within your cities: and I will send the pestilence among you; and you shall be delivered into the hand of the enemy.

(26) When I break your staff of bread, ten women shall bake your bread in one oven, and they shall deliver your bread again by weight: and you shall eat, and not be satisfied.

(27) And if you will not for all this hearken unto me, but walk contrary unto me;

(28) then I will walk contrary unto you in wrath; and I also will chastise you **seven times** for your sins.

Four times in that single passage, addressing specifically the punishments of disobedience, Yahweh promises a sevenfold judgment and punishment for their sins. John's audience, being familiar with the Torah, would have quickly understood the allusion. As we will later see, the judgments dealt by Yahweh were indeed complete and perfect sevenfold.

General Application

One thing that is unique about the content of the seals, as opposed to that of the trumpets and bowls, is the general nature of their judgments. For example, if the second seal represents war and bloodshed, we wouldn't expect *all* bloodshed to be complete prior to the opening of the third seal. Even the staunchest of Futurists wouldn't say that. In addition, if we see any allusion to believers in Yeshua being killed for their faith in the later chapters of the Apocalypse we must conclude that the martyrdom pictured in the fifth seal didn't have to be complete prior to the opening of the sixth.

The judgments of the seals themselves reveal, in general, the types of consequences and events John's audience should expect to see in their near future. They will see war, famine, pestilence, martyrdom, apocalyptic signs in the heavens and on earth, and more. These judgments are outlined with a greater degree of specificity later in the Apocalypse in the eighth, ninth, and sixteenth chapters, et al.

John is using these generic groupings of judgments and afflictions to direct the minds of his audience to Yeshua's prophecies in his Olivet Discourse. There he prophesied of the same things giving very few specifics. The fulfillments of Yeshua's Olivet prophecies are here signified by the unsealing of this judgment scroll. His audience would have immediately recognized the parallels and had their thoughts pointed in the right direction when the specifics of some of these judgments were detailed.

The Four Horsemen

Before going into what the first four seals individually represent it is prudent to give some general details about them and what they are in the entire context of scripture. Zechariah gives us the first account of these four horsemen that is strikingly similar to the account in the Apocalypse.

> Zechariah 1:8-11
> (8) I saw in the night, and, behold, a man riding upon a red horse, and he stood among the myrtle-trees that were in the bottom; and behind him there were horses, red, sorrel, and white.
> (9) Then said I, O my master, what are these? And the angel

that talked with me said unto me, I will show you what these are.

(10) And the man that stood among the myrtle-trees answered and said, These are they whom Yahweh has sent to walk to and fro through the earth.

(11) And they answered the angel of Yahweh that stood among the myrtle-trees, and said, We have walked to and fro through the earth, and, behold, all the earth sits still, and is at rest.

Zechariah 6:1-5
(1) And again I lifted up my eyes, and saw, and, behold, there came four chariots out from between two mountains; and the mountains were mountains of brass.
(2) In the first chariot were red horses; and in the second chariot black horses;
(3) and in the third chariot white horses; and in the fourth chariot grizzled strong horses.
(4) Then I answered and said unto the angel that talked with me, What are these, my master?
(5) And the angel answered and said unto me, These are the four winds of heaven, which go forth from standing before the Master of all the earth.

There are four horsemen here, just like the Apocalypse. From these texts, it is apparent that these four are agents of Yahweh sent forth to accomplish whatever purposes He sets out for them. These horsemen are also given another very specific label – the four winds of heaven. Daniel's prophecy gives us some insight that helps us to better understand how these winds apply to John's symbolism.

Daniel 7:2
(2) Daniel spoke and said, I saw in my vision by night, and, behold, **the four winds of heaven** broke forth upon the great sea.

As we already listed in the table of apocalyptic terminology in the Introduction the "sea" in prophetic and apocalyptic accounts represents a mass of people. In Daniel's account, it appears that the sea represents the people of nations outside of and against Israel. The

THE MYSTERY IS HISTORY

beasts in that chapter come up out of the other nations of the world to become global reigning powers, most of them having specific purposes *against* Israel. It would appear from the passages above that the four horsemen of Yahweh, the four winds of heaven, are used by Him to usher in and exercise His judgments in the earth. Whether they are used for judging Israel itself or the nations that would fight against it, they are used for that purpose.

As it relates to the Apocalypse, we will see that these four horsemen again stir up the seas of people by bringing forth the various judgments they are given power over. The people will be overwhelmed by war, famine, pestilence, deception, and death.

The First Seal

(1) And I saw when the Lamb opened one of the seven seals, and I heard one of the four living creatures saying as with a voice of thunder, Come.
(2) And I saw, and behold, a white horse, and he that sat thereon had a bow; and there was given unto him a crown: and he came forth conquering, and to conquer.

The audience would immediately start recalling Zechariah's prophecy above. In Zechariah's prophecy, the horsemen were sent to quell the anger of Yahweh towards Babylon, who had laid Israel waste[100]. Just like there, the horsemen in this chapter are sent by Yahweh to accomplish his purposes of judgment.

Some eschatologists have commented that this rider is Yeshua, however, given the context of not only the chapter, but the entire judgment written within the scroll, this is unlikely. Yeshua doesn't come on the scene until later. Like each of the first four seals, one of the living creatures that are around the throne called forth the horseman by saying "Come!" This first agent of Yahweh is summoned and given his purpose – to go forth conquering to conquer. Attributes

---

[100] Zechariah 2:6-9.

of this horseman are very telling as it relates to its identity and purpose. First, the horse is white. White is a color throughout the Apocalypse that represents purity. However, the horse being white doesn't mean the purpose of its rider is to bring purity or cleanliness to the objects of his judgment. In fact, we see later in chapter 13 that the second Beast has "two horns like unto a lamb," implying that its overall appearance was that of a lamb, which is white.

This rider also carries a bow. Interestingly enough, he is not said to be carrying any arrows. What good is a bow without arrows? Symbolically this is much more representative of the purpose of the horseman than if he were to be carrying arrows. The rider also wears a crown, which he was given. Unlike most crowns related to conquering this horseman is just *given* it. Taken as a whole, this horseman is one who *appears* to be innocent, and even righteous. He comes forth with a weapon, but not one that can harm people physically. He wears a crown that wasn't won or earned through battle, but was just given to him. His association with the other three horsemen, which come with great and terrible plagues, points to the fact that his mission isn't one for the benefit of those he's sent to. Yet his similar appearance to the horse and its rider in chapter 19 below would seem to link it directly to Yeshua. We must keep these descriptions in mind as we continue in our evaluation of this first seal.

The living creature calling this particular horseman is that which looked like a lion. Peter gives us another clue to the meaning and purpose of this horseman.

1 Peter 5:8-11
(8) Be sober, be watchful: your adversary the devil, as a roaring lion, walks about, seeking whom he may devour,
(9) whom withstand steadfast in your faith, knowing that the same sufferings are accomplished in your brethren who are in the world.
(10) And the Elohim of all grace, who called you unto his eternal glory in Messiah, after that you have suffered a little while, shall himself perfect, establish, strengthen you.
(11) To him *be* the dominion forever and ever. Amein.

Here the devil, as a roaring lion, is linked to the sufferings and persecutions of the brethren in the faith. Yeshua tells us what the disciples were to expect immediately after he left.

Luke 21:8
(8) And he said, Take heed that you be not **led astray**: for many shall come in my name, saying, I am *he*; and, The time is at hand: go you not after them.

Matthew 24:4-5
(4) And Yeshua answered and said unto them, Take heed that no man **lead you astray**.
(5) For many shall come in my name, saying, I am the Messiah; and shall **lead many astray**.

This rider of the white horse represents the spiritual deception that is brought through false messiahs and prophets that were to come after him. This spiritual deception succeeded in leading many astray from Yeshua in that generation. Some may ask, "Why would Yahweh send false prophets or messiahs to his own people?" False prophets were sent by Yahweh in the past for different reasons. Primarily, however, the reason was to test them, to see whether they would cling to Him and love Him.

Deuteronomy 13:1-5
(1) If there arise in the midst of you a prophet, or a dreamer of dreams, and he give you a sign or a wonder,
(2) and the sign or the wonder come to pass, whereof he spoke unto you, saying, Let us go after other elohim, which you have not known, and let us serve them;
(3) you shall not hearken unto the words of that prophet, or unto that dreamer of dreams: for Yahweh your Elohim proves you, to know whether you love Yahweh your Elohim with all your heart and with all your soul.
(4) You shall walk after Yahweh your Elohim, and fear him, and keep his commandments, and obey his voice, and you shall serve him, and cleave unto him.
(5) And that prophet, or that dreamer of dreams, shall be put to

death, because he has spoken rebellion against Yahweh your
Elohim, who brought you out of the land of Egypt, and redeemed
you out of the house of bondage, to draw you aside out of the
way which Yahweh your Elohim commanded you to walk in. So
shall you put away the evil from the midst of you.

Another reason was so that the plans he wanted to accomplish against
certain people would take place. In the following scriptural example,
Yahweh takes the credit for the events and actions that came to pass,
even though the idea itself was presented by an angel.

1 Kings 22:19-23
(19) And *Micaiah* said, Therefore hear you the word of Yahweh:
I saw Yahweh sitting on his throne, and all the host of heaven
standing by him on his right hand and on his left.
(20) And Yahweh said, Who shall entice Ahab, that he may go
up and fall at Ramoth-gilead? And one said on this manner; and
another said on that manner.
(21) And there came forth a spirit, and stood before Yahweh,
and said, I will entice him.
(22) And Yahweh said unto him, Wherewith? And he said, I will
go forth, and will be a lying spirit in the mouth of all his
prophets. And he said, You shall entice him, and shall prevail
also: go forth, and do so.
(23) Now therefore, behold, **Yahweh has put a lying spirit in the
mouth of all these your prophets**; and Yahweh has spoken evil
concerning you.

The false prophets were sent by Yahweh to entice Ahab to fight at
Ramoth-Gilead where he was to be defeated and slain. The spiritual
deception of false messiahs and prophets sent after Yeshua's earthly
ministry was intended to test and prove the faith of the disciples, as
well as make a clear distinction between those who were "elected" and
those who weren't. It is this deception that is represented by the white
horse and its rider.

We find several examples of false prophets, teachers, and messiahs
within the pages of the scriptures themselves spreading this spiritual

deception.

Acts 5:35-37
(35) And he said unto them, You men of Israel, take heed to yourselves as touching these men, what you are about to do.
(36) For before these days rose up Theudas, giving himself out to be somebody; to whom a number of men, about four hundred, joined themselves: who was slain; and all, as many as obeyed him, were dispersed, and came to nothing.
(37) After this man rose up Judas of Galilee in the days of the enrolment, and drew away *some of the* people after him: he also perished; and all, as many as obeyed him, were scattered abroad.

Josephus had the following to say of this Theudas:

"Now it came to pass, while Fadus was procurator of Judea, that a certain magician, whose name was Theudas, persuaded a great part of the people to take their effects with them, and follow him to the river Jordan; for he told them he was a prophet, and that he would, by his own command, divide the river, and afford them an easy passage over it; and many were deluded by his words. However, Fadus did not permit them to make any advantage of his wild attempt, but sent a troop of horsemen out against them; who, falling upon them unexpectedly, slew many of them, and took many of them alive. They also took Theudas alive, and cut off his head, and carried it to Jerusalem. This was what befell the Jews in the time of Cuspius Fadus's government."[101]

We find another account in the book of Acts:

Acts 8:9-11
(9) But there was a certain man, Simon by name, who beforetime in the city used sorcery, and amazed the people of Samaria, giving out that himself was some great one:
(10) to whom they all gave heed, from the least to the greatest,

---

[101] Josephus, Antiquities. 20.5.1. Page 531. *Cf.* Eusebius. Book 2, Chapter 11.

saying, This man is that power of Elohim which is called Great. (11) And they gave heed to him, because that of long time he had amazed them with his sorceries.

This Simon, called "Magus" [the Magician], was a false believer and a deceiver who led many in Samaria and other locations away from the worship of the true Elohim to worship him instead. Almost the entirety of the Clementine Recognitions and Homilies is devoted towards Peter's combating of Simon's false teachings. Eusebius, quoting Irenaeus, gives us additional information regarding this man and his deceptions:

> "And after the ascension of our Lord into heaven, certain men were suborned by demons as their agents, who said that they were gods. These were not only suffered to pass without persecution, but were even deemed worthy of honours by you. Simon, a certain Samaritan of the village called Githon, was one of the number, who, in the reign of Claudius Cesar, performed many magic rites by the operation of demons, was considered a god, in your imperial city of Rome, and was honoured by you with a statue as a god, in the river Tiber (on an island), between the two bridges, having the superscription in Latin, *Simoni Deo Sancto*, which is, 'To Simon the Holy God;' and nearly all the Samaritans, a few also of other nations, worship him, confessing him as the Supreme God."[102]

Yet another example can be found in Acts:

Acts 13:6-12
(6) And when they had gone through the whole island unto Paphos, they found a certain sorcerer, a false prophet, a Jew, whose name was Bar-Jesus;
(7) who was with the proconsul, Sergius Paulus, a man of understanding. The same called unto him Barnabas and Saul, and sought to hear the word of Elohim.
(8) But Elymas the sorcerer (for so is his name by interpretation) withstood them, seeking to turn aside the proconsul from the

---

[102] Eusebius. Book 2, Chapter 13.

faith.

(9) But Saul, who is also *called* Paul, filled with the holy spirit, fastened his eyes on him,

(10) and said, O full of all guile and all villany, you son of the devil, you enemy of all righteousness, will you not cease to pervert the right ways of the Master?

(11) And now, behold, the hand of the Master is upon you, and you shall be blind, not seeing the sun for a season. And immediately there fell on him a mist and a darkness; and he went about seeking some to lead him by the hand.

(12) Then the proconsul, when he saw what was done, believed, being astonished at the teaching of the Master.

This false prophet sought to lead people astray from the faith of Yeshua. Besides these direct accounts and historical testimonies, we have information in other locations in scripture that prove the existence and working of this spiritual deception in the days prior to the war.

1 John 2:18

(18) Little children, it is the last hour: and as you heard that anti-messiah comes, **even now has there arisen many anti-messiahs**; whereby we know that it is **the last hour**.

1 John 4:1-6

(1) Beloved, believe not every spirit, but **prove the spirits,** whether they are of Elohim; because **many false prophets are gone out into the world.**

(2) Hereby you know the spirit of Elohim: every spirit that confesses that Yeshua Messiah is come in the flesh is of Elohim:

(3) and every spirit that confesses not Yeshua is not of Elohim: and this is **the *spirit* of the anti-messiah**, whereof you have heard that it comes; and now it is in the world already.

(4) You are of Elohim, *my* little children, and have overcome them: because greater is he that is in you than he that is in the world.

(5) They are of the world: therefore speak they *as* of the world, and the world hears them.

(6) We are of Elohim: he that knows Elohim hears us; he who is

not of Elohim hears us not. By this we know the spirit of truth, and **the spirit of error**.

Revelation 2:2-3
(2) I know your works, and your toil and patience, and that you canst not bear evil men, and did try them that call themselves apostles, and they are not, and did find them false;
(3) and you have patience and did bear for my name's sake, and have not grown weary.

The belief in a singular "anti-messiah" is one that is quickly disposed of in John's letter quoted above. John's teaching in his letter regards the spiritual deception coming from those who are against messiah, whether they are false prophets or false messiahs. Just as the "wars and rumors of wars" in Yeshua's Olivet Discourse are represented by a single horse and rider in the Apocalypse, the red horse and its rider in the second seal judgment, so the single horse and rider of the first seal can represent an entire host of false prophets, teachers, and apostles.

This seal judgment, like the rest of them, doesn't cease prior to the second seal being broken. The sea continues to be stirred up by the work of this horse and its rider. False prophets and messiahs would continue even until the end of that age and beyond.

"These works, that were done by the robbers, filled the city with all sorts of impiety. And now these impostors and deceivers persuaded the multitude to follow them into the wilderness, and pretended that they would exhibit manifest wonders and signs, that should be performed by the providence of God. And many that were prevailed on by them suffered the punishments of their folly; for Felix brought them back, and then punished them. Moreover, there came out of Egypt about this time to Jerusalem one that said he was a prophet, and advised the multitude of the common people to go along with him to the Mount of Olives, as it was called, which lay over against the city, and at the distance of five furlongs. He said further, that he would show them from here how, at his command, the walls of Jerusalem would fall down; and he promised them that he would procure them an entrance into the city through those walls, when they were fallen down. Now when Felix was informed of these things, he ordered his soldiers to take their weapons, and came against them with a great number of horsemen and footmen from Jerusalem, and attacked the Egyptian and the people that were with him. He also slew four hundred of them, and took two hundred alive. But the Egyptian himself escaped out of the fight, but did not appear any more. And again the robbers stirred up the people to make war with the Romans, and said they ought not to obey them at all; and when any persons would not comply with them, they set fire to their villages, and plundered them."[103]

This Egyptian false prophet arose early in the reign of Nero, before the outbreak of the Jewish rebellion against Rome and the subsequent war.

"A false prophet was the occasion of these people's destruction, who had made a public proclamation in the city that very day, that God commanded them to get upon the temple, and that there they should receive miraculous signs of their deliverance. Now there was then a great number of false prophets suborned by the tyrants to impose on the people, who denounced this to them, that they should wait for deliverance from God; and this was in order to keep them from deserting, and that they might be buoyed up above fear and care by such hopes. Now a man that is in adversity does easily comply with such promises; for when such a seducer makes him believe that he shall be delivered from those miseries which oppress him, then it is that the patient is full of hopes of such his deliverance."[104]

These false prophets were prophesying at the very time that the temple itself was in flames.

From immediately after Yeshua's death and resurrection through the destruction of the temple, Jerusalem, and the Jewish commonwealth, the rider on the white horse, representing the spiritual deception

---

[103] Josephus, Antiquities. 20.8.6. Page 536.
[104] Josephus, Wars. 6.5.2. Page 741.

taught through false prophets, teachers, and apostles, was called and sent forth conquering and to conquer.

The Second Seal

(3) And when he opened the second seal, I heard the second living creature saying, Come.
(4) And another *horse* came forth, a red horse: and to him that sat thereon it was given to take peace from the land, and that they should slay one another: and there was given unto him a great sword.

It couldn't be much clearer than what John wrote. What takes peace from the land and comes along with a great sword more so than war? Yeshua once again didn't leave us in the dark as to when this was to occur.

Luke 21:10-11a
(10) Then said he unto them, Nation shall rise against nation, and kingdom against kingdom;
(11a) and there shall be great earthquakes,

Matthew 24:6-7a
(6) And you shall hear of wars and rumors of wars; see that you be not troubled: for *these things* must come to pass; but the end is not yet.
(7a) For nation shall rise against nation, and kingdom against kingdom;

One need not do anything but a cursory perusal of the historical records such as those of Josephus, Tacitus, Suetonius, Cassius Dio, et al, to see the proliferation of "wars and rumors of wars" during the first century. Josephus specifically provides us with the explicit details of the continual civil wars the Jews waged within Jerusalem. They were, as the second seal indicates, "slaying one another." Yeshua's instruction to his apostles and disciples was to not see all of those as precursors to the end of the age, not the end itself. The sign they were to see, and abomination of desolation they were to look for, would be very clear and apparent so as to not be mistaken by them.

Just like the first seal, these wars and rumors of wars weren't to cease prior to the opening of the third seal. The seals were ongoing judgments merely initiated by their opening.

The Third Seal

(5) And when he opened the third seal, I heard the third living creature saying, Come. And I saw, and behold, a black horse; and he that sat thereon had a balance in his hand.
(6) And I heard as it were a voice in the midst of the four living creatures saying, A measure[105] of wheat for a denarius, and three measures of barley for a denarius; and the oil and the wine hurt you not.

A natural consequence of war is famine and great pestilence that often arises from it. Yeshua prophesied the same.

Luke 21:11b
(11b) and in diverse places famines and pestilences;

Matthew 24:7b
(7b) and there shall be famines and earthquakes in diverse places.

Famines did indeed plague the land of Israel before the war and throughout it. A very severe plague took place during the reign of Claudius Caesar (*ca.* 41-54 CE). This is mentioned in the book of Acts and occasioned the assemblies outside of Israel to take a collection for the brethren in Judea.

Acts 11:28-29
(28) And there stood up one of them named Agabus, and signified by the spirit that there should be a great famine over all

---

[105] Gr. χοῖνιξ, *choinix*.

the world: which came to pass in the days of Claudius.
(29) And the disciples, every man according to his ability,
determined to send relief unto the brethren that dwelt in Judaea.

Testimony of this same famine can be found in the historical record as
well.

"But as to Helena, the king's mother, when she saw that the affairs
of Izates's kingdom were in peace, and that her son was a happy
man, and admired among all men, and even among foreigners, by
the means of God's providence over him, she had a mind to go to the
city of Jerusalem, in order to worship at that temple of God which
was so very famous among all men, and to offer her thank-offerings
there. So she desired her son to give her leave to go thither; upon
which he gave his consent to what she desired very willingly, and
made great preparations for her dismission, and gave her a great
deal of money, and she went down to the city Jerusalem, her son
conducting her on her journey a great way. Now her coming was of
very great advantage to the people of Jerusalem; for whereas a
famine did oppress them at that time, and many people died for
want of what was necessary to procure food withal, queen Helena
sent some of her servants to Alexandria with money to buy a great
quantity of corn, and others of them to Cyprus, to bring a cargo of
dried figs. And as soon as they were come back, and had brought
those provisions, which was done very quickly, she distributed food
to those that were in want of it, and left a most excellent memorial
behind her of this benefaction, which she bestowed on our whole
nation. And when her son Izates was informed of this famine, he
sent great sums of money to the principal men in Jerusalem.
However, what favors this queen and king conferred upon our city
Jerusalem shall be further related hereafter."[106]

"During a scarcity of provisions, occasioned by bad crops for several
successive years, he was stopped in the middle of the forum by the
mob, who so abused him, at the same time pelting him with

---

[106] Josephus, Antiquities. 20.2.5. Page 528.

fragments of bread, that he had some difficulty in escaping into the palace by a back door. He therefore used all possible means to bring provisions to the city, even in winter. He proposed to the merchants a sure profit, by indemnifying them against any loss that might befall them by storms at sea; and granted great privileges to those who built ships for that traffic."[107]

"Several prodigies occurred in that year. Birds of evil omen perched on the Capitol; houses were thrown down by frequent shocks of earthquake, and as the panic spread, all the weak were trodden down in the hurry and confusion of the crowd. Scanty crops too, and consequent famine were regarded as a token of calamity. Nor were there merely whispered complaints; while Claudius was administering justice, the populace crowded round him with a boisterous clamour and drove him to a corner of the forum, where they violently pressed on him till he broke through the furious mob with a body of soldiers. It was ascertained that Rome had provisions for no more than fifteen days, and it was through the signal bounty of heaven and the mildness of the winter that its desperate plight was relieved."[108]

We can read several portions in Josephus' *Wars of the Jews* that are truly amazing as it relates to the severity of the famine in the days of the first Jewish-Roman war.

"After this man there ran away to Titus many of the eminent citizens...and they told him further, that when they were no longer able to carry out the dead bodies of the poor, they laid their corpses on heaps in very large houses, and shut them up therein; as also that a **medimnus of wheat was sold for a talent**; and that when, a while afterward, it was not possible to gather herbs, by reason the city was all walled about, some persons were driven to that terrible distress

---

[107] Suetonius, Claudius. Chapter 19.
[108] Tacitus, Annals. Book 12, Chapter 43.

as to search the common sewers and old dunghills of cattle, and to eat the dung which they got there; and what they of old could not endure so much as to see they now used for food."[109]

The medimnus was the principal dry measure of the Greeks and is equivalent to roughly 11 gallons in the imperial system[110], which is what is used in the United States today. According to the same lexical entry in Smith's dictionary, there are forty-eight χοῖνικες, *choinikes*, per imperial gallon, and thus five hundred twenty-eight in a medimnus. The Greek text of Revelation 6:6 translates the Greek word χοῖνιξ, *choinix*, the singular for χοῖνικες, as "measure" in English. A talent is equivalent to 6,000 drachmae or denarii. Assuming Josephus is referring to a talent of silver, equivalent to about seventy-five pounds, he's saying that you would only get eleven gallons of wheat grains for seventy-five pounds of silver.

The third seal judgment clearly symbolizes the severe famines that were to take place after Yeshua's death and resurrection through the expiration of the war.

The Fourth Seal

(7) And when he opened the fourth seal, I heard the voice of the fourth living creature saying, Come.
(8) And I saw, and behold, a pale horse: and he that sat upon him, his name was Death; and Hades followed with him. And there was given unto them authority over the fourth part of the earth, to kill with sword, and with famine, and with death, and by the wild beasts of the earth.

What are more sequential and consequential results of persecution, war, and famine than death? The severity of the destruction and

---

[109] Josephus, Wars. 5.13.7. Page 726.
[110] Smith. Entry for MEDIMNUS. Page 246.

desolation resulting from the war and the atrocities committed during it is truly staggering. Josephus tells us that there were around 1,100,000 casualties during the siege of Jerusalem alone[111]. Part of that great number were tens of thousands of the people trapped in the city during the siege who were quickly overtaken by famine or the pestilence that resulted therefrom.

What is Hades?

There are varying beliefs about what Hades is and was understood to be in the first century. Some believe that Hades simply refers to the grave. Others would say that Hades refers to a place where the spirits of the dead are held awaiting judgment. There are passages in the New Testament that would lend credence to the latter.

Matthew 10:28
(28) And be not afraid of them that kill the body, but are not able to kill the soul: but rather fear him who is able to destroy both soul and body in Gehenna.

Luke 16:23
And in Hades he lifted up his eyes, being in torments, and sees Abraham afar off, and Lazarus in his bosom.

Revelation 1:17-18
(17) And when I saw him, I fell at his feet as one dead. And he laid his right hand upon me, saying, Fear not; I am the first and the last,
(18) and the Living one; and I was dead, and behold, I am alive for evermore, and I have the keys of death and of Hades.

The verse in Luke and its surrounding context is probably the clearest example one could find to show that Hades could be a holding place for the spirits of the dead. There would appear to be two sections within this Hades, one for the righteous dead, called "Abraham's bosom," and

---

[111] Josephus, Wars. 6.9.3. Page 749.

the other for the unrighteous dead. The fact that Yeshua makes a distinction between a fleshly destruction that can be caused by man and a *spiritual* one that can be caused by Yahweh would also give some support to a "life after death" belief.

However, those who believe that Hades is synonymous with the grave aren't without scriptural support either.

Ecclesiastes 3:19-21
(19) For that which befalls the sons of men befalls beasts; even one thing befalls them: as the one dies, so dies the other; yea, they have all one breath; and man has no preeminence above the beasts: for all is vanity.
(20) All go unto one place; all are of the dust, and all turn to dust again.
(21) Who knows the spirit of man, whether it goes upward, and the spirit of the beast, whether it goes downward to the earth?

Ezekiel 18:4
Behold, all souls are my; as the soul of the father, so also the soul of the son is my: the soul that sins, it shall die.

Psalms 104:29
You hide your face, they are troubled; You take away their breath, they die, And return to their dust.

Ecclesiastes 9:10
Whatsoever your hand finds to do, do *it* with your might; for there is no work, nor device, nor knowledge, nor wisdom, in Sheol, whither you go.

The above passages lead one to the conclusion that Sheol, the Hebrew equivalent of Hades[112], is one and the same as the grave.

---

[112] According to Thayer, entry for Ἅιδης, page 11 – "In the Sept. the Heb. שְׁאוֹל is almost always rendered by this word (once by θάνατος, 2 S. xxi. 6)."

It is not within the scope of this work to perform a comprehensive study of the nature of Sheol, Hades, and the grave. However, whether Hades be a location where the disembodied spirits of dead men and women inhabit, or merely a synonym for the grave in which one is buried after death, one fact remains true – there is an intermediate place between death and eternal life.

The Fifth Seal

(9) And when he opened the fifth seal, I saw underneath the altar the souls of them that had been slain for the word of Elohim, and for the testimony which they held:
(10) and they cried with a great voice, saying, How long, O Master, the holy and true, do you not judge and avenge our blood on them that dwell on the earth?
(11) And there was given them to each one a white robe; and it was said unto them, that they should rest yet for a little time, until their fellow-servants also and their brethren, who should be killed even as they were, should have fulfilled *their course*.

The breaking of this seal reveals the martyrs in Yeshua and their passionate plea to him for justice. Yeshua revealed this fact as a part of his Olivet Discourse.

Luke 21:12-19
(12) But before all these things, they shall lay their hands on you, and shall persecute you, delivering you up to the synagogues and prisons, bringing you before kings and governors for my name's sake.
(13) It shall turn out unto you for a testimony.
(14) Settle it therefore in your hearts, not to meditate beforehand how to answer:
(15) for I will give you a mouth and wisdom, which all your adversaries shall not be able to withstand or to gainsay.
(16) But you shall be delivered up even by parents, and brethren, and kinsfolk, and friends; and *some* of you shall they cause to be put to death.
(17) And you shall be hated of all men for my name's sake.

(18) And not a hair of your head shall perish.
(19) In your patience you shall win your souls.

Matthew 24:9
Then shall they deliver you up unto tribulation, and shall kill you: and you shall be hated of all the nations for my name's sake.

In the fifth seal we see that there were still to be martyrs after its breaking. The persecution of believers hit a great peak under what is known as the "Neronic Persecution," which began in 64 CE under the emperor Nero and didn't end until his suicide in June of 68 CE. More details and historical information on this persecution will be provided in chapter 13 below. Suffice it to say for now, the number of believers slain in the land of Israel and abroad during the period between Yeshua's death and resurrection and the destruction of Jerusalem is staggering.

The Sixth Seal

(12) And I saw when he opened the sixth seal, and there was a great earthquake; and the sun became black as sackcloth of hair, and the whole moon became as blood;
(13) and the stars of the heaven fell unto the earth, as a fig tree casts her unripe figs when she is shaken of a great wind.
(14) And the heaven was removed as a scroll when it is rolled up; and every mountain and island were moved out of their places.
(15) And the kings of the earth, and the princes, and the chief captains, and the rich, and the strong, and every bondman and freeman, hid themselves in the caves and in the rocks of the mountains;
(16) and they say to the mountains and to the rocks, Fall on us, and hide us from the face of him that sits on the throne, and from the wrath of the Lamb:
(17) for the great day of their wrath is come; and who is able to stand?

John is yet again pulling together prophecies and messages here from multiple sources to get his message across. The prophecy of Joel is one of the first that comes to the reader's mind.

> Joel 2:28-32
> (28) And it shall come to pass afterward, that I will pour out my spirit upon all flesh; and your sons and your daughters shall prophesy, your old men shall dream dreams, your young men shall see visions:
> (29) and also upon the servants and upon the handmaids in those days will I pour out my spirit.
> (30) **And I will show wonders in the heavens and in the earth: blood, and fire, and pillars of smoke.**
> (31) **The sun shall be turned into darkness, and the moon into blood, before the great and terrible day of Yahweh comes.**
> (32) And it shall come to pass, that whosoever shall call on the name of Yahweh shall be delivered; for in mount Zion and in Jerusalem there shall be those that escape, as Yahweh has said, and among the remnant those whom Yahweh does call.

Peter quoted this exact same passage in his speech on the day of Pentecost[113] in the first century. The people saw Peter and the disciples and thought they were drunk. The purpose of his speech was two-fold. First, he was telling them with no uncertainty that they were *not* drunk. Second, he was telling them that what they were seeing was a fulfillment of Joel's prophecy above. Peter actually says, "And it shall be in the *last days*, says Elohim..." He then goes on to finish the quote from Joel. Futurists typically concede that the "pour out My spirit upon all flesh" portion of the prophecy was fulfilled at that time in the first century. But, they conveniently push the remaining portion of the prophecy, that which relates to the "great and terrible day of Yahweh," to some unknown time in Peter's future, nineteen centuries of which have already passed. Would it not be more logical and scripturally prudent to believe that Peter quoted the entirety of the prophecy of Joel because all of it was to take place in his day?

---

[113] Acts 2:14-21.

In this seal, John also draws references from Isaiah and Hosea:

Isaiah 34:3-4
(3) Their slain also shall be cast out, and the stench of their dead bodies shall come up; and the mountains shall be melted with their blood.
(4) And **all the host of heaven shall be dissolved**, and **the heavens shall be rolled together as a scroll**; and all their host shall fade away, as the leaf fades from off the vine, **and as a fading *leaf* from the fig-tree**.

Isaiah 2:12-21
(12) For there shall be a **day of Yahweh** of hosts upon all that is proud and haughty, and upon all that is lifted up; and it shall be brought low;
(13) and upon all the cedars of Lebanon, that are high and lifted up, and upon all the oaks of Bashan,
(14) and upon all the high mountains, and upon all the hills that are lifted up,
(15) and upon every lofty tower, and upon every fortified wall,
(16) and upon all the ships of Tarshish, and upon all pleasant imagery.
(17) And the loftiness of man shall be bowed down, and the haughtiness of men shall be brought low; and Yahweh alone shall be exalted in that day.
(18) And the idols shall utterly pass away.
(19) And **men shall go into the caves of the rocks, and into the holes of the earth**, from before the terror of Yahweh, and from the glory of his majesty, when he arises to shake mightily the earth.
(20) In that day men shall cast away their idols of silver, and their idols of gold, which have been made for them to worship, to the moles and to the bats;
(21) **to go into the caverns of the rocks**, and **into the clefts of the ragged rocks**, from before the terror of Yahweh, and from the glory of his majesty, when he arise to shake mightily the earth.

Hosea 10:8
(8) The high places also of Aven, the sin of Israel, shall be

destroyed: the thorn and the thistle shall come up on their altars; and **they shall say to the mountains, Cover us; and to the hills, Fall on us**.

Yeshua also taught on these great phenomena in his discourse on the Mount of Olives and even while being led to the cross.

Matthew 24:32-35
(32) Now from **the fig tree** learn her parable: when her branch is now become tender, and puts forth its leaves, you know that the summer is near;
(33) even so you also, when you see all these things, know you that he is near, *even* at the doors.
(34) Verily I say unto you, This generation shall not pass away, till all these things be accomplished.
(35) Heaven and earth shall pass away, but my words shall not pass away.

Luke 21:29-33
(29) And he spoke to them a parable: Behold **the fig tree**, and all the trees:
(30) when they now shoot forth, you see it and know of your own selves that the summer is now near.
(31) Even so you also, when you see these things coming to pass, know you that **the kingdom of Elohim is near**.
(32) Verily I say unto you, This generation shall not pass away, till all things be accomplished.
(33) Heaven and earth shall pass away: but my words shall not pass away.

Luke 23:29-30
(29) For behold, the days are coming, in which they shall say, Blessed are the barren, and the wombs that never bore, and the breasts that never gave suck.
(30) Then shall they begin *to say to the mountains, Fall on us; and to the hills, Cover us*.

The message of John is very clear. He is drawing upon the teachings of Yeshua and the prophets to tell them one thing – the infamous Day of

Yahweh had come. As we have been thus far we need to view these passages through the apocalyptic lens. Though John and Yeshua may very well be speaking of actual, physical events that were to take place during the time of the end of the age, it is more likely that they are speaking about the prophetic equivalents. See the chart of apocalyptic terminology in the Introduction above for more information.

Earthquakes and famines are likely literal events in this context, though they can refer to the shaking of earthly governments and famines in the spirit or word. Signs appearing in the sun, moon, and stars can also be literal in certain instances, but in this context, it more likely refers to the shaking and eventual destruction of the various classes of people in Israel. From the rich and learned to the poor and ignorant, none are exempt from the coming wrath.

It's very clear that some of the actions referred to in this seal, such as the rolling up of the heavens, cannot be literal. If they were, the heavens would have been rolled up long ago. The mountains would all be melted. Yet that is not what we see. Ezekiel is told to prophesy to the "mountains of Israel."[114] We see later that Yahweh was referring to people, not actual mountains.

These passages go to show us that the destruction or manipulation of earthly or heavenly bodies aren't intended to be literal in apocalyptic or prophetic literature. In many circumstances, however, those apocalyptic actions may very well have real world fulfillments. Context and scope help us determine which of the events are to be interpreted literally. Earthquakes and famines, for instance, are not uncommon events in the span of human history. Looking for fulfillments of those would not be difficult, especially when researching dreadful and awesome wars of the past. Believing that we would actually see the heavens turn over on themselves and roll up as a scroll brings us outside the scope of reality. After all, if the heavens were rolled up here as a part of the sixth seal, what is the purpose of the rest of the Apocalypse? Would not judgment and destruction have been rendered

---

[114] Ezekiel 6:1-6.

upon all at that time?

Nevertheless, Josephus and other historians record remarkable events in history that preceded the war.

> "Thus were the miserable people persuaded by these deceivers, and such as belied God himself; while they did not attend nor give credit to the signs that were so evident, and did so plainly foretell their future desolation, but, like men infatuated, without either eyes to see or minds to consider, did not regard the denunciations that God made to them. Thus there was **a star** resembling a sword, which stood over the city, and **a comet**, that continued a whole year. Thus also before the Jews' rebellion, and before those commotions which preceded the war, when the people were come in great crowds to the feast of unleavened bread, on the eighth day of the month Xanthicus, [Nisan,] and at the ninth hour of the night, so great a light shone round the altar and the holy house, that it appeared to be bright day time; which lasted for half an hour. This light seemed to be a good sign to the unskillful, but was so interpreted by the sacred scribes, as to portend those events that followed immediately upon it. At the same festival also, a heifer, as she was led by the high priest to be sacrificed, brought forth a lamb in the midst of the temple. Moreover, the eastern gate of the inner [court of the] temple, which was of brass, and vastly heavy, and had been with difficulty shut by twenty men, and rested upon a basis armed with iron, and had bolts fastened very deep into the firm floor, which was there made of one entire stone, was seen to be opened of its own accord about the sixth hour of the night. Now those that kept watch in the temple came hereupon running to the captain of the temple, and told him of it; who then came up thither, and not without great difficulty was able to shut the gate again. This also appeared to the vulgar to be a very happy prodigy, as if God did thereby open them the gate of happiness. But the men of learning understood it, that the security of their holy house was dissolved of its own accord, and that the gate was opened for the advantage of their enemies. So **these publicly declared that the signal foreshowed the desolation that was coming upon them.**

Besides these, a few days after that feast, on the one and twentieth day of the month Artemisius, [Jyar,] a certain prodigious and incredible phenomenon appeared: I suppose the account of it would seem to be a fable, were it not related by those that saw it, and were not the events that followed it of so considerable a nature as to deserve such signals; for, before sun-setting, **chariots and troops of soldiers in their armor were seen running about among the clouds, and surrounding of cities.** Moreover, at that feast which we call Pentecost, as the priests were going by night into the inner [court of the temple,] as their custom was, to perform their sacred ministrations, they said that, in the first place, they felt **a quaking,** and heard a great noise, and after that they heard a sound as of a great multitude, saying, "Let us remove from here."

But, what is still more terrible, there was one Jesus, the son of Ananus, a plebeian and a husbandman, who, four years before the war began, and at a time when the city was in very great peace and prosperity, came to that feast whereon it is our custom for everyone to make tabernacles to God in the temple, began on a sudden to cry aloud, 'A voice from the east, a voice from the west, a voice from the four winds, a voice against Jerusalem and the holy house, a voice against the bridegrooms and the brides, and a voice against this whole people!' This was his cry, as he went about by day and by night, in all the lanes of the city. However, certain of the most eminent among the populace had great indignation at this dire cry of his, and took up the man, and gave him a great number of severe stripes; yet did not he either say anything for himself, or anything peculiar to those that chastised him, but still went on with the same words which he cried before. Hereupon our rulers, supposing, as the case proved to be, that this was a sort of divine fury in the man, brought him to the Roman procurator, where he was whipped till his bones were laid bare; yet he did not make any supplication for himself, nor shed any tears, but turning his voice to the most lamentable tone possible, at every stroke of the whip his answer was, 'Woe, woe to Jerusalem!' And when Albinus (for he was then our procurator) asked him, Who he was? and from where he came? and why he uttered such words? he made no manner of reply to what he said, but still did not leave off his melancholy ditty, till

Albinus took him to be a madman, and dismissed him. Now, during all the time that passed before the war began, this man did not go near any of the citizens, nor was seen by them while he said so; but he every day uttered these lamentable words, as if it were his premeditated vow, 'Woe, woe to Jerusalem!' Nor did he give ill words to any of those that beat him every day, nor good words to those that gave him food; but this was his reply to all men, and indeed no other than a melancholy presage of what was to come. This cry of his was the loudest at the festivals; and he continued this ditty for seven years and five months, without growing hoarse, or being tired therewith, until the very time that he saw his presage in earnest fulfilled in our siege, when it ceased; for as he was going round upon the wall, he cried out with his utmost force, 'Woe, woe to the city again, and to the people, and to the holy house!' And just as he added at the last, 'Woe, woe to myself also!' there came a stone out of one of the engines, and smote him, and killed him immediately; and as he was uttering the very same presages he gave up the ghost."[115]

"Prodigies had occurred, which this nation, prone to superstition, but hating all religious rites, did not deem it lawful to expiate by offering and sacrifice. **There had been seen hosts joining battle in the skies, the fiery gleam of arms, the temple illuminated by a sudden radiance from the clouds.** The doors of the inner shrine were suddenly thrown open, and a voice of more than mortal tone was heard to cry that the Gods were departing. At the same instant there was a mighty stir as of departure. Some few put a fearful meaning on these events, but in most there was a firm persuasion, that in the ancient records of their priests was contained a prediction of how at this very time the East was to grow powerful, and rulers, coming from Judaea, were to acquire universal empire. These mysterious prophecies had pointed to Vespasian and Titus, but the common people, with the usual blindness of ambition, had interpreted these

---

[115] Josephus, Wars. 6.5.3. Pages 742-743.

mighty destinies of themselves, and could not be brought even by disasters to believe the truth."[116]

In a futile attempt to convince his fellow Jews in Jerusalem to surrender to Titus, that they all not be destroyed, we read the following.

"The same wonderful sign you had also experience of formerly, when the forementioned king of Babylon made war against us, and when he took the city, and burnt the temple; while yet I believe the Jews of that age were not so impious as you are. Wherefore I cannot but suppose that God is fled out of his sanctuary, and stands on the side of those against whom you fight. Now even a man, if he be but a good man, will fly from an impure house, and will hate those that are in it; and do you persuade yourselves that God will abide with you in your iniquities, who sees all secret things, and hears what is kept most private?"[117]

Josephus himself believed that Elohim had departed from the temple. These signs in the heavens and on earth should have been ones that dissuaded the Jews to go to war with Rome. Yet, we know they did not. The testimonies tell us that Yahweh had left the temple and was sending his angelic armies against Israel to destroy them.

John is trying, through prophetic imagery, to transmit what was to happen in such a way that when it did, all the "pieces of the puzzle" would fall naturally into place. Such it is with the fearful cry to the rocks of those to whom Yahweh's wrath was directed, "Fall on us, and hide us from the face of him that sits on the throne, and from the wrath of the Lamb!" This statement isn't meant to cause one to search through the entirety of history for proof that the Jews acknowledged that the wrath upon them was from "the Lamb." Nor is it something that should be stretched into some unknown time in the future. John is telling his audience that the objects of Yahweh's wrath will be doing anything to try to escape it, including hiding themselves in caves,

---

[116] Tacitus, Histories. Book 5, Chapter 13.
[117] Josephus, Wars. 5.9.4. Page 718.

trusting that the rocks they were made of would protect them. History tells us this couldn't have been farther from the truth towards the end of the war:

"So now the last hope which supported the tyrants, and that crew of robbers who were with them, was in the caves and caverns underground; whither, if they could once fly, they did not expect to be searched for; but endeavored, that after the whole city should be destroyed, and the Romans gone away, they might come out again, and escape from them. This was no better than a dream of theirs; for they were not able to lie hid either from God or from the Romans."[118]

Another account records how Simon, one of the leaders of the rebellion and the head of one of the three final factions in Jerusalem[119], hid himself in an underground cavern and attempted to deceive the Romans even till the end. After he rose from the ground we read the following:

"This rise of his out of the ground did also occasion the discovery of a great number of others of the seditious at that time, who had hidden themselves under ground."[120]

Their cry to the rocks wasn't one that needed to be audible, nor did the phrase "the Lamb" need to be a part of it. They wanted to be hidden from the wrath coming upon them, which Vespasian, Titus, and Josephus all acknowledged was from Elohim, and therefore placed their trust in lifeless stones. The day of vengeance and wrath that the followers of Yeshua had been taught about their entire lives, known as the Day of Yahweh, was come upon them. John carefully pieced together pieces of the prophecies of old and the teachings of Yeshua to convey that message to his audience.

---

[118] Josephus, Wars. 6.7.3. Page 746.
[119] Josephus, Wars. 5.1.4. Page 697.
[120] Josephus, Wars. 7.2.1. Page 752.

One final, yet important verse needs to be discussed here in light of Josephus' historical testimony above.

> 1 Thessalonians 5:3
> When they are saying, **Peace and safety**, then sudden destruction comes upon them, as travail upon a woman with child; and they shall in no wise escape.

Futurists will often say something along the lines of, "There is no place in recorded history, before the war, where the people were saying, 'Peace and safety,' therefore those days couldn't have been the last days. On the contrary it was war and chaos." However, notice what Josephus said above. When speaking of Jesus, son of Ananus, he said, "four years before the war began, and at a time when the city was in **very great peace and prosperity**." Again, we aren't required to have a quote in history of people physically crying, "Peace and safety," though that very well may have been the case. History tells us that was the state of Israel at that time.

CHAPTER SEVEN

The Unanswered Question

Chapter 6 above, at the end of the sixth seal in the very last verse, a question is posed yet never answered – "for the great day of their wrath is come; and **who is able to stand**?" From the perspective of John's audience this would have been a very pivotal time in the reading of the Apocalypse. Thus far they have heard almost nothing but catastrophic and devastating things that were to be happening around and potentially to them.

Most of the assemblies are told about the things they are doing wrong and need to correct. They hear of a great judicial assembly being gathered to mete out the judgments of the Almighty Creator and His Son, Yeshua. They hear of terrifying horses and terrible hardships and plagues that were to be inflicted upon the people and the land. Yet through all of this, nothing encouraging. Then, to wrap it all up, they are left with a rhetorical question, the answer to which would, based on all they had just heard, be "No one!"

This, however, is not the answer John gives. Chapter 7 is a sort of pause in the tale of the judgment of Yahweh upon the people to bring great encouragement to the people and to answer the rhetorical question correctly. Who is able to stand? Those who are sealed and elected by Yahweh to be a part of His kingdom!

The 144,000

(1) After this I saw four angels standing at the four corners of the earth, holding the four winds of the earth, that no wind should blow on the earth, or on the sea, or upon any tree.

(2) And I saw another angel ascend from the sunrising, having the seal of the living Elohim: and he cried with a great voice to the four angels to whom it was given to hurt the earth and the sea,

(3) saying, Hurt not the earth, neither the sea, nor the trees, till we shall have sealed the servants of our Elohim on their foreheads.

(4) And I heard the number of them that were sealed, a hundred and forty and four thousand, sealed out of every tribe of the children of Israel:

(5) Of the tribe of Judah *were* sealed twelve thousand: Of the tribe of Reuben twelve thousand; Of the tribe of Gad twelve thousand;

(6) Of the tribe of Asher twelve thousand; Of the tribe of Naphtali twelve thousand; Of the tribe of Manasseh twelve thousand;

(7) Of the tribe of Simeon twelve thousand; Of the tribe of Levi twelve thousand; Of the tribe of Issachar twelve thousand;

(8) Of the tribe of Zebulun twelve thousand; Of the tribe of Joseph twelve thousand; Of the tribe of Benjamin *were* sealed twelve thousand.

John now prompts his audience to open their minds to the specifics of those who will be able to stand in this time of tribulation and judgment. This chapter contains a contrast exactly like that found in chapter 4 above. John at first *heard* of a certain number of people that are sealed. As we will see later, however, what he *saw* was completely different.

Prior to the sealing of the 144,000 from all tribes we see angels holding back the four winds. These four winds of heaven are mentioned elsewhere in the scriptures as Yahweh's agents for executing his judgments.

Zechariah 6:1-5

(1) And again I lifted up my eyes, and saw, and, behold, there came four chariots out from between two mountains; and the mountains were mountains of brass.

(2) In the first chariot were red horses; and in the second chariot black horses;

(3) and in the third chariot white horses; and in the fourth chariot grizzled strong horses.

(4) Then I answered and said unto the angel that talked with me, What are these, my master?

(5) And the angel answered and said unto me, **These are the four winds of heaven**, which go forth from standing before the Master of all the earth.

The four angels in this chapter are preventing these four winds of heaven from executing the judgments of Yahweh upon the apocalyptic land, sea, and trees until His servants are sealed.

We can search all the records of history that have ever been written and still not find something that directly identifies who these 144,000 people were. We know enough from the symbolism used throughout the Apocalypse and elsewhere in the scriptures, however, to ascertain the meaning of this group.

We must first examine the numbers here involved. Though John writes a specific number of sealed ones for each of the tribes mentioned, this is once again another apocalyptic allusion. The number twelve is of great significance in the scriptures. There were exactly twelve tribes of Israel – Reuben, Simeon, Levi, Judah, Dan, Naphtali, Gad, Asher, Issachar, Zebulun, Joseph, and Benjamin. There were exactly twelve judges of Israel - Othniel, Ehud, Shamgar, Deborah, Gideon, Tola, Jair, Jephthah, Ibzan, Elon, Abdon, and Samson. Yeshua chose exactly twelve apostles – Simon [*a/k/a Cephas, or Peter*], Andrew, James the *son* of Zebedee, John, Philip, Bartholomew, Thomas, Matthew, James the *son* of Alphaeus, Thaddaeus, Simon the Cananaean, and Judas Iscariot[121]. Within the Apocalypse itself we see the number twelve used for the thousands sealed from each tribe in this chapter. In chapter 21 we see it used for the number of gates in the New Jerusalem, the number of the angels guarding those gates, the number of foundations it has, and the number of the thousands of stadia in the measurements of the city[122]. Within the corpus of scripture, the number twelve represents a complete and perfect number.

The number one thousand also has significance beyond its face value.

Exodus 20:4-6
(4) You shall not make unto you a graven image, nor any likeness *of anything* that is in heaven above, or that is in the earth beneath, or that is in the water under the earth:
(5) you shall not bow down yourself unto them, nor serve them; for I Yahweh your Elohim am a jealous Elohim, visiting the iniquity of the fathers upon the children, upon the third and upon the fourth generation of them that hate me,
(6) and showing lovingkindness unto **thousands** of them that love me and keep my commandments.

The word "thousands" here isn't intended to place a limit on the scope Yahweh's mercy and lovingkindness.

Deuteronomy 1:11
Yahweh, the Elohim of your fathers, make you **a thousand times** as many as you are, and bless you, as he has promised you!

Moses' blessing wasn't intended to limit the increase of Israel to only a thousand times, as if that was a maximum to the number of Israelites permitted.

---

[121] Who, after his suicide, was subsequently replaced by only one other individual – Matthias. Acts 1:15-26.
[122] Revelation 21:9-16.

Deuteronomy 7:9-10
(9) Know therefore that Yahweh your Elohim, he is Elohim, the faithful Elohim, who keeps covenant and lovingkindness with them that love him and keep his commandments to **a thousand generations**,
(10) and repays them that hate him to their face, to destroy them: he will not be slack to him that hates him, he will repay him to his face.

This does not mean that Yahweh doesn't keep his covenant with the thousand and first generation.

Psalms 50:10
For every beast of the forest is mine, And the cattle upon **a thousand hills.**

Obviously Yahweh still owns the cattle on the thousand and first hill. More examples of this can be provided, but the above should suffice to show that the word "thousand" isn't to always be interpreted as a fixed number. This is especially true when it is found in prophetic or apocalyptic literature.

What John is telling his audience is that the perfect number of Israelites from the twelve tribes to be sealed and saved will be great, innumerable, and perfect.

The Tribal Mix-Up

One interesting thing that can be found in this passage is the fact that the tribes of Dan and Ephraim were excluded from the list and the tribe of Levi was included. In a similar numbering in the past the tribe of Levi was specifically excluded as they were appointed over the tabernacle of the testimony and the various ministrations therein[123]. They were also not given an inheritance in the land of Israel. In contrast, Dan and Ephraim were included in the numbering of the children of Israel and were allotted a portion of the land of Canaan. How can we explain this apparent conundrum?

---

[123] Numbers 1.

Israel's prophecy over his son Dan as well as their recorded history explains his absence in the numbering of the 144,000.

Genesis 49:16-17
(16) Dan shall judge his people, As one of the tribes of Israel.
(17) Dan **shall be a serpent in the way**, An adder in the path,
That bites the horse's heels, So that his rider falls backward.

The tribe of Dan was the first one to dive headlong into idolatry. Their worship of idols lasted all the way from the time of the Judges until the exile into captivity in Babylon[124]. Ephraim's exclusion is also a symbolic allusion to the teachings of which the Hebrews would have been well-acquainted. We read the following in the scriptures:

Psalms 78:9-17, 65-67
(9) The children of Ephraim, being armed and carrying bows, Turned back in the day of battle.
(10) **They kept not the covenant of Elohim, And refused to walk in his Torah;**
(11) And they forgot his doings, And his wondrous works that he had showed them.
(12) Marvelous things did he in the sight of their fathers, In the land of Egypt, in the field of Zoan.
(13) He cleaved the sea, and caused them to pass through; And he made the waters to stand as a heap.
(14) In the day-time also he led them with a cloud, And all the night with a light of fire.
(15) He cleaved rocks in the wilderness, And gave them drink abundantly as out of the depths.
(16) He brought streams also out of the rock, And caused waters to run down like rivers.
(17) **Yet went they on still to sin against him, To rebel against the Most High in the desert...**
(65) Then the Master awaked as one out of sleep, Like a mighty man that shouts by reason of wine.
(66) And he smote his adversaries backward: He put them to a

---

[124] Judges 18.

perpetual reproach.

(67) Moreover he refused the tent of Joseph, And **chose not the tribe of Ephraim**.

Hosea 5:9-11

(9) **Ephraim shall become a desolation in the day of rebuke**: among the tribes of Israel have I made known that which shall surely be.

(10) The princes of Judah are like them that remove the landmark: I will pour out my wrath upon them like water.

(11) **Ephraim is oppressed, he is crushed in judgment; because he was content to walk after *man's* command**.

John isn't saying that there won't be descendants of Dan or Ephraim that are a part of the ones sealed. He is telling his audience that no spiritual Danite, an *idolater*, will be a part of those sealed for protection and salvation. He is telling them that no spiritual Ephraimite, a covenant-breaking and lawless one, will be a part of the kingdom. The inclusion of Joseph, coupled with Ephraim's exclusion, tells John's audience that those who are like Joseph, humble, loving, and obediently cleaving to Yahweh, are to be a part of the kingdom. Likewise, the inclusion of Levi is John telling them that there will be priests among the sealed ones, or that some of the sealed ones will be priests at some point in the future.

The number 12,000 coming from each tribe was John telling his audience that there will be many thousands from true, obedient Israel who would be sealed, each one having been elected, excluding all idolaters, covenant-breakers, and those who refused to keep His perfect laws in the Torah.

The Great Multitude

(9) After these things I saw, and behold, a great multitude, which no man could number, out of every nation and of *all* tribes and peoples and tongues, standing before the throne and before the Lamb, arrayed in white robes, and palms in their hands;

(10) and they cry with a great voice, saying, Salvation unto our

Elohim who sits on the throne, and unto the Lamb.
(11) And all the angels were standing round about the throne, and *about* the elders and the four living creatures; and they fell before the throne on their faces, and worshipped Elohim,
(12) saying, Amein: Blessing, and glory, and wisdom, and thanksgiving, and honor, and power, and might, *be* unto our Elohim forever and ever. Amein.
(13) And one of the elders answered, saying unto me, These that are arrayed in the white robes, who are they, and from where came they?
(14) And I say unto him, My master, you know. And he said to me, These are they that come out of the great tribulation, and they washed their robes, and made them white in the blood of the Lamb.
(15) Therefore are they before the throne of Elohim; and they serve him day and night in his temple: and he that sits on the throne shall spread his tabernacle over them.
(16) They shall hunger no more, neither thirst anymore; neither shall the sun strike upon them, nor any heat:
(17) for the Lamb that is in the midst of the throne shall be their shepherd, and shall guide them unto fountains of waters of life: and Elohim shall wipe away every tear from their eyes.

Where John had just *heard* the number of those sealed, or elected, he now turns to *see* an innumerable multitude. The number 144,000 symbolized the perfect number of His people that were to be a part of His kingdom, the actual number of those who are to be citizens is uncountable. The actual citizens, though they are all spiritually a part of true Israel, will be from all tribes, peoples, and tongues.

John's vision of this multitude is clearly one of the future, after the tribulations and judgments have all been completed. We know this because the same descriptions of their location and the conditions around them are the same as those of the New Jerusalem in chapter 21.

The New Jerusalem is referred to as Yahweh's tabernacle[125]. The sun will not shine upon them[126]. Every tear will be wiped away[127], and they shall be able to partake of waters of life[128].

The entirety of chapter 7 is sort of "calm before the storm." Just as great blessings were pronounced in the letters to the seven assemblies to those who overcame, so it is here. This is Yeshua's promise and encouragement through John to his servants that despite the trials they undergo they are a part of a kingdom that will never pass away, in which everything that is destructive and wicked in this life will be absent and unwelcome. They have innumerable and immeasurable blessings in their future and that is where their focus should lie, despite the horrible and awesome judgments to be introduced in the chapters to follow.

---

[125] Revelation 21:3.
[126] Revelation 22:5.
[127] Revelation 21:4.
[128] Revelation 21:6, 22:1-2.

CHAPTER EIGHT

Introduction to the Trumpet Judgments

The use of trumpets is found in many places in the scriptures, both realistic and symbolic. As mentioned above in chapter 1, the sound or blowing of a shofar was intended to demand one's undivided attention, to sound the charge for battle and announce or pronounce events. Generally speaking, trumpets were instruments used for proclamations, warnings, and announcements.

In the case of these angels' trumpets, they are proclaiming and announcing the judgments of Yahweh upon the land and the people therein. There is a very important passage of scripture that one must keep in mind while reading through these judgments and those of the seven angels' bowls that come later in the book. John is using vivid imagery to help his readers recall the history of, promises to, and prophecies for Israel.

Familiar Plagues

> Deuteronomy 28:58-61
> (58) If you will not observe to do all the words of this Torah that are written in this book, that you may fear this glorious and fearful name, Yahweh your Elohim;
> (59) then Yahweh will make your plagues wonderful, and the plagues of your seed, even great plagues, and of long

continuance, and sore sicknesses, and of long continuance.
(60) And he will bring upon you again all the diseases of Egypt,
which you were afraid of; and they shall cleave unto you.
(61) Also every sickness, and every plague, which is not written
in the book of this Torah, them will Yahweh bring upon you,
until you be destroyed.

As we proceed through the evaluation of the various judgments in the
Apocalypse we will show, where applicable, which disease or plague of
Egypt is being referred to. The symbolic nature of the Apocalypse
doesn't require that a literal, word-for-word fulfillment be found in
history for each of the events prophesied. Rather, the readers were to
understand the general picture – these are a disobedient and idolatrous
people and the promised plagues are soon to come upon them again. In
addition to parallels to the Egyptian plagues themselves, we will show
how other blessings and promises of Yahweh to his obedient children
are withdrawn because of their continued disobedience and obstinacy.

Partial Scope

The judgments brought about by these trumpet blasts are, unlike the
later bowl judgments, only partial in their scope, affecting only one
third of the things specified. As we will show, these judgments were
intended to be warnings that would incite repentance in the hearts and
minds of those to whom they were directed; however, we can tell that
after the judgments of the first six trumpets were announced, the
afflicted found no place in their hearts for repentance.

Revelation 9:20-21
(20) And the rest of mankind, who were not killed with these
plagues, **repented not** of the works of their hands, that they
should not worship demons, and the idols of gold, and of silver,
and of brass, and of stone, and of wood; which can neither see,
nor hear, nor walk:
(21) and they **repented not** of their murders, nor of their
sorceries, nor of their fornication, nor of their thefts.

Though the entirety of the Apocalypse should once again be viewed through the lens of apocalyptic symbolism, there are literal parallels that can be found in recorded history that show these judgments, announced by the voices of the trumpets, were indeed realities. Historical records that show a literal fulfillment of the various angels' trumpet judgments will be quoted below where applicable.

Chronological Considerations

Upon reading through the judgments of the trumpets in this chapter and the next, then the bowl judgments later in chapter 16, the reader can see that the use of ordinal numbers (first, second, etc.) is common. Ordinal numbers, unlike cardinal numbers (one, two, etc.) relate to order, rank, or position in a series. In virtually every commentary one would read on the Apocalypse the author uses the phrases "First Trumpet," "Second Trumpet," and the like to describe the judgments of the trumpets and bowls. Most readers will be surprised to learn, however, that such phrases do not exist in the Apocalypse. What we do read is "First *angel*," "Second *angel*," etc. This is a significant point that influences how one reads the various plagues in the Apocalypse from a chronological aspect.

The judgments resulting from the blowing these six angels' trumpets are, like the bowls of the seven angels later in chapter 16, intended to be taken together as a whole. Applying the ordinal numbers to the trumpets or bowls themselves naturally causes one to look for each judgment signified thereby to occur sequentially. This, however, is not what John intended. John's intent was to convey that there were going to be six severe, yet partial judgments to come upon the land and the people therein. These judgments are from heaven, not earth, as that is where the angels announcing them dwell.

A clearer way to think about it would be to say something like "the *first* angel announced *one* of the judgments." Then, "the *second* angel announced *another one* of the judgments," and so forth through the sixth angel's trumpet. Taken together as a whole, as John intended them to be, the message to his audience was that there was going to be six different kinds of judgments that were to occur, each one with a divine and heavenly origin, each to be easily seen in the world around them. The judgments themselves are not to be placed into a strict chronological arrangement any more than the Egyptian plagues conveyed by them are in order. The first angel's trumpet judgment is representative of the hail plague, while the second angel's represents the plague of blood. The plague of hail obviously came after the plague of blood, but John didn't care about that. He wasn't emphasizing the order of the judgments themselves. He was emphasizing the fact that there would be several severe judgments inflicted upon the people and that the judgments were of and from the Almighty.

To use a modern example let's imagine that we were going to take a journey through space. While on the spaceship our tour guide stands up and gives us general information about what we are to expect on the journey, but then summons each of his specialists one at a time to provide more specifics on the various sights we'd see. The first specialist tells of the planets we will see and their makeup. The second tells us the same about the stars. The third speaks on meteors and comets. The fourth tells us about the mystical black hole. The fifth tells us about the various star systems that exist and how they all work together. Then finally the sixth tells us about constellations and the tales that have been told about them through the centuries. The order of the specialists' presentations doesn't mean that the first thing we will see on our journey is a planet, or that the sixth thing will be a constellation. The specialists made their presentations in sequential order, but the subjects of their various presentations weren't ever intended to be taken as a strict chronological sequence. Each sight was to be expected, but not necessarily in that order. In fact, we may see a constellation first, then a comet passing by, then a planet, then another comet.

Applying this example to the Apocalypse and the historical fulfillments of its symbols should be much simpler after understanding the above. If the bloody judgment announced by the second and third angels' trumpets is fulfilled in horrific battles and slaughters that doesn't mean there won't be more bloodshed after that battle. There might, for example, be more destruction of nature, as represented by the first angel's trumpet judgment, between the bloody events.

Not wanting to belabor the point any further we'll sum it up by saying that John wasn't telling his audience *the order* in which the judgments were to come, but *the kinds* of judgments they should expect to see. The Apocalypse has within itself a beautiful chronology, as we will see throughout the rest of this work. But the chronological sequence needs to be seen and understood properly. The reader is hereby challenged to once again put aside their preconceived doctrinal biases and view the Apocalypse through new eyes.

The Prayer for Justice Answered

(1) And when he opened the seventh seal, there followed a silence in heaven about the space of half an hour.
(2) And I saw the seven angels that stand before Elohim; and there were given unto them seven trumpets.
(3) And another angel came and stood over the altar, having a golden censer; and there was given unto him much incense, that he should add it unto the prayers of all the saints upon the golden altar which was before the throne.
(4) And the smoke of the incense, with the prayers of the saints, went up before Elohim out of the angel's hand.
(5) And the angel took the censer; and he filled it with the fire of the altar, and cast it upon the earth: and there followed thunders, and voices, and lightnings, and an earthquake.

We saw in chapter 6 above when discussing the fifth seal that the martyrs were pleading with Yeshua to render judgment in their favor. These souls were seen under the altar. The prayers of the saints that ascended unto Elohim as smoke from the incense altar in the tabernacle were finally going to be answered. The angel taking of the fire from that heavenly altar and casting it to the land shows that the answered prayers of the saints is to result in horrible and awesome judgments.

The First Angel's Trumpet

(6) And the seven angels that had the seven trumpets prepared themselves to sound.

(7) And the first sounded, and there followed hail and fire, mingled with blood, and they were cast upon the land: and the third part of the land was burnt up, and the third part of the trees was burnt up, and all green grass was burnt up.

The words "land", "trees", and "grass" are all symbolic. "Land" represents the entirety of Israel and the people therein. "Trees" are representative of people in a high social position. See the table of apocalyptic terminology in the Introduction above for additional information.

Isaiah 2:11-22

(11) The lofty looks of man shall be brought low, and the haughtiness of men shall be bowed down, and Yahweh alone shall be exalted in that day.

(12) For there shall be a day of Yahweh of hosts upon all that is proud and haughty, and upon all that is lifted up; and it shall be brought low;

(13) and upon all the cedars of Lebanon, that are high and lifted up, and upon all the oaks of Bashan,

(14) and upon all the high mountains, and upon all the hills that are lifted up,

(15) and upon every lofty tower, and upon every fortified wall,

(16) and upon all the ships of Tarshish, and upon all pleasant imagery.

(17) And the loftiness of man shall be bowed down, and the haughtiness of men shall be brought low; and Yahweh alone shall be exalted in that day.

(18) And the idols shall utterly pass away.

(19) And men shall go into the caves of the rocks, and into the holes of the earth, from before the terror of Yahweh, and from the glory of his majesty, when he arises to shake mightily the earth.

(20) In that day men shall cast away their idols of silver, and their idols of gold, which have been made for them to worship,

to the moles and to the bats;
(21) to go into the caverns of the rocks, and into the clefts of the
ragged rocks, from before the terror of Yahweh, and from the
glory of his majesty, when he arises to shake mightily the earth.
(22) Cease you from man, whose breath is in his nostrils; for
wherein is he to be accounted of?

Isaiah 37:24
By your servants have you defied the Master, and have said,
With the multitude of my chariots am I come up to the height of
the mountains, to the innermost parts of Lebanon; and I will cut
down the tall cedars thereof, and the choice fir-trees thereof; and
I will enter into its farthest height, the forest of its fruitful field.

"Cedars," "fir-trees" and "oaks" are used above to describe the ones in
exalted positions. Other terms are also used such as "mountains",
"hills", "lofty tower", "ships", etc., each of which can be found in the
table of apocalyptic terminology in the Introduction. The judgment
being wrought is upon all things "proud and haughty." Inanimate
objects are hardly things that can show the human emotion of pride.

"Grass" can represent the commoners in the society.

Isaiah 37:26-27
(26) Hast you not heard how I have done it long ago, and
formed it of ancient times? now have I brought it to pass, that it
should be your to lay waste fortified cities into ruinous heaps.
(27) Therefore their inhabitants were of small power, they were
dismayed and confounded; they were as the grass of the field,
and as the green herb, as the grass on the housetops, and as a
field *of grain* before it is grown up.

Isaiah 40:6-8
(6) The voice of one saying, Cry. And one said, What shall I cry?
All flesh is grass, and all the goodliness thereof is as the flower of
the field.
(7) The grass withers, the flower fades, because the breath of
Yahweh blows upon it; surely the people is grass.

(8) The grass withers, the flower fades; but the word of our Elohim shall stand forever.

Amos 7:1-2
(1) Thus the Master Yahweh showed me: and, behold, he formed locusts in the beginning of the shooting up of the latter growth; and, lo, it was the latter growth after the king's mowings.
(2) And it came to pass that, when they made an end of eating the grass of the land, then I said, O Master Yahweh, forgive, I beseech you: how shall Jacob stand? for he is small.

Revelation 9:4 still speaks of grass existing, so it is likely that the grass destroyed as a part of the judgment of the first angel's trumpet is limited to the one-third part as the rest of the trumpet plagues are. The point of this illustration is to show how no person in the land of Israel, regardless of their social status, will be exempt from the plagues coming upon them. The historical record tells us that this is exactly what happened.

"However, there arose such a Divine storm against them as was instrumental to their destruction; this carried the Roman darts upon them, and made those which they threw return back, and drove them obliquely away from them; nor could the Jews indeed stand upon their precipices, by reason of the violence of the wind, having nothing that was stable to stand upon, nor could they see those that were ascending up to them; so the Romans got up and surrounded them, and some they slew before they could defend themselves, and others as they were delivering up themselves; and the remembrance of those that were slain at their former entrance into the city increased their rage against them now; a great number also of those that were surrounded on every side, and despaired of escaping, threw their children and their wives, and themselves also, down the precipices, into the valley beneath, which, near the citadel, had been dug hollow to a vast depth; but so it happened, that the anger of the Romans appeared not to be so extravagant as was the madness of those that were now taken, while the Romans slew but four thousand, whereas the number of those that had thrown themselves down was found to be five thousand: nor did any one escape except two women, who were the daughters of Philip, and Philip himself was the son of a certain eminent man called Jacimus, who had been general of king Agrippa's army; and these did therefore escape, because they lay concealed from the rage of the Romans when the city was taken; for otherwise they spared not so much as the infants, of which many were flung down by them from the citadel. And thus was Gamala taken on the three and twentieth day of the month Hyperberetens, [Tisri,] whereas the city had first revolted on the four and twentieth day of the month Gorpieus [Elul]."[129]

During this siege and taking of Gamala neither men, nor women, nor children, nor infants were exempt from the punishment. These same cruelties continued throughout the duration of the war.

"While the holy house was on fire, everything was plundered that came to hand, and ten thousand of those that were caught were slain; nor was there a commiseration of any age, or any reverence of gravity, but children, and old men, and profane persons, and priests were all slain in the same manner; so that this war went round all sorts of men, and brought them to destruction, and as well those that made supplication for their lives, as those that defended themselves by fighting."[130]

The righteous chosen and marked in chapter 7 of the Apocalypse are obviously excluded from these plagues.

Again, though it need not be taken literally based on the apocalyptic nature of the book, the destructions mentioned in this passage were realized. Vespasian, Titus, and their armies decimated the land by stripping it of its trees (used for their war engines) and scorching the

---

[129] Josephus, Wars. 4.1.10. Pages 667-668. Gorpieus is the Macedonian equivalent of the Hebrew month Elul.
[130] Josephus, Wars. 6.5.1. Page 741.

grass behind them wherever they went ("scorched earth" method of the Romans).

> "He also **set fire** not only **to the city** [*Gadara*] itself, but **to all the villas and small cities** that were round about it; some of them were quite destitute of inhabitants, and out of some of them he carried the inhabitants as slaves into captivity."[131]

> "And when the resolution was there taken to raise a bank against that part of the wall which was practicable, he sent his whole army abroad to get the materials together. So when they had **cut down all the trees** on the mountains that adjoined to the city, and had gotten together a vast heap of stones, besides the wood they had cut down, some of them brought hurdles, in order to avoid the effects of the darts that were shot from above them."[132]

> "And truly the very view itself of the country was a melancholy thing; for those places which were before adorned with trees and pleasant gardens were now become a desolate country every way, and **its trees were all cut down**: nor could any foreigner that had formerly seen Judea and the most beautiful suburbs of the city, and now saw it as a desert, but lament and mourn sadly at so great a change: for the war had laid all the signs of beauty quite waste: nor if any one that had known the place before, had come on a sudden to it now, would he have known it again; but though he were at the city itself, yet would he have inquired for it notwithstanding."[133] (*Josephus, Wars 6.1.1*)

> "Thence did Simon make his progress over all Idumea, and did not only ravage the cities and villages, but lay waste the whole country; for, besides those that were completely armed, he had forty thousand men that followed him, insomuch that he had not provisions enough to suffice such a multitude. Now, besides this

---

[131] Josephus, Wars. 3.7.1. Pages 645-646.
[132] Josephus, Wars. 3.7.8. Page 647.
[133] Josephus, Wars. 6.1.1. Page 727.

want of provisions that he was in, he was of a barbarous disposition, and bore great anger at this nation, by which means it came to pass that Idumea was greatly depopulated; and as one may see **all the woods behind despoiled of their leaves** by locusts, after they have been there, so was there nothing left behind Simon's army but a desert. Some places they **burnt down**, some they utterly demolished, and whatsoever grew in the country, they either trod it down or fed upon it, and by their marches they made the ground that was cultivated harder and more untractable than that which was barren. In short, there was no sign remaining of those places that had been laid waste, that ever they had had a being."[134]

There is also historical record of bloody rain during Nero's reign.

"Nero... One night he suddenly summoned in haste the foremost senators and knights, as if to make some communication to them regarding the political situation, and then said to them (I quote his exact words): 'I have discovered a way by which the water-organ will produce louder and more musical tones.' In such jests did he indulge even at this crisis. And little did he reck that both sets of doors, those of the mausoleum of Augustus and those of his own bedchamber, opened of their own accord on one and the same night, or that in the Alban territory **it rained so much blood that rivers of it flowed over the land,** or that the sea retreated a long distance from Egypt and covered a great portion of Lycia."[135]

In each of the historical examples above we cannot only see a fulfillment of the destructions announced by the first angel's trumpet, but we can also see John linking these judgments caused by "hail and fire, mingled with blood" to the corresponding plague of Egypt[136]. His message is consistent throughout. The promise of Yahweh to visit His own people with the plagues of Egypt was going to come to pass.

---

[134] Josephus, Wars. 4.8.7. Pages 689-690.
[135] Dio. Book 63, Chapter 26.
[136] Exodus 9:13-35.

The Second Angel's Trumpet

(8) And the second angel sounded, and as it were a great mountain burning with fire was cast into the sea: and the third part of the sea became blood;
(9) and there died the third part of the creatures which were in the sea, *even* they that had life; and the third part of the ships was destroyed.

The nature of this judgment shows that John was clearly referencing the Egyptian plague of blood[137]. Like the apocalyptic plague of hail had just fallen, now the symbolic waters were to be bloodied.

"Mountain," from an apocalyptic/prophetic standpoint, is usually used to describe a people or nation opposed to Elohim. However, it can refer to a people, nation, or kingdom that serves Yahweh.

Jeremiah 51:24-25
(24) And I will render unto Babylon and to all the inhabitants of Chaldea all their evil that they have done in Zion in your sight, says Yahweh.
(25) Behold, I am against you, O destroying **mountain**, says Yahweh, which destroys all the earth; and I will stretch out my hand upon you, and roll you down from the rocks, and will make you a burnt mountain.

Jeremiah 17:3-4
(3) O my **mountain** in the field, I will give your substance and all your treasures for a spoil, *and* your high places, because of sin, throughout all your borders.
(4) And you, even of yourself, shall discontinue from your heritage that I gave you; and I will cause you to serve your enemies in the land which you knows not: for you have kindled a fire in my anger which shall burn forever.

---

[137] Exodus 7:14-25.

Ezekiel 6:2-4

(2) Son of man, set your face toward the **mountains** of Israel, and prophesy unto them,

(3) and say, You **mountains** of Israel, hear the word of the Master Yahweh: Thus says the Master Yahweh to the **mountains** and to the hills, to the watercourses and to the valleys: Behold, I, even I, will bring a sword upon you, and I will destroy your high places.

(4) And your altars shall become desolate, and your sun-images shall be broken; and I will cast down your slain men before your idols.

Ezekiel 36:1, 4-5

(1) And you, son of man, prophesy unto the **mountains** of Israel, and say, You **mountains** of Israel, hear the word of Yahweh...

(4) therefore, you **mountains** of Israel, hear the word of the Master Yahweh: Thus says the Master Yahweh to the **mountains** and to the hills, to the watercourses and to the valleys, to the desolate wastes and to the cities that are forsaken, which are become a prey and derision to the residue of the nations that are round about;

(5) therefore thus says the Master Yahweh: Surely in the fire of my jealousy have I spoken against the residue of the nations, and against all Edom, that have appointed my land unto themselves for a possession with the joy of all their heart, with despite of soul, to cast it out for a prey.

Daniel 2:34-35, 44-45

(34) You saw till that a stone was cut out without hands, which smote the image upon its feet that were of iron and clay, and broke them in pieces.

(35) Then was the iron, the clay, the brass, the silver, and the gold, broken in pieces together, and became like the chaff of the summer threshing-floors; and the wind carried them away, so that no place was found for them: and the stone that smote the image became a great **mountain**, and filled the whole earth...

(44) And in the days of those kings shall the Elohim of heaven set up a kingdom which shall never be destroyed, nor shall the sovereignty thereof be left to another people; but it shall break in

pieces and consume all these kingdoms, and it shall stand forever.

(45) Forasmuch as you saw that a stone was cut out of the **mountain** without hands, and that it broke in pieces the iron, the brass, the clay, the silver, and the gold; the great Elohim has made known to the king what shall come to pass hereafter: and the dream is certain, and the interpretation thereof sure.

Most the occurrences of "mountain(s)" above refers to a people or nation that are destined for destruction. The passage in Daniel refers to a "mountain" that represents the righteous and eternal kingdom that He is to setup after the destruction of the previous kingdom in the vision/dream.

Isaiah 5:30
And they shall roar against them in that day like the roaring of the **sea**: and if one look unto the land, behold, darkness and distress; and the light is darkened in the clouds thereof.

Isaiah 23:9-11
(9) Yahweh of hosts has purposed it, to stain the pride of all glory, to bring into contempt all the honorable of the earth.
(10) Pass through your land as the Nile, O daughter of Tarshish; there is no restraint any more.
(11) He has stretched out his hand over the **sea**, he has shaken the kingdoms: Yahweh has given commandment concerning Canaan, to destroy the strongholds thereof."

Jeremiah 51:28, 42-43
(28) Prepare against her the nations, the kings of the Medes, the governors thereof, and all the deputies thereof, and all the land of their dominion...
(42) The **sea** is come up upon Babylon; she is covered with the multitude of the waves thereof.
(43) Her cities are become a desolation, a dry land, and a desert, a land wherein no man dwells, neither doth any son of man pass thereby."

Daniel 7:2-3

(2) Daniel spoke and said, I saw in my vision by night, and, behold, the four winds of heaven broke forth upon the great **sea**.

(3) And four great beasts came up from the **sea**, diverse one from another."

The "sea" in the above passage refers to a large multitude of people. It isn't necessarily specific to any particular nation or people.

The point of John's illustration of the second angel's trumpet judgment is to tell the people that a great nation, one opposed to Elohim (i.e. Rome), will be thrown (i.e. under the control of Yahweh) into the multitude of the people of the land (Israel). The result of this will be the death of a third of the creatures in the sea (i.e. the people of Israel), which causes the sea to become bloody, and a destruction of a third of the ships, or towns, which are "carriers" of the creatures in the multitude of people.

Again, though a literal fulfillment is not necessary to explain the meaning of this judgment, it can once again be found in the pages of history. Josephus records that Vespasian's first campaign was through the northernmost region of Israel – Galilee. At that time, there were three main divisions of Israel – Galilee in the North, Judea in the South, and Samaria between them[138]. Vespasian systematically besieged and destroyed the cities of Galilee until he had conquered it all[139]. Included in these were great slaughters along the coast of the Mediterranean Sea and in the Lake of Gennesareth.

> "Now as those people of Joppa were floating about in this **sea**, in the morning there fell a violent wind upon them; it is called by those that sail there 'the black north wind,' and there dashed their ships one against another, and dashed some of them against the rocks, and carried many of them by force, while they strove against the

---

[138] Josephus, Wars. 3.3. Pages 641-642.
[139] Josephus, Wars. 4.2.5. Page 669.

opposite waves, into the main sea; for the shore was so rocky, and had so many of the enemy upon it, that they were afraid to come to land; nay, the waves rose so very high, that they drowned them; nor was there any place whither they could fly, nor any way to save themselves; while they were thrust out of the **sea**, by the violence of the wind, if they staid where they were, and out of the city by the violence of the Romans. And much lamentation there was when the **ships were dashed against one another**, and a terrible noise when they were **broken to pieces**; and some of the multitude that were in them were covered with waves, and so perished, and a great many were embarrassed with shipwrecks. But some of them thought that to die by their own swords was lighter than by the sea, and so they killed themselves before they were drowned; although the greatest part of them were carried by the waves, and dashed to pieces against the abrupt parts of the rocks, insomuch that **the sea was bloody a long way, and the maritime parts were full of dead bodies**; for the Romans came upon those that were carried to the shore, and destroyed them; and the number of the bodies that were thus thrown out of the sea was four thousand and two hundred."[140]

The Third Angel's Trumpet

(10) And the third angel sounded, and there fell from heaven a great star, burning as a torch, and it fell upon the third part of the rivers, and upon the fountains of the waters;
(11) and the name of the star is called Wormwood: and the third part of the waters became wormwood; and many men died of the waters, because they were made bitter."

The key to understanding the fulfillment of this angel's trumpet judgment is to seek the identity of this mysterious star called "Wormwood." A literal fulfillment of this would be impossible for many reasons. One reason is that if a star of virtually any size blew through our atmosphere and struck the earth, the earth would surely be destroyed immediately thereafter. This action would obviously

---

[140] Josephus, Wars. 3.9.3. Page 658.

make the subsequent judgments pointless as all life would be extinguished. Another reason is the inability to have a single star poison or "make bitter" one-third of the rivers and streams on the planet. There is no single location where a falling star could land to affect one-third of the fountains, streams, and rivers.

The identity of "Wormwood" here can be found throughout the scriptures.

> Deuteronomy 29:14-15, 18
> (14) Neither with you only do I make this covenant and this oath,
> (15) but with him that stands here with us this day before Yahweh our Elohim, and also with him that is not here with us this day...
> (18) lest there should be among you man, or woman, or family, or tribe, whose heart turns away this day from Yahweh our Elohim, to go to serve the elohim of those nations; lest there should be among you a root that bears gall and **wormwood**."

Moses' warning against idolatry and turning away from obedience to Yahweh came along with a promise of wormwood. He warned them against doing such things telling them that if they did roots that "bear gall and wormwood" would rise among them.

> Lamentations 3:15, 19
> (15) He has filled me with bitterness, he has sated me with **wormwood**...
> (19) Remember my affliction and my misery, the **wormwood** and the gall."

Jeremiah is speaking here after the destruction of Israel and Jerusalem by Babylon. "Wormwood and gall" are here equated with "affliction and misery." Yahweh's warning through Moses was that affliction and misery would come upon them for their disobedience.

> Jeremiah 9:13-15
> (13) And Yahweh says, Because they have forsaken my Torah

which I set before them, and have not obeyed my voice, neither
walked therein,
(14) but have walked after the stubbornness of their own heart,
and after the Ba'alim, which their fathers taught them;
(15) therefore thus says Yahweh of hosts, the Elohim of Israel,
Behold, I will feed them, even this people, with **wormwood**, and
give them water of gall to drink."

Jeremiah 23:15
Therefore thus says Yahweh of hosts concerning the prophets:
Behold, I will feed them with **wormwood**, and make them drink
the water of gall; for from the prophets of Jerusalem is
ungodliness gone forth into all the land."

Affliction, misery, bitterness – all are descriptions of "wormwood."
John's mention of wormwood in this third judgment was to cause his
readers to recall the passages of scripture above and the
warnings/promises therein. He is once again showing them that the
disobedience of the people is causing the prophesied consequences to
come upon them.

"Rivers" are also used to represent people and/or armies.

Isaiah 8:7
Now therefore, behold, the Master brings up upon them the
waters of the **River**, strong and many, even the king of Assyria
and all his glory: and it shall come up over all its channels, and
go over all its banks."

Ezekiel 29:2-5
(2) Son of man, set your face against Pharaoh king of Egypt, and
prophesy against him, and against all Egypt;
(3) speak, and say, Thus says the Master Yahweh: Behold, I am
against you, Pharaoh king of Egypt, the great monster that lies
in the midst of his **rivers**, that has said, My **river** is my own, and I
have made it for myself.
(4) And I will put hooks in your jaws, and I will cause the fish of
your **rivers** to stick unto your scales; and I will bring you up out

of the midst of your **rivers**, with all the fish of your **rivers** which stick unto your scales.

(5) And I will cast you forth into the wilderness, you and all the fish of your **rivers**: you shall fall upon the open field; you shall not be brought together, nor gathered; I have given you for food to the beasts of the earth and to the birds of the heavens."

The star of the third angel's trumpet judgment isn't literally poisoning the rivers and streams of the world. The star represents a chief individual in a particular nation or kingdom. The illustration here is that a leader of some sort is going to bring about great and bitter affliction and misery upon the people. Rivers and fountains either feed or are fed by seas. This "wormwood" was to affect those that stream to the multitude of Israel.

A literal fulfillment of this in the historical record can be found in the fact that Vespasian, while in Galilee, besieged Gennesareth.

"Now this lake of Gennesareth is so called from the country adjoining to it. Its breadth is forty furlongs, and its length one hundred and forty; its waters are sweet, and very agreeable for drinking, for they are finer than the thick waters of other fens; the lake is also pure, and on every side ends directly at the shores, and at the sand; it is also of a temperate nature when you draw it up, and of a more gentle nature than river or fountain water, and yet always cooler than one could expect in so diffuse a place as this is...It is divided into two parts by **the river Jordan**...But now, when the vessels were gotten ready, Vespasian put upon ship-board as many of his forces as he thought sufficient to be too hard for those that were upon the lake, and set sail after them...As for those that endeavored to come to an actual fight, the Romans ran many of them through with their long poles. Sometimes the Romans leaped into their ships, with swords in their hands, and slew them; but when some of them met the vessels, the Romans caught them by the middle, and destroyed at once their ships and themselves who were taken in them. And for such as were drowning in the sea, if they lifted their heads up above the water, they were either killed by darts, or caught by the vessels; but if, in the desperate case they were in, they attempted to swim to their enemies, the Romans **cut off either their heads or their hands;** and indeed they were destroyed after various manners everywhere, till the rest being put to flight, were forced to get upon the land, while the vessels encompassed them about [on the sea]: but as many of these were repulsed when they were getting ashore, they were killed by the darts upon the lake; and the Romans leaped out of their vessels, and destroyed a great many more upon the land: one might then see **the lake all bloody, and full of dead bodies,** for not one of them escaped. And **a terrible stink,** and a very sad sight there was on the following days over that country; for as for the shores, they were full of shipwrecks, and of **dead bodies all swelled;** and as **the dead bodies were inflamed by the sun,** and putrefied, they corrupted the air, insomuch that the misery was not only the object of commiseration to the Jews, but to those that hated them, and had been the authors of that misery. This was the upshot of the sea-fight. The number of the slain, including those that were killed in the city before, was six thousand and five hundred."[141]

This lake was fed by the Jordan river and then feeds Jordan river on the south side. It was full of blood and putrefied bodies that would surely have been carried down the river and to its various branches. This is also told to us in Josephus' history.

"Now this destruction that fell upon the Jews, as it was not inferior to any of the rest in itself, so did it still appear greater than it really was; and this, because not only the whole country through which they fled was filled with slaughter, and Jordan could not be passed over, by reason of the dead bodies that were in it, but because the lake Asphaltiris was also full of dead bodies, that were carried down into it by the river."[142]

The imagery of the judgment of the third angel's trumpet, like that of the second. was intended to recall the first plague inflicted upon Egypt

---

[141] Josephus, Wars. 3.10.7-9. Pages 662-663.
[142] Josephus, Wars. 4.7.6. Page 685.

– the plague of blood. However, as per the word of Yahweh in Deuteronomy 28:59, the plague was made "wonderful."

The Fourth Angel's Trumpet

(12) And the fourth angel sounded, and the third part of the sun was smitten, and the third part of the moon, and the third part of the stars; that the third part of them should be darkened, and the day should not shine for the third part of it, and the night in like manner.

The darkening or covering of the heavenly bodies is very common in prophetic and apocalyptic literature.

Isaiah 13:9-11
(9) Behold, the day of Yahweh comes, cruel, with wrath and fierce anger; to make the land a desolation, and to destroy the sinners thereof out of it.
(10) For the **stars of heaven and the constellations thereof shall not give their light**; the sun shall be darkened in its going forth, and the **moon shall not cause its light to shine**.
(11) And I will punish the world for their evil, and the wicked for their iniquity: and I will cause the arrogance of the proud to cease, and will lay low the haughtiness of the terrible."

Isaiah, based on verse 1 of this chapter, is speaking of the destruction of Babylon.

Isaiah 24:19-23
(19) The earth is utterly broken, the earth is rent asunder, the earth is shaken violently.
(20) The earth shall stagger like a drunken man, and shall sway to and fro like a hammock; and the transgression thereof shall be heavy upon it, and it shall fall, and not rise again.
(21) And it shall come to pass in that day, that Yahweh will punish the host of the high ones on high, and the kings of the earth upon the earth.
(22) And they shall be gathered together, as prisoners are

gathered in the pit, and shall be shut up in the prison; and after many days shall they be visited.

(23) Then the **moon** shall be confounded, and the **sun** ashamed; for Yahweh of hosts will reign in mount Zion, and in Jerusalem; and before his elders shall be glory.

Joel 2:10, 28-32

(10) The earth quakes before them; the heavens tremble; the **sun and the moon are darkened**, and the **stars withdraw their shining**...

(28) And it shall come to pass afterward, that I will pour out my spirit upon all flesh; and your sons and your daughters shall prophesy, your old men shall dream dreams, your young men shall see visions:

(29) and also upon the servants and upon the handmaids in those days will I pour out my spirit.

(30) And I will show wonders in the heavens and in the earth: blood, and fire, and pillars of smoke.

(31) The **sun shall be turned into darkness**, and the **moon into blood**, before the great and terrible day of Yahweh comes.

(32) And it shall come to pass, that whosoever shall call on the name of Yahweh shall be delivered; for in mount Zion and in Jerusalem there shall be those that escape, as Yahweh has said, and among the remnant those whom Yahweh doth call."

Ezekiel 32:7-8

(7) And when I shall extinguish you, I will cover the heavens, and **make the stars thereof dark**; I will **cover the sun with a cloud**, and the **moon shall not give its light**.

(8) All the bright lights of heaven will I make dark over you, and set darkness upon your land, says the Master Yahweh."

The imagery used by the prophets in these instances is intended to illustrate the downfall of nations or leaders of nations. We know that these changes in the motions and/or appearances of the various heavenly bodies themselves aren't literal because of what Yahweh told us through Jeremiah:

Jeremiah 31:35-36
(35) Thus says Yahweh, who giveth the **sun for a light by day**, and the ordinances of the **moon and of the stars for a light by night**, who stirs up the sea, so that the waves thereof roar; Yahweh of hosts is his name:
(36) If these ordinances depart from before me, says Yahweh, then the seed of Israel also shall cease from being a nation before me forever."

The "ordinances" of the day, night, and the lighting thereof by the sun, moon, and stars, are never to cease. If any of the above passages were literal, that would have happened repeatedly. Frederick Farrar, the author of a commentary on the Apocalypse, states the following:

"...ruler after ruler, chieftain after chieftain of the Roman Empire and the Jewish nation was assassinated and ruined. Gaius, Claudius, Nero, Galba, Otho, Vitellius, all died by murder or suicide; Herod the Great, Herod Antipas, Herod Agrippa, and most of the Herodian princes, together with not a few of the leading High Priests of Jerusalem, perished from disgrace, or in exile, or by violent hands. All these were quenched suns and darkened stars."[143]

Though a literal rendering was likely not the author's intent, literal fulfillments of these types of events were also recorded in history.

"At the close of the year people talked much about prodigies, presaging impending evils. Never were **lightning flashes** more frequent, and a **comet** too appeared, for which Nero always made propitiation with noble blood."[144]

"Besides the manifold vicissitudes of human affairs, there were **prodigies in heaven and earth**, the warning voices of the **thunder,**

---

[143] Farrar. Pages 264-265.
[144] Tacitus, Annals. Book 15, Chapter 47.

and other intimations of the future, auspicious or gloomy, doubtful or not to be mistaken. Never surely did more terrible calamities of the Roman People, or evidence more conclusive, prove that the gods take no thought for our happiness, but only for our punishment."[145]

"But the shame that would attend them in case they returned without doing anything at all so for overcame that their repentance, that they lay all night before the wall, though in a very bad encampment; for there broke out a prodigious storm in the night, with the utmost violence, and **very strong winds,** with the **largest showers of rain,** with continual **lightnings,** terrible **thunderings,** and **amazing concussions and bellowings of the earth,** that was in an **earthquake.** These things were a manifest indication that some destruction was coming upon men, when the system of the world was put into this disorder; and anyone would guess that these wonders foreshowed some grand calamities that were coming."[146]

---

[145] Tacitus, History. Book 1, Chapter 3.
[146] Josephus, Wars. 4.4.5. Page 678.

CHAPTER NINE

The Three Woes

The judgments of the last angels' trumpets are also identified as the three "woes." The Greek word οὐαί, from which the word "woe" comes, is used as an exclamation of grief[147]. We find it used repeatedly by Yeshua in the New Testament. The infamous "Woe to you scribes and Pharisees!" is but one example. However, just like many other symbols used in the Apocalypse, John is referencing texts from Old Testament prophets to tell his readers what is coming upon the people of the land and why. Isaiah makes this very clear in the following passage and his exclamations are surprisingly similar to the descriptions found in the fifth and sixth angels' trumpet judgments below.

Isaiah 5:8-30
(8) **Woe** unto them that join house to house, that lay field to field, till there be no room, and you be made to dwell alone in the midst of the land!
(9) In my ears says Yahweh of hosts, Of a truth many houses shall be desolate, even great and fair, without inhabitant.
(10) For ten acres of vineyard shall yield one bath, and a homer of seed shall yield but an ephah.

---

[147] Thayer. Entry for οὐαί. Page 461.

(11) **Woe** unto them that rise up early in the morning, that they may follow strong drink; that tarry late into the night, till wine inflame them!

(12) And the harp and the lute, the tabret and the pipe, and wine, are in their feasts; but they regard not the work of Yahweh, neither have they considered the operation of his hands.

(13) Therefore my people are gone into captivity for lack of knowledge; and their honorable men are famished, and their multitude are parched with thirst.

(14) Therefore Sheol has enlarged its desire, and opened its mouth without measure; and their glory, and their multitude, and their pomp, and he that rejoices among them, descend into it.

(15) And the mean man is bowed down, and the great man is humbled, and the eyes of the lofty are humbled:

(16) but Yahweh of hosts is exalted in justice, and Elohim the Holy One is sanctified in righteousness.

(17) Then shall the lambs feed as in their pasture, and the waste places of the fat ones shall wanderers eat.

(18) **Woe** unto them that draw iniquity with cords of falsehood, and sin as it were with a cart rope;

(19) that say, Let him make speed, let him hasten his work, that we may see it; and let the counsel of the Holy One of Israel draw near and come, that we may know it!

(20) **Woe** unto them that call evil good, and good evil; that put darkness for light, and light for darkness; that put bitter for sweet, and sweet for bitter!

(21) **Woe** unto them that are wise in their own eyes, and prudent in their own sight!

(22) **Woe** unto them that are mighty to drink wine, and men of strength to mingle strong drink;

(23) that justify the wicked for a bribe, and take away the righteousness of the righteous from him!

(24) Therefore as the tongue of fire devours the stubble, and as the dry grass sinks down in the flame, so their root shall be as rottenness, and their blossom shall go up as dust; because they have rejected the Torah of Yahweh of hosts, and despised the word of the Holy One of Israel.

(25) Therefore is the anger of Yahweh kindled against his people, and he has stretched forth his hand against them, and has smitten them; and the mountains tremble, and their dead bodies are as refuse in the midst of the streets. For all this his anger is not turned away, but his hand is stretched out still.
(26) And he will lift up an ensign to the nations from far, and will hiss for them from the end of the earth; and, behold, they shall come with speed swiftly.
(27) None shall be weary nor stumble among them; none shall slumber nor sleep; neither shall the girdle of their loins be loosed, nor the latchet of their shoes be broken:
(28) whose arrows are sharp, and all their bows bent; their horses' hoofs shall be accounted as flint, and their wheels as a whirlwind:
(29) their roaring shall be like a lioness, they shall roar like young lions; yea, they shall roar, and lay hold of the prey, and carry it away safe, and there shall be none to deliver.
(30) And they shall roar against them in that day like the roaring of the sea: and if one look unto the land, behold, darkness and distress; and the light is darkened in the clouds thereof."

Repeatedly Isaiah proclaims his grief at the atrocities committed by his people and the judgments coming as a result thereof. Verses 20, 21, and 22 are especially interesting for a few reasons. First, these are the last three "woes" in the series and they each begin a verse in consecutive order. Second, the judgments and punishments detailed after the woes are strikingly similar to those inflicted by the Romans. "Fire devours the stubble," "they have rejected the Torah of Yahweh," "He has stretched forth His hand against them," "their dead bodies are as refuse in the midst of the streets," etc., are all examples of things that occurred during the invasion of the Romans into Israel and/or the siege of Jerusalem itself.

Examples from the historical record relating to the burning of towns and villages and the absolute devastation of wildlife have already been given above regarding the first angel's trumpet judgment. But are there examples we can find showing that the others also had literal fulfillments corresponding to the symbols given?

"But these zealots came at last to that degree of barbarity, as **not to bestow a burial** either on those slain in the city, or on those that lay along the roads; but as if they had made an agreement to **cancel** both **the laws of their country** and the laws of nature, and, at the same time that they defiled men with their wicked actions, they would pollute the Divinity itself also, **they left the dead bodies to putrefy under the sun**; and the same punishment was allotted to such as buried any as to those that deserted, which was no other than death; while he that granted the favor of a grave to another would presently stand in need of a grave himself. To say all in a word, no other gentle passion was so entirely lost among them as mercy; for what were the greatest objects of pity did most of all irritate these wretches, and they transferred their rage from the living to those that had been slain, and from the dead to the living. Nay, the terror was so very great, that he who survived called them that were first dead happy, as being at rest already; as did those that were under torture in the prisons, declare, that, upon this comparison, those that lay unburied were the happiest. These men, therefore, trampled upon all the laws of men, and **laughed at the laws of God**; and for the oracles of the prophets, **they ridiculed them as the tricks of jugglers**; yet did these prophets foretell many things concerning [the rewards of] virtue, and [punishments of] vice, which when these zealots violated, they occasioned the fulfilling of those very prophecies belonging to their own country; for there was a certain ancient oracle of those men, that the city should then be taken and the sanctuary burnt, by right of war, when a sedition should invade the Jews, and their own hand **should pollute the temple of God.** Now while these zealots did not [quite] disbelieve these predictions, they made themselves the instruments of their accomplishment."[148]

---

[148] Josephus, Wars. 4.6.3. Pages 682-683.

"He also jested upon him, and told him that he might now see whether those to whom he intended to go over would send him any succors or not; but still **he forbade their dead bodies should be buried.**"[149]

"[*Titus speaking*]...for it is unbecoming you, who are Romans and my soldiers, who have in peace been taught how to make wars, and who have also been used to conquer in those wars, to be inferior to Jews, either in action of the hand, or in courage of the soul, and this especially when you are at the conclusion of your victory, and **are assisted by God himself**; for as to our misfortunes, they have been owing to the madness of the Jews, while their sufferings have been owing to your valor, and to the assistance God has afforded you; for as to the seditions they have been in, and the famine they are under, and the siege they now endure, and the fall of their walls without our engines, what can they all be but **demonstrations of God's anger against them**, and of **his assistance afforded us?**"[150]

The people ridiculed and mocked the laws and teachings of Elohim, disregarding and disobeying them at every turn. The body count was so high and the terror of the people so great that they couldn't even bury the dead. Instead they left them to rot in the city streets, just as the prophecy of Isaiah said. Likewise, the hand of Yahweh was stretched forth against the people. A fact recognized by even the invading general himself.

Third, the woes of Isaiah state that these destroyers were to be called from the "ends of the earth." Another familiar passage comes to mind here.

Deuteronomy 28:49-51
(49) Yahweh will bring a nation against you from far, from the **end of the earth**, as the **eagle** flies; a nation whose tongue you shall not understand;

---

[149] Josephus, Wars. 5.13.1. Page 724.
[150] Josephus, Wars. 6.1.5. Pages 728-729.

(50) a nation of fierce countenance, that shall not regard the person of the old, nor show favor to the young,
(51) and shall eat the fruit of your cattle, and the fruit of your ground, until you be destroyed; that also shall not leave you grain, new wine, or oil, the increase of your cattle, or the young of your flock, until they have caused you to perish.

Not only does the prophecy of Moses in this chapter of Deuteronomy mirror the people of and destruction wrought by the Roman Empire, but this passage actually states that this terrible nation was to be brought to them as the **eagle** flies. Is it mere coincidence that it is an eagle that brings the warning of the three "woes" to come in chapter 9[151]? Is it mere coincidence that the symbol found on the Roman ensigns carried throughout their campaign was an eagle? We think not.

In summary, we can see that these three "woes" were to be announcements of intensified judgments that were to be inflicted directly on the people. Many more "woes" can be found throughout the scriptures in the books of Isaiah, Jeremiah, Ezekiel, Amos, Hosea, et al.

The Fifth Angel's Trumpet

(1) And the fifth angel sounded, and I saw a star from heaven fallen unto the earth: and there was given to him the key of the pit of the abyss.
(2) And he opened the pit of the abyss; and there went up a smoke out of the pit, as the smoke of a great furnace; and the sun and the air were darkened by reason of the smoke of the pit.
(3) And out of the smoke came forth locusts upon the earth; and power was given them, as the scorpions of the earth have power.
(4) And it was said unto them that they should not hurt the

---

[151] Revelation 8:13.

grass of the earth, neither any green thing, neither any tree, but only such men as have not the seal of Elohim on their foreheads.

(5) And it was given them that they should not kill them, but that they should be tormented five months: and their torment was as the torment of a scorpion, when it strikes a man.

(6) And in those days men shall seek death, and shall in no wise find it; and they shall desire to die, and death flees from them.

(7) And the shapes of the locusts were like unto horses prepared for war; and upon their heads as it were crowns like unto gold, and their faces were as men's faces.

(8) And they had hair as the hair of women, and their teeth were as the teeth of lions.

(9) And they had breastplates, as it were breastplates of iron; and the sound of their wings was as the sound of chariots, of many horses rushing to war.

(10) And they have tails like unto scorpions, and stings; and in their tails is their power to hurt men five months.

(11) They have over them as king the angel of the abyss: his name in Hebrew is Abaddon, and in the Greek tongue he has the name Apollyon.

(12) The first Woe is past: behold, there come yet two Woes hereafter."

As an initial note regarding this angel's trumpet judgment we must recognize is that it is focused on the release and description of the demonic host and its leader, not the actual carrying out of their mission. Unlike the judgment of the sixth angel's trumpet, where it states that a third part of men *were killed*, this judgment says that "in *those* days men shall seek death," etc., as if it wasn't going to come to pass immediately after their release. This trumpet announces their release, while the carrying out of their mission isn't to take place until some undefined time in their future.

Each of the symbols signified in this judgment – the star, the abyss, the host of locusts, the angelic king – are once again full of symbolism. The "star" represents, in this case, an angel from heaven with the keys to the "abyss." This same angel is found in Revelation 20:1 in the binding of the dragon. There is no reason to assume that this angel is a wicked one just because it opens the abyss.

The "abyss" is the habitation of the dead, Satan, and his demonic host. Luke 8:31 tells us that this "abyss" is something that the "Legion" of demons cast out of the demoniac requested not to be cast to. The abyss is the place from where the Beast arises and the place where Satan is cast to be bound for the thousand-year period. Thus, it is clear this is no human host. That does not, however, preclude these demons from inhabiting or influencing men that they may accomplish their purpose.

The locusts here are not real locusts. Locusts, by nature, feed on crops. These locusts are instead given permission to torment mankind whilst prohibited from destroying actual crops. Apocalyptically speaking, the mission of these locusts was to destroy a specific kind of people. The five-month period, whether literal in history, is antitypical of the period of time that locusts are present in Israel.

Verse 5 contains a very interesting phrase that reads very strangely in the American Standard Version above. It says, "it was *given to them...*" The Greek verb used in for "given," δίδωμι, *didomi*, is indeed the one that means "to give." However, in this context, the Lexham English Bible provides us with a more appropriate translation given its contextual usage – "and it was *granted to them* that they should not kill them." The phrase implies that the demonic host wasn't given an explicit command to abstain from killing, but they actually *requested permission* to not have to kill them, but rather to torture them. Their request was then "granted" to them. This account is not unlike the one we find in the book of Job:

> Job 1:11-12
> (11) But put forth your hand now, and touch all that he has, and he will renounce you to your face.
> (12) And Yahweh said unto Satan, Behold, all that he has is in your power; only upon himself put not forth your hand. So Satan went forth from the presence of Yahweh.

Satan basically requested to test Job's faithfulness by questioning whether it was legitimate due to Yahweh's hand of protection over him. Satan's request, like the demons' of the locust host in this chapter, was granted to him. We see another similar account of these ideas or petitions being presented to Yahweh for Him to grant or deny permission:

1 Kings 22:19-23
(19) And Micaiah said, Therefore hear you the word of Yahweh: I saw Yahweh sitting on his throne, and all the host of heaven standing by him on his right hand and on his left.
(20) And Yahweh said, Who shall entice Ahab, that he may go up and fall at Ramoth-gilead? And one said on this manner; and another said on that manner.
(21) And there came forth a spirit, and stood before Yahweh, and said, I will entice him.
(22) And Yahweh said unto him, Wherewith? And he said, I will go forth, and will be a lying spirit in the mouth of all his prophets. And he said, You shall entice him, and shall prevail also: go forth, and do so.
(23) Now therefore, behold, Yahweh has put a lying spirit in the mouth of all these your prophets; and Yahweh has spoken evil concerning you.

Yahweh granted the angel permission to carry out his idea.

It is noteworthy to mention that just because these locust demons didn't kill men themselves that doesn't mean men couldn't commit murder or suicide as a result of their torments. We know that when demons would possess people in the past they had the power to injure and very likely kill them if they so desired. One example of this in found in the account of the demon-possessed man of the Garasenes, who, because he was controlled by the Legion of demons within him[152], bruised himself with stones[153]. Matthew 17:14-21 also tells us of a boy who had a demon in him that threw him often into the fire. The

---

[152] Luke 8:30.
[153] Mark 5:1-20.

passage in 1 Kings 22 above tells us that though the lying spirits didn't kill Ahab or his men themselves in that battle, they were nevertheless killed as a result of their faith in the false prophecy.

In addition to the eighth Egyptian plague[154] John is clearly alluding to the prophecies of Joel and Isaiah when describing this demonic host.

Joel 1:4-7
(4) That which the palmer-worm has left has the **locust** eaten; and that which the **locust** has left has the canker-worm eaten; and that which the canker-worm has left has the caterpillar eaten.
(5) Awake, you drunkards, and weep; and wail, all you drinkers of wine, because of the sweet wine; for it is cut off from your mouth.
(6) For **a nation is come up upon my land**, strong, and without number; **his teeth are the teeth of a lion**, and **he has the jaw-teeth of a lioness**.
(7) He has laid my vine waste, and barked my fig-tree: he has made it clean bare, and cast it away; the branches thereof are made white."

Joel 2:1-11
(1) Blow you the trumpet in Zion, and sound an alarm in my holy mountain; let all the inhabitants of the land tremble: for the day of Yahweh comes, for it is near at hand;
(2) a day of darkness and gloominess, a day of clouds and thick darkness, as the dawn spread upon the mountains; a great people and a strong; there has not been ever the like, neither shall be any more after them, even to the years of many generations.
(3) A fire devours before them; and behind them a flame burns: the land is as the garden of Eden before them, and behind them a desolate wilderness; yea, and none has escaped them.
(4) The appearance of them is as the appearance of horses; and as horsemen, so do they run.

---

[154] Exodus 10:1-20.

(5) Like the noise of chariots on the tops of the mountains do they leap, like the noise of a flame of fire that devours the stubble, as a strong people set in battle array.

(6) At their presence the peoples are in anguish; all faces are waxed pale.

(7) They run like mighty men; they climb the wall like men of war; and they march everyone on his ways, and they break not their ranks.

(8) Neither doth one thrust another; they march everyone in his path; and they burst through the weapons, and break not off their course.

(9) They leap upon the city; they run upon the wall; they climb up into the houses; they enter in at the windows like a thief.

(10) The earth quakes before them; the heavens tremble; the sun and the moon are darkened, and the stars withdraw their shining.

(11) And Yahweh utters his voice before his army; for his camp is very great; for he is strong that executes his word; for the day of Yahweh is great and very terrible; and who can abide it?"

Isaiah 14:29-31

(29) Rejoice not, O Philistia, all of you, because the rod that smote you is broken; for out of the serpent's root shall come forth an adder, and his fruit shall be a fiery flying serpent.

(30) And the first-born of the poor shall feed, and the needy shall lie down in safety; and I will kill your root with famine, and your remnant shall be slain.

(31) Howl, O gate; cry, O city; you are melted away, O Philistia, all of you; for there comes a **smoke** out of the north, and there is no straggler in his ranks."

Isaiah uses "smoke" here, not to describe a literal smoke as from a burning fire, but rather an innumerable horde of creatures so dense that it would appear as smoke and cover all things in its path. The descriptions of Joel's locust army are utilized directly in portions of the fifth angel's trumpet judgment. In using the blended descriptions of the eighth Egyptian plague and the locust armies of Joel, John is clearly illustrating how a vast demonic host was to be released and allowed to sow destruction and torment for a definite period of time.

Why illustrate using a demonic host, though? Yeshua gave the following prophecy as it related to that generation of people:

Matthew 12:43-45
(43) But the unclean spirit, when he is gone out of the man, passes through waterless places, seeking rest, and finds it not.
(44) Then he says, I will return into my house from where I came out; and when he is come, he finds it empty, swept, and garnished.
(45) Then goes he, and takes with himself seven other spirits more evil than himself, and they enter in and dwell there: and the last state of that man becomes worse than the first. Even so shall it be also unto **this evil generation**."

Yeshua was addressing this message to certain scribes and Pharisees who were asking for a sign from him[155]. He came and "cleaned house" of the demons that were dwelling so comfortably and securely in Israel. However, just as he prophesied, after he left that generation of people became more and more demonic even unto the end. After going through vivid details of the utterly demonic behaviors and actions happening during the Jewish-Roman war Josephus states the following:

"It is therefore impossible to go distinctly over every instance of these men's iniquity. I shall therefore speak my mind here at once briefly: - That neither did any other city ever suffer such miseries, **nor did any age ever breed a generation more fruitful in wickedness that this was, from the beginning of the world.**"[156]

"I suppose, that had the Romans made any longer delay in coming against these villains, the city would either have been swallowed up by the ground opening upon them, or been overflowed by water, or else been destroyed by such thunder as the country of Sodom perished by, **for it had brought forth a generation of men much**

---

[155] Luke 12:38.
[156] Josephus, Wars. 5.10.5. Page 720.

more atheistical than were those that suffered such punishments; for by their madness it was that all the people came to be destroyed."[157]

Many more gruesome actions can be found in the first and tenth chapters of Josephus' fifth book on the Wars of the Jews. We would be astonished if one could read of the horrors found therein, perpetrated by the seditious and wicked, and not see the clear effects of the release of this demonic force from the abyss. Though the actions of this demonic host were carried out by the hands of men, their possession of or influence over those men was ultimately what was controlling them. This angel's trumpet judgment, unlike the rest of them, doesn't limit its effects to a third of anything. This is very telling in that it again points to the fact that their mission wasn't to be carried out until later and this trumpet was only announcing their release from the abyss and supplying clues to John's audience regarding the demon general's identity.

Abaddon and His Host

As we read above, the demonic host's request to torment the people was granted, but they were specifically told that they couldn't inflict their torments upon any but those who didn't have the seal of Elohim on their foreheads or hands. The leader of this vast host is called "Abaddon," or in Greek "Apollyon." In both languages the word means "destroyer" or "destruction." From this designation it is clear that this demon general had his focus on one thing, destroying all people, places, or things over which he was given permission. Although it is clear that the origin and nature of this leader and his host are infernal and spiritual, there are very interesting parallels in history that would point us to potential identities of both, in addition to the time their appointed mission was carried out. We must at this time remind the reader that John's intent is to show the heavenly origin of the demonic judgments announced by the fifth angel's trumpet. He was telling his audience that they would see or hear of things that would, in all ways,

---

[157] Josephus, Wars. 5.13.6. Page 726.

be consistent with those that demon-possessed people would inflict or partake in.

We see the descriptions of Titus and the Roman host he commanded in 70 CE match the descriptions of Abaddon and the demonic host in striking ways. Josephus provides us with a detailed description of the dress and appearance of the Roman armies:

> "When, after this, they are gone out of their camp, they all march without noise, and in a decent manner, and everyone keeps his own rank, as if they were going to war. The **footmen are armed with breastplates and head-pieces,** and have swords on each side; but the sword which is upon their left side is much longer than the other, for that on the right side is not longer than a span. Those foot-men also that are chosen out from the rest to be about the general himself have a lance and a buckler, but the rest of the foot soldiers have a spear and a long buckler, besides a saw and a basket, a pick-axe and an axe, a thong of leather and a hook, with provisions for three days, so that a footman hath no great need of a mule to carry his burdens. The horsemen have a long sword on their right sides, axed a long pole in their hand; a shield also lies by them obliquely on one side of their horses, with three or more darts that are borne in their quiver, having broad points, and not smaller than spears. **They have also head-pieces and breastplates,** in like manner as have all the footmen. And for those that are chosen to be about the general, their armor no way differs from that of the horsemen belonging to other troops; and he always leads the legions forth to whom the lot assigns that employment."[158]

> "A resolution was now taken by Titus to relax the siege for a little while, and to afford the seditious an interval for consideration, and to see whether the demolishing of their second wall would not make them a little more compliant, or whether they were not somewhat afraid of a famine, because the spoils they had gotten by rapine would not be sufficient for them long; so he made use of this

---

[158] Josephus, Wars. 3.5.5. Pages 643-644.

relaxation in order to compass his own designs. Accordingly, as the usual appointed time when he must distribute subsistence money to the soldiers was now come, he gave orders that the commanders should put the army into battle-array, in the face of the enemy, and then give every one of the soldiers their pay. So the soldiers, according to custom, opened the cases wherein their arms before lay covered, and marched with their **breastplates** on, as did the horsemen lead their horses in their **fine trappings**. Then did **the places that were before the city shine very splendidly for a great way**; nor was there anything so grateful to Titus's own men, or so terrible to the enemy, as that sight. **For the whole old wall, and the north side of the temple, were full of spectators, and one might see the houses full of such as looked at them**; nor was there any part of the city which was not covered over with their multitudes; nay, a very great consternation seized upon the hardiest of the Jews themselves, when they saw all the army in the same place, together with the fineness of their arms, and the good order of their men. And I cannot but think that the seditious would have changed their minds at that sight, unless the crimes they had committed against the people had been so horrid, that they despaired of forgiveness from the Romans; but as they believed death with torments must be their punishment, if they did not go on in the defense of the city, they thought it much better to die in war."[159]

"Hereupon Titus ordered those whose business it was to read the list of all that had performed great exploits in this war, whom he called to him by their names, and commended them before the company, and rejoiced in them in the same manner as a man would have rejoiced in his own exploits. He also put on their heads **crowns of gold**, and **golden ornaments about their necks**, and gave them long spears of gold, and ensigns that were made of silver, and removed every one of them to a higher rank; and besides this, he plentifully distributed among them, out of the spoils, and the other prey they had taken, silver, and gold, and garments."[160]

---

[159] Josephus, Wars. 5.9.1. Pages 714-715.
[160] Josephus, Wars. 7.1.3. Page 751.

The host of the Roman armies were so beautifully and fancifully dressed that their splendor shone a great distance. The Israelites shut up in Jerusalem couldn't help but wonder at the spectacle they saw. The glory of the Roman army itself was enough to fill the people with a very great fear, even in the hearts of the boldest and bravest of their soldiers.

Just as the demonic host was decked in glory with crowns and great breastplates, so were the Roman legions. Just as the demons of the abyss were seen with the faces of men, the army of Titus consisted of valiant men. Just as the lion's teeth of Joel 1:6 quoted above relate to the arms of the invading nation, so did the Roman's weapons of warfare cause those looking on to stand in awe. Just as the demonic locusts had tails to inflict damage so did the Roman legions march with their war engines (catapults, trebuchets, etc.) towards the rear of their rank and file[161].

While the physical host of the Romans took five months to seize and ultimately demolish Jerusalem[162] the demons behind them performed things in the city that would seem like science fiction if it weren't that they were recorded in history. Here we see a shocking account of just some of the atrocities that were committed within the city:

> "It was now a miserable case, and a sight that would justly bring tears into our eyes, how men stood as to their food, while the more powerful had more than enough, and the weaker were lamenting [for want of it.] But the famine was too hard for all other passions, and it is destructive to nothing so much as to modesty; for what was otherwise worthy of reverence was in this case despised; insomuch that **children pulled the very morsels that their fathers were eating out of their very mouths,** and what was still more to be pitied, **so did the mothers do as to their infants;** and when those that were most dear were perishing under their hands, they were not ashamed to take from them the very last drops that might preserve their lives:

---

[161] Josephus, Wars. 3.6.2. Page 645.
[162] From April 14, 70 CE to September 1, 70 CE.

and while they ate after this manner, yet were they not concealed in so doing; but the seditious everywhere came upon them immediately, and snatched away from them what they had gotten from others; for when they saw any house shut up, this was to them a signal that the people within had gotten some food; whereupon **they broke open the doors, and ran in, and took pieces of what they were eating almost up out of their very throats, and this by force: the old men, who held their food fast, were beaten; and if the women hid what they had within their hands, their hair was torn for so doing; nor was there any commiseration shown either to the aged or to the infants, but they lifted up children from the ground as they hung upon the morsels they had gotten, and shook them down upon the floor.** But still they were more barbarously cruel to those that had prevented their coming in, and had actually swallowed down what they were going to seize upon, as if they had been unjustly defrauded of their right. **They also invented terrible methods of torments to discover where any food was, and they were these to stop up the passages of the privy parts of the miserable wretches, and to drive sharp stakes up their fundaments; and a man was forced to bear what it is terrible even to hear,** in order to make him confess that he had but one loaf of bread, or that he might discover a handful of barley-meal that was concealed; and **this was done when these tormentors were not themselves hungry;** for the thing had been less barbarous had necessity forced them to it; **but this was done to keep their madness in exercise,** and as making preparation of provisions for themselves for the following days. These men went also to meet those that had crept out of the city by night, as far as the Roman guards, to gather some plants and herbs that grew wild; and when those people thought they had got clear of the enemy, they snatched from them what they had brought with them, even while they had frequently entreated them, and that by calling upon the tremendous name of God, to give them back some part of what they had brought; though these would not give them the least crumb, and they were to be well contented that they were only spoiled, and not slain at the same time.

These were the afflictions which the lower sort of people suffered from these tyrants' guards; but for the men that were in dignity, and withal were rich, they were carried before the tyrants themselves; some of whom were falsely accused of laying treacherous plots, and so were destroyed; others of them were charged with designs of betraying the city to the Romans; but the readiest way of all was this, to suborn somebody to affirm that they were resolved to desert to the enemy. And he who was utterly despoiled of what he had by Simon was sent back again to John, as of those who had been already plundered by Jotre, **Simon got what remained; insomuch that they drank the blood of the populace to one another, and divided the dead bodies of the poor creatures between them**; so that although, on account of their ambition after dominion, they contended with each other, yet did they very well agree in their wicked practices; for he that did not communicate what he got by the miseries of others to the other tyrant seemed to be too little guilty, and in one respect only; and he that did not partake of what was so communicated to him grieved at this, as at the loss of what was a valuable thing, that he had no share in such barbarity."[163]

"Nor was there any lamentations made under these calamities, nor were heard any mournful complaints; but the famine confounded all natural passions; for those who were just going to die looked upon those that were gone to rest before them with dry eyes and open mouths. A deep silence also, and **a kind of deadly night, had seized upon the city**; while yet the robbers were still more terrible than these miseries were themselves; for **they brake open those houses which were no other than graves of dead bodies, and plundered them of what they had; and carrying off the coverings of their bodies, went out laughing, and tried the points of their swords in their dead bodies; and, in order to prove what metal they were made of they thrust some of those through that still lay alive upon the ground; but for those that entreated them to lend them their right hand and their sword to dispatch them, they were too proud to grant their requests, and left them to be consumed by the famine.** Now every one of these died with their eyes fixed upon the temple, and left the seditious alive behind them. Now the seditious at first

---

[163] Josephus, Wars. 5.10.3-4. Pages 719-720.

gave orders that the dead should be buried out of the public treasury, as not enduring the stench of their dead bodies. But afterwards, when they could not do that, **they had them cast down from the walls into the valleys beneath...**

...So Caesar went his rounds through the legions, and hastened on the works, and showed the robbers that they were now in his hands. But these men, and these only, were incapable of repenting of the wickednesses they had been guilty of; and **separating their souls from their bodies, they used them both as if they belonged to other folks, and not to themselves. For no gentle affection could touch their souls, nor could any pain affect their bodies,** since they could still tear the dead bodies of the people as dogs do, and fill the prisons with those that were sick."[164]

The barbarities of the zealots and seditious within the walls of Jerusalem were incomprehensible. Children were stealing food from their fathers. Women doing the same from their own children. The seditious, just for sport and not out of necessity, would seal the urinary tracts of men or shove stakes up their anuses in order to acquire whatever food they may have had, if even a mere handful of barley. They drank blood. They sliced up dead bodies, and the bodies of those yet alive but succumbing to the deadly famine, again, all for sport. At the end of this discourse Josephus actually tells us these acts were committed by ones who had, as it were, *separated their souls from their bodies, and used them as though they belonged to others.* Can we see a description of demonic activities more apparent than in these accounts?

But, what of the identity of Abaddon, the destroyer? It is interesting to read that Titus, in order to satisfy the seemingly insatiable lust of his soldiers for death and destruction, ordered the absolute destruction of Jerusalem and the temple:

"Now as soon as the army had no more people to slay or to plunder,

---

[164] Josephus, Wars. 5.12.3-4. Pages 723-724.

because there remained none to be the objects of their fury, (for they would not have spared any, had there remained any other work to be done,) **Caesar gave orders that they should now demolish the entire city and temple,** but should leave as many of the towers standing as were of the greatest eminency; that is, Phasaelus, and Hippicus, and Mariamne; and so much of the wall as enclosed the city on the west side. This wall was spared, in order to afford a camp for such as were to lie in garrison, as were the towers also spared, in order to demonstrate to posterity what kind of city it was, and how well fortified, which the Roman valor had subdued; **but for all the rest of the wall, it was so thoroughly laid even with the ground by those that dug it up to the foundation, that there was left nothing to make those that came thither believe it had ever been inhabited.** This was the end which Jerusalem came to **by the madness of those that were for innovations;** a city otherwise of great magnificence, and of mighty fame among all mankind."[165]

Thus, the great demon general's mission of destruction was complete. The release of the host of the abyss was announced by the fifth angel's trumpet with their mission to be accomplished and completed during and after the siege and destruction of Jerusalem. "In those days," as prophesied by John in verse 6 of this chapter, the people would eagerly desire death yet not find it. History also confirms this by giving us yet more information on what was going on in the city after the siege had been formed:

"And now, as the city was engaged in a war on all sides, from these treacherous crowds of wicked men, the people of the city, between them, were like a great body torn in pieces. The aged men and the women were in such distress by their internal calamities, **that they wished for the Romans, and earnestly hoped for an external war,** in order to their delivery from their domestical miseries. The citizens themselves were under a terrible consternation and fear; nor had they any opportunity of taking counsel, and of changing their conduct; nor were there any hopes of coming to an agreement with

---

[165] Josephus, Wars. 7.1.1. Pages 750-751.

their enemies; nor could such as had a mind flee away; for guards were set at all places, and the heads of the robbers, although they were seditious one against another in other respects, yet did they agree in killing those that were for peace with the Romans, or were suspected of an inclination to desert them, as their common enemies. They agreed in nothing but this, to kill those that were innocent. The noise also of those that were fighting was incessant, both by day and by night; but the lamentations of those that mourned exceeded the other; nor was there ever any occasion for them to leave off their lamentations, because their calamities came perpetually one upon another, although the deep consternation they were in prevented their outward wailing; but being constrained by their fear to conceal their inward passions, **they were inwardly tormented**, without daring to open their lips in groans. Nor was any regard paid to those that were still alive, by their relations; nor was there any care taken of burial for those that were dead; the occasion of both which was this, that everyone despaired of himself; for those that were not among the seditious had no great desires of anything, as expecting for certain that they should very soon be destroyed; but for the seditious themselves, they fought against each other, while they trod upon the dead bodies as they lay heaped one upon another, and taking up a mad rage from those dead bodies that were under their feet, became the fiercer thereupon. They, moreover, **were still inventing somewhat or other that was pernicious against themselves; and when they had resolved upon anything, they executed it without mercy, and omitted no method of torment or of barbarity.**"[166]

The atrocities committed within the walls of Jerusalem, which caused such a great degree of mourning and lamentation, caused the people who were internally tormented by them to desire the slaughter of the Roman armies to the thought of remaining in their miseries. Yet, their desires were not, as John told his audience, granted them. The Romans wouldn't break through the walls until almost five months later. Until that time, the sting of famine and pestilence, and the stench of death

---

[166] Josephus, Wars. 5.1.5. Page 698.

around them would torment them.

The demon host from the abyss were granted permission to use the hordes of the Romans and the multitudes of the zealots and the seditions to inflict great and terrible torments upon the apostate and lawless Jews, with the great destroyer, Abaddon or Apollyon, leading the charge.

The Sixth Angel's Trumpet

(13) And the sixth angel sounded, and I heard a voice from the horns of the golden altar which is before Elohim,

(14) one saying to the sixth angel that had the trumpet, Loose the four angels that are bound at the great river Euphrates.

(15) And the four angels were loosed, that had been prepared for the hour and day and month and year, that they should kill the third part of men.

(16) And the number of the armies of the horsemen was twice ten thousand times ten thousand: I heard the number of them.

(17) And thus I saw the horses in the vision, and them that sat on them, having breastplates as of fire and of hyacinth and of brimstone: and the heads of the horses are as the heads of lions; and out of their mouths proceeds fire and smoke and brimstone.

(18) By these three plagues was the third part of men killed, by the fire and the smoke and the brimstone, which proceeded out of their mouths.

(19) For the power of the horses is in their mouth, and in their tails: for their tails are like unto serpents, and have heads; and with them they hurt."

There is great significance in an often-overlooked portion of this judgment – the voice from the four horns of the golden altar. This altar is said to be the one which "is before Elohim." This golden altar is none other than the altar of sweet incense described in Exodus 30:1-10. But what is so important about the voice coming from the horns of the altar? The sin-offering, detailed in Leviticus 4, required that the blood of the sacrifice be brought into the holy place and smeared upon the incense altar.

The sin-offering was intended to expiate sins committed in ignorance, not willful sin as Israel in the first century were guilty of. However, the voice coming from the horns of the altar here isn't one of acceptance. Rather, the punishments for their guilt were being proclaimed from the very place where it used to be expiated.

In addition, the offering of strange fire upon this altar was what caused the deaths of Nadab and Abihu, the sons of Aaron the high priest. Like the fire that came forth from Yahweh to devour them the massive army led by the four angels bound at the Euphrates are said to have breathed "fire, smoke, and brimstone."

The description of the appearance of this force is not unlike that given above for the locust army of the fifth angel's trumpet judgment. These similarities, in addition to the fact that this vast host is also led by angelic generals, points to this also being a supernatural, spiritual force. Unlike the demonic host mentioned above, though, there is a specific number given by John here. The Greek text of this number is δύο μυριάδες μυριάδων, most often translated "twice ten thousand times ten thousand,"[167] "two myriads of myriads,"[168] or even "two hundred million."[169] Similar descriptions are found elsewhere in the scriptures. Revelation 5:11 speaks of an innumerable host of angels surrounding the throne. The author of Hebrews also uses the same terminology.

Hebrews 12:22
...but you are come unto mount Zion, and unto the city of the living Elohim, the heavenly Jerusalem, and to **innumerable** hosts of angels...

Are there a fixed number of angels in heaven? Probably. If so, that

---

[167] American Standard Version, English Standard Version, Rotherham Bible
[168] J.P. Green's Literal Version, Young's Literal Translation
[169] New American Standard Bible

would obviously make them "numerable" from a technical standpoint, but, continuing his constant use of symbolism, John isn't trying to give an actual number for the people to watch out for. It is intended to convey that these four angels went and gathered a host so large that John had to be told the number, one that would otherwise be innumerable by simply viewing it. This host was given the permission to kill a third part of man.

Symbolic meanings aside, do we have any historical evidence for such a vast host coming against Israel? Indeed, we do!

> "But as to Titus, he sailed over from Achaia to Alexandria, and that sooner than the winter season did usually permit; so he took with him those forces he was sent for, and marching with great expedition, he came suddenly to Ptolemais, and there finding his father, together with the two legions, the fifth and the tenth, which were the most eminent legions of all, he joined them to that fifteenth legion which was with his father; eighteen cohorts followed these legions; there came also five cohorts from Cesarea, with one troop of horsemen, and five other troops of horsemen from Syria. Now these ten cohorts had severally a thousand footmen, but the other thirteen cohorts had no more than six hundred footmen apiece, with a hundred and twenty horsemen. There were also a considerable number of auxiliaries got together, that came from the kings Antiochus, and Agrippa, and Sohemus, each of them contributing one thousand footmen that were archers, and a thousand horsemen. Malchus also, the king of Arabia, sent a thousand horsemen, besides five thousand footmen, the greatest part of which were archers; so that the whole army, including the auxiliaries sent by the kings, as well horsemen as footmen, when all were united together, amounted to sixty thousand, besides the servants, who, as they followed in vast numbers, so because they had been trained up in war with the rest, ought not to be distinguished from the fighting men; for as they were in their masters' service in times of peace, so did they undergo the like dangers with them in times of war, insomuch that they were inferior to none, either in skill or in strength, only they were subject

to their masters."[170]

In addition to understanding the vastness of this host notice also that four foreign kings that are specifically named – Antiochus, Agrippa, Sohemus, and Malchus. The Antiochus here is Antiochus IV, king of Commagene, the capitol of which lied on the Euphrates. Sohemus was the king of Emesa, located in Syria[171]. Malchus, in the passage above quoted, was the king of Arabia. Finally, the "Agrippa" here mentioned is Herod Agrippa II, who was king over Chalcis in Syria[172]. These four kings could have very well been possessed or used by the angelic generals released from the Euphrates.

Three legions, twenty-three cohorts, six troops of Syrian horseman, thousands of archers, thousands of unmentioned servants trained just as their masters, along with auxiliaries from numerous other allied forces, could most definitely have formed an "innumerable host."

From a purely practical aspect, the belief that John's 200,000,000-man army is to be literal is completely inviable. There are several things that need to be taken into consideration here. One must determine how many men are on the planet now, then how many of those are of fighting age (i.e. remove the aged, the young boys, and the babies), the amount of food/provisions required to feed the 200,000,000 men, their horses, their beasts of burden, and so forth. Even with the population of the entire world being over seven billion as of the time of this work, a 200,000,000-man army is impossible.

Persistent Impenitence

At the beginning of this chapter we stated that the judgments that resulted from the blowing the angels' trumpets were partial in their scope, essentially being a cumulative "last-ditch" effort to exhort the people to repentance. As we saw in 9:20-21, however, they did not heed

---

[170] Josephus, Wars. 3.4.2. Page 642.
[171] Josephus, Wars. 7.7.1. Page 761.
[172] Josephus, Antiquities. 20.1.3. Page 526.

the call and remained impenitent. As detailed above Vespasian began his campaign by invading Galilee, a third part of the nation of Israel, systematically conquering and destroying it. His son, Titus, tells us something very interesting regarding the reason for Vespasian's actions.

> "At this time my father [Vespasian] came into this country, not with a design to punish you for what you had done under Cestius, but to **admonish** you; for had he come to overthrow your nation, he had run directly to your fountain-head, and had immediately laid this city waste; whereas he went and burnt **Galilee** and the neighboring parts, and thereby **gave you time for repentance**; which instance of humanity you took for an argument of his weakness, and nourished up your impudence by our mildness."[173]

Even the pagan emperor to-be, who recognized that Elohim assisted him in his conquering of the Jewish people, realized that repentance had been offered to them. The outcome of their lack of repentance was apparent.

---

[173] Josephus, Wars. 6.6.2. Pages 744-745.

CHAPTER TEN

The Angel and the Scroll

(1) And I saw another strong angel coming down out of heaven, arrayed with a cloud; and the rainbow was upon his head, and his face was as the sun, and his feet as pillars of fire;

(2) and he had in his hand a little scroll open: and he set his right foot upon the sea, and his left upon the earth;

(3) and he cried with a great voice, as a lion roars: and when he cried, the seven thunders uttered their voices.

(4) And when the seven thunders uttered *their voices*, I was about to write: and I heard a voice from heaven saying, Seal up the things which the seven thunders uttered, and write them not.

(5) And the angel that I saw standing upon the sea and upon the earth lifted up his right hand to heaven,

(6) and swore by him that lives forever and ever, *who created the heaven and the things that are therein, and the earth and the things that are therein, and the sea and the things that are therein,* that there shall be delay no longer:

(7) but in the days of the voice of the seventh angel, when he is about to sound, then is finished the mystery of Elohim, according to the good tidings which he declared to his servants the prophets.

(8) And the voice which I heard from heaven, *I heard it* again speaking with me, and saying, Go, take the scroll which is open

in the hand of the angel that stands upon the sea and upon the earth.

(9) And I went unto the angel, saying unto him that he should give me the little scroll. And he says unto me, Take it, and eat it up; and it shall make your belly bitter, but in your mouth it shall be sweet as honey.

(10) And I took the little scroll out of the angel's hand, and ate it up; and it was in my mouth sweet as honey: and when I had eaten it, my belly was made bitter.

(11) And they say unto me, You must prophesy again over many peoples and nations and tongues and kings.

Commentators traditionally identify the strong angel in this chapter as one of two different characters - a mighty ministering angel of Yahweh, or the Son Yeshua himself. We won't spend any more time on this topic other than to say that though we believe it to be a ministering angel, one's conclusion is largely irrelevant. In this instance, it isn't the giver of the message that is of importance or the focus of this chapter. The message itself is what is important and emphasized.

John is calling upon two prophetic accounts in this chapter.

Daniel 12:4-7

(4) But you, O Daniel, shut up the words, and **seal the scroll**, even to the time of the end: many shall run to and fro, and knowledge shall be increased.

(5) Then I, Daniel, looked, and, behold, there stood other two, the one on the brink of the river on this side, and the other on the brink of the river on that side.

(6) And one said to the man clothed in linen, who was above the waters of the river, How long shall it be to the end of these wonders?

(7) And I heard the man clothed in linen, who was above the waters of the river, when **he held up his right hand and his left hand unto heaven**, and swore by **him that lives forever** that it shall be for a time, times, and a half; and when they have made an end of breaking in pieces the power of the holy people, all these things shall be finished.

In this passage, the time elements and prophetic significance of which we will detail more in chapter 12 below, we see several similarities with the account in the Apocalypse. In both instances an angel is delivering the message. In both instances the angels are raising their hands to swear by Him who is heaven, who is said to be the one who "lives forever." In both instances a scroll is mentioned. The most significant difference is that Daniel is told to seal the scroll and John is told to reveal what is in the scroll. It is our belief that these scrolls are one and the same. As we will detail below, Daniel's prophecy speaks of the same exact period for which John was prophesying.

Ezekiel 2:8-3:3
(8) But you, son of man, hear what I say unto you; be not you rebellious like that rebellious house: **open your mouth, and eat** that which I give you.
(9) And when I looked, behold, a **hand was put forth unto me**; and, lo, a roll of a scroll was therein;
(10) and he spread it before me: and it was written within and without; and there were written therein **lamentations**, and **mourning, and woe.**
(3:1) And he said unto me, Son of man, eat that which you find; **eat this roll**, and go, speak unto the house of Israel.
(2) So I opened my mouth, and he caused me to eat the roll.
(3) And he said unto me, Son of man, cause your belly to eat, and fill your bowels with this roll that I give you. Then did I eat it; and **it was in my mouth as honey for sweetness**.

Again, this account is strikingly similar to the one in the Apocalypse. Just as Ezekiel was given a scroll and told to eat it, so was John. Just as Ezekiel's scroll was as sweet as honey in his mouth, so was John's. Ezekiel's scroll was written inside and out with lamentations, mourning, and woes, all things which could readily be considered bitter.

Both scrolls are as sweet as honey because all the words and commands of Yahweh are such.

Psalms 19:9-10
(9) The fear of Yahweh is clean, enduring forever: The ordinances of Yahweh are true, *and* righteous altogether.

(10) More to be desired are they than gold, yea, than much fine gold; **Sweeter also than honey** and the droppings of the honeycomb.

However, the consequences of the words are bitter, filled with sadness and pain. John is telling his audience that Daniel's sealed book is about to be opened. Though they are blessed to taste of the sweetness of Yahweh's words through Yeshua, they are to expect that the unrolling of the scroll and reading of the words therein will result in great bitterness, lamentations, mourning, and woes.

As we detailed at the end of the previous chapter, Israel's last chance at repentance had come and gone, remaining unheeded. Thus, the message delivered by this strong angel was the one containing the final judgments of Yahweh. Though He gracefully stayed His hand to give them one last chance to turn from their wicked and idolatrous ways, their time had run out. "There shall be no more delay;" their judgment is upon them.

CHAPTER ELEVEN

Introduction to the Two Witnesses

The Apocalypse, being a truly amazing work, shows us yet again how the symbols represented in this chapter can have both symbolic and literal representations. Symbolically, we can see in the account of the two witnesses various aspects of, or expectations for, the assembly of Yeshua in John's day:

(1) The illustration of measuring a something with a reed is found elsewhere in the scriptures[174] referring symbolically to the counting of people.

(2) The "holy city," the true Zion, the children of Yahweh being trampled underfoot by the nations, symbolizes how the assemblies in John's day were going to undergo trials and tribulations at the hand of the spiritual Beast.

(3) The Two Witnesses are described as "lampstands," a term which was previously applied to the assemblies[175]. The assemblies were to be Yahweh's agents to bring the announcements of judgment and repentance to the nations.

(4) The Witnesses, the assemblies of Yeshua, were going to be given over to the Beast to be persecuted and in many cases

---

[174] Zechariah 2.
[175] Revelation 1:20.

destroyed.

(5) The resurrection of the Two Witnesses symbolizes how even the incalculable wickedness of the spiritual Beast will not be able to prevent the resurrection of the assemblies of Yeshua from death, only a short time after their destruction.

(6) The earth, apocalyptically representing a part of the religio-political system in Israel/Jerusalem, quaked to its foundations due to the preaching of the message of Yeshua through the assemblies.

From a literal perspective, we can see amazing parallels as well. Wherever literalism is intended John goes to great efforts to make this clear in the text. Several of these details aid us in concluding that the literal city and temple are also what is being referenced:

(1) The illustration of measuring a temple with a reed is also found in the scriptures[176], but referring to the measurement of a literal, physical temple.

(2) The holy city is trampled underfoot by the nations, which implies a literal city upon which to trample and literal feet with which to trample it.

(3) The Two Witnesses, described in detail below, were to minister, work miracles, die, and resurrect three and a half days later in a literal city, specified as the one "where their Master was crucified," which could be none other than Jerusalem.

(4) There was to be a literal earthquake that would shake the city and cause the deaths of several thousands of people. This destruction of the city and people was a "tithe" of the total destruction that was to take place later. Those who didn't die as a result of this earthquake praised Elohim for sparing their lives.

---

[176] Ezekiel 40-48.

The Existence of the Temple

(1) And there was given me a reed like unto a rod: and one said, Rise, and measure the temple of Elohim, and the altar, and them that worship therein.

(2) And the court which is without the temple leave without, and measure it not; for it has been given unto the nations: and the holy city shall they tread under foot forty and two months.

This passage goes a long way in proving the date of the writing of the Apocalypse. The fact that the temple and holy city are here mentioned, as well as the current existence of the city of Jerusalem in verse 8, points to the fact that both were still in existence at the time the Apocalypse was authored. If John had written it at a time after the destruction of both the temple and Jerusalem the passage loses much of its meaning. After all, if the later dating were accurate, the city and the temple would have both been immeasurable, ruinous heaps of stone and ash. Therefore, outside of some fanciful conjecture about John speaking of a Jerusalem and temple in his distant future, the simplest interpretation of the passage requires that both were still standing at the time the Apocalypse was penned. We are not alone in this belief. Alfred Edersheim, a 19th century Jewish convert to Christianity, wrote two very significant works on the life and practices of the Jews in the times of Yeshua who scholars to this day still trust. He states the following in one of those.

"Indeed, the Apocalypse, as a whole, may be likened to the Temple services in its mingling of prophetic symbols with worship and praise. But it is specially remarkable, that the Temple-references with which the Book of Revelation abounds are generally to minutiae, which a writer who had not been as familiar with such details, as only personal contact and engagement with them could have rendered him, would scarcely have even noticed, certainly not employed as part of his imagery. They come in naturally, spontaneously, and so unexpectedly, that the reader is occasionally in danger of overlooking them altogether; and in language such as a professional man would employ, which would come to him from the previous exercise of his calling. Indeed, some of the most striking of these references could not have been understood at all without the professional treatises of the Rabbis on the Temple and its services. Only the studied minuteness of Rabbinical descriptions, derived from the tradition of eye-witnesses, does not leave the same impression as the unstudied illustrations of St. John.

These naturally suggest the twofold inference that the **Book of Revelation** and the Fourth Gospel **must have been written before the Temple services had actually ceased**, and by one who had not merely been intimately acquainted with, but probably at one time an actor in them."[177]

Applying this clear terminology and illustration to some unknown time in the future would not only make its relevance to John's contemporaries null and void, but would also remove any ability to "read and keep" the prophecy.

The Identity of the Two Witnesses

(3) And I will give unto my two witnesses, and they shall prophesy a thousand two hundred and threescore days, clothed in sackcloth.
(4) These are the two olive trees and the two candlesticks, standing before the Master of the earth.
(5) And if any man desires to hurt them, fire proceeds out of their mouth and devours their enemies; and if any man shall desire to hurt them, in this manner must he be killed.
(6) These have the power to shut the heaven, that it rain not during the days of their prophecy: and they have power over the waters to turn them into blood, and to smite the earth with every plague, as often as they shall desire.
(7) And when they shall have finished their testimony, the beast that comes up out of the abyss shall make war with them, and overcome them, and kill them.
(8) And their dead bodies *lie* in the street of the great city, which spiritually is called Sodom and Egypt, where also their

---

[177] Edersheim. Chapter 7. Pages 112-113.

CHAPTER ELEVEN

Master was crucified.

(9) And from among the peoples and tribes and tongues and nations do *men* look upon their dead bodies three days and a half, and suffer not their dead bodies to be laid in a tomb.

(10) And they that dwell on the earth rejoice over them, and make merry; and they shall send gifts one to another; because these two prophets tormented them that dwell on the earth.

(11) And after the three days and a half the breath of life from Elohim entered into them, and they stood upon their feet; and great fear fell upon them that beheld them.

(12) And they heard a great voice from heaven saying unto them, Come up here. And they went up into heaven in the cloud; and their enemies beheld them.

The identity of the Two Witnesses of this chapter has been and will, to some degree, continue to be a mystery. This is because the very nature of the descriptions blend many different symbols and reference several different Old Testament characters or passages. The phrase "two olive trees and two candlesticks" bears a striking resemblance to the account of Joshua and Zerubbabel[178]. The most compelling similarity being that both these Two Witnesses and the two characters in Zechariah's prophecy "stand by the Master of the earth." The symbolism of fire-breathing humans likewise isn't new.

Jeremiah 5:14
Wherefore thus says Yahweh, the Elohim of hosts, Because you speak this word, behold, **I will make my words in your mouth fire,** and this people wood, and it shall devour them.

Though there are instances of literal fire coming upon men as the result of someone's word[179] it would be unlike someone who is to minister the gospel of Yeshua to these people to choose instead to engulf them in flame. Then the powers they have to shut up heaven so that it doesn't rain or turn waters to blood clearly bring the prophets

---

[178] Zechariah 4.
[179] Numbers 16:29-35; 2 Kings 1:9-12.

Elijah and Moses to mind.

We find the detailed evaluation of this topic by James Stuart Russell[180] very convincing and would like to share it here. We encourage the reader to carefully examine each part of Russell's evaluation, the text and the footnotes, to ensure a full and proper understanding of his position is understood.

Episode of the Two Witnesses.

CHAP. xi. 3–13.—'And I will give [power] unto my two witnesses, and they shall prophesy a thousand two hundred and threescore days, clothed in sackcloth. These are the two olive trees, and the two candlesticks standing before the Lord of the earth. And if any man willeth to hurt them, fire proceedeth out of their mouth, and devoureth their enemies: and if any man willeth to hurt them, he must in this manner be killed. These have

---

[180] Russell. Pages 430-444.

power to shut heaven, that it rain not in the days of their prophecy: and have power over the waters to turn them into blood, and to smite the earth [land] with every plague, as often as they will. And when they have finished their testimony, the beast that ascendeth out of the abyss shall make war against them, and overcome them, and kill them. And their dead body shall lie in the [broad] street of the great city, which spiritually is called Sodom and Egypt, where also their 'Lord was crucified. And they of the people and kindreds and tongues and nations shall see their dead bodies three days and an half, and shall not suffer their dead bodies to be put in graves. And they that dwell upon the earth shall rejoice over them, and make merry, and shall send gifts one to another; because these two prophets tormented them that dwelt upon the earth. And after three days and an half the Spirit of life from God entered into them, and they stood upon their feet; and great fear fell upon them which saw them. And they heard a great voice from heaven saying unto them, Come up hither. And they ascended up to heaven in a cloud; and their enemies beheld them. And the same hour was there a great earthquake, and the tenth part of the city fell, and in the earthquake were slain of men seven thousand: and the remnant were affrighted, and gave glory to the God of heaven.'

We now enter upon the investigation of one of the most difficult problems contained in Scripture, and one which has exercised, we may even say baffled, the research and ingenuity of critics and commentators up to the present hour. Who are the two witnesses? Are they mythical or historical persons? Are they symbols or actual realities? Do they represent principles or individuals? The conjectures, for they are nothing more, which have been propounded on this subject, form one of the most curious chapters in the history of Biblical interpretation. So complete is the bewilderment, and so unsatisfactory the explanation, that many consider the problem insoluble, or conclude that the witnesses have never yet appeared, but belong to the unknown future.

It is one of the tests of a true theory of interpretation that it should be a good working hypothesis. When the right key to the Apocalypse is found it will open every lock. If this prophetic vision be, as we believe it to be, the reproduction and expansion of the prophecy on the Mount of Olives; and if we are to look for the *dramatis personæ* who appear in its scenes within the limits of the period to which that prophecy extends, then the area of investigation becomes very restricted, and the probabilities of discovery proportionately increased. In the inquiry respecting the identity of the two witnesses we are shut up almost to a point of time. Some of the data are precise enough. It will be seen that the *period* of their prophesying is antecedent to the sounding of the seventh trumpet, that is, just previous to the catastrophe of Jerusalem. The *scene* of their prophesying also is not obscurely indicated : it is ' the great city, which spiritually is called Sodom and Egypt, where also their Lord was crucified.' Notwithstanding Alford's objections, which appear to have really no weight, there can be no reasonable doubt that *Jerusalem* is the place intended, according to the general consent of almost all commentators and the obvious requirements of the passage. The question then is, What two persons, living in the last days of the Jewish commonwealth and in the city of Jerusalem, can be found to answer the description of the two witnesses as given in the vision? That description is so marked and minute that their identification ought not to be difficult. There are seven leading characteristics :—

1. They are witnesses of Christ.
2. They are two in number.
3. They are endowed with miraculous powers.
4. They are symbolically represented by the two olive-trees and the two candlesticks seen in the vision of Zechariah. (Zech. iv.)
5. They prophesy in sackcloth, *i.e.* their message is one of woe.
6. They die a violent death in the city, and their dead bodies are treated with ignominy.
7. After three days and a half they rise from the dead, and are taken up to heaven.

Before proceeding further in the inquiry it may be well to notice the following remarks of Dr. Alford on the subject, with which we cordially agree :—

' *The two witnesses, etc.* No solution has ever been given of this portion of the prophecy. Either the two witnesses are literal,—two individual men,—or they are symbolical,—two individuals taken as the concentration of principles and characteristics, and this either in themselves, or as representing men who embodied those principles and characteristics. . . . The article τοῖς seems as if the two witnesses were well known, and distinct in their individuality. The δυοῖν is essential to the prophecy, and is not to be explained away. No interpretation can be right which does not, either in individuals, or in characteristic lines of testimony, retain and bring out this dualism.'

On the statement 'clothed in sackcloth' (in token of need of repentance and of approaching judgment), Alford says :—

'Certainly this portion of the prophetic description strongly favours the individual interpretation. For, first, it is hard to conceive how whole bodies of men and churches could be thus described; and, secondly, the principal symbolical interpreters have left out, or passed very slightly, this important particular. One does not see how bodies of men who lived like other men (their being the victims of persecution is another matter) can be said to have prophesied *clothed in sackcloth*.'

Again, on the fifth verse :—

'This whole description is most difficult to apply on the allegorical interpretation ; as is that which follows, and, as might have been expected, the allegorists halt and are perplexed exceedingly. The double announcement here seems to stamp the literal sense, and the εἴ τις and δεῖ αὐτὸν ἀποκτανθῆναι are decisive against any mere national application of the words. *Individuality* could not be more strongly indicated.'

Again, on the miraculous powers ascribed to the witnesses :—

'All this points out the spirit and power of Moses, combined with that of Elias. And, undoubtedly, it is in these two directions that we must look for the two witnesses, or lines of witnesses. The one impersonates the law, the other the prophets. The one reminds us of the prophet whom God should raise up like unto Moses ; the other of Elias the prophet, who should come before the great and terrible day of the Lord.' *

Entirely concurring in these observations, which state the problem fairly, and conclusively set aside any allegorical interpretation as incompatible with the plain requirements of the case, we now proceed to search for the two witnesses of Christ who testified for their Lord and sealed their testimony

* See Greek Testament *in loc.*

29

with their blood, in Jerusalem, in the last days of the Jewish
polity, *and we have no hesitation in naming St. James* and
St. Peter as the persons indicated.

1. *St. James.*

We know as a matter of fact and of history that in the
last days of Jerusalem there lived in that city a Christian
teacher eminent for his sanctity, a faithful witness of Christ,
endowed with the gifts of prophecy and miracles, who prophesied in sackcloth, and who sealed his testimony with his
blood, being murdered in the streets of Jerusalem towards
the closing days of the Jewish commonwealth. This was
' James, a servant of God, and of the Lord Jesus Christ.'*

---

* We have two accounts of the death of St. James—one given by Josephus
and the other by Hegesippus, a Christian writer of the second century. The
notice of Josephus is as follows :—

'Ananus [the high-priest], judging that he had found a fitting opportunity, in
consequence of Festus having died, and Albinus (his successor) being still on
the way, convoked an assembly of the judges; and having brought before them
the brother of Jesus who was called Christ, James by name, and certain others,
he laid an accusation against them as breakers of the law, and delivered them
up to be stoned to death.'—Antiquities, xx. 9, 1.

We give the narrative of Hegesippus from Alford's Prolegomena to the
Epistle of James (Greek Testament, vol. iv. pp. 97, 98):—

' Further particulars of his death are given us from Hegesippus, by Eusebius
(H. E. ii. 23), but they do not seem to tally with the above account in Josephus.
According to Hegesippus, whose narrative is full of strange expressions and
savours largely of the fabulous, some of the seven sects of the people asked
James, " What is the door of Jesus ?" And by his preaching to them Jesus as
the Christ, so many of them believed on Him that, *many of the rulers also
believing, there was a tumult of the Jews and of the Scribes and Pharisees,
saying that all the people were in danger of expecting* [the coming of] *Jesus the
Christ.* On this they invited James to deter the people from being thus
deceived, standing on *the wing of the temple* at the Passover, that he might be
seen and heard by all. But, the story proceeds, when he was set there, and
appealed to by them to undeceive the people. he *answered with a loud voice,
Why ask ye me concerning Jesus the Son of man ? for He sitteth in heaven at the
right hand of the Almighty Power, and will soon come in the clouds of heaven.*
On this, many were confirmed in their belief, and glorified God for his testimony and cried, Hosanna to the Son of David. Whereat the Scribes and
Pharisees said to one another, *We did wrong in affording such testimony to
Jesus ; but let us go up and throw him down, that they may be deterred by fear
from believing him. So they cried out, saying, Oh ! oh ! the Just one has gone*

Let us see how this name fulfils the requirements of the problem. It is impossible to conceive a more adequate representative of the old prophets and of the law of Moses than the Apostle James. That he was a faithful witness of Christ in Jerusalem is unquestionable. His habitual, if not his fixed, residence was there: his relation to the church of Jerusalem makes this all but certain. No man of that day had a better title to be called an Elijah. No silken courtier, no prophesier of smooth things, but ascetic in his habits, stern and bold in his denunciation of sin,—a man whose

mad. So they went up, and cast him down, and said one to another, *Let us stone James the just. And they began to stone him, since he was not killed by the fall, but, turning, got upon his knees, saying, I beseech thee, O Lord God the Father, forgive them, for they know not what they do.* And while they were stoning him, a priest, one of the sons of Rechab, cried out, *What do ye? The Just one is praying for you!* And a certain man among them, seizing a fuller's mallet, *with which garments are pressed, brought it down on the head of the Just one: and thus he suffered martyrdom. And they buried him on the spot; and his monument is still standing near the temple.*

'This last sentence seems wholly inexplicable, considering that long before it was written both city and temple were destroyed. And the more so, as Hegesippus proceeds to say that immediately upon St. James's martyrdom Vespasian formed the siege of the city. He adds: *So wonderful a man was James, and so extolled for his righteousness above all others, that sensible men, even among the Jews themselves, considered that this was the cause of the siege of Jerusalem, which took place immediately after his martyrdom, and which was brought upon them by nothing else than on account of the crime perpetrated on him.* And he quotes from Josephus: *These things befell the Jews to avenge James the just, who was the brother of Jesus called Christ, inasmuch as the Jews put that most just man to death;* but no such passage is now found in Josephus.'

Upon the whole we are inclined to think the story of Hegesippus neither fabulous nor incredible. There may be slight inaccuracies, such as the statement about the martyr's pillar or monument; but it has an air of truthfulness and circumstantiality which commend it to respect. The expression about 'the door of Jesus,' which has occasioned so much perplexity, is, we venture to think, susceptible of an easy explanation. In his epistle, St. James had written, 'Behold, the Judge is standing before the door.' The Jews, perhaps in mockery, demanded, 'What is the door of Jesus?' *i.e.* by what way will He come in? This gave the apostle occasion to bear his testimony, which he did with the results described. We cannot help thinking Hegesippus more accurate than Josephus in this instance, for the time at which the latter places the murder of James, viz. at the death of Festus, can hardly be possible. The Epistle of James is evidently written close upon the siege of Jerusalem; and we may easily suppose that the expected appearing of the Son of man would be the general theme in Jerusalem.

29 *

knees were callous, like those of a camel, with much prayer; whose unflinching. integrity and primitive sanctity won for him even in that wicked city the appellation of *the Just*: was not this the manner of man to 'torment them that dwelt in the land,' and to answer to the description of a witness of Christ? We can still hear the echo of those stern rebukes which galled the proud and covetous men who 'oppressed the hireling in his wages,' and which predicted the swiftly-coming wrath which was now so near,—'Go to, ye rich men, weep and howl for your miseries which are coming on. Ye heaped up treasures in the last days.' Who can with greater probability be named as one of the two prophet witnesses of the last days than James of Jerusalem, 'the Lord's brother'?

Concerning the exact time and manner of the martyrdom of this witness there may be some doubt, but of the fact itself, and of its having taken place in the city of Jerusalem, there can be none. Thus far, at all events, St. James, in the manner of his life and of his death, answers with remarkable fitness to the description of the witnesses given in the Apocalypse.

The following observations by Dr. Schaff place in a striking light the life and work of St. James of Jerusalem, and are eminently appropriate to the subject under discussion:—

'There was a necessity for the ministry of James. If any could win over the ancient covenant people it was he. It pleased God to set so high an example of Old Testament piety in its purest form among the Jews, to make conversion to the Gospel, even at the eleventh hour, as easy as possible for them. But when they would not listen to the voice of this last messenger of peace, then was the measure of the divine patience exhausted, and the fearful and long-threatened judgment broke forth. And thus was the mission of James fulfilled. He was not to outlive the destruction of the Holy City and the temple. According to Hegesippus, he was martyred in the year before that event, viz. A.D. 69.'[*]

2. *St. Peter.*

But who is the other witness? Here we seem to be left wholly in the dark. Stuart indeed suggests that we may

---

[*] Schaff's History of the Apostolic Church, vol. i. p. 314.

regard the number *two* as merely symbolical; but this seems an unwarrantable supposition. Besides, as the Old Testament prototypes of the witnesses, 'the two anointed ones' of Zechariah's vision, were two persons, Zerubbabel and Joshua, it is only congruous that the witnesses of the Apocalypse should be two persons. Undoubtedly the second witness, like the first, must be sought among the apostles. They were pre-eminently Christ's witnesses, and possessed in the highest degree the miraculous endowments ascribed to the witnesses in the Apocalypse.*

Now, what other apostle besides St. James had a recognised connection with the church of Jerusalem; dwelt statedly in that city; lived up to the eve of the dissolution of the Jewish polity; died a martyr's death; and suffered in Jerusalem? It may seem to some a wild conjecture to suggest the name of *St. Peter*, as we venture to do; but it is by no means a random guess, and we solicit a candid consideration of the arguments in favour of the suggestion.

If it should appear that the habitual or fixed residence of St. Peter was in Jerusalem; that there was an intimate, if not an official, connection between him and the church of that city; and that St. Peter was in Jerusalem on the eve of the Jewish revolt: all these circumstances would lend great probability to the supposition that St. Peter was the other witness associated with St. James.

What, then, are the facts of the case as shown in the New Testament?

1. We find St. Peter the most prominent person at the original founding of the church of Jerusalem on the day of Pentecost.

* There is a remarkable coincidence between the description of the witnesses in Rev. xi. 3 and our Lord's language respecting the apostles in Acts i. 8 :—

Acts i. 8.—'And *ye shall receive power* after that the Holy Ghost is come upon you; and *ye shall be witnesses unto me*, both in Jerusalem,' etc.

Rev. xi. 3.—'And *I will give* [*power*] *unto my two witnesses*, and they shall prophesy a thousand two hundred and threescore days, clothed in sackcloth.'

2. We find St. Peter summoned before the Sanhedrim as the representative of the Christians in Jerusalem (Acts iv. 8; v. 29).

3. When the church of Jerusalem was dispersed after the death of Stephen, St. Peter, with the other apostles, continued in Jerusalem (Acts viii. 1).

4. St. Peter was delegated, along with St. John, to visit the Samaritans converted by the preaching of Philip. After fulfilling their mission they returned to Jerusalem (Acts viii. 25).

5. When St. Peter was called by a divine revelation to Cæsarea to preach the Gospel to Cornelius we find that he returned from Cæsarea to Jerusalem (Acts xi. 2).

6. It was in Jerusalem that St. Peter was apprehended and imprisoned by Herod Agrippa I. after the martyrdom of St. James ' the brother of John ' (Acts xii. 3).

7. On St. Paul's conversion we are told that ' he did not go up to Jerusalem to them which were apostles before him' (Gal. i. 17): which implies that there were apostles residing in that city.

8. Three years after his conversion St. Paul goes up to Jerusalem. For what purpose? 'To see Peter;' and he adds,—' I abode with him fifteen days,' implying that St. Peter's stated abode was in Jerusalem. On this occasion St. Paul saw only one other apostle, viz. ' James, the Lord's brother' (Gal. i. 18, 19).

9. Fourteen years afterwards St. Paul again visits Jerusalem. Whom does he find there? '*James, Cephas,* and John, who seemed to be pillars' (Gal. ii. 1, 9).

10. When Paul and Barnabas were deputed by the church of Antioch to go to Jerusalem to consult the apostles and elders respecting the imposition of the Jewish ritual upon the Gentile converts, what apostles did they find in Jerusalem on that occasion? St. Peter and St. James. (Acts xv. 2, 7, 13.)

11. We find St. Peter and St. James taking a leading part

in the discussion of the question referred to them by the church of Antioch; no other apostles being named as present. (Acts xv. 6-22.)

12. That St. Peter and St. James had an official and recognised connection with the church of Jerusalem is presumable from the terms of the letter addressed to the Gentile churches in Antioch, etc. The document is styled ' the decrees of the apostles and elders which are in Jerusalem' [τῶν ἐν 'Ιεροσολύμοις], implying their fixed abode there. (See Steiger on 1 Peter v. 31.)

13. Judas and Silas, having delivered the epistle to the church of Antioch, return to Jerusalem, ' *unto the apostles* ' (Acts xv. 33).

14. We infer that St. Peter was associated with St. James in the church of Jerusalem from the fact that St. Peter, when miraculously brought out of prison, sent a special message to St. James and the brethren,—' Go, shew these things unto James, and to the brethren ' (Acts xii. 17).

15. St. Peter (in 1 Peter v. 13) sends a salutation from ' his son Marcus.' If this means John surnamed Mark, as is most probable, we know that his home was in Jerusalem, where his mother had a house. (Acts xii. 12.)

16. If it shall appear (as we hope to show) that the Babylon of 1 Peter v. 13 is really Jerusalem, it will be a decisive proof that St. Peter's habitual place of residence was in that city. The complete evidence, however, of the identity of Babylon with Jerusalem must be reserved until we come to the consideration of Rev. xvi. xvii.

17. A comparison of the epistles of St. James and St. Peter shows that both are addressed to the same class of persons, viz. Jewish believers of the dispersion. (James i. 1; 1 Peter i. 1.) It is very suggestive, in connection with this inquiry, to find these two apostles dwelling in the same city, officially connected with the same church, associated in the same work, addressing the believing Jews in foreign lands, and bearing

witness to the same great truths in advanced age, almost at
the close of their life, and on the eve of that great catastrophe
which buried the city, the temple, and the nation in one
common ruin.

18. Finally, it may be affirmed that, whether these probabilities amount to demonstration or not, no man could be named
more answerable to the character of a witness for Christ in
the last days of Jerusalem than St. Peter. Of course, we
reject as unhistorical and incredible the lying legends of tradition which assign to him a bishopric and a martyrdom in
Rome. The imposture has received only too respectful treatment at the hands of critics and commentators. It is more
than time that it should be relegated to the limbo of fable, with
other pious frauds of the same character. That St. Peter's
stated abode was in Jerusalem is, we think, proved. That he
lived up to the verge of the Jewish revolt and war is evident
from his epistles. That he died a martyr's death we know
from our Lord's prediction ; and in his case we may well say
that the proverb would hold good, 'It cannot be that a prophet
perish out of Jerusalem.' As we read his epistles, and view
them as the testimony of one of the two apostolic witnesses of
Christ in the doomed city, a new emphasis is imparted to his
prophetic warnings. What a new light breaks in upon the
mysterious utterance which anticipates his own and his
country's fate, 'The time is come when judgment must begin
at the house of God: and if it first begin at *us!*' How
appalling the description of the evil times and evil men, as
he saw them in the last days, with his own eyes, in Jerusalem!
While the last chapter might be the final testimony of the
prophet-witness to the guilty land and city ; the last warning-
cry before the fiery storm of vengeance burst : ' The day of
the Lord *will come* as a thief in the night,' etc. (2 Pet. iii. 10).

Let us now see how far the requirements of the apocalyptic
description are met by this identification of the two witnesses
as St. James and St. Peter.

They are two in number : 'Individual men, well known, and distinct in their individuality,' as Alford truly says they must be. They are more than this,—they are fellow-servants and brethren in Christ, associated in the same work, the same church, the same city. The *dualism*, which Alford says is essential to the right interpretation, is perfect. Still more than this,—' The one impersonates the law, the other the prophets.' Who could be a better representative of the law than St. James ? though he does not the less impersonate the prophets. St. James indeed strongly reminds us of Elias, who might have been his model ; the stern ascetic, whose mighty achievements in prayer he commemorates in his epistle. St. Peter also, who may be called the founder of the Jewish Christian church, reminds us of Moses, the founder of the ancient Jewish church. What the old prophets were to Israel, St. James and St. Peter were to their own generation, and especially to Jerusalem, the chief scene of their life and labours. The period of their prophecy is also remarkable ; it is for the space of a thousand two hundred and threescore days, or three years and a half, representing the duration of the Jewish war. They prophecy in sackcloth : that is, their message is of coming judgment; the denunciation of the wrath of God. They are likened to the two olive-trees and the two candlesticks seen in the vision of Zechariah : that is, they are 'the two anointed ones ' on whom the unction of the Spirit has been poured, the feeders and lights of the Christian church, as Zerubbabel and Joshua were the feeders and lights of Israel in their day. They are endowed with miraculous powers, a characteristic which must not be explained away, and which will apply only to apostolic witnesses. They are to seal their testimony with their blood, and thus far we find St. James and St. Peter perfectly fulfil the conditions of the problem. We are sure that they were both martyrs of Christ, and that too in the last days of the Jewish commonwealth. As regards the place where St. James's blood was shed we have credible historical evidence that it was in Jerusalem. But here the light fails us, and henceforth we are compelled to grope and feel our way. Of the death of St. Peter we possess no record; but the very silence is suggestive. That the two chief persons in the church of Jerusalem should fall victims to a suspicious government, or to popular fury, at the moment when revolution was on the point of breaking out, or had already broken out, is only too probable; that their dead bodies should lie unburied is in accordance with what actually occurred in many instances during that fearful period of lawless barbarity which preceded the fall of Jerusalem: but though we can go thus far we can go no farther. The martyred witnesses are raised again to life after three days and a half; they stand up on their feet, to the consternation of their enemies and murderers; they ascend to heaven in a cloud, in view of those who exulted over their dead bodies. If we are asked, Did this miracle take place with respect to the martyred witnesses of Christ, St. James and St. Peter? we can only answer, We do not know. There is no evidence one way or another. We only know that it was a distinct promise of Christ that at His coming the living saints should be caught up to meet the Lord in the air. If such a thing might take place on the large scale of tens of thousands, and hundreds of thousands, there is no difficulty in supposing that it might take place in the case of two individuals. If the ascension of Christ Himself is a credible fact, it is not easy to see why the ascension of His two witnesses may not also be a literal fact. But we do not dogmatise on the subject: the facts are before us, and must be left to make their own impression on the mind of the reader. It does not seem possible to resolve the whole into allegory. Where we have found so much already of substantial fact and credible history, it seems inconsistent and unreasonable to sublimate the conclusion into mere metaphor and symbol. We therefore quit the subject with this one observation: Four-fifths at least of the description in the Apocalypse suit the known history of

St. James and St. Peter, and no one can allege that the remainder may not be equally appropriate.

There remains, however, one circumstance to which we have not adverted, viz. the enemy by whom the witnesses are slain. We read in ver. 7, 'And when they shall have finished their testimony, the wild beast that cometh up from the abyss shall make war upon them, and shall overcome them, and kill them.' This is the first mention made of a being that occupies a large space in the subsequent part of the Book of Revelation—'the wild beast from the abyss.' Here he is introduced proleptically, that is by anticipation. We shall have much to say respecting this portentous being in the sequel, and only now allude to the subject in order to note the fact that, whatever the symbol may mean, it points to a powerful and deadly antagonist to Christ and His people; and that to the agency of this monster the death of the two witnesses is ascribed.

The ascension of the martyred witnesses to heaven is immediately followed by an act of judgment inflicted on the guilty city in which their blood was shed :—

CHAP. xi. 13.—'And in that same hour there was a great earthquake, and the tenth part of the city fell, and there were slain in the earthquake seven thousand men, and the remnant were affrighted, and gave glory to the God of heaven.'

It is difficult to see how this can be regarded as merely symbolical. It is a remarkable fact that we find in Josephus an account of an incident which occurred during the Jewish war which in many respects bears a striking resemblance to the events described in this passage. On that fatal occasion, when the Idumean force was treacherously admitted into the city by the Zealots, a fearful earthquake took place, and in the same night a great massacre of the inhabitants of the city was perpetrated by these brigands. The statement of Josephus is as follows :—

' During the night a terrific storm arose ; the wind blew with tempestuous violence, and the rain fell in torrents ; the lightnings flashed without inter-

444   THE PAROUSIA IN THE APOCALYPSE.

mission, accompanied by fearful peals of thunder, and the quaking earth resounded with mighty bellowings. The universe, convulsed to its very base, appeared fraught with the destruction of mankind, and it was easy to conjecture that these were portents of no trivial calamity.' *

Taking advantage of the panic caused by the earthquake, the Idumeans, who were in league with the Zealots, who occupied the temple, succeeded in effecting an entrance into the city, when a fearful massacre ensued. 'The outer court of the temple,' says Josephus, 'was inundated with blood, and the day dawned upon eight thousand five hundred dead.' †

We do not quote this as the fulfilment of the scene in the vision, although it may be so; but to show how much the symbols resemble actual historical facts.

So ends the vision of the sixth seal with these impressive words, ' The second woe is past ; behold, the third woe cometh quickly.'

James and Peter. Are there any two individuals more qualified for this calling than them? James, the brother of Yeshua, was entrusted with the leadership of the first assembly of Yeshua after his death and resurrection. He was considered by all to be a pious man who devoted himself to prayer and worship. Simon Peter, one of the twelve apostles hand-picked by Yeshua, was told that he would be one of the foundations upon which the entire assembly of Yeshua would be built. These two men were trustworthy, bold leaders who were intimate with Yeshua's teachings, called to positions of great authority, and filled with the spirit of Yahweh completely.

We know from two historical witnesses that the death of James was perpetrated by the hands of lawless Jews. The Beast, described in vivid detail in Chapter 13 below, though representative of a literal being in the time of John, is also a spiritual being or influence. It is by this wicked influence and power that those lawless Jews thought it fit and just to put such a one as James to death.

As Russell says, we have no account of the death of Peter in Jerusalem.

However, he provides compelling evidence that the tradition of his death occurring in Rome is a historical fable. After all the scriptures confirm that after each ministry expedition he returned to his home, Jerusalem. We are, however, provided with plenty of historical evidence regarding the death of James the Just, the brother of Yeshua. Since his death, when properly dated, ties into the timing of the resurrection of the first fruits detailed in chapter 12 below, we feel it is prudent to belabor the point a little longer.

Russell quotes several lines of Hegesippus' commentary above, taken from Eusebius' Ecclesiastical History[181]. While Hegesippus' statement about the tombstone of James is questionable, as Russell also notes above, his statements about the timing and manner of death of James are supported by several other historical accounts.

"But, as to the manner of James's death, it has been already stated in the words of Clement that **he was thrown from a wing of the temple and beaten to death with a club.**"[182]

"This James was of so shining a character among the people, on account of his righteousness, that Flavius Josephus, when, in his twentieth book of the Jewish Antiquities, he had a mind to set down what was the cause, why the people suffered such miseries, till the very holy house was demolished, he said, that these things befell them by the anger of God, on account of what they had dared to do to James, the brother of Jesus, who was called Christ; and wonderful it is, that while he did not receive Jesus for Christ, he did nevertheless bear witness that James was so righteous a man. He says farther, that **the people thought they had suffered these things for the sake of James.**"[183]

"Now this writer [*Josephus*], although not believing in Jesus as the Christ, in seeking after the cause of the fall of Jerusalem and the

---

[181] Eusebius. Book 2, Chapter 23, Verse 18.
[182] Clement of Alexandria; quoted in Eusebius. Book 2, Chapter 23, Verse 3.
[183] Origen, Matthew. Book 2, Chapter 17.

destruction of the temple, whereas he ought to have said that the conspiracy against Jesus was the cause of these calamities befalling the people, since they put to death Christ, who was a prophet, says nevertheless – being, although against his will, not far from the truth – **that these disasters happened to the Jews as a punishment for the death of James the Just,** who was a brother of Jesus (called Christ)."[184]

"Josephus also has not hesitated to add this testimony in his works: **'These things,'** said he, **'happened to the Jews to avenge James the Just,** who was the brother of him that is called the Christ, and whom the Jews had slain, notwithstanding his pre-eminent justice.'"[185]

It is possible that Eusebius' quote above was taken from Origen's writings, which came earlier. Regardless, it seems highly unlikely that Origen would have manufactured these quotes of Josephus, even though they aren't found in any extant manuscripts of Josephus' writings today. If he had chosen to falsify or add to Josephus' writings, he wouldn't have gone to the lengths he did to explain Josephus' mistake in crediting the destruction of Jerusalem to James' death instead of Yeshua's. If his personal belief was that the destruction came upon the Jews because of their murder of Yeshua, as he so clearly states, his falsified statements would have been worded accordingly. In other words, if his intent was to convince his audience that even a staunch Jew like Josephus recognized the destruction of his people came upon them for Yeshua's murder, he failed.

Returning to Hegesippus' account, for some unknown reason Russell stopped the quote a couple lines short of the end. The missing sentences are extremely important as it relates to the time of James' death and the timeline of the Apocalypse.

---

[184] Origen, Celsus. Book 1, Chapter 47.
[185] Eusebius. Book 2, Chapter 23, Verse 20.

"He became a faithful **witness**, both to the Jews and Greeks, that Jesus is the Christ. **Immediately after this, Vespasian invaded and took Judea.**"[186]

As a part of the note from Alford's "Prolegomena to the Epistle of James" quoted in Russell's evaluation above, we read, "And the more so, Hegesippus proceeds to say that immediately upon St. James's martyrdom Vespasian **formed the siege of the city**." That is not, however, what Hegesippus said. He said that immediately after James' death Vespasian began his invasion and subsequent taking of Judea, not the city of Jerusalem itself. Historically speaking this is a difference of almost two years. Josephus also gives us an account of James' judgment.

"Festus was now dead, and Albinus was but upon the road; so he assembled the Sanhedrin of judges, and brought before them the brother of Jesus, who was called Christ, whose name was James, and some others, [or, some of his companions]; and when he had formed an accusation against them as breakers of the law, **he delivered them to be stoned**: but as for those who seemed the most equitable of the citizens, and such as were the most uneasy at the breach of the laws, they disliked what was done; they also sent to the king [Agrippa], desiring him to send to Ananus that he should act so no more, for that what he had already done was not to be justified; nay, some of them went also to meet Albinus, as he was upon his journey from Alexandria, and informed him that it was not lawful for Ananus to assemble a Sanhedrin without his consent. Whereupon Albinus complied with what they said, and wrote in anger to Ananus, and threatened that he would bring him to punishment for what he had done; on which king Agrippa took the high priesthood from him, when he had ruled but three months, and made Jesus, the son of Damneus, high priest."[187]

There is an *apparent* contradiction between Josephus' account of James'

---

[186] Eusebius. Book 2, Chapter 23, Verse 18.
[187] Josephus, Antiquities. 20.9.1. Page 538.

judgment and *supposed* death and those quoted from Clement, Origen, Hegesippus, and Eusebius above. This *apparent* contradiction needs to be addressed. Commentators, historians, and scholars alike have all interpreted Josephus' statement above to mean that James, the brother of Yeshua, was actually stoned to death at that moment in time. The year of this unlawful convening of the Sanhedrin and judgment of James is agreed upon by most to be 62 CE. Therefore, most also date the death of James to the same year. However, Josephus' account does not state that James and the others with him were stoned, only that they were *delivered* over to be stoned. As admitted in the gospels, the Jews, while under Roman control, didn't have the authority to put people to death.

> John 18:31
> Pilate therefore said unto them, Take him yourselves, and judge him according to your law. The Jews said unto him, **It is not lawful for us to put any man to death**.

Given that the rebellion of the Jews against Rome had not yet begun by 62 CE, it is unlikely that they would suddenly feel free to put a group of people to death without their Roman governor's permission. The "most equitable of the citizens" mentioned by Josephus didn't send to Albinus and Agrippa with complaints regarding the unlawful and unjust deaths of a group of people. They sent complaints to them regarding the unlawful convening of the Sanhedrin. Surely the former would have been considered more severe to both Albinus and Agrippa than a convening of a judgment body! This is especially true when one considers the fact that the Jews considered James a very pious man. If the equitable citizens were appalled and angered by the convening of the Sanhedrin, surely they would have been more so with the unjust killing of such a righteous man. William Whiston, arguably the most well-known translator of the works of Josephus, argues the same himself in detail in another work of his called "Primitive Christianity Revived."[188]

---

[188] Whiston. Chapter 1. Pages 42-46.

What this proper understanding of Josephus' testimony does is bring all the accounts into harmony with one another. The *apparent* contradiction disappears and we are left with a congruent and seamless timeline once again. James was condemned to be stoned in 62 CE. His sentence was never carried out, however, because the false judicature's ruling was deemed unlawful given Ananus' lack of authority to convene a Sanhedrin or execute the death penalty apart from the Roman governor's permission. From the accounts above we can safely conclude that James, during the feast of Passover, was called before the people in the city to testify concerning Yeshua, after doing so was cast down from the pinnacle of the temple, stoned, and then beaten to death. Immediately after this horrific event Vespasian's invasion of Judea began. Josephus tells us when that happened.

> "In the meantime, an account came that there were commotions in Gall, and that Vindex, together with the men of power in that country, had revolted from Nero; which affair is more accurately described elsewhere. This report, thus related to Vespasian, excited him to go on briskly with the war...**at the beginning of the spring** he took the greatest part of his army, and led it from Cesarea to Antipatris..."[189]

The account of Vespasian's conquest continues throughout that book of the Wars. This invasion began in the spring of 68 CE, a time which will become much more impactful as chapter 12 is read below.

We believe that one other important matter in this account of the Two Witnesses needs to be addressed further. We are told that these Two Witnesses would die and remain as such for three and a half days, after which they would be raised from the dead. There is obviously no historical record of this, else the books we have would be full of accounts of the event. How can this be explained?

There is an important concept that both the reader and skeptic may well remember. *The absence of evidence is not the evidence of absence.* It's

---

[189] Josephus, Wars. 4.8.1. Page 686.

like the old saying, "If a tree falls in the woods and no one is around to hear it does it make a sound?" Physics demands that the falling of a tree be the cause of a sound. However, no confirmation or evidence of the sound can be provided because no one was present when it fell. The preponderance of the evidence we have in favor of the demands of physics require us to acknowledge with certainty that the falling of the tree did indeed make a sound. Likewise, the evidence regarding the identity of the Two Witnesses provided above, despite the absence of evidence regarding their resurrection, require us to consider James and Peter as extremely likely and qualified candidates.

Futurists may say, "Surely there would be a record of such an amazing and unprecedented event!" However, let them be reminded that outside of the historical works of followers of Yeshua we have only one historical testimony of his resurrection. That account is found in work of Josephus and is greatly disputed.[190] There are several explanations that may be offered for this silence, however.

First, it is possible that unbelieving historians may have considered testimonies to such an event as fantastic and unrealistic, therefore not worthy of their fact-based histories. Second, since the testimonies to the resurrection would have been started and perpetuated by Yeshua's followers, they may have considered them too biased to be reliable. Third, like many believing Jews in the days of the apostles, including those we read about in Hegesippus, there may have been secular historians who believed upon Yeshua but, having fear of shame, ridicule, and persecution, remained silent. Fourth, the works of secular or profane historians that provided testimony to the resurrection are no longer extant. Fifth, none of the historians were among the ones present to see this resurrection, and the people that would have been able to give an account of it were killed in the siege.

Regardless of whether any of these explanations are accurate we can

---

[190] Evidence on the historicity and reliability of this quote is provided by Whiston in his first Dissertation in the Appendix in Josephus, Wars, Pages 815-822.

know from the preponderance of the evidence that the resurrection did indeed occur. If the plethora of different works such as the gospels and epistles in our New Testament aren't enough we have the simple fact that a faith in Yeshua as the son of Elohim and Messiah still exists today. Given the number of accounts we find in histories of Josephus regarding so-called "prophets" and "messiahs"[191], none of them have followers existing to this day. Yeshua, however, despite being the poor son of a first century carpenter, has had dozens and dozens of historical accounts recorded of him and has followers in the billions today. Josephus, in contrast to the other prophets and messiahs he writes of, gives us an account of the same, almost as though he was surprised.

> "Now there was about this time Yeshua, a wise man, if it be lawful to call him a man; for he was a doer of wonderful works, a teacher of such men as receive the truth with pleasure. He drew over to him both many of the Jews and many of the Gentiles. He was [the] Christ. And when Pilate, at the suggestion of the principal men amongst us, had condemned him to the cross, those that loved him at the first did not forsake him; for he appeared to them alive again the third day; as the divine prophets had foretold these and ten thousand other wonderful things concerning him. **And the tribe of Christians, so named from him, are not extinct at this day.**"[192]

Just as we look for the preponderance of the evidence in the case of the resurrection we must do so here. If two people in history so clearly match the descriptions given of the Two Witnesses, but we are missing historical testimony to the event of their resurrection, that absence of evidence doesn't equate to evidence of it not occurring. It just so happens, however, that the conclusions drawn in chapter 12 below will lend great support to the resurrection of these two witnesses occurring in early spring of 68 CE, just as Vespasian's invasion of Judea began.

---

[191] Josephus, Wars. 2.13.4-5. Page 614; 6.5.3. Pages 742-743; et. al.
[192] Josephus, Antiquities. 18.3.3. Page 480.

The Great Earthquake

(13) And in that hour there was a great earthquake, and the tenth part of the city fell; and there were killed in the earthquake seven thousand persons: and the rest were affrighted, and gave glory to the Elohim of heaven.
(14) The second Woe is past: behold, the third Woe comes quickly.

Just as specified in the table of apocalyptic terminology found in the Introduction, great shakings of the earth or heavenly bodies represent the shaking of political bodies eventually to result in their destruction. We read above that many early "church fathers," quoting Josephus, stated that the death of James was the eventual or final event resulting in the final destruction of Jerusalem and the temple. However, this particular quaking is only partial in nature, affecting but a tenth of the city. The numbers "one-tenth" and "seven thousand" are highly symbolic. As any diligent student of the scriptures will readily acknowledge, one-tenth is the number representing the amount of the offerings given to the Levites from the other tribes for their service in the tabernacle[193]. The number seven thousand is the number of perfection or completion, seven, multiplied by one thousand, signifying a great, yet perfect number of people. Symbolically speaking, it appears John is telling his audience that the Levites, the tribe from which the priests were taken, were at that time going to have a tenth taken *from* them, as opposed to given *to* them.

At about this same time in history, very near the time the two witnesses were put to death, we read of an awesome earthquake that took many lives.

"But the shame that would attend them in case they returned without doing anything at all so for overcame that their repentance, that they lay all night before the wall, though in a very bad encampment; for there broke out a prodigious storm in the night, with the utmost violence, and **very strong winds**, with the **largest**

---

[193] Leviticus 27:30-32; Numbers 18:21.

showers of rain, with continual **lightnings,** terrible **thunderings,** and **amazing concussions and bellowings of the earth,** that was in an **earthquake.** These things were a manifest indication that some destruction was coming upon men, when the system of the world was put into this disorder; and anyone would guess that these wonders foreshowed some grand calamities that were coming."[194]

Under the cover of this storm the Idumeans, joined by the zealots, stormed the outer temple slaughtering the people therein. When all was said and done, eighty-five hundred people were dead[195], seven thousand of which may have been those specified in the Apocalypse.

The Seventh Angel's Trumpet

(15) And the seventh angel sounded; and there followed great voices in heaven, and they said, The kingdom of the world is become *the kingdom* of our Master, and of his Messiah: and he shall reign forever and ever.
(16) And the four and twenty elders, who sit before Elohim on their thrones, fell upon their faces and worshipped Elohim,
(17) saying, We give you thanks, O Yahweh Elohim, the Almighty, who are and who were; because you have taken your great power, and did reign.
(18) And the nations were enraged, and your wrath came, and the time of the dead to be judged, and *the time* to give their reward to your servants the prophets, and to the saints, and to them that fear your name, the small and the great; and to destroy them that destroy the earth.
(19) And there was opened the temple of Elohim that is in heaven; and there was seen in his temple the ark of his covenant; and there followed lightnings, and voices, and thunders, and an earthquake, and great hail.

The blowing of this trumpet marked a pivotal event in history, possibly

---

[194] Josephus, Wars. 4.4.5. Page 678.
[195] Josephus, Wars. 4.5.1. Page 679.

the most pivotal event, second only to the death and resurrection of Yeshua. Prior to this the enemy, the Dragon, Satan and his minions had been given rule over the kingdoms of the world. If this were not so, how could he have offered them as a gift to Yeshua?

Matthew 4:8-9
(8) Again doth the Devil take him to a very high mount, and doth shew to him **all the kingdoms of the world** and the glory of them,
(9) and says to him, '**All these to you I will give**, if falling down you may bow to me.'

Satan cannot offer and give Yeshua what was not his to give. At the time that this seventh trumpet sounded the final transference of power occurred. Daniel also speaks of this wondrous event.

Daniel 2:40-45
(40) And the fourth kingdom shall be strong as iron, forasmuch as iron breaks in pieces and subdues all things; and as iron that crushes all these, shall it break in pieces and crush.
(41) And whereas you saw the feet and toes, part of potters' clay, and part of iron, it shall be a divided kingdom; but there shall be in it of the strength of the iron, forasmuch as you saw the iron mixed with miry clay.
(42) And as the toes of the feet were part of iron, and part of clay, so the kingdom shall be partly strong, and partly broken.
(43) And whereas you saw the iron mixed with miry clay, they shall mingle themselves with the seed of men; but they shall not cleave one to another, even as iron doth not mingle with clay.
(44) And in the days of those kings shall the Elohim of heaven set up a kingdom which shall never be destroyed, nor shall the sovereignty thereof be left to another people; but it shall break in pieces and consume all these kingdoms, and it shall stand forever.
(45) Forasmuch as you saw that a stone was cut out of the mountain without hands, and that it broke in pieces the iron, the brass, the clay, the silver, and the gold; the great Elohim has made known to the king what shall come to pass hereafter: and

the dream is certain, and the interpretation thereof sure.

The first of the five kingdoms of this dream is the Babylonian empire. Babylon was conquered by the second kingdom, the Medo-Persian empire. Medo-Persia was conquered by the third kingdom, the Grecian empire, which included the later portions under the Ptolemaic and Seleucid dynasties. The fourth kingdom was none other than the Roman empire, the ten toes of which represented the ten provinces of Rome existing in Yeshua's and John's day (more details will be provided later). Then the fifth and final kingdom is that of the small stone, which will grow to be a mountain, and last until eternity. Something is unique about how that final kingdom is described, though. Unlike the successive nature of the first four kingdoms, the eternal kingdom is to be set up "in the days of those [ten] kings." That fourth kingdom and its ten toes aren't to come to an end first. Can this be any more descriptive of the timing of the establishment of the kingdom of heaven during the time of Yeshua and the first Jewish-Roman war?

The blowing of the seventh trumpet established this everlasting kingdom as the final ruling authority over the earth. This kingdom, unlike the others, was not made with hands. It wasn't a kingdom that could be seen, as though it were constructed by men. Did not Yeshua testify of the same regarding his kingdom?

John 18:33-36
(33) Pilate therefore entered again into the Praetorium, and called Yeshua, and said unto him, Art you the King of the Jews?
(34) Yeshua answered, Say you this of yourself, or did others tell it you concerning me?
(35) Pilate answered, Am I a Jew? Your own nation and the chief priests delivered you unto me: what have you done?
(36) Yeshua answered, My kingdom is not of this world: if my kingdom were of this world, then would my servants fight, that I should not be delivered to the Jews: but now is my kingdom not from here.

The immediate fall and destruction of Rome, or any subsequent ruling authority or kingdom on earth, need not be necessary for this kingdom to be the true and only power. At its inception, the kingdom here solidified was indeed a small one. However, the gospel message spread like a wildfire and continues in power to this day. As more and more followers of Yeshua die, they enter that kingdom and begin ruling and reigning with him. More details on this topic will be discussed later in this work.

Has the Kingdom of Heaven Come Already?

The temporal nature of John the Baptist's and Yeshua's teachings on the kingdom of Elohim[196], among other passages and teachings, demand that its coming be in their very near future. Consider the most hermeneutically simple rendering of the following passages:

Matthew 3:1-2
(1) And in those days comes John the Baptist, preaching in the wilderness of Judaea, saying,
(2) Repent you; for the kingdom of heaven is **at hand**.

Matthew 4:17
From that time began Yeshua to preach, and to say, Repent you; for the kingdom of heaven is **at hand**.

Matthew 10:5-7
(5) These twelve Yeshua sent forth, and charged them, saying, Go not into *any* way of the Gentiles, and enter not into any city of the Samaritans:
(6) but go rather to the lost sheep of the house of Israel.
(7) And as you go, preach, saying, The kingdom of heaven is **at hand**.

Mark 1:14-15
(14) Now after John was delivered up, Yeshua came into Galilee, preaching the gospel of Elohim,
(15) and saying, The time is fulfilled, and the kingdom of Elohim

---

[196] Also called the "kingdom of heaven."

is **at hand**: repent you, and believe in the gospel.

The phrase "at hand" was discussed in the Introduction. In this context, it is used to denote an event to take place in the very near future. Consider also the following verse:

Matthew 10:23
But when they persecute you in this city, flee into the next: for truly I say unto you, **You shall not have gone through the cities of Israel, till the Son of man be come.**

The coming of the kingdom not made with hands, to come during the time of the ten kings represented by the statue in Nebuchadnezzar's dream, was to occur within the very lifetimes of the twelve apostles to whom this statement was addressed.

Mark 8:38
For whosoever shall be ashamed of me and of my words **in this adulterous and sinful generation**, the Son of man also shall be ashamed of him, when he comes in the glory of his Father with the holy angels.

Matthew 16:27-28
(27) For the Son of man shall come in the glory of his Father with his angels; and *then shall he render unto every man according to his deeds.*
(28) Truly I say unto you, **There are some of them that stand here, who shall in no wise taste of death, till they see the Son of man coming in his kingdom.**

Matthew 26:63-64
(63) But Yeshua held his peace. And the high priest said unto him, I adjure you by the living Elohim, that you tell us whether you are the Messiah, the Son of Elohim.
(64) Yeshua says unto him, You have said: nevertheless I say unto you, Henceforth **you shall see** *the Son of man sitting at the right hand of Power,* and *coming on the clouds of heaven.*
Luke 23:27-31

(27) And there followed him a great multitude of the people, and of women who bewailed and lamented him.

(28) But Yeshua turning unto them said, Daughters of Jerusalem, weep not for me, **but weep for yourselves, and for your children**.

(29) For behold, the days are coming, in which they shall say, Blessed are the barren, and the wombs that never bore, and the breasts that never gave suck.

(30) Then shall they begin *to say to the mountains, Fall on us; and to the hills, Cover us.*

(31) For if they do these things in the green tree, what shall be done in the dry?

That adulterous generation, those that *stood there* with Yeshua, *the high priest* Yeshua spoke to, all of those were to see him coming in his kingdom with glory and power. Those statements, if taken to mean some unknown time in the future, would have in the end meant absolutely nothing to those to whom they were spoken. The woman who were lamenting him were told to weep for *themselves* and *their children.* His instruction was not addressed to some distant generation of women and children. That statement would once again have been pointless and meaningless, and Yeshua is not one to do things without point and meaning.

All the passages above are shown to prove that the coming and establishment of Yeshua's kingdom did indeed occur during the first century, very near the time of the destruction of the temple and Jerusalem in 70 CE.

Immediate Outcome or Progressive Regeneration?

The following passage is very powerful and compelling as it relates to the purpose and timeframe of the kingdom of heaven.

Matthew 19:28-30

(28) And Yeshua said unto them, Truly I say unto you, that you who have followed me, **in the regeneration** when the Son of man shall sit on the throne of his glory, you also shall sit upon twelve

thrones, judging the twelve tribes of Israel.

(29) And every one that has left houses, or brethren, or sisters, or father, or mother, or children, or lands, for my name's sake, shall receive a hundredfold, and shall inherit eternal life.

(30) But many shall be last *that are* first; and first *that are* last.

The concept of *regeneration* is not taught today. Traditional Christian and/or Messianic doctrine would have us believe that when Yeshua returns all his enemies are immediately destroyed[197] and his kingdom and Torah are immediately those controlling the earth. However, that is not what Yeshua taught. Here we are told that his kingdom would be one of regeneration. The world, which had long been engulfed in every form of wickedness, was now to go through a regeneration period wherein the absolute rule of the kingdom in the heavenly realm would be realized in the earthly.

Yeshua tells us the order of operations as it relates to heavenly and earthly events. The following verses are quoted in three different versions to show how many translations, as literal as they may be, often don't bring out the true force of the Greek text here.

Matthew 16:18-19 (American Standard Version)

(18) And I also say unto you, that you are Peter, and upon this rock I will build my assembly; and the gates of Hades shall not prevail against it.

(19) I will give unto you the keys of the kingdom of heaven: and whatsoever you shall bind on earth shall be bound in heaven; and whatsoever you shall loose on earth shall be loosed in heaven.

Matthew 16:18-19 (Young's Literal Translation)

(18) 'And I also say to you, that you are a rock, and upon this rock I will build my assembly, and gates of Hades shall not prevail against it;

(19) and I will give to you the keys of the reign of the heavens,

---

[197] Their teaching excepting death as the final enemy. *Cf.* 1 Corinthians 15:26.

and whatever you may bind upon the earth shall be **having been bound in the heavens**, and whatever you may loose upon the earth shall be having been loosed in the heavens.'

Matthew 16:18-19 (J.P. Green's Literal Version)
(18) And I also say to you that you are Peter, and on this rock I will build My assembly, and *the* gates of Hades will not prevail against her.
(19) And I will give to you the keys of the kingdom of Heaven. And whatever you bind on earth shall occur, **having been bound in Heaven**. And whatever you may loose on the earth shall be, having been loosed in Heaven.

The traditional phrase for which the force is not brought forth in most translations is "whatsoever **you shall bind** on earth **shall be bound** in heaven." The tense, voice, and mood of the Greek verbs in question, in addition to the positions of the words in most English translations, really prevent the reader from grasping the impact of this teaching. J.P. Green's translation is the clearest, most literal, and easiest to read translation here. What Yeshua is telling us through his words to Peter is that whatever he binds, shall be bound. But, those things that Peter binds would have *already been bound* in heaven. Things occur in the heavenly realm first, the results of which trickle down to the earthly. They are bound in heaven even before Peter binds them on earth. This order seems very foreign to many given the fact that it implies a level of control that is well outside of our hands. However, the truth remains the same. The heavenly rules over the earthly just as a king does over his servants. So it is with the kingdom of heaven.

Some may ask, Futurists especially, "Why then has it taken so long for the regeneration to happen and why don't we see its completion yet?" The answer to that question is simple, yet likely not very fulfilling to our personal desires. We will let the words of Nebuchadnezzar and Paul speak for us here.

Daniel 4:34-35
(34) And at the end of the days I, Nebuchadnezzar, lifted up my eyes unto heaven, and my understanding returned unto me, and

I blessed the Most High, and I praised and honored him that lives forever; for his dominion is an everlasting dominion, and his kingdom from generation to generation;

(35) and all the inhabitants of the earth are reputed as nothing; and **he does according to his will in the army of heaven, and among the inhabitants of the earth; and none can stay his hand**, or say unto him, What do you?

Romans 9:14-24

(14) What shall we say then? Is there unrighteousness with Elohim? Elohim forbid.

(15) For he says to Moses, *I will have mercy on whom I have mercy, and I will have compassion on whom I have compassion*[198].

(16) So then it is not of him that wills, nor of him that runs, but of Elohim that has mercy.

(17) For the scripture says unto Pharaoh, *For this very purpose did I raise you up, that I might show in you my power, and that my name might be published abroad in all the earth.*

(18) **So then he has mercy on whom he will, and whom he will be hardens.**

(19) You will say then unto me, Why does he still find fault? For who withstands his will?

(20) Nay but, O man, who are you that replies against Elohim? Shall the thing formed say to him that formed it, Why did you make me thus?

(21) Or **has not the potter a right over the clay, from the same lump to make one part a vessel unto honor, and another unto dishonor**?

(22) What if Elohim, willing to show his wrath, and to make his power known, endured with much longsuffering vessels of wrath fitted unto destruction:

(23) and that he might make known the riches of his glory upon vessels of mercy, which he afore prepared unto glory,

(24) *even* us, whom he also called, not from the Jews only, but also from the Gentiles?

---

[198] Exodus 33:19.

The answer is, "Because that is His perfect will." Maybe it is because there is one individual to be born 500 years from now that He wants to hear and accept the gospel to be a part of His kingdom. Maybe He wants to empower His people and watch as they overcome evil with good through His spirit and word. Maybe He, as the Creator of all things, just enjoys watching His creation and doesn't want it to end yet. After all, though history has seen wickedness proliferate, it has also seen its defeat. In all of this, though it may be confusing to us, we need to do as our Master taught us and pray, "Your will be done, as in heaven, so on earth."[199]

A Preview of Coming Events

We find it important to emphasize here that the verses in this section of chapter 11 encompass, as is very evident, a span of time greater than an instant. John manages to weave together events that occur later in chapters 12, 14, 16, and 19 all together in a very succinct manner. Verses 18 and 19 make this clear because it speaks of the coming of Yahweh's wrath (found in the seven angels' bowl judgments in chapter 16), the resurrection and judgment of the dead (found in chapters 12, 14, and 20), and the destruction of those who destroy the land (found in chapters 16 and 19). John basically gives his audience a brief prelude to what they should expect to see and hear in the duration of the Apocalypse, all of which were triggered by the blowing of this final judgment trumpet.

Verse 15 states that the kingdoms have been transferred to Yahweh and Yeshua, which is a preview of what happens in chapter 12 verse 10 after Satan is cast down from heaven having lost the battle with Michael. Verse 18 tells us of the reward being given to the saints and other faithful ones, which we know from the context of the scriptures is eternal life. Yet, we don't see the resurrection verses until the man-child of chapter 12 and the harvest of chapter 14, both of which we will detail more below. Verse 18 also mentions the judgment of the dead, which isn't detailed until chapter 20. Many future events separated by

---

[199] Matthew 6:10.

different spaces of time are being prefigured and summed up in this verse.

Verse 19 is probably the most powerful example, though. First, he tells us that the temple of Elohim in heaven is opened and the ark of the covenant becomes visible. Later in chapters 15 and 16 we read that the seven angels who carry the bowls of Yahweh's wrath come forth from the temple. John is seeing that the place from which the final judgments of Yahweh will come has been opened. Second, he tells his audience that *after* the temple in heaven was opened there were lightnings, voices, thunders, an earthquake, and great hail. We read the following in chapter 16 below:

> (17) And the seventh poured out his bowl upon the air; and **there came forth a great voice out of the temple**, from the throne, saying, **It is done**:
> (18) and **there were lightnings**, and **voices**, and **thunders**; and **there was a great earthquake**, such as was not since there were men upon the earth, so great an earthquake, so mighty.
> (19) And the great city was divided into into three parts, and the cities of the nations fell: and Babylon the great was remembered in the sight of Elohim, to give unto her the cup of the wine of the fierceness of his wrath.
> (20) And every island fled away, and the mountains were not found.
> (21) **And great hail**, *every stone* about the weight of a talent, came down out of heaven upon men: and men blasphemed Elohim because of **the plague of the hail**; for the plague thereof is exceeding great.

John is clearly summarizing the events that his audience were to expect to hear throughout the rest of the Apocalypse. He sets all of the major themes that are later broken down into much greater detail. In a very real sense, John is supplying his audience with an outline as to how they are to understand various events mentioned later in the Apocalypse. As we proceed through this work and come to each individual portion of this rich, interwoven message, we will present again the relevant portions of the information above to refresh the mind of the reader.

CHAPTER TWELVE

Heavenly Signs

A few different views exist regarding the identity of some of the characters in this passage, but only a couple of them are the most widely accepted. Many traditional Christian commentators believe, especially those of the Catholic denomination, that the woman signified here is Mary, the mother of Yeshua, and the man-child brought forth by her is none other than Yeshua himself. However, contextually this makes no sense. The remaining passages in this chapter do not support this view. Instead, we must take the signs individually and establish who they are presenting within the entire context of scripture.

The Woman

(1) And a great sign was seen in heaven: a woman arrayed with the sun, and the moon under her feet, and upon her head a crown of twelve stars;
(2) and she was with child; and she cries out, travailing in birth, and in pain to be delivered.

First, John sees a woman arrayed with the sun, standing on the moon, and wearing a crown of stars. The symbols here used immediately bring to mind Joseph's dreams.

Genesis 37:9-10
(9) And he dreamed yet another dream, and told it to his brethren, and said, Behold, I have dreamed yet a dream: and, behold, **the sun and the moon and eleven stars** made obeisance to me.
(10) And he told it to his father, and to his brethren; and his father rebuked him, and said unto him, What is this dream that you have dreamed? Shall I and your mother and your brethren indeed come to bow down ourselves to you to the earth?

In this context, his brothers and his father all understood the sun to represent Israel, the moon to represent Rachel, and the eleven stars to represent Joseph's brothers. We must remember that John's goal in using the signs and symbols within the Apocalypse is to bring things like Joseph's dream to the forefront of their minds. These signs and symbols, when taken together, identify the woman very clearly to the reader. Given the signs above, the fact that she is provided with divine protection, and that her children are those who hold to the testimony of Yeshua and obey the commandments of Elohim[200], this woman is none other than Zion, the representation of the true body of believers. This becomes even clearer as we see who the man-child is further down.

The Dragon

(3) And there was seen another sign in heaven: and behold, a great red dragon, having seven heads and ten horns, and upon his heads seven diadems.
(4) And his tail draws the third part of the stars of heaven, and did cast them to the earth: and the dragon stands before the woman that is about to be delivered, that when she is delivered he may devour her child.

Little mystery surrounds the identity of this symbol. He is clearly identified as the Devil, Satan, only six verses later. This is the same one

---

[200] Revelation 12:6, 14-17.

who is found in the following chapter standing on the sand of the sea calling forth the first wild Beast. It is the same one bound in Chapter 20 and later cast into the lake of fire.

The description of the dragon and his actions doesn't stop at just words, though. We must remember that the dragon, and later the first and second Beasts, are spiritual creatures that influence real people and direct them where they would. In this case, we read that the dragon drew a third of the stars out of heaven with his tail and cast them to the land. What are these stars? Why does it specify that he drew them down with his tail and not his head or hands? Once again, the truth lies in history.

The path that Vespasian took as he was conquering Galilee is very detailed in the work of Josephus. The map below illustrates this path.

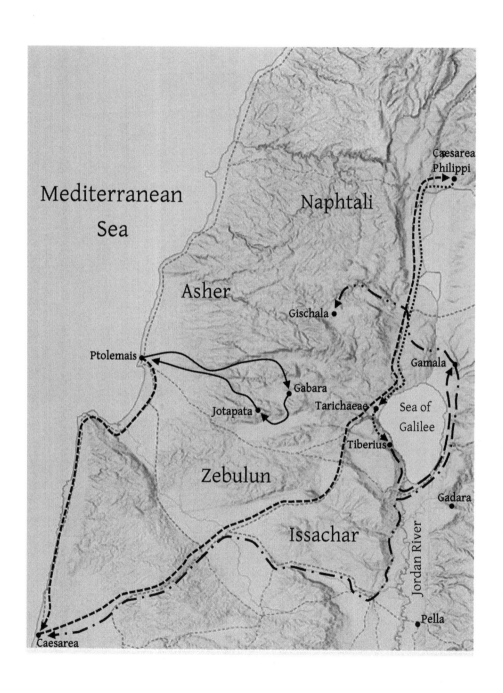

Vespasian met his son Titus with several legions and auxiliaries from neighboring confederates at Ptolemais[201]. From there his army marched upon a city called Gabara[202], which he took with ease[203]. After that he marched towards the city defended by Josephus, Jotapata[204], and after a 47-day siege seized it by force, burning it to the ground[205]. Vespasian returned to Ptolemais. This path is shown on the map as the solid (——) line.

After this he turned South down the coast to arrive at Caesarea[206]. From there he desired to see the kingdom of Herod Agrippa he traveled to Caesarea Philippi in the Northernmost part of Israel to the East[207]. This path is shown on the map as the short-dashed (----) line.

While in Caesarea Philippi he prepared for the siege against Tiberius and Taricheae, the former of which surrendered[208]. This path is shown on the map as the dotted (·······) line. After taking both of those cities he continued his march around the Sea of Galilee to Gamala, also conquering it[209]. This path is shown on the map as the long-dashed (— —) line.

The final city remaining in Galilee who still withstood the Romans was Gischala, to which Vespasian sent Titus. Gischala was also taken by force[210]. Vespasian decided to retire back to Caesarea to rest his troops. Titus' path is shown as the long-dash-dot-dot (— · ·) line and Vespasian's path is shown as the long-dash-dot (— ·) on the map.

---

[201] Josephus, Wars. 3.4.2. Page 642.
[202] Gadara is typically used here but is inaccurate since it is too far a distance from Jotapata for a one-day march and that Vespasian proceeds to demolish Gadara less than a year later.
[203] Josephus, Wars. 3.7.1. Page 645.
[204] Known today as Yodfat.
[205] Josephus, Wars. 3.7.3-36. Pages 646-654.
[206] Josephus, Wars. 3.9.1. Page 658.
[207] Josephus, Wars. 3.9.7. Page 659.
[208] Josephus, Wars. 3.9.7-3.10.1. Pages 659-670.
[209] Josephus, Wars. 4.1.1-10. Pages 664-668.
[210] Josephus, Wars. 4.2.1-5. Pages 668-669.

Vespasian and his armies systematically dismantled and destroyed all the chief and controlling cities of Galilee. Galilee was the home of four out of the twelve tribes, or *one-third* of them. We must be consistent with the use of the word "star" in this chapter of the Apocalypse. We see that Asher, Zebulun, Naphtali, and Issachar were all "stars" cast down by the dragon.

What is meant by the dragon's tail? The tail of any creature is something that is behind it. Vespasian's campaign was to turn towards Jerusalem having left everything behind him, in the tail of his massive host, conquered and destroyed. John is telling his audience that the driving spiritual force behind Vespasian and his conquering Roman force, Satan, the dragon, is going to decimate one-third of the land consisting of one third of the tribes of Israel.

The Man-Child

(5) And she was delivered of a son, a man child, who is to rule all the nations with a rod of iron: and her child was caught up unto Elohim, and unto his throne.
(6) And the woman fled into the wilderness, where she has a place prepared of Elohim, that there they may nourish her a thousand two hundred and threescore days.

We have now reached one of the events that John gave as merely a preview in the account of the seventh angel's trumpet above. Isaiah gives us great insight in one of his prophecies that helps us to identify both the woman and her child.

Isaiah 66:7-8
(7) Before she travailed, she brought forth; before her pain came, she was delivered of a **man-child**.
(8) Who has heard such a thing? who has seen such things? Shall a land be born in one day? shall a nation be brought forth at once? for as soon as **Zion** travailed, she brought forth **her children**.

We see here that Zion gives birth twice, once before she travailed, and one as a result of that later travailing. The first birth is only one child, a man-child. This birth takes place *before* the woman, Zion, travails in the pains of tribulation. The man-child referred to here is Yeshua. The second birth is multiple children, representing a group of people.

Unlike the verse in Isaiah, however, the woman in Revelation 12 gives birth to a man-child *after* travailing. If we continue to use Isaiah's prophecy above to help us interpret what John meant, just as his audience in the past would have done, we must agree that the man-child of verse 5 is to be a group of people. These people are those who are followers of Yeshua obedient to the commandments of Elohim, just like the woman and the rest of her children.

We are told that the man-child is immediately caught up to Elohim and his throne. He is also said to be one who is to rule the nations with a rod of iron. Revelation 2:27 says the same of those who keep Yeshua's words till the end and overcome. Knowing that at this time death or Hades was still a necessary intermediate between temporal and eternal life, the people who made up this man-child were those followers of Yeshua who had already died. The fact that the throne is here mentioned and that the temple in heaven now opened was mentioned just a few verses prior, it is apparent that this group was taken from the earthly realm wherein it was born to the heavenly one where Yahweh is.

The man-child represents, as it were, a first fruits of the resurrection of the dead. More on this resurrection and how it relates to the timing of the resurrection of the Two Witnesses will be detailed later in this chapter. The woman, representing heavenly Zion[211], the fullness of the body of believers, brought forth a first-born child, who was resurrected from the dead unto eternal life in the heavenly realm. We see this same group of first fruits mentioned later in the Apocalypse[212], which we will discuss more below. It is likely that this group consisted of many or most of the apostles and disciples of Yeshua and the many

---

[211] *Cf.* Hebrews 12:22.
[212] Revelation 14:1-5, 15:2.

thousands who believed upon Yeshua because of their message, especially those who were martyred as a part of the fifth seal. This group is what is to be known later, in chapter 20, as the "first resurrection."

The War in Heaven

(7) And there was war in heaven: Michael and his angels *going forth* to war with the dragon; and the dragon warred and his angels;

(8) and they prevailed not, neither was their place found any more in heaven.

(9) And the great dragon was cast down, the old serpent, he that is called the Devil and Satan, the deceiver of the whole world; he was cast down to the earth, and his angels were cast down with him.

(10) And I heard a great voice in heaven, saying, Now is come the salvation, and the power, and the kingdom of our Elohim, and the authority of his Messiah: for the accuser of our brethren is cast down, who accuses them before our Elohim day and night.

(11) And they overcame him because of the blood of the Lamb, and because of the word of their testimony; and they loved not their life even unto death.

(12) Therefore rejoice, O heavens, and you that dwell in them. Woe for the earth and for the sea: because the devil is gone down unto you, having great wrath, knowing that he has but a short time.

This is not the first time we hear of a time where Michael stands up to fight for the people of Yahweh. Remember, John is making every attempt possible to bring to the minds of his audience the prophecies and teachings they were all so familiar with. This is to both convey the purpose and intent of the things coming upon Israel and to reveal the fulfilments of many prophecies, blessings, and curses pronounced in the scriptures. Because of this, we must direct ourselves briefly to an evaluation of Daniel's prophecies in Chapters 11 and 12 in his work.

The Willful King

For brevity's sake, we are not going to go through the text and ancient fulfillments of the prophecies contained in the first thirty-five verses of Daniel 11. Instead, it will suffice to say that the persons and events outlined therein are those of the Persian and Grecian empires, and subsequently the Ptolemaic and Seleucid dynasties. The historical record, if studied carefully, displays that fact in vivid detail. However, we encounter a rather peculiar phrase at the beginning of verse 36 that marks a transition in time and focus. We will begin quotes of the relevant passages from that point.

> Daniel 11:36-39
> (36) And the king shall do according to his will; and he shall exalt himself, and magnify himself above every elohim, and shall speak marvelous things against the Elohim of elohim; and he shall prosper till the indignation be accomplished; for that which is determined shall be done.
> (37) Neither shall he regard the elohim of his fathers, nor the desire of women, nor regard any elohim; for he shall magnify himself above all.
> (38) But in his place shall he honor the elohim of fortresses; and an elohim whom his fathers knew not shall he honor with gold, and silver, and with precious stones, and pleasant things.
> (39) And he shall deal with the strongest fortresses by the help of a foreign elohim: whosoever acknowledges *him* he will increase with glory; and he shall cause them to rule over many, and shall divide the land for a price.

Who then is this king mentioned if not one of the kings of the south or kings of the north? The simple answer – Vespasian. We must examine the details to show how this is proven to be true.

Unlike every other occurrence of the phrase "the king" in the verses 5-35 of that chapter, the one at the beginning of verse 36 isn't suffixed by "of the south" or "of the north." That Vespasian did "according to his will" requires no explanation. Any Caesar of Rome did exactly as he saw fit. This king is said to "magnify himself above every god." Can we find any evidence in history to support that Vespasian did this?

"Having, therefore, entered on a civil war, and sent forward his generals and forces into Italy, he himself, in the meantime, passed over to Alexandria, to obtain possession of the key of Egypt. Here having entered alone, without attendants, the temple of Serapis, to take the auspices respecting the establishment of his power, and having done his utmost to propitiate the deity, upon turning round, [his freedman] Basilides appeared before him, and seemed to offer him the sacred leaves, chaplets, and cakes, according to the usage of the place, although no one had admitted him, and he had long laboured under a muscular debility, which would hardly have allowed him to walk into the temple; besides which, it was certain that at the very time he was far away. Immediately after this, arrived letters with intelligence that Vitellius's troops had been defeated at Cremona, and he himself slain at Rome. **Vespasian**, the new emperor, having been raised unexpectedly from a low estate, **wanted something which might clothe him with divine majesty and authority**. This, likewise, was now added. A poor man who was blind, and another who was lame, came both together before him, when he was seated on the tribunal, imploring him to heal them, and saying that they were admonished in a dream by the god Serapis to seek his aid, who assured them that he would restore sight to the one by anointing his eyes with his spittle, and give strength to the leg of the other, if he vouchsafed but to touch it with his heel. At first he could scarcely believe that the thing would any how succeed, and therefore hesitated to venture on making the experiment. At length, however, by the advice of his friends, he made the attempt publicly, in the presence of the assembled multitudes, and it was crowned with success in both cases. About the same time, at Tegea in Arcadia, by the direction of some soothsayers, several vessels of ancient workmanship were dug out of a consecrated place, on which there was an effigy resembling Vespasian."[213]

"In the months during which Vespasian was waiting at Alexandria for the periodical return of the summer gales and settled weather at

---

[213] Suetonius, Vespasian. Chapter 7.

sea, many wonders occurred which seemed to point him out as the object of the favour of heaven and of the partiality of the Gods. One of the common people of Alexandria, well-known for his blindness, threw himself at the Emperor's knees, and implored him with groans to heal his infirmity. This he did by the advice of the God Serapis, whom this nation, devoted as it is to many superstitions, worships more than any other divinity. He begged Vespasian that he would deign to moisten his cheeks and eye-balls with his spittle. Another with a diseased hand, at the counsel of the same God, prayed that the limb might feel the print of a Caesar's foot. At first Vespasian ridiculed and repulsed them. They persisted; and he, though on the one hand he feared the scandal of a fruitless attempt, yet, on the other, was induced by the entreaties of the men and by the language of his flatterers to hope for success. At last he ordered that the opinion of physicians should be taken, as to whether such blindness and infirmity were within the reach of human skill. They discussed the matter from different points of view. "In the one case," they said, "the faculty of sight was not wholly destroyed, and might return, if the obstacles were removed; in the other case, the limb, which had fallen into a diseased condition might be restored, if a healing influence were applied; such, perhaps, might be the pleasure of the Gods, and the Emperor might be chosen to be the minister of the divine will; at any rate, **all the glory of a successful remedy would be Caesar's**, while the ridicule of failure would fall on the sufferers." And so Vespasian, supposing that all things were possible to his good fortune, and that nothing was any longer past belief, with a joyful countenance, amid the intense expectation of the multitude of bystanders, accomplished what was required. The hand was instantly restored to its use, and the light of day again shone upon the blind. Persons actually present attest both facts, even now when nothing is to be gained by falsehood."[214]

Vespasian in this one account in history not only boldly entered the temple of the "highest" god in their society, as if having dominion, but claimed responsibility for divine acts such as healing. We have no

---

[214] Tacitus, Histories. Book 4, Chapter 81.

reference to provide to verify that Vespasian spoke "marvelous things against the God of gods," but given what he accepted as worship above, and that Suetonius, quoted above, titles his book "Divus Vespasianus"[215], we feel it is unnecessary given the additional evidence offered below.

If indeed Vespasian is the one referred to here, and our conclusion that the "time of indignation" was referring to the destruction of Jerusalem and the Jewish commonwealth, he most definitely "prospered" until that indignation was accomplished.

Much obscurity revolves around the phrase "god of fortresses," but several viable explanations can be provided to show that Vespasian did indeed honor that "god." The god Serapis referenced in both historical passages above was a Greco-Egyptian god, not a Roman one. Where his "fathers" devoted their worship to themselves or the Roman gods Vespasian showed openly his devotion to Serapis. It is also possible that Vespasian was overly devoted to many gods at once, which wouldn't be unlike a pagan. The wealth he procured from his campaigns in Israel were, after all, placed in a newly built temple[216]. His worship of the "god of fortresses" and devotion of wealth to it could also be a symbol of him exalting himself and adorning his war machine, at any expense necessary, with anything it needed or desired. Habakkuk 1:11 tells us that there were those "whose might is his god." We are told that Vespasian was also one who "increased" many with glory, caused them to rule over many, and divided the land for a price.

> "And now, when Vespasian had given answers to the embassages, and had **disposed of the places of power** justly, and **according to every one's deserts**..."[217]

---

[215] Latin for "Divine Vespasian."
[216] Josephus, Wars. 7.5.7. Page 758.
[217] Josephus, Wars. 4.11.1. Page 694.

Vespasian was already in the habit of justly dividing power and glory to those worthy under his rule.

> "About the same time it was that Caesar sent a letter to Bassus, and to Liberius Maximus, who was the procurator [of Judea], and **gave order that all Judea should be exposed to sale** for he did not found any city there, but reserved the country for himself."[218]

Josephus here tells us plainly that Vespasian ordered that the land of Judea be put up for sale. Can there be a more direct fulfillment of Daniel's prophecy?

Daniel 11:40-45
(40) And at the time of the end shall the king of the south contend with him; and the king of the north shall come against him like a whirlwind, with chariots, and with horsemen, and with many ships; and he shall enter into the countries, and shall overflow and pass through.
(41) He shall enter also into the glorious land, and many countries shall be overthrown; but these shall be delivered out of his hand: Edom, and Moab, and the chief of the children of Ammon.
(42) He shall stretch forth his hand also upon the countries; and the land of Egypt shall not escape.
(43) But he shall have power over the treasures of gold and of silver, and over all the precious things of Egypt; and the Libyans and the Ethiopians shall be at his steps.
(44) But tidings out of the east and out of the north shall trouble him; and he shall go forth with great fury to destroy and utterly to sweep away many.
(45) And he shall plant the tents of his palace between the sea and the glorious holy mountain; yet he shall come to his end, and none shall help him.

---

[218] Josephus, Wars. 7.6.6. Page 761.

The Final King of the North

In this passage the king of the south is representative of Israel, and specifically the rulers, zealots, and rebels. These "kings" of Israel contended with the Romans by sedition, deceit, and murder. The king of the north, Vespasian again, brings his entire war machine against Israel by land and by sea. He enters the glorious land, which could be none other than Israel, and many shall be overthrown. Edom, Moab, and Ammon remained untouched in the war as Vespasian had no need to expand his forces to the East of the Jordon, where those three peoples resided. As we read in another quote above Vespasian had control over Egypt and its wealth, and the borders of the Roman empire extended to the southern border of Egypt, adjacent to Libya and near Ethiopia. As we also read above, Vespasian and his generals often took camp at places like Ptolemais and Caesarea, both cities located "between the sea [*Mediterranean*] and the glorious holy mountain [*earthly Zion*]."

All the above very clearly paints a historical picture that identifies Vespasian as this final king. But, what's even more compelling is what we are told in the next chapter. When understanding this final king to be Vespasian, the meaning and context of Daniel 12, and several other parts of the Apocalypse become much clearer.

Daniel 12:1-13
(1) And at that time shall Michael stand up, the great prince who stands for the children of your people; and there shall be a time of trouble, such as never was since there was a nation even to that same time: and at that time your people shall be delivered, every one that shall be found written in the book.
(2) And many of them that sleep in the dust of the earth shall awake, some to everlasting life, and some to shame and everlasting contempt.
(3) And they that are wise shall shine as the brightness of the firmament; and they that turn many to righteousness as the stars forever and ever.
(4) But you, O Daniel, shut up the words, and seal the book, even to the time of the end: many shall run to and fro, and knowledge shall be increased.

(5) Then I, Daniel, looked, and, behold, there stood other two, the one on the brink of the river on this side, and the other on the brink of the river on that side.

(6) And one said to the man clothed in linen, who was above the waters of the river, How long shall it be to the end of these wonders?

(7) And I heard the man clothed in linen, who was above the waters of the river, when he held up his right hand and his left hand unto heaven, and swore by him that lives forever that it shall be for a time, times, and a half; and when they have made an end of breaking in pieces the power of the holy people, all these things shall be finished.

(8) And I heard, but I understood not: then said I, O my master, what shall be the issue of these things?

(9) And he said, Go your way, Daniel; for the words are shut up and sealed till the time of the end.

(10) Many shall purify themselves, and make themselves white, and be refined; but the wicked shall do wickedly; and none of the wicked shall understand; but they that are wise shall understand.

(11) And from the time that the continual *burnt-offering* shall be taken away, and the abomination that makes desolate set up, there shall be a thousand and two hundred and ninety days.

(12) Blessed is he that waits, and comes to the thousand three hundred and five and thirty days.

(13) But go you your way till the end be; for you shall rest, and shall stand in your lot, at the end of the days.

Michael and the Time of Trouble

At the time of this final king, Vespasian, Michael will stand up for the chosen people. Is this not the same Michael we see in Revelation 12:7? We have arrived perfectly at the same point in the historical record with Vespasian marching forward leading his host towards Jerusalem. The chronological intersection between these two prophecies, separated by hundreds of years, and the historical record, cannot be ignored or underemphasized. After Michael stands up, as if to train and ready his army for the spiritual war to end all spiritual wars, a time of trouble was to come upon Daniel's people like had never happened until that day. The atrocities that transpired because of the first Jewish-Roman war causes it to meet that criteria perfectly.

What we read next in Daniel's prophecy sheds great light upon portions of the Apocalypse that we have only touched upon briefly, or haven't yet discussed at all. Thus, this will serve as a sort of prelude to what is to come later in this commentary. Daniel is told that during this time of trouble his people will be delivered, all of those who are found written in the book. Immediately after he is told that many will rise, some to life, and others to shame and everlasting contempt. Does this not sound familiar?

> Revelation 20:11-15
> (11) And I saw a great white throne, and him that sat upon it, from whose face the earth and the heaven fled away; and there was found no place for them.
> (12) And I saw the dead, the great and the small, standing before the throne; and **books were opened: and another book was opened, which is *the book* of life**: and the dead were judged out of the things which were written in the books, according to their works.
> (13) And the sea gave up the dead that were in it; and death and Hades gave up the dead that were in them: **and they were judged every man according to their works**.
> (14) And death and Hades were cast into the lake of fire. This is the second death, *even* the lake of fire.
> (15) **And if any was not found written in the book of life, he was cast into the lake of fire**.

Here we see a resurrection of the dead, which are judged according to their works. Some were to obtain eternal life; those whose names were found written in the book of life. Others were to be raised, judged worthy of death, and destroyed for all eternity. Again, remember, John is using imagery and prophetic terminology in the Apocalypse to point his readers to familiar passages of scripture. His audience would have understood John's illustrations here as fulfillments of what Daniel had prophesied about hundreds of years earlier, which they had been taught since they were just children.

Daniel is then told to seal up the book as it was not yet time for all the information to be disclosed. Many more events in history had to transpire before the entire stage was set. As if all the information provided by Daniel's prophecies weren't enough to point us to a singular place in history, we have a linen-clad man who gives us yet another clue. He responds to the second man clothed in linen, who had asked "How long shall it be to the *end* of these wonders?", saying, "A time, times, and a half; and when they have made an end of breaking in pieces the power of the holy people, *all these things* shall be finished." The phrase "time, times, and a half" is another phrase used elsewhere[219] referring to 1,260 days, three and a half years, or forty-two months. The man clothed in linen tells the other one that after three and a half years *all* the things previously mentioned in the prophecy were to be *finished*. This means a resurrection and judgment of the righteous and unrighteous dead, as well as the shattering of the power of the Israelites, the set-apart people of Yahweh, was to have been accomplished.

Most Futurists unnecessarily place these events anachronistically into some unknown time period yet to come. However, to do so is to divorce the events and timeline from the context of Daniel's prophecy with no clear break in the text. The beginning of verse 1 in chapter 12 makes the continuous time progression very clear by saying "At that time," meaning at the time that final king of the north is.

The 1,290 and 1,335 Day Period

After questioning the man in linen further, Daniel is given yet another time clue. He is told about two periods of time, 1,290 days and 1,335 days, both to be counted from the time the continual offering is taken away and an abomination of desolation setup. These times have great

---

[219] Revelation 12:14. *Cf.* Revelation 12:6, 13:5.

significance as it relates to the Jewish war. Josephus tells us that the removal of the "Daily Sacrifice" occurred on the seventeenth day of the month Panemus[220]. According to very detailed Babylonian cuneiform tablets, containing calendrical observations for over 700 years, that day equates to July 14, 70 CE[221]. Josephus also tells us that the day the temple was destroyed was the tenth day of Lous[222], August 6, the exact same day that it was destroyed by the Babylonians hundreds of years earlier[223]. Something extremely abominable occurred on this same day.

> "And now the Romans, upon the flight of the seditious into the city, and upon the burning of the holy house itself, and of all the buildings round about it, **brought their ensigns to the temple and set them over against its eastern gate; and there did they offer sacrifices to them,** and there did they make Titus imperator with the greatest acclamations of joy."[224]

The same actions, the setting up of abominable things[225] in the temple and offering sacrifices to them, were cumulatively labeled "an abomination of desolation" before[226]. Beginning the 1,335-day count from then gets us to a very profound date. Using the same cuneiform tablets above, the 1,335th day would be April 1, 74 CE[227], which was the

---

[220] Josephus, Wars. 6.2.1. Page 731. Panemus is the Macedonian equivalent to the Hebrew month Tammuz.

[221] Parker & Dubberstein. Page 47. At that time the way that the Jews calculated their months, by visual observation of the new crescent moon, was identical to that which was recorded in the cuneiform tablets.

[222] Lous is the Macedonian equivalent to the Hebrew month Av.

[223] Josephus, Wars. 6.4.5. Page 739.

[224] Josephus, Wars. 6.6.1. Page 743.

[225] That the ensigns of the Romans were abominations to the Jews see: Josephus, Antiquities. 18.3.1. Pages 479-480, and Josephus, Antiquities. 18.5.3. Pages 484-485.

[226] 1 Maccabees 1:54-59.

[227] For evidence of 74 CE being the final year of the Jewish war instead of the traditional 73 CE see Campbell and Cotton.

15[228] of the month of Nisan[228], or the first day of the feast of unleavened bread[229]. Amazingly enough, Josephus tells us of this exact same date.

> "Yet was there an ancient woman, and another who was of kin to Eleazar, and superior to most women in prudence and learning, with five children, who had concealed themselves in caverns underground, and had carried water thither for their drink, and were hidden there when the rest were intent upon the slaughter of one another. Those others were nine hundred and sixty in number, the women and children being withal included in that computation. **This calamitous slaughter was made on the fifteenth day of the month Xanthicus**[230]."[231]

This refers to the destruction of the final Jewish stronghold in Israel, Masada, the fall of which marked the official end of the war.

All the above information regarding the prophecies at the end of Daniel chapter 11 through chapter 12 is provided to show one thing. They align perfectly with the timeline of the destruction of the temple and city of Jerusalem and the end of the Jewish commonwealth.

The Flight of Zion

(13) And when the dragon saw that he was cast down to the earth, he persecuted the woman that brought forth the man *child*.

(14) And there were given to the woman the two wings of the great eagle, that she might fly into the wilderness unto her place, where she is nourished for a time, and times, and half a time, from the face of the serpent.

(15) And the serpent cast out of his mouth after the woman

---

[228] *Heb.* Aviv.

[229] Leviticus 23:6. This day was one where each person was required to rest from their labors.

[230] Xanthicus is the Macedonian equivalent of the Hebrew month Nisan.

[231] Josephus, Wars. 7.9.1. Page 769.

water as a river, that he might cause her to be carried away by the stream.

(16) And the earth helped the woman, and the earth opened her mouth and swallowed up the river which the dragon cast out of his mouth.

(17) And the dragon waxed wroth with the woman, and went away to make war with the rest of her seed, that keep the commandments of Elohim, and hold the testimony of Yeshua.

Here we now move back into the text of Revelation. In verses 7-9 we see the battle alluded to in Daniel 12:1, where the armies of Yahweh, led by Michael, conquer Satan and his angels and cast them out of heaven. Where we saw the kingdoms of the world become those of Yahweh and his Messiah's at the blowing of the seventh trumpet we see in more detail here. As mentioned in a previous chapter above, Satan was once given control over the kingdoms of the world. That control has now been stripped.

Though it is not stated explicitly, verse 11 would seem to say that there were certain believers who had already overcome the enemy through their faithfulness unto death. It may very well be that the man-child resurrected previously in chapter 12 represent the first martyrs of Messiah. Overcoming by their constant faith and trust in Yeshua allowed them to be a part of that resurrection and subsequent beginning of the rule of Messiah over his newly all-powerful kingdom.

The time has now come for the woman who gave birth to the man-child to flee from the dragon into the wilderness. This is none other than the historical event of the Hebrew followers of Yeshua fleeing from Jerusalem and Judea to Pella. We read the following in the writings of Eusebius and Epiphanius:

"The whole body, however, of the church at Jerusalem, having been commanded by a divine revelation given to men of approved piety there before the war, **removed from the city and lived at a certain town beyond the Jordan called Pella**. Here, those who believed in Christ removed from Jerusalem, as if holy men had entirely abandoned the royal city itself and the whole land of Judea."[232]

"This sect of Nazoraeans is to be found in Beroea near Coelesyria, in the Decapolis near Pella, and in Bashanitis at the place called Cocabe - Khokhabe in Hebrew. For that was its place of origin, **since all the disciples had settled in Pella after their remove from Jerusalem**— Christ having told them to abandon Jerusalem and withdraw from it **because of the siege it was about to undergo**. And they settled in Peraea for this reason and, as I said, lived their lives there. It was from this that the Nazoraean sect had its origin."[233]

"Their origin came **after the fall of Jerusalem**. For since **practically all who had come to faith in Christ had settled in Peraea then, in Pella**, a town in the 'Decapolis' the Gospel mentions, which is near Batanaea and Bashanitis - as they had moved there then and were living there, this provided an opportunity for Ebion."[234]

"So Aquila, while he was in Jerusalem, also saw the disciples of the disciples of the apostles flourishing in the faith and working great signs, healings, and other miracles. For they were such as had **come back from the city of Pella** to Jerusalem and were living there and teaching. **For when the city was about to be taken and destroyed by the Romans**, it was revealed in advance to all the disciples by an angel of God that they should remove from the city, as it was going to be completely destroyed. They sojourned as emigrants in Pella, the city above mentioned, in Transjordania. And this city is said to be of the Decapolis. But after the destruction of Jerusalem, when they had returned to Jerusalem, as I have said, they wrought great signs, as I have already said."[235]

Now, one thing needs to be pointed out regarding Eusebius' statement. As one will notice when reading the four texts above, Eusebius states

---

[232] Eusebius. Book 3, Chapter 5, Verse 3.
[233] Epiphanius, Panarion. Book 1, Section 2, Part 29, 7:7-8.
[234] Epiphanius, Panarion. Book 1, Section 2, Part 30, 2:7.
[235] Epiphanius, On Weights and Measures. Chapter 15.

that the fleeing to Pella took place *before* the war. However, Epiphanius states, as if casually stating the accepted tradition with no theological intent, that the fleeing took place *just prior to the siege of Jerusalem* itself. This siege didn't take place until almost three years after the war began.

It is our understanding that the fleeing of the Hebrew assembly to Pella didn't take place until mid-late spring, 68 CE. Jonathan Bourgel put together an amazing treatise on this topic[236]. In our opinion the historical information provided by Bourgel proves the exodus from Jerusalem did indeed take place in 68 CE, not the traditional 66 CE, which is based solely on Eusebius' writings. Bourgel argues, amongst other things, that the historical record of the fleeing of the Hebrew assembly from Jerusalem can be found in Josephus' work wherein he mentions many deserters from the city just prior to its siege.

> "And now the commanders joined in their approbation of what Vespasian had said, and it was soon discovered how wise an opinion he had given. **And indeed many there were of the Jews that deserted every day, and fled away from the zealots,** although their flight was very difficult, since they had guarded every passage out of the city, and slew every one that was caught at them, as taking it for granted they were going over to the Romans; yet did he who gave them money get clear off, while he only that gave them none was voted a traitor."[237]

> "But because the city had to struggle with three of the greatest misfortunes, war, and tyranny, and sedition, it appeared, upon the comparison, that the war was the least troublesome to the populace of them all. **Accordingly, they ran away from their own houses to foreigners, and obtained that preservation from the Romans which they despaired to obtain among their own people.**"[238]

---

[236] Bourgel.
[237] Josephus, Wars. 4.6.3. Page 682.
[238] Josephus, Wars. 4.7.1. Page 683.

"These things were told Vespasian by **deserters**; for although the seditious watched all the passages out of the city, and destroyed all, whosoever they were, that came thither, **yet were there some that had concealed themselves, and when they had fled to the Romans,** persuaded their general to come to their city's assistance, and save the remainder of the people; informing him withal, that it was upon account of the people's good-will to the Romans that many of them were already slain, and the survivors in danger of the same treatment."[239]

Here we see again that there were many of those who were in the city that fled to the Romans. None of the texts above state that these deserters joined the forces of the Romans, but that they had simply chosen to surrender and not be a part of the war against Rome. Is it possible that the Jerusalem assembly was a part of these deserters?

Prior to these passages in Josephus' work he also tells us the following:

"Nor could anyone escape, unless he were very inconsiderable, either on account of the meanness of his birth, or on account of his fortune."[240]

Though the flight of deserters from the city was notably very difficult, being a mere commoner of no merit or, as Josephus puts it, being "fortunate," allowed open escape as they were of no value whatsoever to the zealots. We know that the disciples of Yeshua sold everything they owned and were instructed to take nothing with them when the time for their flight was upon them[241]. We also know that what Josephus called "fortunate," Yeshua called "elected."

We read the following in Josephus' account very shortly after the accounts of these deserters:

---

[239] Josephus, Wars. 4.7.3. Page 684.
[240] Josephus, Wars. 4.6.1. Page 682.
[241] Matthew 24:15-18.

"And now the war having gone through all the mountainous country, and all the plain country also, **those that were at Jerusalem were deprived of the liberty of going out of the city;** for as to such as had a mind to desert, they were watched by the zealots; and as to such as were not yet on the side of the Romans, **their army kept them in, by encompassing the city round about on all sides.**"[242]

Here we see a direct and explicit mention of Jerusalem being surrounded by armies, just as Yeshua mentioned in his Olivet Discourse. The historian Luke tells us the following in the gospel named for him.

Luke 21:20
But when you see Jerusalem compassed with armies, then know that her desolation is at hand.

The Greek verb translated as "compassed" in the American Standard Version above is κυκλόω, *kukloo*, and means "*to surround, encircle, encompass.*"[243] Here the American Standard Version, like most other versions of the Bible, translates the verb using the past tense. However, this is an inaccurate translation given the Greek tense, voice, and mood in the original. The form of the verb used in this verb, κυκλουμένην, *kukloumenen*, is in the present tense, the passive voice, and the participle mood. The present tense in Greek means that the action of the verb is ongoing. The passive voice means that the action verb is being performed upon the subject, not performed by the subject (in this case, Jerusalem). The participle voice is best understood as an "-ing" verb in English (shout*ing*, runn*ing*, listen*ing*, etc.). Once again J.P. Green's Literal Version gives us the most accurate translation of this verse.

Luke 21:20
And when you see Jerusalem **being encircled** by armies, then recognize that its destruction has come near.

---

[242] Josephus, Wars. 4.9.1. Page 688.
[243] Thayer. Entry for κυκλόω. Page 364.

The encircling or encompassing that Yeshua is warning them of in this passage isn't one that is to be complete at the time of their fleeing. It is to be clearly visible, yet unfinished. The quote from Josephus above regarding Jerusalem being completely encompassed by armies is the state of affairs *after* the believers had already fled. Vespasian's campaign against Judea was about to begin. Prior to proceeding, however, he wanted to ensure there was no one left behind him that would interrupt or deter him from destroying Jerusalem.

> "However, he was obliged first to overthrow what remained elsewhere, and to leave nothing out of Jerusalem behind him that might interrupt him in that siege. Accordingly, he marched against Gadara, the metropolis of Perea, which was a place of strength, and entered that city on the fourth day of the month Dystrus [Adar]."[244]

The fourth day of Dystrus[245] that year was February 26, 68 CE. The map on the following page shows his campaign[246] after he took Gadara, as well as the cities he conquered before Josephus' statement.

---

[244] Josephus, Wars. 4.7.3. Page 684.
[245] Dystrus is the Macedonian equivalent to the Hebrew month Adar.
[246] Josephus, Wars. 4.8.1. Pages 685-686.

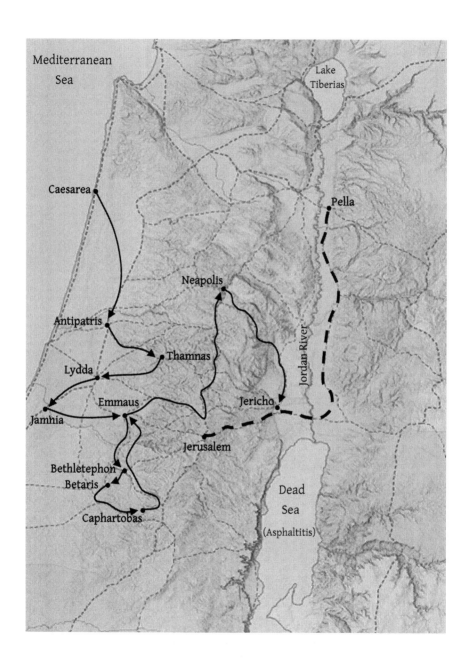

The first thing to be pointed out in the map is that Jerusalem was indeed being strategically surrounded or encircled by the Roman armies. Emmaus, Bethletephon, Betaris, Caphartobas, and Jericho are all cities or villages that controlled passage in and out of Jerusalem. However, something else needs to be pointed out on the map. Notice how the path of Vespasian, shown as the **solid** lines on the map, looks very similar to a river in its winding path. The dragon, the driving force behind the armies of Vespasian, was directing his path in such a way as to try to engulf as much of Judea as possible in an inevitably fruitless attempt to prevent the woman's flight to the wilderness. We read the following regarding what Vespasian and his armies encountered as they approached Jericho:

> "Hereupon **a great multitude prevented their approach**, and came out of Jericho, and fled to those mountainous parts that lay over against Jerusalem, while that part which was left behind was in a great measure destroyed; they also found the city desolate."[247]

On the map above we have outlined our proposed route for the woman's exodus from Jerusalem using a **dashed** line. Jonathan Bourgel has the following to say regarding our proposal:

> "It is reasonable to suppose that the Jewish-Christians, after fleeing from Jerusalem, would have encountered the Roman forces east of the Holy City, probably in Jericho where we know that Vespasian placed garrisons (*BJ* IV, 486). This could explain why the Jewish-Christians were subsequently sent to Peraea, unlike many other deserters who were settled in the coastal cities. Although they were considered as defeated persons, we think it is likely that the Jewish deserters did negotiate the terms of their surrender with the Roman authorities."[248]

---

[247] Josephus, Wars. 4.8.2. Page 686.
[248] Bourgel. Page 129.

This same route out of the city, east, towards the Mount of Olives, the Kidron Valley and the plain of Jericho, had been taken before[249]. In fact, Zechariah prophesied about this very event while telling about a coming "Day of Yahweh" in his future:

> Zechariah 14:4-5
> (4) And his feet shall stand in that day upon the mount of Olives, which is **before Jerusalem on the east**; and **the mount of Olives shall be cleft in the midst thereof toward the east and toward the west**, *and there shall be* a very great valley; and half of the mountain shall remove toward the north, and half of it toward the south.
> (5) And you shall flee by the valley of my mountains; for the valley of the mountains shall reach unto Azel; yea, you shall flee, like as you fled from before the earthquake in the days of Uzziah king of Judah; and Yahweh my Elohim shall come, and all the holy ones with you.

The woman fled out of Jerusalem to the east, passing over the Mount of Olives. The splitting of the mount as mentioned in Zechariah's prophecy isn't a literal rending of rock. It is prophetic language signifying that Yahweh is to come down and make the way easy for the believers fleeing to Pella. This isn't the first time that the phrase is used to mean the same thing[250]. Half of the Mount of Olives apocalyptically moved towards the north and half towards the south signifying that an east-to-west path would be opened and safe for them to flee through. That is the exact direction the woman took.

The forces of Vespasian that were forced to halt because of the multitude of people who were fleeing from Jericho could very well be what is represented by the land opening its mouth and swallowing the river in Revelation 12:16. The Jerusalem assembly then did one of two things. They deserted to the Romans, negotiating the terms of their submission by requesting that they be allowed to settle in Pella, a

---

[249] 2 Samuel 15:13-37; 2 Kings 25:4-5.
[250] Isaiah 31:4; Micah 1:3-4; Habakkuk 3:6.

Roman-guarded town in Perea; or, more likely, they were able to escape the city safely and, due to the halting of Vespasian's army, pass securely through the now deserted Jericho into the plain across the Jordan following it all the way up to Pella. Given the perfection of the timeline laid out in the Apocalypse thus far, we conclude that as the Jerusalem assembly noticed the towns surrounding the city falling one by one to Vespasian, they gathered their things and prepared to leave. Their poor and lowly state, as well as their election by Yeshua, allowed them passage out of the city to the east, where they passed through the Kidron Valley, through the deserted city of Jericho, and up the plain next to the Jordan to finally settle in Pella.

The Resurrections – Part I

We must now take some time to bring several topics discussed in this and the previous chapter together for a clearer and more complete understanding. As we concluded in chapter 11 above, the Two Witnesses' resurrections would have taken place towards the beginning of the spring of 68 CE, about the same time that Vespasian began his invasion of Judea. The first day of the biblical new year in 68 CE would have been on Thursday, March 24, 68 CE[251]. Moving forward with our conclusion that James the Just, the brother of Yeshua, was indeed one of the Two Witnesses, we know from the historical testimonies already quoted that he was martyred on the day of Passover in that year. That would have been on Wednesday, April 6, 68 CE. We conclude that three and a half days later, just as the scriptures tell us, the Two Witnesses were resurrected. This would have been on Sunday, April 10, on the first day of the week, the same day of the week and year that their Messiah was raised thirty-eight years earlier. That is also the day of the year that the first fruits of the barley harvest were waved.

We also conclude that after this, the resurrection of the first fruits of the spiritual wheat harvest, represented by the man-child in John's

---

[251] Parker & Dubberstein. Page 47.

vision, took place on the exact day in the biblical year it was supposed to. As the scriptures instruct us[252] we are to count fifty days from the day that the barley first fruits are waved to celebrate to the Feast of Weeks[253]. On that day in the biblical year the first fruits of the wheat harvest were waved. Counting forward fifty days from April 10, 68 CE, we arrive at Sunday, May 29. That is the day that the 144,000 first fruits were resurrected. Shortly after that, and before Nero's suicide on June 9 just eleven days later[254], Zion took her flight from Jerusalem across the Jordan and up to Pella, where they were protected by Yahweh.

Between the testimonies of Eusebius, Epiphanius and Josephus we believe the conclusion is apparent. The Hebrew assembly at Jerusalem, the true Zion, fled from the city just as their Messiah commanded them to do, and that just as "her desolation was at hand." This evidence not only aligns Yeshua's prophecy and the historical record perfectly, but it allows the constant and progressive timeline of the Apocalypse to continue to flow seamlessly.

---

[252] Leviticus 23:15-22.

[253] *Heb.* שָׁבֻעוֹת, *shavuot.*

[254] Jerusalem was already encompassed by armies by this time. Josephus, Wars. 4.9.2. Page 688.

CHAPTER THIRTEEN

The First Beast

(1) And he stood upon the sand of the sea. And I saw a beast coming up out of the sea, having ten horns and seven heads, and on his horns ten diadems, and upon his heads names of blasphemy.

(2) And the beast which I saw was like unto a leopard, and his feet were as *the feet* of a bear, and his mouth as the mouth of a lion: and the dragon gave him his power, and his throne, and great authority.

(3) And *I saw* one of his heads as though it had been smitten unto death; and his death-stroke was healed: and the whole earth wondered after the beast;

(4) and they worshipped the dragon, because he gave his authority unto the beast; and they worshipped the beast, saying, Who is like unto the beast? and who is able to war with him?

(5) and there was given to him a mouth speaking great things and blasphemies; and there was given to him authority to continue forty and two months.

(6) And he opened his mouth for blasphemies against Elohim, to blaspheme his name, and his tabernacle, *even* them that dwell in the heaven.

(7) And it was given unto him to make war with the saints, and to overcome them: and there was given to him authority over every tribe and people and tongue and nation.

(8) And all that dwell on the earth shall worship him, *every one* whose name has not been written from the foundation of the world in the book of life of the Lamb that has been slain.
(9) If any man has an ear, let him hear.
(10) If any man *is* for captivity, into captivity he goes: if any man shall kill with the sword, with the sword must he be killed. Here is the patience and the faith of the saints.

Many have speculated about the identity of this important antagonistic character in the Apocalypse. From theories about certain popes of the Catholic church, to different countries in world-wide government alliances such as the European Union or the United Nations, the speculation abounds. However, such theories, mostly put forward and held by Futurists, have no basis in fact and are unable to be proven correct or disproven. We believe that the taking of this Beast's identity out of the context of John's audience has been the primary cause for such speculation. To resolve this, we must attempt to interpret the symbolism put forward in this chapter in view of who existed in the first century as well as any relevant religious and/or political situations that were present.

We are first told that this Beast arises out of the sea. We have already discussed above how the sea symbolizes the peoples of various nations. That this sea is referring to the nations outside of Israel is made clear by the origin of the second Beast – the land [*of Israel*]. The seven heads and ten horns are very important aspects of the Beast that greatly aid in identifying this creature. If we hold to the entire supposition of this work, we must look to characters or peoples who existed in the first century.

Before relating the characteristics of the Beast in this chapter to anything and/or anyone specific in history we must first emphasize the prophetic and apocalyptic symbolism involved. The fact that the Beast is said to have seven heads, each of them decked in crowns, tells us that the rule of this Beast was complete. There was nothing that was not under its power or control. The terrible and powerful nature of this Beast is known by the fact that it is said to contain various aspects of all the beasts in Daniel's vision[255]. Blasphemies being spoken against Elohim and overcoming the saints both necessitate that this Beast be one that is not of Yahweh. In short, John is continuing his use of apocalyptic language to ensure the clandestine nature of the Apocalypse is maintained.

The seven heads of the Beast are most clearly representative of the first seven emperors of the Roman Empire – Julius[256], Augustus, Tiberius, Gaius, Claudius, Nero, and Galba. These seven heads are also said to represent seven kings and seven mountains[257]. The seven kings are obviously the previously mentioned emperors. The mountains are representative of the seven hills upon which Rome was built – Aventine, Caelian, Capitoline, Esquiline, Palatine, Quirinal, and Viminal. In the same passage, we are told that in the time John was writing the Apocalypse five of those kings had fallen, one was, and one was yet to come. Seeing that the external and internal evidence point to the earlier dating of the Apocalypse as being the correct one, the identity of these kings is again confirmed. At the time of John's writing the first five emperors of Rome had fallen (i.e. died). The one who was existing was Nero. The one yet to come was Galba, who was to only reign for a short time. Galba's reign lasted seven years and seven months[258]. On the seven heads were names of blasphemy. The title "Augustus," with which all but Julius were surnamed, means "venerated one" or "one to be venerated." Emperors of Rome believed themselves to either be gods, or to be transformed into gods upon their death[259].

---

[255] Daniel 7:1-8.

[256] A common belief is that Augustus was officially the first emperor of Rome. Evidence that Julius was indeed the first emperor can be found in many historical facts. First, Suetonius authored his work "The Twelve Caesars" and had Julius listed first. Second, Dio Cassius, in his work "Roman History" numbers Julius as the first Caesar. Third, Josephus calls Augustus the second, Tiberius the third, and Gaius the fourth emperor of Rome (Antiquities 18.2.2 & 18.6.10); the only one prior to Augustus being Julius.

[257] Revelation 17:9-10.

[258] Josephus, Wars. 4.9.2. Page 688.

[259] Suetonius, Vespasian. Chapter 23.

The ten horns of the Beast are the ten imperial provinces in Rome, which existed in the time of John. Strabo gives us the details on these:

> "But at the outset Caesar organized the Provinces of the People by creating, first, two consular provinces; I mean (1) Libya, in so far as it was subject to the Romans, except the part which was formerly subject to Juba and is now subject to Ptolemy his son, and (2) the part of Asia that lies this side the Halys River and the Taurus, except the countries of the Galatians and of the tribes which had been subject to Amyntas, and also of Bithynia and the Propontis; and, secondly, **ten praetorial provinces**, first, in Europe and the islands near it, I mean (1) Iberia Ulterior, as it is called, in the neighbourhood of the Baetis and Anas Rivers, (2) Narbonitis in Celtica, (3) Sardo together with Cyrnus, (4) Sicily, (5 and 6) Macedonia and, in Illyria, the country next to Epeirus, (7) Achaea as far as Thessaly and Aetolia and Acarnania and certain Epeirotic tribes which border on Macedonia, (8) Crete along with Cyrenaea, (9) Cypros, and (10) Bithynia along with the Propontis and certain parts of the Pontus. But the rest of the Provinces are held by Caesar; and to some of these he sends as curators men of consular rank, to others men of praetorian rank, and to others men of the rank of knights. Kings, also, and potentates and decarchies are now, and always have been, in Caesar's portion."[260]

These ten provinces, though having leadership appointed for their own governance, were still ruled over by Caesar. These ten horns of the Beast are also called ten kings[261]. The ten kings were to lend their power to the Beast for a short time. Likewise, the ten praetorial provinces would have lent whatever resources necessary to Rome proper in times of war, including their armed forces.

We also read that one of the heads of the Beast sustained a fatal head wound. If the Beast represents the Roman Empire, and each head represents a different emperor, we must look to see whether something

---

[260] Strabo. Book 17, Chapter 3, Section 25.
[261] Revelation 17:12-13.

that could be considered a "death-stroke" was inflicted upon one of the emperors or during the time of their reign. It just so happens that the ancient historians tell us that an individual emperor, Nero, and Rome itself, was dealt that death-stroke during his reign. The result of this death-stroke appeared to be the fall and ultimate death of the Empire itself.

Nero committed suicide in June of 68 CE after a reign of thirteen years and eight days[262]. His death ended the Julio-Claudian reign, severing the line of succession from the founding fathers of the Empire. After his death, the Empire went into a state of chaos it had never seen. Civil wars, heavenly phenomena, and anarchy are just a few of the things that broke loose in Rome. Historians thought it would lead to its demise.

"I am entering on the history of a period rich in disasters, frightened in its wars, torn by civil strife, and even in peace full of horrors. Four emperors perished by the sword. There were three civil wars; there were more with foreign enemies; there were often wars that had both characters at once. There was success in the East, and disaster in the West. There were disturbances in Illyricum; Gaul wavered in its allegiance; Britain was thoroughly subdued and immediately abandoned; the tribes of the Suevi and the Sarmatae rose in concert against us; the Dacians had the glory of inflicting as well as suffering defeat; the armies of Parthia were all but set in motion by the cheat of a counterfeit Nero. Now too Italy was prostrated by disasters either entirely novel, or that recurred only after a long succession of ages; cities in Campania's richest plains were swallowed up and overwhelmed; Rome was wasted by conflagrations, its oldest temples consumed, and the Capitol itself fired by the hands of citizens. Sacred rites were profaned; there was profligacy in the highest ranks; the sea was crowded with exiles, and its rocks polluted with bloody deeds. In the capital there were yet worse horrors. Nobility, wealth, the refusal or the acceptance of office, were grounds for accusation, and virtue

---

[262] Suetonius, Nero. Chapter 49; Josephus, Wars. 4.9.2. Page 688.

ensured destruction. The rewards of the informers were no less odious than their crimes; for while some seized on consulships and priestly offices, as their share of the spoil, others on procuratorships, and posts of more confidential authority, they robbed and ruined in every direction amid universal hatred and terror. Slaves were bribed to turn against their masters, and freedmen to betray their patrons; and those who had not an enemy were destroyed by friends.

Yet the age was not so barren in noble qualities, as not also to exhibit examples of virtue. Mothers accompanied the flight of their sons; wives followed their husbands into exile; there were brave kinsmen and faithful sons in law; there were slaves whose fidelity defied even torture; there were illustrious men driven to the last necessity, and enduring it with fortitude; there were closing scenes that equalled the famous deaths of antiquity. Besides the manifold vicissitudes of human affairs, there were prodigies in heaven and earth, the warning voices of the thunder, and other intimations of the future, auspicious or gloomy, doubtful or not to be mistaken. Never surely did more terrible calamities of the Roman People, or evidence more conclusive, prove that the Gods take no thought for our happiness, but only for our punishment."[263]

Josephus also acknowledged the well-known existence of these civil wars.

"I have omitted to give an exact account of them, because they are well known by all, and they are described by a great number of Greek and Roman authors; yet for the sake of the connexion of matters, and that my history may not be incoherent, I have just touched upon everything briefly."[264]

During the period between Nero's suicide and the appointment of Vespasian as emperor, also known as the "Year of the Four Emperors,"

---

[263] Tacitus, Histories. Book 1, Chapters 2-3.
[264] Josephus, Wars. 4.9.2. Page 688.

Rome was in a constant state of flux. It was unsettled, disturbed, engulfed in civil and foreign wars, devoid of peace, lacking security, and saw the rise and violent death of three different emperors – Galba, Otho, and Vitellius. Nero and Rome had been dealt a death-stroke. It wasn't until Vespasian took the reins that the death-stroke was healed and the world again stood amazed at the Beast.

> "The empire, which had been long thrown into a disturbed and unsettled state, by the rebellion and violent death of its three last rulers, was at length restored to peace and security by the Flavian family."[265]

After the account of the fatal wound being healed we read that the Beast was given authority for forty-two months, which included the authority to make war with the saints and overcome them. Nero, on July 19, 64 CE, started a fire in Rome that ended up burning and/or destroying ten of the fourteen districts[266]. It was believed by many that Nero himself was responsible for the fire[267]. However, to shift the blame away from himself he directed his persecution towards the followers of Yeshua. The following historical accounts record the details of what is now known as the "Neronic Persecution":

> "He likewise inflicted punishments on the Christians, a sort of people who held a new and impious superstition."[268]

> "But all human efforts, all the lavish gifts of the emperor, and the propitiations of the gods, did not banish the sinister belief that the conflagration was the result of an order. Consequently, to get rid of the report, Nero fastened the guilt and inflicted the most exquisite tortures on a class hated for their abominations, called Christians by the populace. Christus, from whom the name had its origin, suffered the extreme penalty during the reign of Tiberius at the hands of one

---

[265] Suetonius, Vespasian. Chapter 1.
[266] Tacitus, Annals. Book 15, Chapter 40.
[267] Tacitus, Annals. Book 15, Chapter 38; Dio. Book 62, Chapter 57, Section 16; Suetonius, Nero. Chapters 38-39.
[268] Suetonius, Nero. Chapter 16.

of our procurators, Pontius Pilatus, and a most mischievous superstition, thus checked for the moment, again broke out not only in Judaea, the first source of the evil, but even in Rome, where all things hideous and shameful from every part of the world find their centre and become popular. Accordingly, an arrest was first made of all who pleaded guilty; then, upon their information, an immense multitude was convicted, not so much of the crime of firing the city, as of hatred against mankind. Mockery of every sort was added to their deaths. Covered with the skins of beasts, they were torn by dogs and perished, or were nailed to crosses, or were doomed to the flames and burnt, to serve as a nightly illumination, when daylight had expired."[269]

"As to Nero, I shall not say that he was the worst of kings, but that **he was worthily held the basest of all men, and even of wild beasts**. It was he who first began a persecution; and I am not sure but he will be the last also to carry it on, if, indeed, we admit, as many are inclined to believe, that he will yet appear immediately before the coming of Antichrist... **He first attempted to abolish the name of Christian**."[270]

Nero was the first true, pagan persecutor of the followers of Yeshua. As Severus tells us, he made it his goal to *abolish* the name of "Christian," the name given by the nations to the followers of Yeshua. This persecution is very likely the one addressed in the seven letters of chapters 2 and 3 above, as well as that which is found in several epistles in the New Testament. Severus also states plainly in the next chapter of his work:

"It was accordingly believed that, even if he did put an end to himself with a sword, his wound was cured, and his life preserved, according to that which was written regarding him – '**And his**

---

[269] Tacitus, Annals. Book 15, Chapter 44.
[270] Severus, Sacred History. Book 2, Chapter 28.

mortal wound was healed' – to be sent forth again near the end of the world, in order that he may practice the mystery of iniquity."[271]

The exact beginning of this brutal persecution of believers is not recorded. However, we do know it was sometime after the fire destroyed most of Rome. If it is assumed that it took several months for the rumors of Nero's responsibility in the fire to spread and for any subsequent investigations to take place, it is possible that the persecution and turning towards the believers didn't take place until late fall. Counting backwards forty-two months from his death in June of 68 CE we get to November 64 CE.

It is amazing how Nero, the one so perfectly meeting the criteria set out in every other aspect of the Beast's description, was also considered a beast by others in his day.

"Moreover, in traversing more of the earth than any man yet has visited, I have seen hosts of Arabian and Indian wild beasts; but as to **this wild beast**, which many call a tyrant, I know not either how many heads he has, nor whether he has crooked talons and jagged teeth. In any case, though this monster is said to be a social beast and to inhabit the heart of cities, yet he is also much wilder and fiercer in his disposition than animals of the mountain and forest, that whereas you can sometimes tame and alter the character of lions and leopards by flattering them, this one is only roused to greater cruelty than before by those who stroke him, so that he rends and devours all alike. And again there is no animal anyhow of which you can say that it ever devours its own mother, but **Nero** is gorged with such quarry."[272]

The Second Beast

(11) And I saw another beast coming up out of the land; and he had two horns like unto a lamb, and he spoke as a dragon.

---

[271] Severus, Sacred History. Book 2, Chapter 29.
[272] Apollonius. Book 4, Chapter 38.

(12) And he exercises all the authority of the first beast in his sight. And he makes the land and them that dwell therein to worship the first beast, whose death-stroke was healed.
(13) And he does great signs, that he should even make fire to come down out of heaven upon the land in the sight of men.
(14) And he deceives them that dwell on the land by reason of the signs which it was given him to do in the sight of the beast; saying to them that dwell on the land, that they should make an image to the beast who has the stroke of the sword and lived.
(15) And it was given *unto him* to give breath to it, *even* to the image of the beast, that the image of the beast should both speak, and cause that as many as should not worship the image of the beast should be killed.

To ascertain the identity of this second Beast we need to closely examine its various characteristics. First, unlike the first Beast, this one is said to rise up out of the land. Second, this Beast is one who appears innocent, yet speaks as though he were Satan, the dragon. Third, this second Beast has the authority of the first Beast. Fourth, this Beast uses its power and authority to direct the people of the land to obey and otherwise worship the first Beast. Fifth, this Beast is endowed with special powers that are intended to deceive the people and cause the deceived to worship and venerate the first Beast. Those who resisted this Beast's deceptions were killed. We also know that elsewhere this Beast is labeled as the False Prophet[273].

We must seek to identify this Beast while keeping consistent with John's use of apocalyptic terminology. Consequently, we must first understand that this Beast was to be one arising from the land, Israel. John's use of the lamb symbol here recalls the only other character labeled as such in the Apocalypse, Yeshua. Some form of identity or similarity must exist between these two lambs for the symbolism to be retained. Obviously the first lamb representing Yeshua is holy and good and this lamb is the antithesis. The power and authority given to this second Beast was the same as that of the first Beast, which was the

---

[273] Revelation 16:3, 19:20, 20:10.

same as that of the Dragon, or Satan. The signs and deceptive actions of the second Beast mentioned in this chapter, as well as the clear labeling of it as the "False Prophet" later in the Apocalypse, are intended to bring a couple different things to the mind of John's audience. First, similar to what he did in describing the Two Witnesses in chapter 11 above, he wishes to convey the apparent powers given to this Beast. However, just as the signs and wonders performed by the Two Witnesses aren't intended to be literal, such as breathing fire, the signs and wonders displayed by this second Beast need not be either. Second, the mention of this Beast leading of the deceived to the worship of someone or something other than Yahweh is intended to remind them of the commands and warnings against such in the Torah.

After all the above is considered, in addition to the scriptures provided below, the identity of this Beast reveals itself. It is none other than the false religious system through which the Dragon has, and will continue to lead people away from the worship of the one true Elohim, Yahweh Almighty, and the faith in his son Yeshua as the prophesied Messiah. Its two horns represent false apostles and false messiahs. John once again pointed his audience back to Yeshua's Olivet Discourse in using this symbolism.

Matthew 24:23-25
(23) Then if any man shall say unto you, Lo, here is the Messiah, or, Here; believe *it* not.
(24) For there shall arise **false messiahs, and false prophets**, and **shall show great signs and wonders; so as to lead astray**, if possible, even the elect.
(25) Behold, I have told you beforehand.

Mark 13:21-23
(21) And then if any man shall say unto you, Lo, here is the Messiah, Lo, there; believe *it* not:
(22) for there shall arise **false messiahs and false prophets**, and **shall show signs and wonders, that they may lead astray**, if possible, the elect.
(23) But take you heed: behold, I have told you all things beforehand.

Yeshua revealed to his disciples exactly what this second Beast was to look like. The apostle John likewise told us to guard ourselves from the same:

1 John 2:18-19,22-23
(18) Little children, it is the last hour: and as you heard that anti-messiah comes, **even now have there arisen many anti-messiahs**; whereby we know that it is the last hour.
(19) They went out from us, but they were not of us; for if they had been of us, they would have continued with us: but *they went out*, that they might be made manifest that they all are not of us...
(22) Who is the liar but he that denies that Yeshua is the Messiah? **This is the anti-messiah**, *even* he that denies the Father and the Son.
(23) Whosoever denies the Son, the same has not the Father: he that confesses the Son has the Father also.

1 John 4:1-3
(1) Beloved, believe not every spirit, but prove the spirits, whether they are of Elohim; because many **false prophets** are gone out into the world.
(2) Hereby know you the spirit of Elohim: every spirit that confesses that Yeshua Messiah is come in the flesh is of Elohim:
(3) and every spirit that confesses not Yeshua is not of Elohim: and **this is the *spirit* of the anti-messiah**, whereof you have heard that it comes; and now it is in the world already.

False prophets and false messiahs are not only allowed by Yahweh but are at times even sent by Him to try and prove his children. John's mention of the actions and purpose of the deceptive works of the second Beast immediately recalls the following passage.

Deuteronomy 12:32-13:5[274]
(32) Everything I command you, that shall you observe to do:

---

[274] Deuteronomy 12:32 is actually 13:1 in the Hebrew text, and therefore should be read as a part of the context relating to dealing with false prophets.

you shall not add thereto, nor diminish from it.

(1) If there arise in the midst of you a prophet, or a dreamer of dreams, and he give you a sign or a wonder,

(2) and the sign or the wonder come to pass, whereof he spoke unto you, saying, Let us go after other elohim, which you have not known, and let us serve them;

(3) you shall not hearken unto the words of that prophet, or unto that dreamer of dreams: for Yahweh your Elohim proves you, to know whether you love Yahweh your Elohim with all your heart and with all your soul.

(4) You shall walk after Yahweh your Elohim, and fear him, and keep his commandments, and obey his voice, and you shall serve him, and cleave unto him.

(5) And that prophet, or that dreamer of dreams, shall be put to death, because he has spoken rebellion against Yahweh your Elohim, who brought you out of the land of Egypt, and redeemed you out of the house of bondage, to draw you aside out of the way which Yahweh your Elohim commanded you to walk in. So shall you put away the evil from the midst of you.

This warning from Yahweh is glaringly similar to the actions of the second Beast. The command warns the people against prophets who would come and attempt, through prophecies or miraculous works, to lead them towards the worship of other gods. This is exactly what the second Beast does. He comes and performs miraculous works to deceive the people into serving and worshiping the first Beast. Those who were obedient to Yeshua and to Yahweh's commands would have recognized this. As we see these false prophets were sent by and under the control of Yahweh. Likewise, the actions of the Beasts in the Apocalypse are under His control and direction.

Though John's main intent is to bring Yeshua's prophecies to the minds of his audience through symbolism, there are accounts in the scriptures and in the historical record that show us how real these symbols were. Rather than repeat the accounts here we refer the reader to the section called "The First Seal" in chapter 6 above. We would like to quote a few very compelling historical records to the account of Simon Magus.

"This man, then, was glorified by many as if he were a god; and he taught that it was himself who appeared among the Jews as the Son, but descended in Samaria as the Father while he came to other nations in the character of the Holy Spirit. He represented himself, in a word, as being the loftiest of all powers, that is, the Being who is the Father over all, and he allowed himself to be called by whatsoever title men were pleased to address him."[275]

"This Simon's father was Antonius, and his mother Rachel. By nation he is a Samaritan, from a village of the Gettones; by profession a magician, yet exceedingly well trained in the Greek literature; desirous of glory, and **boasting above all the human race;** so that he wishes himself to be believe to be an exalted power, which is above God the Creator, and **to be thought to be the Christ,** and to be called the Standing One."[276]

"'Only, however, on condition,' says he, 'that you confer the chief place upon me, Simon, who by magic are am able to show many signs and prodigies, by means of which either my glory or our sect may be established. For I am able to render myself invisible to those who wish to lay hold of me, and again to be visible when I am willing to be seen...I can make the barriers open of their own accord; **I can render statues animated, so that those who see suppose that they are men**...I shall be **worshipped as God;** I shall have divine honours publicly assigned to me, so that **an image of me shall be set up,** and I **shall be worshipped and adored as God.** And what need of more words?'"[277]

Meander, the successor to Simon, was also described by Irenaeus.

"The successor of this man was Menander, also a Samaritan by birth, and he, too, was a perfect adept in the practice of magic. **He affirms** that the primary Power continues unknown to all, but **that he**

---

[275] Irenaeus, Against Heresies. Book 1, Chapter 23, Section 1.
[276] Recognitions, Latin. Book 2, Chapter 7.
[277] Recognitions, Latin. Book 2, Chapter 9.

himself is the person who has been sent forth from the presence of the invisible beings as a **saviour,** for the deliverance of men. The world was made by angels, whom, like Simon, he maintains to have been produced by Ennoea. He gives, too, as he affirms, by means of that magic which he teaches, knowledge to this effect, that one may overcome those very angels that made the world; **for his disciples obtain the *resurrection* by being baptized into him,** and can die no more, but remain in the possession of immortal youth."[278]

How remarkable are the similarities between these false prophets and their deceptive works to those described in the Apocalypse and Yeshua's prophecy! Simon Magus, as is detailed in chapter 6 above, was well known by the disciples. So, it would not be unlike John to allude to him symbolically in the Apocalypse by mentioning the ability to animate statues. Likewise, both Simon and Meander thought themselves to be the Messiah, with salvation being only through themselves. History and the scriptures are ripe with examples of this lamb-like religious system, the powers of which are exemplified by and displayed through false prophets and false messiahs. John's audience would have been well aware of Yeshua's warning against these types.

Matthew 7:15
Beware of false prophets, who come to you in sheep's clothing, but inwardly are ravening wolves.

The Mark of the Beast

(16) And he causes all, the small and the great, and the rich and the poor, and the free and the bond, that there be given them a mark on their right hand, or upon their forehead;
(17) and that no man should be able to buy or to sell, save he that has the mark, *even* the name of the beast or the number of his name.
(18) Here is wisdom. He that has understanding, let him count the number of the beast; for it is the number of a man: and his

---

[278] Irenaeus, Against Heresies. Book 1, Chapter 23, Section 5.

number is Six hundred and sixty and six.

Just as speculative theories abound regarding the identity of the first Beast, so it is with this riddle about his name and the number of his name. Before delving into the historical fulfillment of this mark we must first address the message John is conveying to his audience symbolically here. Deuteronomy 6:4-8, known best as the "Shema" today, was an inward and outward sign clearly representing one's allegiance to the one true Elohim, Yahweh. Just as we read below that the mark of the Beast is said to be placed upon the hands and foreheads of those who worship him, the "mark" of Yahweh was placed on the hands and foreheads of His servants. In both cases the hands are representative of one's actions and the foreheads of one's thoughts. To be a true follower of Yahweh one must devote all their actions and their thoughts to Him by the keeping of all His commandments and laws contained in the Torah. The keeping of the weekly seventh-day Sabbath, amongst other things, is spoken of as one of these signs[279].

Similar to the mark of Yahweh in the keeping of His commandments and loving obedience to him, the mark of the Beast is the worship and subservience to the enemies of Yahweh. Idolatry can come in many forms, but any one of them sets one in opposition to Yahweh and in submission to the Beast.

Once again, though, the symbolism of the Apocalypse also has a literal fulfillment in history. The first textual clue John provides relates in some way to buying and selling, or conducting commerce in general. The following image is taken from an article published online written by Stewart James Felker[280].

---

[279] Exodus 31:12-17.
[280] Felker.

(Image courtesy of Shimon Gibson, from the official press release)

The Latin inscription on this first century coin reads NERO CAESAR AVG IMP. As the article details, this means "Nero Caesar Augustus, Imperator."

When referring to the inability to buy or sell without accepting the mark of the beast John was likely not referring to an absolute restriction on commerce altogether. Rather, continuing in his apocalyptic symbolism he was giving yet another clue to his audience to aid them in identifying this Beast. They would have recalled an important teaching of Yeshua's:

Matthew 22:17-22
(17) Tell us therefore, What do you think? Is it lawful to give tribute unto **Caesar**, or not?
(18) But Yeshua perceived their wickedness, and said, Why make you trial of me, you hypocrites?
(19) Show me the tribute money. And they brought unto him a

denarius.

(20) And he says unto them, **Whose is this image and superscription?**

(21) They say unto him, Caesar's. Then says he unto them, Render therefore unto Caesar the things that are Caesar's; and unto Elohim the things that are Elohim's.

(22) And when they heard it, they marveled, and left him, and went away.

Yeshua specifically mentions the image *and* superscription on the Roman coins. It is very likely that the coin pictured is one that would have been familiar to Yeshua and the apostles, though with a different emperor's name and image. In John's day, the coin would have been identical to the above. In referring to this coinage, he is also giving them the identity of the Beast in no uncertain terms, yet still masking it to those who were unfamiliar with Yeshua's teachings.

Next, John provides information regarding the identity of the Beast in the form of gematria[281]. Stuart Russell once again provides an amazing yet simple evaluation of this topic that we feel will sufficiently prove its accuracy[282].

The Number of the Beast.

We now come to a question which has exercised the ingenuity of critics and commentators almost since the day it was first propounded, and which even yet can hardly be said to be solved, viz. the name or number of the beast. Without

---

[281] Gematria is a numerological system whereby each Hebrew letter is represented by a number.

[282] Russell. Pages 462-465.

wasting time on the various answers that have been given,
it may suffice to make one or two preliminary remarks on the
conditions of the problem.

1. It is evident that the writer considered that he was giving
   sufficient data for the identification of the person intended. It is also presumable that he meant not to
   puzzle, but to enlighten, his readers.

2. It is equally evident that the explanation does not lie on
   the surface. It requires wisdom to understand his
   words : it is only the man 'who hath understanding'
   that is competent to solve the problem.

3. It is plain that what he intends to convey to his readers
   is the name of the person symbolised by the beast.
   His *name* expresses a certain *number;* or, the letters
   which form his name, when added together, amount to
   a certain numerical value.

4. The name or number is that of a *man,*—*i.e.* it is not a
   beast, nor an evil spirit, nor an abstraction, but a
   person, a living *man.*

5. The number which expresses the name is, in Greek
   characters, χ ξ ς, or in numerical value six hundred
   threescore and six.

We have already, on entirely independent grounds, arrived
at the conclusion that by the apocalyptic beast is intended
the reigning emperor, Nero. It is his name, therefore, that
ought to fulfil, not indeed obviously, nor without some research, yet satisfactorily and conclusively, all the conditions
of the problem. That emperor's name would be written in
three ways, according as it was expressed in one or other of
the three languages, the Latin, the Greek, or the Hebrew :
in Latin, *Nero Cæsar;* in Greek, Νερων Καισαρ; in Hebrew,
נרונ קסר

St. John was not writing to Romans, nor in the Latin
tongue, so that the first form may be at once set aside. He
was writing, however, in Greek, and to readers well acquainted

with Greek, though most of them probably of Jewish blood. It is probable that most of them would at once, and instinctively, pronounce the dreaded name. If so they would feel at a loss, for the Greek letters $N \epsilon \rho \omega \nu$ $K \alpha \iota \sigma \alpha \rho$ would not make up the number required.

But if this had been all that was necessary, the name would have lain upon the surface, patent and palpable to the dullest apprehension. It would have required neither wisdom nor understanding to read the riddle. The reader must try another method. St. John was a Hebrew, and though he wrote in Greek characters, his thoughts were Hebrew, and the Hebrew form of the Imperial name and title was familiar to him and to his Hebrew-Christian friends both in Asia Minor and in Judea. It might not unnaturally occur to the reflecting reader to calculate the value of the letters which expressed the emperor's name in Hebrew. And the secret would stand disclosed :—

נ = 50	ק = 100
ר = 200	ס = 60
ו = 6	ר = 200
נ = 50	
———	———
306	+ 360 = 666.[*]

Here, then, is a number which expresses a *name;* the name of a *man,* of *the* man who, of all then living, best deserved to be called a wild beast: the head of the Empire, the master of the world; claiming to be a god, receiving divine honours, persecuting the saints of the Most High; in short, answering in every particular to the description in the apocalyptic vision.

[*] The name of Nero as given above occurs in the Talmud, and in other Rabbinical writings. It may be proper to add, for the information of the general reader, that in both the Hebrew and the Greek language the letters of the alphabet are used as figures or numerals, and the letters of the Hebrew form of the words 'Nero Cæsar' have the value of 666. For a more full investigation of this subject see Stuart on the Apocalypse, Excursus iv. 'On the Number of the Beast.'

If it should be asked, Why should the prophet wrap up his
meaning in enigmas? why should he not expressly name
the individual he means? First, the Apocalypse is a book
of symbols: everything in it is expressed in imagery, which
requires translation into ordinary language. But, secondly,
it would not have been safe to speak more plainly. To have
openly stated the name of the tyrant, after describing and
designating him in the manner employed in the Apocalypse,
would have been rash and imprudent in the extreme. Like
St. Paul when describing ' the man of sin,' St. John veils his
meaning under a disguise, which the heathen Greek or Roman
would probably fail to penetrate, but which the instructed
Christian of Judea or Asia Minor would readily see through.

It is a strong confirmation of the accuracy of this interpretation that we have another enigmatical description of
the very same personage from the hand of St. Paul. We
have already seen the proof that 'the man of sin' delineated in
1 Thess. ii. is no other than Nero, and the comparison of the
two portraitures shows how striking is their resemblance to
one another and to the original. This correspondence cannot be a curious coincidence merely; it can only be accounted
for by the supposition that both apostles had the same individual in view. *

We would like to provide one more piece of evidence that support ours
and Mr. Russell's conclusions regarding the number of the Beast's
name. The following image is taken directly from the Dead Sea Scrolls
Digital Library[283]. It is known as the MUR 18 papyrus as it was found in
the caves near Murabba'at. The scroll is dated to the second year of
Nero (ca. 55-56 CE). Outlined is the Aramaic phrase נרון קסר, NRON QSR.
The last two consonants are damaged, but enough is visible to
determine that there are no letters between the Samekh and Resh.

---

[283] http://www.deadseascrolls.org.il/explore-the-archive/manuscript/MUR18-
1

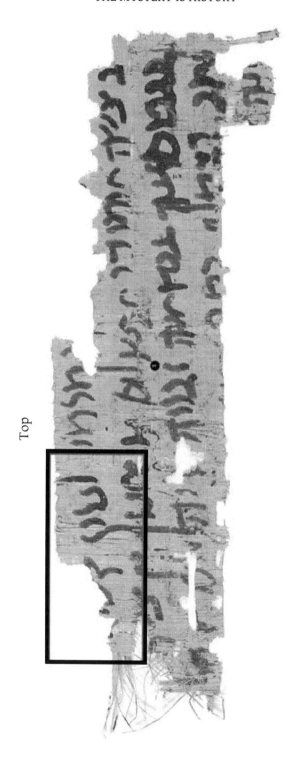

Top

This ancient manuscript provides us with compelling archaeological evidence that supports our conclusion. In a sense, John is saying, "The name of the Beast has something to do with how you buy and sell. Take the coins out of your pouches and look at them. If you were to take that name and convert it in our language to numbers, you would arrive at six hundred sixty-six." He provides them with two witnesses for this identity. There is only one individual living in their day that could possibly meet all the criteria John provided. The identity of the Beast as determined by the entire context of chapter 13 and the number of his name points conclusively to Nero Caesar.

CHAPTER FOURTEEN

The Heavenly First Fruits

(1) And I saw, and behold, the Lamb standing on the mount Zion, and with him a hundred and forty and four thousand, having his name, and the name of his Father, written on their foreheads.

(2) And I heard a voice from heaven, as the voice of many waters, and as the voice of a great thunder: and the voice which I heard *was* as *the voice* of harpers harping with their harps:

(3) and they sing as it were a new song before the throne, and before the four living creatures and the elders: and no man could learn the song save the hundred and forty and four thousand, *even* they that had been purchased out of the earth.

(4) These are they that were not defiled with women; for they are virgins. These *are* they that follow the Lamb whithersoever he goes. These were purchased from among men, *to be* the first fruits unto Elohim and unto the Lamb.

(5) And in their mouth was found no lie: they are without blemish.

We touched briefly on this group of people in chapter 12 above. These are definitely people who were at one point in the earthly realm but are now part of the heavenly. As we know that John is in the spirit when seeing this vision, we can safely conclude that the Mount Zion upon which Yeshua is standing is not the earthly one. After all, the earthly mountain was at that time engulfed in treachery, famine, rapines, murders, idolatry, atheism, and any other number of abominations. The mount upon which the Lamb is standing is one in the heavenly realm. The following passage in the book of Hebrews will be referenced several times through the following chapters. The content contained within this passage has caused some to question whether the author of Hebrews was familiar with and/or alluded directly to the Apocalypse[284].

Hebrews 12:18-24
(18) For you are not come unto *a mount* that might be touched, and that burned with fire, and unto blackness, and darkness, and tempest,
(19) and the sound of a trumpet, and the voice of words; which *voice* they that heard entreated that no word more should be spoken unto them;
(20) for they could not endure that which was enjoined, *If even a beast touch the mountain, it shall be stoned*;
(21) and so fearful was the appearance, *that* Moses said, *I exceedingly fear* and quake:
(22) but you are come unto mount Zion, and unto the city of the living Elohim, the heavenly Jerusalem, and to innumerable hosts of angels,
(23) to the festal gathering, and the assembly of the firstborn who are enrolled in heaven, and to Elohim the Judge of all, and to the spirits of just men made perfect,
(24) and to Yeshua the mediator of a new covenant, and to the blood of sprinkling that speaks better than *that of* Abel.

Either the author of Hebrews was familiar with the Apocalypse, John was familiar with the letter to the Hebrews, or both received the same insight into the future heavenly realm independently. Whichever one chooses to believe, the glaring similarities cannot be missed. To come unto the Zion mentioned in Hebrews is to come unto all the things mentioned after it – the heavenly Jerusalem, innumerable hosts of angels, the festal gathering, the assembly of the firstborn, Elohim the

---

[284] Russell. Pages 469-470; Desperez. Page 484; et al.

Judge of all, the spirits of just men made perfect, and to Yeshua the Messiah himself. The phrases that are relevant to this group of first fruits are "mount Zion," "the spirits of just men made perfect," and "Yeshua, the mediator of a new covenant." This group of first fruits is, as we mentioned above in chapter 12, the man-child born of the true assembly of believers, Zion. These are the first fruits of the resurrection, a vision of the spirits of just men made perfect. Given the following verse, it is not unlikely that these first fruits also contained the just dead who lived prior to Yeshua's death and resurrection, in addition to the believers and apostles mentioned in chapter 12:

Hebrews 11:39-40
(39) And these all, having had witness borne to them[285] through their faith, received not the promise,
(40) Elohim having provided some better thing concerning us, that apart from us they should not be made perfect.

Their virginity need not mean one that was true in their earthly lives. Rather, just as Babylon is called the "Mother of all Harlots"[286] because of her idolatrous fornication, these first fruits were ones who "followed the Lamb withersoever" he went. They did not stray off the straight and narrow path to the service of another Elohim. Instead, they followed the instruction of their master and worshipped only the true Elohim, Yahweh[287].

The Messages of the Three Angels

(6) And I saw another angel flying in mid heaven, having eternal good tidings to proclaim unto them that dwell on the earth, and unto every nation and tribe and tongue and people;
(7) and he says with a great voice, Fear Elohim, and give him glory; for the hour of his judgment is come: and worship him that made the heaven and the earth and sea and fountains of

---

[285] Those included are ones like Noah, Abraham, Moses, Jacob, Enoch, et al.
[286] Revelation 17:5.
[287] Matthew 4:10; John 4:23-24, 17:3, 20:17.

waters.

(8) And another, a second angel, followed, saying, Fallen, fallen is Babylon the great, that has made all the nations to drink of the wine of the wrath of her fornication.

(9) And another angel, a third, followed them, saying with a great voice, If any man worships the beast and his image, and receives a mark on his forehead, or upon his hand,

(10) he also shall drink of the wine of the wrath of Elohim, which is prepared unmixed in the cup of his anger; and he shall be tormented with fire and brimstone in the presence of the holy angels, and in the presence of the Lamb:

(11) and the smoke of their torment goes up forever and ever; and they have no rest day and night, they that worship the beast and his image, and whoso receives the mark of his name.

(12) Here is the patience of the saints, they that keep the commandments of Elohim, and the faith of Yeshua.

The message of the first angel would seem to be one displaying that indeed Yeshua's prophecy has been fulfilled.

Matthew 24:14
And this gospel of the kingdom shall be preached in the whole world for a testimony unto all the nations; and then shall the end come.

This angel's message is confirming Yeshua's words. The time of the end has now arrived since the gospel has been preached to all that dwell in the land, and to every nation, tongue and people. The second part of the angel's message isn't that far separate to the message of the gospel itself – "Repent, for the kingdom of heaven is at hand!"

The message of the second angel is clearly a prophetic utterance. We know this because Babylon is still in existence at the end of chapter 16 when she was "remembered in the sight of Elohim," and her destruction isn't detailed until the end of chapter 17 through chapter 18. Rather, the fall of Babylon is as good as done.

The message of the third angel is yet another against idolatry. "Don't succumb to the enemy! Don't give up the fight! Don't give in to the Beast to avoid earthly punishment at the cost of a punishment that lasts for eternity!" In the midst of this warning can also be found a promise, though. The patience of the saints will result in them being able to see, in this life or the one to come, the absolute and permanent destruction of the Beast and his kingdom.

A Blessed Death

(13) And I heard a voice from heaven saying, Write, Blessed are the dead who die in the Master from henceforth: yea, says the spirit, that they may rest from their labors; for their works follow with them.

One may rightfully ask, "Why are those who die in the Master from that moment forward more blessed than those who died in him before? Why are they more blessed than the righteous saints before Yeshua?" The simple answer is because the intermediate place between death and the afterlife, whether it be Hades as mentioned in chapter 6 above or simply the grave, has now been destroyed. This is done after the judgment of the resurrected dead takes place, which will be detailed in chapter 20 below. The saints of old mentioned in Hebrews 11:39-40 above couldn't have been raised apart from those in Yeshua because Yeshua needed to go first. Only he conquered death and the grave.

Death used to come hand-in-hand with fear and in that fear people were held in bondage.

Hebrews 2:14-15
(14) Since then the children are sharers in flesh and blood, he also himself in like manner partook of the same; that through death he might bring to nothing him that had the power of death, that is, the devil;
(15) and might deliver all them who through fear of death were all their lifetime subject to bondage.

The power of death, fear, has now been destroyed and the bondage of the grave it resulted in has been loosed. Those who died in the Master after that point in time and those who die now in him, which includes us, are more blessed because we needn't wait to enter the kingdom. Unlike the saints of old, we enter immediately into the kingdom that was prepared for us before the foundation of the world.

Matthew 25:31-34
(31) But when the Son of man shall come in his glory, and all the angels with him, then shall he sit on the throne of his glory:
(32) and before him shall be gathered all the nations: and he shall separate them one from another, as the shepherd separates the sheep from the goats;
(33) and he shall set the sheep on his right hand, but the goats on the left.
(34) Then shall the King say unto them on his right hand, **Come, you blessed of my Father, inherit the kingdom prepared for you from the foundation of the world.**

The verses after this teaching of Yeshua speak of the works of the people that caused the King to allow them entrance into the kingdom. This passage is remarkably similar to the one in Daniel 12 that we discussed in chapter 12 above. When Yeshua came in his glory those who had died were raised. Those who did righteously were raised to eternal life and those who did the opposite were raised to shame and everlasting contempt. This judgment, however, didn't include everyone who was to die from that moment forward. Instead, we have no need of a resurrection from the dead as they did. When we die we immediately see our judgment take place. If, as the Apocalypse tells us, we die "in the Master," we will be blessed and immediately see the reward of our works and we will rest from our labors in the kingdom of heaven. Paul of Tarsus was another one who understood this properly.

1 Corinthians 15:35-46
(35) But someone will say, How are the dead raised? and with what manner of body do they come?
(36) You foolish one, that which you yourself sow is not quickened except it die:
(37) and that which you sow, you sow not the body that shall be, but a bare grain, it may chance of wheat, or of some other

kind;

(38) but Elohim gives it a body even as it pleased him, and to each seed a body of its own.

(39) All flesh is not the same flesh: but there is one *flesh* of men, and another flesh of beasts, and another flesh of birds, and another of fishes.

(40) There are also celestial bodies, and bodies terrestrial: but the glory of the celestial is one, and the *glory* of the terrestrial is another.

(41) There is one glory of the sun, and another glory of the moon, and another glory of the stars; for one star differs from another star in glory.

(42) So also is the resurrection of the dead. It is sown in corruption; it is raised in incorruption:

(43) it is sown in dishonor; it is raised in glory: it is sown in weakness; it is raised in power:

(44) **it is sown a natural body; it is raised a spiritual body**. If there is a natural body, there is also a spiritual *body*.

(45) So also it is written, The first *man* Adam *became a living soul*. The last Adam *became* a life-giving spirit.

(46) Howbeit that is not first which is spiritual, but that which is natural; then that which is spiritual.

Yeshua's resurrection was bodily that in every way he might fulfill his promises and prophecies. The tomb would be empty and his body would not see decay[288]. We, however, have no need to be raised again in our earthly bodies. When death takes our mortal bodies, we are immediately given new spiritual, eternal bodies, and become "equal unto the angels."

Luke 20:34-38
(34) And Yeshua said unto them, The sons of this world marry, and are given in marriage:

(35) but they that are accounted worthy to attain to that world, and the resurrection from the dead, neither marry, nor are given in marriage:

---

[288] Acts 2:29-31.

(36) for neither can they die any more: for they are **equal unto the angels**; and are **sons of Elohim**, being **sons of the resurrection**.
(37) But that the dead are raised, even Moses showed, in *the place concerning* the Bush, when he calls Yahweh *the Elohim of Abraham, and the Elohim of Isaac, and the Elohim of Jacob*.
(38) Now he is not the Elohim of the dead, but of the living: for all live unto him.

Yeshua says the following in response to Martha's mournful plea for her dead brother Lazarus:

John 11:25-26
(25) Yeshua said unto her, I am the resurrection, and the life: he that believes on me, though he dies, yet shall he live;
(26) and whosoever lives and believes on me shall never die. Do you believe this?

Yeshua here tells us of the two different results of death. There are those who were to believe upon and follow Yeshua, then die and remain dead (physically and spiritually) until they were resurrected at his second appearing. To them he is "the resurrection." Then there were (are) those who were (are) to believe upon and follow him, then die and transition directly into eternal life spiritually. To them he is "the life."

The Harvest of the Wheat

(14) And I saw, and behold, a white cloud; and on the cloud *I saw* one sitting like unto a son of man, having on his head a golden crown, and in his hand a sharp sickle.
(15) And another angel came out from the temple, crying with a great voice to him that sat on the cloud, Send forth your sickle, and reap: for the hour to reap is come; for the harvest of the earth is ripe.
(16) And he that sat on the cloud cast his sickle upon the earth; and the earth was reaped.

We come now to another event that was prefigured in the account of the seventh angel's trumpet in chapter 11 above. Before moving forward with any detailed explanations of the fulfillments of this passage we need to briefly discuss the harvest cycle in Israel. The first harvest each scriptural year was that of the barley. A first fruits offering from this harvest was a requirement under the commands in the Torah[289]. Once the first fruits were offered the rest of the barley could be harvested. We see a fulfillment of this agricultural type within the pages of scripture. Yeshua was the first fruits of the spiritual barley harvest. After he was resurrected, symbolizing the waving of the first fruits offering, the remaining barley harvest took place:

Matthew 27:51-53
(51) And behold, the veil of the temple was rent in two from the top to the bottom; and the earth did quake; and the rocks were rent;
(52) and the tombs were opened; and **many bodies of the saints that had fallen asleep were raised**;
(53) and coming forth out of the tombs **after his resurrection** they entered into the holy city and appeared unto many.

Though the identity of these saints is not given, it is not in the least unlikely that they were those such as Abraham, Isaac, Jacob, David, Samuel, Elijah, and other righteous men and women of the past. Thus, the barley harvest type was then fulfilled. The next harvest in Israel is the wheat harvest, which begins mid-late Spring and lasts for around seven weeks. Just like the barley harvest a first fruits offering was required before the full wheat harvest could ensue[290]. This first fruits offering is represented by the 144,000 that were raised to life in chapter 12. This is the same group that was sealed in chapter 7, against whom the locust army of the fifth angel's trumpet judgment had no authority. That demonic army, whose mission was to destroy Jerusalem through the Roman armies, wasn't permitted to touch them. John wasn't saying

---

[289] Leviticus 23:9-11.
[290] Leviticus 23:15-16.

the 144,000 wouldn't die at all, but that their days would be shortened[291] (*i.e.* they would die before the final tribulation of the siege of Jerusalem). That same group of people are called first fruits at the beginning of this chapter. After the first fruits are offered the rest of the wheat harvest can begin. The final harvest in Israel is that of the grapes, figs, olives, and other summer fruits. This is a type of what is discussed further down in this chapter.

At this point in the chapter we see the full harvest of wheat being completed. Here we see one harvest consisting of two types, the both of which are mentioned in Daniel 12 and by Yeshua in the passage just quoted above. This harvest is a perfect fulfillment of Yeshua's parable of the wheat and tares[292]. His interpretation of that parable to his disciples is as follows:

Matthew 13:36-43
(36) Then he left the multitudes, and went into the house: and his disciples came unto him, saying, Explain unto us the parable of the tares of the field.
(37) And he answered and said, He that sows the good seed is the Son of man;
(38) and the field is the world; and the good seed, these are the sons of the kingdom; and the tares are the sons of the evil *one*;
(39) and the enemy that sowed them is the devil: and **the harvest is the end of the age**; and the reapers are angels.
(40) As therefore the tares are gathered up and burned with fire; so shall it be **in the end of the age**.
(41) The Son of man shall send forth his angels, and they shall gather out of his kingdom all things that cause stumbling, and them that do iniquity,
(42) and shall cast them into the furnace of fire: there shall be the weeping and the gnashing of teeth.
(43) Then shall *the righteous shine forth as the sun* in the kingdom of their Father. He that has ears, let him hear.

---

[291] Matthew 24:22; Mark 13:20.
[292] Matthew 13:24-30.

It may take reading this explanation by Yeshua of his parable several times to fully grasp the fulfillments of it here in the Apocalypse. First, the identity of the angel that was "like unto a son of man" is revealed. Some believe it refers to Yeshua himself[293]. Yeshua, however, taught something different. We see above that he taught that the reapers are angels. The angel that is like a son of man in chapter 14 is being commanded to reap by another angel. Yeshua taught that *he* would be the one commanding the angels to reap, not the other way around. Thus we can conclude that the instruction given to both of these angels, including the one that was "like unto a son of man," came from Yeshua himself.

Yeshua also tells us that harvest would not contain only the righteous, but also those who were unrighteous. This is yet another mirror to what we are told in Daniel, showing us that Daniel's prophecy and Yeshua's parable are speaking of the same time. Here is another teaching of Yeshua that says the same thing:

John 5:28-29
(28) Marvel not at this: for the hour comes, in which all that are in the tombs shall hear his voice,
(29) and shall come forth; they that have done good, unto **the resurrection of life**; and they that have done evil, unto **the resurrection of judgment**.

Farther down in the parable of the wheat and the tares we see yet another direct reference by Yeshua to the prophecy of Daniel. Daniel tells us that "they that are wise shall shine as the brightness of the firmament; and they that turn many to righteousness as the stars forever and ever."[294] Yeshua tells us "Then shall the righteous shine forth as the sun." These two accounts are direct parallels. When the full wheat harvest was reaped, righteous and unrighteous dead were raised alike and judged accordingly. The righteous dead consisted of those who were dead in the Master from his death and resurrection

---

[293] Russell. Pages 417-418.
[294] Daniel 12:3.

until that moment. We are not provided with any specific time elements in this passage on the resurrection of the remaining dead that would help us pinpoint a specific time in history when it occurred. There are several verses of scripture, however, that lead us to conclude it took place on the "last day."[295]. Which is the "last day," though?

As we read above in chapter 12, the man clothed in linen in Daniel 12 said that "*all* these things shall be finished," one of which included "them that sleep in the dust of the earth shall awake, some to everlasting life, and some to shame and everlasting contempt." This "breaking in pieces the power of the holy people" must have been complete prior to the continual offering being taken away, since the context of Daniel's prophecy shifts at that point[296]. The most significant date prior to that point was the beginning of the siege of Jerusalem on April 14, 70 CE, which was the day of Passover. The timing of this event will be outlined in detail in the chapters that follow. That date and how it relates to the "last day" is very significant. The number forty is used several times in the scriptures to signify a period of trial, repentance or judgment[297]. We know that Yeshua was crucified and died on the day of Passover, April 7, 30 CE[298]. Just as Yeshua promised, the sign of Jonah was that which would be given to that generation. Yeshua's ministry was three years[299], each day of Jonah's preaching corresponding to a year. Like the period the Ninevites were given to repent, forty days, the Israelites were given forty years. Eusebius confirms that this was indeed the historical tradition:

> "Yet it may be proper to mention, also, what things occurred that show the benignity of that all-gracious Providence that had deferred their destruction for **forty years** after their crimes against Christ."[300]

---

[295] John 6:39-40, 44, 54, 7:37, 11:24, 12:48.
[296] Daniel 12:11.
[297] Exodus 24:18; Ezekiel 4:6; Jonah 3:4; Matthew 4:1-11.
[298] Finegan. Pages 359-369; Jones. Pages 220-238.
[299] From Passover, 27 CE through Passover, 30 CE.
[300] Eusebius. Book 3, Chapter 7, Section 8.

Thus, the "last day," on which the resurrection of the dead was to take place, was the final day of that period of repentance, or the day on which the siege of Jerusalem began.

A common doctrinal belief and stronghold needs to be briefly addressed here before moving on. Since most followers of Yeshua believe that *all* must be resurrected *from the dead*, they believe that this reaping of the spiritual harvest must take place at the end of all time. In the mind of a Futurist this would be at or just before Yeshua's coming to setup his kingdom on the earth. However, that doctrinal belief is a misconception. It is one that has been perpetuated for centuries because the truth of the fulfillment of the prophecies in the Apocalypse has been lost, or even rejected for the same period of time. Despite the common belief, a resurrection of the dead does *not* need to take place at the end of all time. As we have already outlined in detail above, we are told that there is a more blessed death for those in the Master than those who had died prior to then. The prophecies throughout the scriptures regarding the resurrection of the dead were required to be fulfilled. Yeshua was to be raised from the dead as the first fruits[301]. Then there were the resurrections of the righteous and unrighteous dead. All the necessary scriptures concerning those can be found and will be discussed in detail in the section entitled "The Resurrections – Part II" in chapter 20 below. However, once the prophecies of the resurrections were fulfilled, there is no further need for a resurrection from the grave.

As we said, more evidence regarding the fulfillment of the resurrection of the dead will be discussed below in chapter 20. For now, though, let it be sufficient to say that the wheat harvest in this chapter of the Apocalypse must require, per Yeshua's teachings and the types of the agricultural harvests, that both righteous and unrighteous dead were raised as a part of the reaping.

---

[301] Psalms 16:10; Psalms 22; Isaiah 53; et. al.

The Harvest of the Grapes

(17) And another angel came out from the temple which is in heaven, he also having a sharp sickle.

(18) And another angel came out from the altar, he that has power over fire; and he called with a great voice to him that had the sharp sickle, saying, Send forth your sharp sickle, and gather the clusters of the vine of the earth; for her grapes are fully ripe.

(19) And the angel cast his sickle into the earth, and gathered the vintage of the earth, and cast it into the winepress, the great *winepress*, of the wrath of Elohim.

(20) And the winepress was trodden without the city, and there came out blood from the winepress, even unto the bridles of the horses, as far as a thousand and six hundred furlongs.

Immediately our minds are called back to a situation very similar to this one in Israel's past. Israel is on many occasions called a "vineyard" in the scriptures. One for which Yahweh took great effort to plant, protect, and cause to grow. Yet, when the vineyard's yield was sour grapes, we are told that he threw those grapes into a winepress and trod it.

Isaiah 5:1-6

(1) Let me sing for my well-beloved a song of my beloved touching his vineyard. My well-beloved had a **vineyard** in a very fruitful hill:

(2) and he dug it, and gathered out the stones thereof, and planted it with the choicest vine, and built a tower in the midst of it, and also hewed out a winepress therein: and he looked that it should bring forth grapes, and it brought forth wild grapes.

(3) And now, O inhabitants of Jerusalem and men of Judah, judge, I pray you, between me and **my vineyard**.

(4) What could have been done more to **my vineyard**, that I have not done in it? wherefore, when I looked that it should bring forth grapes, brought it forth wild grapes?

(5) And now I will tell you what I will do to my vineyard: I will take away the hedge thereof, and it shall be eaten up; I will break down the wall thereof, and **it shall be trodden down**:

(6) and I will lay it waste; it shall not be pruned nor hoed; but

there shall come up briers and thorns: I will also command the clouds that they rain no rain upon it.

Lamentations 1:15
(15) The Master has set at nothing all my mighty men in the midst of me; He has called a solemn assembly against me to crush my young men: **The Master has trodden as in a winepress the virgin daughter of Judah**.

Isaiah prophesied of the treading of Israel in the winepress of Yahweh's wrath and Jeremiah lamented it after it happened. This prophecy and lamentation related specifically to Jerusalem and Judea being destroyed by Nebuchadnezzar, king of Babylon. We see the same thing happening in the Apocalypse.

In contrast to the wheat harvest, which we have seen clearly represented the resurrection of both righteous and unrighteous *dead*, the treading of the winepress is representative of the destruction of the wicked, lawless, and rebellious ones who were yet *alive*. We are told that the treading of these sour grapes was to take place outside of the city.

The harvest cycle of Israel, being a type of the order of events here in the Apocalypse, tells us that after the resurrection of the dead on April 14, 70 CE, the harvest of the vintage was to be reaped. John use of the phrase "without [*outside*] the city" would have had a significant impact on his audience. The author of the book of Hebrews tells us the following:

Hebrews 13:12
Wherefore Yeshua also, that he might sanctify the people through his own blood, suffered **without the gate**.

Yeshua was crucified and died outside of the city. An astounding historical parallel is found within the pages of Josephus' work.

"So now Titus's banks were advanced a great way, notwithstanding his soldiers had been very much distressed from the wall. He then sent a party of horsemen, and ordered they should lay ambushes for those that went out into the valleys to gather food. Some of these were indeed fighting men, who were not contented with what they got by rapine; but the greater part of them were poor people, who were deterred from deserting by the concern they were under for their own relations; for they could not hope to escape away, together with their wives and children, without the knowledge of the seditious; nor could they think of leaving these relations to be slain by the robbers on their account; nay, the severity of the famine made them bold in thus going out; so nothing remained but that, when they were concealed from the robbers, they should be taken by the enemy; and when they were going to be taken, they were forced to defend themselves for fear of being punished; as after they had fought, they thought it too late to make any supplications for mercy; **so they were first whipped, and then tormented with all sorts of tortures, before they died, and were then crucified before the wall of the city.** This miserable procedure made Titus greatly to pity them, while **they caught every day five hundred Jews**; nay, some days they caught more: yet it did not appear to be safe for him to let those that were taken by force go their way, and to set a guard over so many he saw would be to make such as great deal them useless to him. The main reason why he did not forbid that cruelty was this, that he hoped the Jews might perhaps yield at that sight, out of fear lest they might themselves afterwards be liable to the same cruel treatment. So the soldiers, out of the wrath and hatred they bore the Jews, **nailed those they caught, one after one way, and another after another, to the crosses,** by way of jest, when their multitude was so great, **that room was wanting for the crosses, and crosses wanting for the bodies.**"[302]

In the same way that Yeshua was tortured and crucified so were the wicked who fled from the city. These horrendous punishments were inflicted upon no less than five hundred people every day. Can we think of any more just punishment for the torture and crucifixion of their Messiah, the very Son of Yahweh, than for them to be tortured

---

[302] Josephus, Wars. 5.11.1. Page 720.

and slain in the exact same way? This calamity took place, as we should expect by now, in the perfect chronological place as it relates to the types found in the harvests. This treading of the winepress outside of the city took place after the completion of the wheat harvest. The winepress of the wrath of Yahweh was indeed tread without the city and the blood flowed for a long way.

CHAPTER FIFTEEN

The Resurrected Saints

(1) And I saw another sign in heaven, great and marvelous, seven angels having seven plagues, *which are* the last, for in them is finished the wrath of Elohim.

(2) And I saw as it were a sea of glass mingled with fire; and them that come off victorious from the beast, and from his image, and from the number of his name, standing by the sea of glass, having harps of Elohim.

(3) And they sing the song of Moses the servant of Elohim, and the song of the Lamb, saying, Great and marvelous are your works, O Yahweh Elohim, the Almighty; righteous and true are your ways, you King of the ages.

(4) Who shall not fear, O Yahweh, and glorify your name? *for you only are holy; for all the nations shall come and worship before you; for your righteous acts have been made manifest.*

The group of saints pictured here are no different than the 144,000 pictured in verses 1-5 in chapter 14 above. Both were obviously victorious over the Beast and his image; both are pictured with harps; and both were singing songs to Elohim. Where they are portrayed by John in chapter 14 in a fashion introducing his audience to his harvest fulfillments, that being that they are the first fruits of the wheat harvest, they are here pictured in the context of the seven angels with the seven last plagues of judgment. Where they were pictured in chapter 14 as standing on mount Zion, the place of their eternal rest, here they stand on a sea of fiery glass, which was last mentioned in chapter 4 regarding the convening of the heavenly court. The wheat and grape harvests are now finished and the time has come for the last of the wrath of Yahweh to be poured out.

The Seven Angels and the Final Plagues

(5) And after these things I saw, and the temple of the tabernacle of the testimony in heaven was opened:
(6) and there came out from the temple the seven angels that had the seven plagues, arrayed with *precious* stone, pure *and* bright, and girt about their breasts with golden girdles.
(7) And one of the four living creatures gave unto the seven angels seven golden bowls full of the wrath of Elohim, who lives forever and ever.
(8) And the temple was filled with smoke from the glory of Elohim, and from his power; and none was able to enter into the temple, till the seven plagues of the seven angels should be finished.

John uses the phrases "seven angels" and "seven plagues" three times in this passage. He is emphasizing to his audience that the wrath due the persecutors of the followers of Yeshua is soon to come to a complete and perfect end. John is bringing to the minds of his audience the record of Isaiah's vision and commission from the Almighty.

Isaiah 6:1-13
(1) In the year that king Uzziah died I saw Yahweh sitting upon a throne, high and lifted up; and his train filled the temple.
(2) Above him stood the seraphim: each one had six wings; with twain he covered his face, and with twain he covered his feet, and with twain he did fly.
(3) And one cried unto another, and said, Holy, holy, holy, is Yahweh of hosts: the whole earth is full of his glory.
(4) And the foundations of the thresholds shook at the voice of him that cried, and **the house was filled with smoke**.

(5) Then said I, Woe is me! for I am undone; because I am a man of unclean lips, and I dwell in the midst of a people of unclean lips: for my eyes have seen the King, Yahweh of hosts.
(6) Then flew one of the seraphim unto me, having a live coal in his hand, which he had taken with the tongs from off the altar:
(7) and he touched my mouth with it, and said, Lo, this has touched your lips; and your iniquity is taken away, and your sin forgiven.
(8) And I heard the voice of the Master, saying, Whom shall I send, and who will go for us? Then I said, Here am I; send me.
(9) And he said, Go, and tell this people, Hear you indeed, but understand not; and see you indeed, but perceive not.
(10) Make the heart of this people fat, and make their ears heavy, and shut their eyes; lest they see with their eyes, and hear with their ears, and understand with their heart, and turn again, and be healed.
(11) Then said I, Master, how long? And he answered, Until cities be waste without inhabitant, and houses without man, and the land become utterly waste,
(12) and Yahweh have removed men far away, and the forsaken places be many in the midst of the land.
(13) And if there be yet a tenth in it, it also shall in turn be eaten up: as a terebinth, and as an oak, whose stock remains, when they are felled; so the holy seed is the stock thereof.

He is also reminding them of Yeshua's teaching on Isaiah's prophecy and who he said it applied to.

Matthew 13:10-15
(10) And the disciples came, and said unto him, Why speak you unto them in parables?
(11) And he answered and said unto them, Unto you it is given to know the mysteries of the kingdom of heaven, but to them it is not given.
(12) For whosoever has, to him shall be given, and he shall have abundance: but whosoever has not, from him shall be taken away even that which he has.
(13) Therefore speak I to them in parables; because seeing they see not, and hearing they hear not, neither do they understand.

(14) And unto them is fulfilled the prophecy of Isaiah, which says, *By hearing you shall hear, and shall in no wise understand; And seeing you shall see, and shall in no wise perceive:*
(15) *For this people's heart is waxed gross, And their ears are dull of hearing, And their eyes they have closed; Lest haply they should perceive with their eyes, And hear with their ears, And understand with their heart, And should turn again, And I should heal them.*

Yeshua made it clear. The prophecy in Isaiah was fulfilled in the rebellious and stubborn people in his day. John completely understood this. Thus, he also understood that the remaining portion of Isaiah's prophecy was also to be fulfilled in that generation. Cities were to be destroyed and left uninhabited. The land was to be utterly wasted. The people would be carried away into captivity by the hand of Yahweh. All those calamities befell the wicked and rebellious people during the war.

CHAPTER SIXTEEN

Introduction to the Bowl Judgments

Now is a good time to remind the reader that John's primary intent of the Apocalypse is to convey the righteous judgments of Yahweh and Yeshua via prophetic and apocalyptic symbolism. Though there are astounding real-life historical events that underlie virtually every symbol, John is mainly trying to tell his audience that the curses promised the children of Israel for disobedience were coming upon them.

> Deuteronomy 28:60-61
> (60) And he will bring upon you again **all the diseases of Egypt**, which you were afraid of; and they shall cleave unto you.
> (61) Also **every sickness**, and **every plague**, which is not written in the book of this Yahweh, them will Yahweh bring upon you, until you be destroyed.

Where the judgments caused by the seven angels' trumpets in chapters 8 and 9 above were partial in their scope, in an attempt to give the people one final chance at repentance, the judgments of the seven angels' bowls are complete. The wrath of the Almighty fills the bowls to the brim and the resulting judgments are the complete removal of the blessings they were promised repeatedly if they only obeyed Him.

Some believe that the seven bowl judgments are merely a

recapitulation of the seven angels' trumpet judgments[303], though in many ways abbreviated. Where the themes and similarities of them cannot be denied, we believe it is pulling the context and flow of the Apocalypse out of historical timeline unnecessarily. It is true that dreams and visions are frequently given in duplicate throughout the scriptures. Joseph's dreams in Gen. 37:1-11, Pharaoh's dreams in Gen. 41:1-36, and Daniel's dreams in Dan. 2:31-45 and Dan. 7:15-28 are all examples. Each contain different symbols, all pairs referring to the other in the pair. However, it is also possible, and in fact more likely that the bowls are the result of the actions of the still unrepentant people.

It is important to note that the judgments contained in these bowls were to be inflicted upon the people, not the city. We will see later in chapters 17 and 18 that the city itself receives its own judgment. Seeing as Jerusalem has now been fully encompassed by armies, the punishments inflicted by these bowls were upon the people within the city. In addition, let the reader remember that the outpouring of the bowls is a vision seen in heaven. As we pointed out in the Introduction to the trumpet judgments in chapter 8 above, each of the bowls were likely to have been poured out in the heavens before any earthly events took place. In addition, it is the angels that John lists in the chronological order, not the content of the judgments they are announcing. Just like the trumpets above, there are no phrases such as "First bowl," or "Second bowl," etc. All the judgments poured out of the bowls need to be taken together as a whole. We need not look for a completion of the plague of the first bowl before seeing the beginning of the second, and so forth.

The First Angel's Bowl

(1) And I heard a great voice out of the temple, saying to the seven angels, Go you, and pour out the seven bowls of the wrath of Elohim into the earth.
(2) And the first went, and poured out his bowl into the earth;

---

[303] Russell. Pages 476-477; Chilton.

and it became a noisome and grievous sore upon the men that
had the mark of the beast, and that worshipped his image.

The "noisome and grievous sore" recalls the corresponding plague of
Egypt[304]. These plagues coming upon them were an exact fulfillment of
that spoken by Moses hundreds of years earlier.

Deuteronomy 28:20-22
(20) Yahweh will send upon you cursing, discomfiture, and
rebuke, in all that you put your hand unto to do, until you be
destroyed, and until you perish quickly; because of the evil of
your doings, whereby you have forsaken me.
(21) Yahweh will make **the pestilence** cleave unto you, until he
has consumed you from off the land, where you go in to possess
it.
(22) Yahweh will smite you with consumption, and with fever,
and with inflammation, and with fiery heat, and with the sword,
and with blasting, and with mildew; and they shall pursue you
until you perish.

In recording what happened during the beginning stages of the siege
on Jerusalem, we read the following.

"Now the number of those that were carried captive during this
whole war was collected to be ninety-seven thousand; as was the
number of those that perished during the whole siege eleven
hundred thousand, the greater part of whom were indeed of the
same nation [with the citizens of Jerusalem], but not belonging to
the city itself; for they were come up from all the country to the
feast of unleavened bread, and were on a sudden shut up by an
army, which, at the very first, occasioned so great a straitness
among them, that there came **a pestilential destruction** upon them,
and soon afterward such a famine, as destroyed them more
suddenly."[305]

---

[304] Exodus 9:8-12.
[305] Josephus, Wars. 6.9.3. Page 749.

Once the city was surrounded and no one was permitted to leave without dying a horrific death, the famine and death spread throughout the city and a pestilence consequently came.

The Second Angel's Bowl

(3) And the second poured out his bowl into the sea; and it became blood as of a dead man; and every living soul died, *even* the things that were in the sea.

Unlike the waters being turned to blood as in the second and third angels' trumpet judgments, this blood as specifically called "blood of a dead man." Blood that flowed in lakes and rivers, though voluminous during this time, wasn't the same. This blood was one as found around a dead body. Thick, coagulated, baked by the sun, and stagnant would be the blood John was referring to. This horrid sight had already been witnessed in other parts of the city.

"But these zealots came at last to that degree of barbarity, as not to bestow a burial either on those slain in the city, or on those that lay along the roads; but as if they had made an agreement to cancel both the laws of their country and the laws of nature, and, at the same time that they defiled men with their wicked actions, they would pollute the Divinity itself also, they **left the dead bodies to putrefy under the sun.**"[306]

This bloody judgment was later magnified greatly as this second bowl.

Remember that the sea being referred to in the Apocalypse is the people of Israel themselves. Where the second angel's trumpet judgment affected one third of the sea, this judgment was poured out upon the whole sea. The visitation of the Egyptian plague of blood upon wicked and rebellious Israel was no longer one intended to bring about repentance; it was to completely exhaust the wrath of Yahweh.

---

[306] Josephus, Wars. 4.6.3. Page 682.

The conquering of Israel outside of Jerusalem already having been accomplished, all the people within the city itself were now being affected in some way by this complete plague. The staggering historical fulfillment of this is recorded by Josephus.

"Insomuch that many persons who came thither with great zeal from the ends of the earth, to offer sacrifices at this celebrated place, which was esteemed holy by all mankind, fell down before their own sacrifices themselves, and **sprinkled that altar** which was venerable among all men, both Greeks and Barbarians, **with their own blood;** till the dead bodies of strangers were mingled together with those of their own country, and those of profane persons with those of the priests, and **the blood of all sorts of dead carcasses stood in lakes in the holy courts themselves.**"[307]

"But as for the legions that came running thither, neither any persuasions nor any threatenings could restrain their violence, but each one's own passion was his commander at this time; and as they were crowding into the temple together, many of them were trampled on by one another, while a great number fell among the ruins of the cloisters, which were still hot and smoking, and were destroyed in the same miserable way with those whom they had conquered; and when they were come near the holy house, they made as if they did not so much as hear Caesar's orders to the contrary; but they encouraged those that were before them to set it on fire. As for the seditious, they were in too great distress already to afford their assistance [towards quenching the fire]; they were everywhere slain, and everywhere beaten; and as for a great part of the people, they were weak and without arms, and **had their throats cut wherever they were caught.** Now **round about the altar lay dead bodies heaped one upon another,** as at the steps going up to **it ran a great quantity of their blood,** whither also the dead bodies that were slain above [on the altar] fell down."[308]
"Yet was the misery itself more terrible than this disorder; for one

---

[307] Josephus, Wars. 5.1.3. Page 697.
[308] Josephus, Wars. 6.4.6. Page 740.

would have thought that the hill itself, on which the temple stood, was seething hot, as full of fire on every part of it, that **the blood was larger in quantity than the fire,** and those that were slain more in number than those that slew them; for **the ground did nowhere appear visible, for the dead bodies that lay on it;** but the soldiers went over heaps of those bodies, as they ran upon such as fled from them."[309]

"But although they had this commiseration for such as were destroyed in that manner, yet had they not the same for those that were still alive, but they ran every one through whom they met with, and **obstructed the very lanes with their dead bodies,** and made **the whole city run down with blood,** to such a degree indeed that **the fire of many of the houses was quenched with these men's blood.**"[310]

The judgment represented by this bowl could not have manifested itself in a more real way than it did at that time. All the places that were once considered set-apart, all the streets of the holy city, were now covered with the coagulating and stagnant blood of the men and women who had dared to rebel against Yahweh. John's mention of "every living soul" dying doesn't mean every person on the planet died at that moment. It means that not one soul that was then in the city was left unaffected by the atrocities inflicted therein. The very spirits within them were either destroyed by their own swords, or those of the Romans, or they were brought to death via captivity and enslavement.

The Third Angel's Bowl

(4) And the third poured out his bowl into the rivers and the fountains of the waters; and it became blood.
(5) And I heard the angel of the waters saying, Righteous are you, who are and who were, you Holy One, because you did thus judge:

---

[309] Josephus, Wars. 6.5.1. Page 741.
[310] Josephus, Wars. 6.8.5. Page 748.

(6) for they poured out the blood of saints and prophets, and
blood have you given them to drink: they are worthy.

In this bowl, we see the plague of blood affecting not only moving
water but water sources themselves. Jerusalem, like many other
ancient cities, had water supply systems that are vastly more primitive
than ours are today. Their water supplies came from wells dug within
or without the city itself, or from runoff pools that collected the rain
water. Dr. E. W. G. Masterman wrote an excellent paper detailing the
water supply and return systems of Ancient Jerusalem[311]. In his
introductory paragraph, he states that the work done to maintain a
steady supply of water in the city "is witnessed by the **numberless**
remains of ancient **aqueducts, tunnels, pools,** and **cisterns, on** and
beneath the surface at **almost every spot** in and close around the Holy
City." Fountains and pools in certain parts of the city, when
overflowing, would fill others farther down. Aqueducts, subterranean
or other, would connect these cisterns and pools.

After reading the paper above and applying it to the scope of the third
bowl judgment the meaning becomes clear. The outpouring of blood
detailed in the second bowl would inevitably flow down into the pools,
cisterns, and aqueducts in the city. Thus, the very fountains that once
contained water used for life were now polluted with the stagnant and
unclean blood of the slain.

Once again John was reminding his audience of the curses of
disobedience promised by Yahweh. As we read in Deuteronomy 28
above all the plagues of Egypt were stored up for them if they defied
Him and disobeyed His commands.

Exodus 7:19
And Yahweh said unto Moses, Say unto Aaron, Take your rod,
and stretch out your hand over the waters of Egypt, over their
rivers, over their **streams**, and over their **pools**, and over all their
ponds of water, that they may become blood; and there shall be

---

[311] Masterman.

blood throughout all the land of Egypt, both in **vessels of wood** and in **vessels of stone**.

Just as the plague of blood inflicted upon the Egyptians affected their water sources, flowing and standing, so would the blood represented in this bowl judgment do to the water sources and supplies of the city.

The Fourth Angel's Bowl

(8) And the fourth poured out his bowl upon the sun; and it was given unto it to scorch men with fire.
(9) And men were scorched with great heat: and they blasphemed the name of Elohim who has the power over these plagues; and they repented not to give him glory.

John is stating that yet another blessing of Yahweh would be removed because of the wickedness of the people.

Deuteronomy 28:22
Yahweh will smite you with consumption, and with fever, and with inflammation, and **with fiery heat**, and with the sword, and with blasting, and with mildew; and they shall pursue you until you perish.

Psalms 121:5-6
(5) Yahweh is your keeper: Yahweh is your shade upon your right hand.
(6) The **sun shall not smite you** by day, Nor the moon by night.

Isaiah 49:8-10
(8) Thus says Yahweh, In an acceptable time have I answered you, and in a day of salvation have I helped you; and I will preserve you, and give you for a covenant of the people, to raise up the land, to make them inherit the desolate heritages:
(9) saying to them that are bound, Go forth; to them that are in darkness, Show yourselves. They shall feed in the ways, and on all bare heights shall be their pasture.
(10) They shall not hunger nor thirst; **neither shall the heat nor**

sun smite them: for he that has mercy on them will lead them, even by springs of water will he guide them.

This personification of the sun "smiting" His people was something that was held back, but only if the people were living in obedience to Yahweh's commands. As we read in the table of apocalyptic terminology in the Introduction the sun represents kings. Where obedient Israel was divinely protected from the smiting of the kings of foreign nations, that protection was now lifted. The pagan kings of Rome and her allies were given permission and power by Yahweh to bring a great smiting upon Israel. Israel's adulterous and idolatrous ways resulted in the removal of the protective blessing, thus the sun would now be permitted to "smite" them.

John isn't telling the people he's writing to that they will see solar flares reaching down to the earth to turn men into ash. He isn't telling them that they should expect to see a lot of sun-burnt people. He isn't telling them to look for intercontinental ballistic missiles falling from the sky upon a nation. He is continuing his discourse on how Yahweh is systematically removing the blessings that He so graciously lavished upon His children because they have persisted in disobedience. The blessing of protection, however, is restored to those who are in Yeshua, who through faith and obedience to him and Yahweh's commandments will enter joyously into the kingdom of heaven.

Revelation 7:16-17
(16) They shall hunger no more, neither thirst anymore; **neither shall the sun strike upon them, nor any heat**:
(17) for the Lamb that is in the midst of the throne shall be their shepherd, and shall guide them unto fountains of waters of life: and Elohim shall wipe away every tear from their eyes.

The Fifth Angel's Bowl

(10) And the fifth poured out his bowl upon the throne of the beast; and his kingdom was darkened; and they gnawed their tongues for pain,
(11) and they blasphemed the Elohim of heaven because of their

pains and their sores; and they repented not of their works.

The fifth bowl is an amazing example showing us that the agents of Yahweh's wrath, the Roman Empire in this instance, aren't free from their own punishments. This was true of Nebuchadnezzar king of Babylon and Cyrus king of Persia in the past. Both were used as agents of Yahweh's wrath or liberation, yet both came to their ultimate destruction as they were still defiant to Him and His ways. Likewise, the kingdom of the Beast, Rome, was afflicted with torments that caused a great darkness to fall upon it.

We briefly detailed in chapter 13 above how the head of the Beast that was struck with a fatal wound represented Nero and his suicide in June of 68 CE. After this event the Roman Empire was greatly shaken and historians record how its recovery may have been impossible. This chaos lasted over a year and therefore meets the timeline of the Apocalypse perfectly. During this year known as the "Year of the Four Emperors" there were numerous wars being fought, both foreign and civil[312]. Galba, the successor immediately after Nero, was murdered via plot by the next emperor to be – Otho[313]. After a reign of just ninety-five days Otho committed suicide[314]. A general of Rome by the name of Vitellius was the next one to take the throne of the Empire[315]. Then, despite the desperate attempts of Vitellius[316] to reverse the declaration of Vespasian as emperor by his troops[317], Vespasian ended up being victorious. He put a strangle-hold on the Capitol by stopping the supply of corn to Rome from Egypt, having been in control of Alexandria[318]. In Rome, Vitellius ordered the burning of the renowned and cherished temple of Jupiter[319]. The day after Vitellius was killed Vespasian was officially recognized as emperor by the Roman Senate.

---

[312] Tacitus, Histories. Book 1, Chapters 2-3.
[313] Suetonius, Otho. Chapter 7.
[314] Suetonius, Otho. Chapter 11.
[315] Suetonius, Vitellius. Chapter 11.
[316] Suetonius, Vitellius. Chapter 15.
[317] Josephus, Wars. 4.10.3-4. Pages 692-693.
[318] Josephus, Wars. 4.10.5. Page 693.
[319] Suetonius, Vitellius. Chapter 15; Tacitus, Histories. Book 3, Chapters 71-73.

The plague of darkness represented by the fifth bowl was poured out upon the kingdom of the Beast at the same time the other plagues were affecting the people in the city of Jerusalem.

There is, however, an alternate view of this fifth bowl judgment that we should present. It is noteworthy that those upon whom this fifth plague was inflicted had sores just as those in the first bowl judgment did. Though we believe Jerusalem cannot, in the context of the Apocalypse, be considered the throne of the first Beast, it is most definitely the throne of the second. As we have shown above the second Beast is the false religious system originating out of apostate Israel; its two horns being false prophets and false messiahs. The Beast in the description of the fifth bowl judgment is often *assumed* to be the first Beast. However, there is nothing else in the context of that passage that would indicate it is the first Beast and not the second that is being referred to.

The conditions within the city during the time of the march of Titus to Jerusalem and throughout the siege was a gruesome and terrible one indeed. History records the absolute atrocities that were committed therein as well as the deep fear and consternation that the people within were feeling.

"And now, as the city was engaged in a war on all sides, from these treacherous crowds of wicked men, the people of the city, between them, were like a great body torn in pieces. The aged men and the women were in such distress by their internal calamities, that they wished for the Romans, and earnestly hoped for an external war, in order to their delivery from their domestical miseries. The citizens themselves were under a terrible consternation and fear; nor had they any opportunity of taking counsel, and of changing their conduct; nor were there any hopes of coming to an agreement with their enemies; nor could such as had a mind flee away; for guards were set at all places, and the heads of the robbers, although they were seditious one against another in other respects, yet did they agree in killing those that were for peace with the Romans, or were suspected of an inclination to desert them, as their common enemies. They agreed in nothing but this, to kill those that were innocent. The noise also of those that were fighting was incessant, both by day and by night; but the lamentations of those that mourned exceeded the other; nor was there ever any occasion for them to leave off their lamentations, because their calamities came perpetually one upon another, although the deep consternation they were in prevented their outward wailing; but being constrained by their fear to conceal their inward passions, they were inwardly tormented, without daring to open their lips in groans. :Nor was any regard paid to those that were still alive, by their relations; nor was there any care taken of burial for those that were dead; the occasion of both which was this, that everyone despaired of himself; for those that were not among the seditious had no great desires of anything, as expecting for certain that they should very soon be destroyed; but for the seditious themselves, they fought against each other, while they trod upon the dead bodies as they lay heaped one upon another, and taking up a mad rage from those dead bodies that were under their feet, became the fiercer thereupon. They, moreover, were still inventing somewhat or other that was pernicious against themselves; and when they had resolved upon anything, they executed it without mercy, and omitted no method of torment or of barbarity."[320]

"As now the war abroad ceased for a while, the sedition within was revived; and on the feast of unleavened bread, which was now come, it being the fourteenth day of the month Xanthicus, [Nisan,] when it is believed the Jews were first freed from the Egyptians, Eleazar and his party opened the gates of this [inmost court of the] temple, and admitted such of the people as were desirous to worship God into it. But John made use of this festival as a cloak for his treacherous designs, and armed the most inconsiderable of his own party, the greater part of whom were not purified, with weapons concealed under their garments, and sent them with great zeal into the temple, in order to seize upon it; which armed men, when they were gotten in, threw their garments away, and presently appeared in their armor. Upon which there was a very great disorder and

---

[320] Josephus, Wars. 5.1.5. Page 698.

disturbance about the holy house; while the people, who had no concern in the sedition, supposed that this assault was made against all without distinction, as the zealots thought it was made against themselves only. So these left off guarding the gates any longer, and leaped down from their battlements before they came to an engagement, and fled away into the subterranean caverns of the temple; while the people that stood trembling at the altar, and about the holy house, were rolled on heaps together, and trampled upon, and were beaten both with wooden and with iron weapons without mercy. Such also as had differences with others slew many persons that were quiet, out of their own private enmity and hatred, as if they were opposite to the seditious; and all those that had formerly offended any of these plotters were now known, and were now led away to the slaughter; and when they had done abundance of horrid mischief to the guiltless, they granted a truce to the guilty, and let those go off that came out of the caverns."[321]

The once holy city, the city set upon a hill, the city intended to be the source of light and truth to the whole world, was now enveloped in utter fear, oppression, and darkness. Heartless murders, rape, theft, and any other number of barbarities were perpetrated upon those within the city regardless of age or gender. There was no place that was safe for hiding, including the innermost court of the temple itself. Any light of hope that remained within the walls was snuffed out and covered by the mournful cries and bloodshed that now reigned.

Given what we have in recorded history and the scriptures, we conclude that the darkness of the fifth plague refers to the consequences of the persistent blasphemous actions by apostate and impenitent Israel. Although substantial information exists to show that the darkness of the fifth plague could have been referring to the chaos and seeming demise of the Roman Empire, its application to those in Jerusalem, the throne of the second Beast, better fits the entire context and goal of the Apocalypse. After all, the scriptures are more concerned with what happens to, with, or for Yahweh's chosen people.

---

[321] Josephus, Wars. 5.3.1. Pages 701-702.

Darkness and confusion engulfed the throne of the second Beast's kingdom causing the people to grope around in spiritual darkness cursing Yahweh for their sores, blaspheming Him the entire time.

The Sixth Angel's Bowl

(12) And the sixth poured out his bowl upon the great river, the *river* Euphrates; and the water thereof was dried up, that the way might be made ready for the kings that *come* from the sunrising.

(13) And I saw *coming* out of the mouth of the dragon, and out of the mouth of the beast, and out of the mouth of the false prophet, three unclean spirits, as it were frogs:

(14) for they are spirits of demons, working signs; which go forth unto the kings of the whole world, to gather them together unto the war of the great day of Elohim, the Almighty.

(15) (Behold, I come as a thief. Blessed is he that watches, and keeps his garments, lest he walk naked, and they see his shame.)

(16) And they gathered them together into the place which is called in Hebrew Har-Magedon.

Here we see yet another highly apocalyptic passage from John. This bowl judgment is multi-faceted. First, the bowl is poured upon the Euphrates river. John's intent is not to convey that the river itself, which set the northernmost border of Israel, was to actually become a dry bed. Rather, the speed by which the troops that were to be called from the regions across the Euphrates would be such that it would seem the river itself dried up to allow them swifter passage. The historical record tells us that troops that marched with Titus to Jerusalem for the siege consisted not only of Roman legions but of auxiliaries from nations across the Euphrates.

"He found in Judaea three legions, the 5th, the 10th, and the 15th, all old troops of Vespasian's. To these he added the 12th from **Syria,** and some men belonging to the 18th and 3rd, whom he had withdrawn from Alexandria. This force was accompanied by twenty cohorts of allied troops and eight squadrons of cavalry, by the two kings Agrippa and Sohemus, by the auxiliary forces of king

Antiochus, by a **strong contingent of Arabs,** who hated the Jews with the usual hatred of neighbours, and, lastly, by many persons brought from the capital and from Italy by private hopes of securing the yet unengaged affections of the Prince."[322]

"Vespasian... Envoys had come from king Vologesus to offer him **40,000 Parthian cavalry**...He therefore entrusted Titus with the main strength of the army to complete what had yet to be done in the Jewish war."[323]

"...Vespasian as their emperor...the army in Judaea, where he then was, also swore allegiance to him...promised to join him with the Syrian army, and, among the allied kings, Vologesus, king of the **Parthians,** offered him a reinforcement of **forty thousand archers**."[324]

These soldiers came from Syria, Arabia, and Parthia, which are all countries across the Euphrates towards the "sunrising" [East].

John then tells us that he saw frogs coming out of the three apocalyptic antagonists with the mission to gather forces from the whole world to gather them for battle. First, John's use of frogs as representations of these demonic spirits need not be overlooked. Frogs were the second plague inflicted upon Egypt[325]. We read in that passage the following regarding what the frogs would do:

Exodus 8:3-4
(3) and the river shall swarm with frogs, which shall go up and come into your house, and into your bedchamber, and upon your bed, and into the house of your servants, and upon your people, and into your ovens, and into your kneading-troughs:
(4) and the frogs shall come up both upon you, and upon your people, and upon all your servants.

[322] Tacitus, Histories. Book 5, Chapter 1.
[323] Tacitus, Histories. Book 4, Chapter 51.
[324] Suetonius. Vespasian, Chapter 6.
[325] Exodus 8:1-15.

John's use of frog imagery here is to let his audience know that nothing will escape the forces gathered against the wicked and rebellious of the land. No house will be safe. Every room of every house will be searched and those hiding therein will be enslaved or killed. Regardless of one's societal position, whether they be elders, priests, women, children, slave, or free, all will be affected by the judgment of the sixth bowl.

The number of frogs and the historical record once again perfectly coincide. The following information shows how completely set the stage was for the siege against the holy city.

"...for Titus, when he had gotten together part of his forces about him, and had ordered the rest to meet him at Jerusalem, marched out of Cesarea. He had with him those **three legions** that had accompanied his father when he laid Judea waste, together with that twelfth legion which had been formerly beaten with Cestius; which legion, as it was otherwise remarkable for its valor, so did it march on now with greater alacrity to avenge themselves on the Jews, as remembering what they had formerly suffered from them. Of these legions he ordered **the fifth** to meet him, by going through Emmaus, and **the tenth** to go up by Jericho; he also moved himself, together with the rest; besides whom, marched those auxiliaries that came from the kings, being now more in number than before, together with a considerable number that came to his assistance from Syria. Those also that had been selected out of these four legions, and sent with Mucianus to Italy, had their places filled up out of these soldiers that came out of Egypt with Titus; who were two thousand men, chosen out of the armies at Alexandria. There followed him also three thousand drawn from those that guarded the river Euphrates; as also there came Tiberius Alexander, who was a friend of his, most valuable, both for his good-will to him, and for his prudence."[326]

Titus began his march toward Jerusalem with several Roman legions as

---

[326] Josephus, Wars. 5.1.6. Pages 698-699.

well as the auxiliaries from across the Euphrates. However, he ordered that two other legions, the fifth and the tenth, meet him instead at Jerusalem. The former through Emmaus to the west of Jerusalem, where it was encamped[327], and the latter through Jericho to the east. The following map illustrates this.

[327] Josephus, Wars. 4.8.1. Page 686.

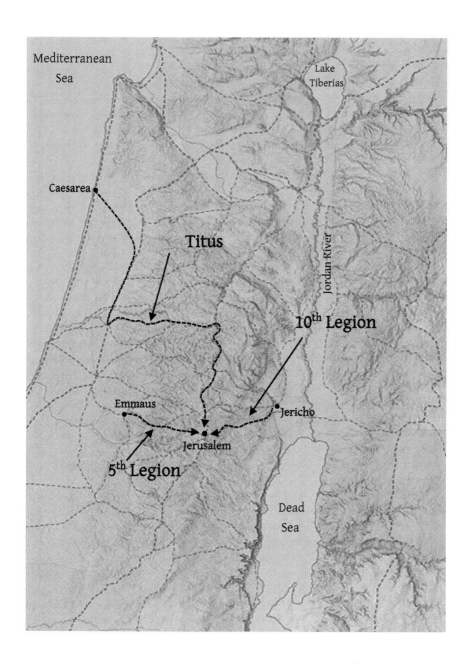

In addition to the three legions being called to meet at Jerusalem, we learn from Tacitus that the armies rallying against the city were from three different regions in the world:

> "He found in Judaea three legions, the fifth, the tenth, and the fifteenth, all old troops of Vespasian's. To these he added the twelfth from Syria, and some men belonging to the eighteenth and third, whom he had withdrawn from Alexandria. This force was accompanied by twenty cohorts of allied troops and eight squadrons of cavalry, by the two kings Agrippa and Sohemus, by the auxiliary forces of king Antiochus, by a strong contingent of Arabs, who hated the Jews with the usual hatred of neighbours, and, lastly, by many persons brought from the capital and from Italy by private hopes of securing the yet unengaged affections of the Prince. With this force Titus entered the enemy's territory, preserving strict order on his march, reconnoitring every spot, and always ready to give battle. At last he encamped near Jerusalem."[328]

Those three demonic frog spirits truly went to the world to call them for battle. Not only did Titus call his forces together from three different locations, but the forces were made up of hosts from three different regions of the known world – Italy to the North; Arabia, Parthia, and Syria to the East; and Egypt to the South. The fifth legion set its camp at a place called Scopus, a hill located west of the city with a great view. The tenth legion from Jericho was stationed on the Mount of Olives to the east of the city.

Armageddon

Many fantastical tales have developed over the years regarding this mystical place called Armageddon. However, John wasn't trying to keep his audience in the dark. Though he continued to use apocalyptic terminology, the goal of the Apocalypse was to reveal, not hide. In

---

[328] Tacitus, Histories. Book 5, Chapter 1.

verse 16 John gives us a very important clue that tells us how to interpret this symbol. He tells us that the name of the place of the gathering of these forces is to be interpreted from Hebrew. In Hebrew, the name is הַר-מְגִדּוֹן, har-megidon. Har means "mountain."[329] Megidon comes from the verb גָדַד, gadad, which, in this context[330], means "to crowd in great numbers into one place."[331]

From geography and the scriptures, we can discern that John isn't talking about a literal mountain. In the scriptures, Megiddo wasn't a mountain at all. It was a valley or plain.

> 2 Chronicles 35:22
> Nevertheless Josiah would not turn his face from him, but disguised himself, that he might fight with him, and hearkened not unto the words of Neco from the mouth of Elohim, and came to fight in **the valley of Megiddo**.

Even if the phrase was intended to refer to a valley next to a mountain called Megiddo, there is one huge problem with it from a geographic and topographic perspective. Today Megiddo, known in Israel as *Tel-Megiddo*[332], is only a thirty-five-acre mound, and that is at its base. The top of the mound is only around fifteen acres. If the traditional Futurist interpretation is correct, it would mean that a vast host of armies gathered from around the world would be gathering on top of a hill with a fifteen-acre space. This is unfeasible if not impossible.

John is telling his audience once again, similar to the number of the Beast in chapter 13 above, to peer through his words to the true meaning. The Hebrews to whom this was written would have understood the meaning of the words. John was telling them the vast host was to gather at the "place of crowds." At that time, it was Jerusalem. Jerusalem sat on the top of a mountain. During the siege, it

---

[329] Gesenius. Entry for הַר. Page 230.
[330] See also Jeremiah 5:7 and Micah 4:14 (*Heb*).
[331] Gesenius. Entry for גָדַד. Page 158.
[332] Literally "Hill of Megiddo."

was crowded with people celebrating the Feast of Unleavened Bread.

"As now the war abroad ceased for a while, the sedition within was revived; and **on the feast of unleavened bread**, which was now come, it being the fourteenth day of the month Xanthicus, [Nisan,] when it is believed the Jews were first freed from the Egyptians, Eleazar and **his party opened the gates of this** [inmost court of the] **temple, and admitted such of the people as were desirous to worship God into it.**"[333]

"Now the number of those that were carried captive during this whole war was collected to be ninety-seven thousand; as was the number of those that perished during the whole siege eleven hundred thousand, the greater part of whom were indeed of the same nation, but not belonging to the city itself; **for they were come up from all the country to the feast of unleavened bread**, and were on a sudden shut up by an army, which, at the very first, occasioned so great a straitness among them, that there came a pestilential destruction upon them, and soon afterward such a famine, as destroyed them more suddenly. And that this city could contain so many people in it, is manifest by that number of them which was taken under Cestius, who being desirous of informing Nero of the power of the city, who otherwise was disposed to contemn that nation, entreated the high priests, if the thing were possible, to take the number of their whole multitude. So these high priests, upon the coming of that feast which is called the Passover, when they slay their sacrifices, from the ninth hour till the eleventh, but so that a company not less than ten belong to every sacrifice, (for it is not lawful for them to feast singly by themselves,) and many of us are twenty in a company, found the number of sacrifices was two hundred and fifty-six thousand five hundred; which, upon the allowance of no more than ten that feast together, amounts to two millions seven hundred thousand and two hundred persons that

---

were pure and holy."[334]

It was commanded in the Torah that the men of Israel were to appear before Yahweh three times a year[335]. Hundreds of thousands of Jews would have flocked to their metropolis to celebrate this most holy time. John's message through the symbolism of "Armageddon" was that the beastly armies united against apostate Israel were going to converge on a single site, the place where Israelites flood to in droves, making it a mountain of crowded gatherings – Jerusalem. Armageddon = *Har-Megidon* = Mountain of Crowds = Jerusalem during festival times. The mysticism behind the "Battle of Armageddon" needs to be immediately forsaken. John's message is consistent and seamless. Judgment is coming upon the rebellious children of Israel and it will come to the peak of its crescendo after the armies are gathered to their capitol.

The Seventh Angel's Bowl

(17) And the seventh poured out his bowl upon the air; and there came forth a great voice out of the temple, from the throne, saying, It is done:

(18) and there were lightnings, and voices, and thunders; and there was a great earthquake, such as was not since there were men upon the earth, so great an earthquake, so mighty.

(19) And the great city was divided into into three parts, and the cities of the nations fell: and Babylon the great was remembered in the sight of Elohim, to give unto her the cup of the wine of the fierceness of his wrath.

(20) And every island fled away, and the mountains were not found.

(21) And great hail, *every stone* about the weight of a talent, comes down out of heaven upon men: and men blasphemed Elohim because of the plague of the hail; for the plague thereof is exceeding great.

---

[334] Josephus, Wars. 6.9.3. Page 749.
[335] Exodus 34:22; Deuteronomy 16:16-17.

The occurrence of the phrase "It is done" in this passage is very revealing. We can obviously discern from the remainder of the passage and from the fact that there are yet five chapters left in the Apocalypse that the "end" has not yet come. Just like the sounding of the trumpets in chapters 8, 9, and 11 above, the events which are represented by the seven angels' bowl judgments need not take place immediately after the bowl is poured out and be completed before the next bowl is poured. In fact, though the timeline of the events in history do occur chronologically in relation to their representations in the bowl judgments, it is likely each of the bowls were poured out in the heavenly realm prior to any of them having any effect on earth. After all, "what is bound on earth *shall have been bound* in heaven." Daniel declares the same of the kingdoms of the beasts represented in his vision:

> Daniel 7:9-12
> (9) I beheld till thrones were placed, and one that was ancient of days did sit: his raiment was white as snow, and the hair of his head like pure wool; his throne was fiery flames, *and* the wheels thereof burning fire.
> (10) A fiery stream issued and came forth from before him: thousands of thousands ministered unto him, and ten thousand times ten thousand stood before him: the judgment was set, and the books were opened.
> (11) I beheld at that time because of the voice of the great words which the horn spoke; I beheld even till the beast was slain, and its body destroyed, and it was given to be burned with fire.
> (12) **And as for the rest of the beasts, their dominion was taken away: yet their lives were prolonged for a season and a time.**

The beasts' dominions were their rule over the kingdoms of the world. Yet, the lives of the beasts represented their physical existence in the world. The setting up of the kingdom of heaven on the earth didn't instantly kill the beasts. They were permitted to continue in existence. But, their authority over the kingdoms of the world was stripped.

At the time that Titus was approaching the city for the siege, it was divided into three factions, each warring brutally against the other.

"And now there were **three treacherous factions** in the city, the one parted from the other. **Eleazar** and his party, that kept the sacred first-fruits, came against John in their cups. Those that were with **John** plundered the populace, and went out with zeal against Simon. This **Simon** had his supply of provisions from the city, in opposition to the seditious. When, therefore, John was assaulted on both sides, he made his men turn about, throwing his darts upon those citizens that came up against him, from the cloisters he had in his possession, while he opposed those that attacked him from the temple by his engines of war. And if at any time he was freed from those that were above him, which happened frequently, from their being drunk and tired, he sallied out with a great number upon Simon and his party; and this he did always in such parts of the city as he could come at, till he set on fire those houses that were full of corn, and of all other provisions. The same thing was done by Simon, when, upon the other's retreat, he attacked the city also; as if they had, on purpose, done it to serve the Romans, by destroying what the city had laid up against the siege, and by thus cutting off the nerves of their own power. Accordingly, it so came to pass, that all the places that were about the temple were burnt down, and were become an intermediate desert space, ready for fighting on both sides of it; and that almost all that corn was burnt, which would have been sufficient for a siege of many years. So they were taken by the means of the famine, which it was impossible they should have been, unless they had thus prepared the way for it by this procedure."[336]

As noted in the table of apocalyptic terms in the Introduction, great shakings or quakings of the heavens or the earth symbolize the shaking of kingdoms so as to destroy or distract them. This great earthquake in verse 18, which divided the "great city" into three parts was a shaking of the governing bodies of Israel to such a degree that three factions of the same people waged war against themselves, and that with the Romans at their door step. John could also be pointing his audience back to Ezekiel's prophecy made hundreds of years earlier.

---

[336] Josephus, Wars. 5.1.4. Pages 697-698.

Ezekiel 5:1-5

(1) And you, son of man, take you a sharp sword; *as* a barber's razor shall you take it unto you, and shall cause it to pass upon your head and upon your beard: then take your balances to weigh, and divide the hair.

(2) A **third part shall you burn in the fire in the midst of the city**, when the days of the siege are fulfilled; and you shall take **a third part, and smite with the sword round about it**; and **a third part you shall scatter to the wind**, and I will draw out a sword after them.

(3) And you shall take thereof a few in number, and bind them in your skirts.

(4) And of these again shall you take, and cast them into the midst of the fire, and burn them in the fire; therefrom shall a fire come forth into all the house of Israel.

(5) Thus says the Master Yahweh: This is Jerusalem; I have set her in the midst of the nations, and countries are round about her.

Yahweh specifically tells Ezekiel that the actions he is to take relate to Jerusalem. The city is divided into thirds, each third being judged in a different way. John's reference here to the prophecy of Ezekiel is revealing in a couple ways. First, it identifies the "great city" of verse 19 specifically with Jerusalem. The label "great city" will be evaluated further in chapter 17 below. Second, it once again gives John's audience insight into what they should expect to see happen to the inhabitants of Jerusalem. They will be slain by the sword, burned with fire, and brought into captivity into a foreign nation. There is yet another explanation for the city being divided into three, which we will detail shortly.

After this, Babylon was remembered in the sight of Elohim. As soon as Titus and the Roman legions had settled themselves and a battle plan was established, the siege began. Josephus gives an amazing account of the damage the war engines of the tenth legion, stationed on the Mount of Olives to the east of Jerusalem, caused.

"The engines, that all the legions had ready prepared for them, were admirably contrived; but still more extraordinary ones belonged to the tenth legion: those that threw darts and those that threw stones were more forcible and larger than the rest, by which they not only repelled the excursions of the Jews, but drove those away that were upon the walls also. Now the stones that were cast were of the weight of a talent, and were carried two furlongs and further. The blow they gave was no way to be sustained, not only by those that stood first in the way, but by those that were beyond them for a great space. As for the Jews, they at first watched the coming of the stone, for it was of a white color, and could therefore not only be perceived by the great noise it made, but could be seen also before it came by its brightness; accordingly the watchmen that sat upon the towers gave them notice when the engine was let go, and the stone came from it, and cried out aloud, in their own country language, 'THE SON COMETH' so those that were in its way stood off, and threw themselves down upon the ground; by which means, and by their thus guarding themselves, the stone fell down and did them no harm. But the Romans contrived how to prevent that by blacking the stone, who then could aim at them with success, when the stone was not discerned beforehand, as it had been till then; and so, they destroyed many of them at one blow."[337]

There are a few very telling parallels within this record to the account in verse 21. First, the hail stones thrown by this engine were specifically stated to be the weight of a talent. Second, the color of the stones, prior to the Romans coloring them for disguise, was white, just like hail. Third, and the most striking of them all, is that the Jews shouted, "The *Son* Cometh," or, "The Son is Coming" when they saw the great stone hurling towards them. In his translation of Josephus' work William Whiston provides us with a very detailed footnote regarding this translation.

"What should be the meaning of this signal or watchword, when the watchmen saw a stone coming from the engine, 'The Son Cometh,' or what mistake there is in the reading, I cannot tell. The MSS. Both

---

[337] Josephus, Wars. 5.6.3. Page 710.

Greek and Latin, all agree in this reading: and I cannot approve of any groundless conjectural alteration of the text from *huios* to *ios*, that not the *son* or a *stone*, but that the *arrow* or *dart* comes; as has been made by Dr. Hudson, and not corrected by Havercamp. Had Josephus written even the first edition of these books of the *War* in pure Hebrew, or had the Jews then used the pure Hebrew at Jerusalem, the Hebrew word for a son is so like that for a stone, *ben* and *eben*, that such a correction might have been more easily admitted. But Josephus wrote his former edition for the use of the Jews beyond Euphrates, and so in the Chaldee language, as he did this second edition in the Greek language; and *bar* was the Chaldee word for *son*, instead of the Hebrew *ben*, and was used, not only in Chaldea, etc., but in Judea also, as the New Testament informs us: Dio also lets us know, that the very Romans at Rome pronounced the name of Simon the son of Gioras, *Bar Poras* for *Bar Gioras*, as we learn from Xiphiline, p. 217. Roland takes notice, 'that many will here look for a mystery, as though the meaning were, that the Son of God came now to take vengeance on the sins of the Jewish nation;" which is indeed the truth of the fact, but hardly what the Jews could now mean: unless possibly by way of derision of Christ's threatening so often that he would come at the head of the Roman army for their destruction. But even this interpretation has but a very small degree of probability. If I were to make an emendation by mere conjecture, I would read *petros* instead of *huios*, though the likeness be not so great as in *ios*; because that is the word used by Josephus just before, as has been already noted on this very occasion, while *ios*, an arrow or dart, is only a poetical word, and never used by Josephus elsewhere, and is indeed no way suitable to the occasion, this engine was not throwing arrows or darts, but great stones, at this time."

Whiston's great defense here leads us to believe that the translation "The Son is Coming" is indeed what Josephus intended. The blasphemy of the men as a result of this hail plague may very well have been their boastful mocking of the war engines of the Romans. Regardless of whether one considers the translation of that phrase accurate doesn't remove the unbelievable accuracy of the historical record as compared to the text of the Apocalypse. The timeline has remained completely consistent. Titus and his forces all gathered together at the "place of crowds," *Har-Megidon*, and the deadly onslaught of the siege had begun.

After Titus' engines had been setup, we read the following:

> "Then did Titus set his engines at proper distances, so much nearer to the wall, that the Jews might not be able to repel them, and gave orders they should go to work; and when thereupon **a prodigious noise echoed** round about from **three places**, and that on the sudden there was a great noise made by the citizens that were within the city, and no less a terror fell upon the seditious themselves; whereupon both sorts, seeing the common danger they were in, contrived to make a like defense. So **those of different factions cried out one to another**, that they acted entirely as in concert with their enemies; whereas they ought however, notwithstanding God did not grant them a lasting concord, in their present circumstances, to lay aside their enmities one against another, and to unite together against the Romans."[338]

The talent-sized stones thrown by these engines were the first of the attacks upon the city, the beginning of the end. This passage shows yet another example of the great city being divided into three parts. The great shaking of the apocalyptic heavens had become a shocking and awesome reality to the people of the city. The attack had begun and the cries of fear for their lives echoed through the city from the three different parts. The time of the utter destruction and desolation of Babylon the great city had come.

At this point we believe it is of great prudence to look back at the final verses of this chapter, those pertaining to the seventh angel's bowl, to compare them to what Yeshua said of his second appearing.

> (17) And the seventh poured out his bowl upon the air; and **there came forth a great voice out of the temple**, from the throne, saying, **It is done**:

---

[338] Josephus, Wars. 5.6.4. Page 711.

(18) and **there were lightnings**, and **voices**, and **thunders**; and **there was a great earthquake**, such as was not since there were men upon the earth, so great an earthquake, so mighty.
(19) And the great city was divided into three parts, and the cities of the nations fell: and Babylon the great was remembered in the sight of Elohim, to give unto her the cup of the wine of the fierceness of his wrath.
(20) And every island fled away, and the mountains were not found.
(21) And **great hail**, *every stone* about the weight of a talent, comes down out of heaven upon men: and men blasphemed Elohim because of **the plague of the hail**; for the plague thereof is exceeding great.

The three accounts of Yeshua's return in judgment all speak of very similar things:

Matthew 24:29-30
(29) But immediately after the tribulation of those days *the sun shall be darkened, and the moon shall not give her light, and the stars shall fall* from **heaven**, and **the powers of the heavens shall be shaken:**
(30) and then shall appear the sign of the Son of man in heaven: and then shall all the tribes of the earth mourn, and they shall see the *Son of man coming on the clouds of heaven* with power and great glory.

Mark 13:24-26
(24) But in those days, after that tribulation, *the sun shall be darkened, and the moon shall not give her light,*
(25) *and the stars shall be falling* from **heaven**, and **the powers that are in the heavens shall be shaken.**
(26) And then shall they see *the Son of man coming in clouds* with great power and glory.

Luke 21:25-27
(25) And **there shall be signs in sun and moon and stars**; and **upon the earth distress of nations**, in perplexity for **the roaring of the sea and the billows;**

(26) **men fainting for fear, and for expectation of the things which are coming on the world: for the powers of the heavens shall be shaken.**

(27) And then shall they see *the Son of man coming in a cloud* with power and great glory.

Yeshua himself is bringing in prophecies from Isaiah spoken hundreds of years earlier. The context of these passages is essential so we've chosen to quote significant portions of them here. Let the reader take the time to soak the messages of these prophecies in and remember that the "earth" in these prophetic utterances very often refer specifically to the "land" of Israel.

Isaiah 13:10-16
(10) For the **stars of heaven and the constellations thereof shall not give their light; the sun shall be darkened in its going forth,** and **the moon shall not cause its light to shine.**
(11) And I will punish the world for *their* evil, and the wicked for their iniquity: and I will cause the arrogance of the proud to cease, and will lay low the haughtiness of the terrible.
(12) I will make a man more rare than fine gold, even a man than the pure gold of Ophir.
(13) Therefore **I will make the heavens to tremble, and the land shall be shaken out of its place**, in the wrath of Yahweh of hosts, and in the day of his fierce anger.
(14) And it shall come to pass, that as the chased roe, and as sheep that no man gathers, they shall turn every man to his own people, and shall flee every man to his own land.
(15) **Every one that is found shall be thrust through; and every one that is taken shall fall by the sword.**
(16) **Their infants also shall be dashed in pieces before their eyes; their houses shall be rifled, and their wives ravished.**

Isaiah 24:1-13, 17-23
(1) Behold, Yahweh **makes the land empty, and makes it waste,** and **turns it upside down, and scatters abroad the inhabitants thereof.**
(2) And it shall be, as with **the people,** so with **the priest;** as with **the servant,** so with **his master;** as with **the maid,** so with **her**

mistress; as with **the buyer**, so with **the seller;** as with **the creditor**, so with **the debtor;** as with **the taker of interest**, so with **the giver of interest** to him.

(3) The **land shall be utterly emptied**, and **utterly laid waste**; for Yahweh has spoken this word.

(4) **The land mourns and fades away, the world languishes and fades away, the lofty people of the land do languish.**

(5) **The land also is polluted under the inhabitants thereof;** because they have transgressed the Torah, violated the statutes, broken the everlasting covenant.

(6) Therefore has **the curse devoured the land**, and they that dwell therein are found guilty: therefore **the inhabitants of the land are burned**, and **few men left**.

(7) The new wine mourns, the vine languishes, all the merry-hearted do sigh.

(8) The mirth of tabrets ceases, the noise of them that rejoice ends, the joy of the harp ceases.

(9) They shall not drink wine with a song; strong drink shall be bitter to them that drink it.

(10) **The waste city is broken down; every house is shut up**, that no man may come in.

(11) There is a **crying in the streets** because of the wine; **all joy is darkened, the mirth of the land is gone**.

(12) In **the city is left desolation, and the gate is smitten with destruction**.

(13) For thus shall it be in the midst of the land among the peoples, as the shaking of an olive-tree, as the gleanings when the vintage is done...

(17) Fear, and the pit, and the snare, are upon you, O inhabitant of the earth.

(18) And it shall come to pass, that he who flees from the noise of the fear shall fall into the pit; and he that comes up out of the midst of the pit shall be taken in the snare: for the windows on high are opened, and **the foundations of the land tremble**.

(19) **The land is utterly broken, the land is rent asunder, the land is shaken violently**.

(20) The land shall stagger like a drunken man, and shall sway to and fro like a hammock; and the transgression thereof shall be heavy upon it, and it shall fall, and not rise again.

(21) And it shall come to pass in that day, that **Yahweh will punish the host of the high ones on high**, and **the kings of the land upon the land.**
(22) And they shall be gathered together, as prisoners are gathered in the pit, and **shall be shut up in the prison**; and after many days shall they be visited.
(23) Then **the moon shall be confounded**, and **the sun ashamed**; for Yahweh of hosts will reign in mount Zion, and in Jerusalem; and before his elders shall be glory.

Can one read the prophecies of Yeshua and Isaiah above and *not* see the absolute desolation and destruction of Jerusalem therein? The signs and events outlined in the last few verses of this chapter of the Apocalypse aren't speaking of actual earthquakes, lightning, and mountains or islands moving out of their places. These are speaking of the absolute shaking that was to happen to the apocalyptic heavenly and earthly bodies. The people of all echelons of society, from the priests to the foot washers, were to be punished. Every established institution, religious or political, was to be brought low and destroyed. All these things occurred after Yeshua's coming in his kingdom and the inflicting of the final judgments upon Jerusalem.

The historical information provided in this chapter and the ones previous detail explicitly how even the literal renderings of these passages were fulfilled upon Israel and Jerusalem. The land was emptied and laid waste. The houses were rifled, the infants were dashed to pieces, and the wives were ravished. The curses of Deuteronomy 28 devoured the land and the inhabitants were burned. The Romans thrust anyone they found through with the sword.

As if more evidence needed to be provided we find yet another amazing parallel at the end of Isaiah 24. There we are told that Yahweh is to reign in Mount Zion and in Jerusalem. This obviously can't be in the city or with the people that were just spoken of as being utterly laid waste and destroyed. Yahweh reigning here is in the new Jerusalem. The next chapter in Isaiah makes this even clearer as it discusses the final abolition of death itself. This concept will be discussed in chapters 21 and 22 below, but for now it should suffice to say that the order of

Isaiah's prophecies is perfectly aligned with the destruction of Jerusalem and the setting up of the new kingdom. First the old, wicked, and rebellions city is destroyed, then the new and righteous city is established and inhabited by Elohim.

Let the reader now recall our brief discussion on the preview of future events that John supplied his readers with in the account of the seventh angel's trumpet in chapter 11 above. Verse 19 of that chapter spoke of the same great and terrible heavenly and earthly signs that we see taking place in this final bowl judgment. John wasn't telling his audience in chapter 11 that they should expect to see those lightnings, voices, etc., immediately after the blowing of the seventh angel's trumpet. He was giving his audience the information they needed to weave the various accounts describing the coming of Yeshua together, each of which followed the sounding of the seventh angel's trumpet. The events mentioned in this account of the seventh angel's bowl is one of those.

Yeshua's Coming With the Clouds

In Revelation 1:7 above, we read the following:

Behold, he comes with the clouds, and **every eye shall see him,** and they that pierced him; and all the tribes of the earth shall mourn over him. Even so, Amein.

This "coming with the clouds" concept is found several other times in the scriptures and refers to judgment coming upon that nation via another's military force. This is a very important point that we need to emphasize. Most followers of Yeshua, Futurist or otherwise, place the second coming, or more correctly "appearing"[339], in Revelation 19 when we see him riding a white horse from heaven. However, the following passages of scripture tell us how "clouds" were understood in prophetic terms:

---

[339] Gr. Παρουσία.

Isaiah 19:1
(1) The burden of Egypt. Behold, **Yahweh rides upon a swift cloud**, and comes unto Egypt: and the idols of Egypt shall tremble at his presence; and the heart of Egypt shall melt in the midst of it.

Jeremiah 4:13
(13) Behold, **he shall come up as clouds**, and his chariots *shall be* as the whirlwind: his horses are swifter than eagles. Woe unto us! for we are ruined.

Ezekiel 30:2-4
(2) Son of man, prophesy, and say, Thus says the Master Yahweh: Wail you, Alas for the day!
(3) For the day is near, even the day of Yahweh is near; **it shall be a day of clouds**, a time of the nations.
(4) And a sword shall come upon Egypt, and anguish shall be in Ethiopia, when the slain shall fall in Egypt; and they shall take away her multitude, and her foundations shall be broken down.

Joel 2:1-2
(1) Blow you the trumpet in Zion, and sound an alarm in my holy mountain; let all the inhabitants of the land tremble: for the day of Yahweh comes, for it is near at hand;
(2) a day of darkness and gloominess, **a day of clouds** and thick darkness, as the dawn spread upon the mountains; **a great people and a strong**; there has not been ever the like, neither shall be any more after them, even to the years of many generations.

Zephaniah 1:14-16
(14) The great day of Yahweh is near, it is near and hastes greatly, *even* the voice of the day of Yahweh; the mighty man cries there bitterly.
(15) That day is a day of wrath, a day of trouble and distress, a day of wasteness and desolation, a day of darkness and gloominess, **a day of clouds** and thick darkness,
(16) a day of the trumpet and alarm, against the fortified cities, and against the high battlements.

Most of the passages above, with the exceptions of Isaiah 19:1 and possibly Joel 2:1-2, refer to the coming of the Babylonian kingdom, ruled by Nebuchadnezzar, to destroy Jerusalem and the temple. Jeremiah 4:13 is very telling in that it specifically says "he shall come up as clouds," referring to Nebuchadnezzar and his hosts. Each of these prophecies use the word "clouds" in reference to a day or days coming wherein the people and nation specified were to be destroyed by a foreign army. There is no difference here in Revelation 16. The "clouds" that Yeshua came with were the hosts of the Roman armies.

That Yeshua's coming at the pouring out of this seventh angel's bowl is one of judgment and vengeance is proven by the descriptions he himself gave as well as the prophets before him. This is what Yeshua had to say about his appearing in his response to his apostles' question:

Matthew 24:27-31
(27) For as the lightning comes forth from the east, and is seen even unto the west; so shall be the coming of the Son of man.
(28) Wherever the carcass is, there will the eagles be gathered together.
(29) But immediately after the tribulation of those days *the sun shall be darkened, and the moon shall not give her light, and the stars shall fall* from heaven, and the powers of the heavens shall be shaken:
(30) and then shall appear the sign of the Son of man in heaven: and then shall all the tribes of the earth mourn, and they shall see the **Son of man coming on the clouds of heaven with power and great glory**.
(31) And he shall send forth his angels with *a great sound of a trumpet,* and *they shall gather together* his elect from the four winds, from one end of heaven to the other.

Mark 13:24-27
(24) But in those days, after that tribulation, *the sun shall be darkened, and the moon shall not give her light,*
(25) *and the stars shall be falling* from heaven, and the powers that are in the heavens shall be shaken.
(26) And then shall they see **the Son of man coming in clouds**

with great power and glory.
(27) And then shall he send forth the angels, and shall gather together his elect from the four winds, from the uttermost part of the earth to the uttermost part of heaven.

Luke 21:25-28
(25) And there shall be signs in sun and moon and stars; and upon the earth distress of nations, in perplexity for the roaring of the sea and the billows;
(26) men fainting for fear, and for expectation of the things which are coming on the world: for the powers of the heavens shall be shaken.
(27) And then shall they see *the Son of man coming in a cloud* **with power and great glory**.
(28) But when these things begin to come to pass, look up, and lift up your heads; because your redemption draws near.

Yeshua made it perfectly clear that his appearing would be, like the other prophetic examples before him, with the clouds. People would see and understand the vengeance coming upon them because of the prophetic imagery they were familiar with. Yeshua's "coming on the clouds of heaven" is an apocalyptic way of saying that his appearing will be one of judgment, vengeance and wrath, not of salvation and mercy as it was the first time.

Yeshua's and John's use of the cloud imagery as it relates to his appearing is also intended to bring their audiences back to the prophecies in Daniel.

Daniel 7:13-14
(13) I saw in the night-visions, and, behold, **there came with the clouds of heaven one like unto a son of man**, and he came even to the ancient of days, and they brought him near before him.
(14) And there was given him dominion, and glory, and a kingdom, that all the peoples, nations, and languages should serve him: his dominion is an everlasting dominion, which shall not pass away, and his kingdom that which shall not be destroyed.

We have addressed several portions of this prophecy in different chapters above. However, in this instance we need to focus on the fact that this son of man is coming with the clouds of heaven, just as Yeshua did. In this prophecy, the son of man is coming to receive the kingdom of heaven, the one that is to rule over all and last unto eternity. Yeshua also spoke the following parable about coming in his kingdom, which contains some very powerful truths.

Matthew 21:33-45

(33) Hear another parable: There was a man that was a householder, who *planted a vineyard, and set a hedge about it, and dug a winepress in it, and built a tower,* and let it out to husbandmen, and went into another country.

(34) And when the season of the fruits drew near, he sent his servants to the husbandmen, to receive his fruits.

(35) And the husbandmen took his servants, and beat one, and killed another, and stoned another.

(36) Again, he sent other servants more than the first: and they did unto them in like manner.

(37) But afterward he sent unto them his son, saying, They will reverence my son.

(38) But the husbandmen, when they saw the son, said among themselves, This is the heir; come, let us kill him, and take his inheritance.

(39) And they took him, and cast him forth out of the vineyard, and killed him.

(40) When therefore the master of the vineyard shall come, what will he do unto those husbandmen?

(41) They say unto him, He will miserably destroy those miserable men, and will let out the vineyard unto other husbandmen, who shall render him the fruits in their seasons.

(42) Yeshua said unto them, Did you never read in the scriptures, *The stone which the builders rejected, The same was made the head of the corner; This was from Yahweh, And it is marvelous in our eyes?*

(43) Therefore say I unto you, The kingdom of Elohim shall be taken away from you, and shall be given to a nation bringing forth the fruits thereof.

(44) And he that falls on this stone shall be broken to pieces: but

on whomsoever it shall fall, it will scatter him as dust.
(45) And when the chief priests and the Pharisees heard his
parables, they perceived that he spoke of them.

Let's closely evaluate this parable. The man, the householder, is
Yahweh. The servants he sent were his prophets of old. The
husbandmen were the corrupt, idolatrous, and wicked Jews of the past
who hated, slandered, and killed Yahweh's prophets. The son is
Yeshua. Again, the husbandmen, the wicked Jews, murdered the heir
to the throne of the kingdom. The master of the vineyard is once again
Yahweh.

When the chief priests and Pharisees, who were listening on, were
asked by Yeshua, "What would the master do to those husbandmen?,"
they suddenly understood the parable. Yeshua told them that the
kingdom they thought was theirs to rule over was to be snatched from
them. They realized that Yeshua was referring to *them*, the ones
standing there before him, the chief priests and Pharisees of *that*
generation. Within the same generation of those wicked husbandmen,
those corrupt Jews who were listening on, the master of the vineyard
would return. At that time, He would take the kingdom from them,
give it to another people, and destroy them. That is exactly what
happened at the appearing of Yeshua coming on the apocalyptic clouds
of heaven.

A brief recapitulation of the chronological record surrounding these
events is now merited. Referring to the passages in Matthew, Mark,
and Luke above, we can see that he said he would appear again after
that time of great tribulation had passed and the heavens had been
utterly shaken. In taking the three accounts together we can discern
that the period of the tribulation was to last right up until the coming
of Yeshua. After the Jerusalem assembly had fled from the city in mid-
late spring of 68 CE, their tribulation was over, but the tribulation
within Judea and Jerusalem was far from over. From that point forward
the focus was solely on pouring out the final judgments upon the
wicked and rebellious children of Israel.

After Vespasian was made aware of Nero's suicide he made haste to return to Rome to settle affairs there. This was the time we've discussed above known as the "Year of the Four Emperors." This was a period of great chaos, war, and death for both Rome and Israel. Galba had taken the throne of Rome. At that time, Titus was commanded by his father to go to Rome to greet the new emperor. While on the way Galba was killed after having reigned for only seven months and seven days. Josephus then tells us the following:

> "And now they were both in suspense about the public affairs, the Roman empire being then in a fluctuating condition, and **did not go on with their expedition against the Jews**, but thought that to make any attack upon foreigners was now unseasonable, on account of the solicitude they were in for their own country."[340]

Thus, the war against the Jews by the Romans was temporarily suspended. However, the war between the Jews themselves was hardly over. The spiritual Dragon and Beast were still wreaking havoc wherever they could. An intelligent and courageous man by the name of Simon ben Giora began an expedition throughout Idumea and the lower parts of Judea. While doing so he amassed a great army upwards of twenty thousand. He led his armies into various cities, overcoming them, and destroying everything of nature, leaving behind him, as it was, a desert. His wife was seized by the zealots, which enraged him greatly. His actions taken against the people in Jerusalem after her capture was described by Josephus as one "like wild beasts when they are wounded." Appalled by the severity of his punishments the people and the zealots agreed to release his wife to him, at which point he calmed down a little. At this point civil war and sedition prevailed in Judea and Jerusalem.[341]

Meanwhile, in Rome, after Galba's death, Otho had taken the reins of the Empire. Wars and slaughters occurred between his faction and those who sided with another one vying for the throne, Vitellius. After a reign of only three months and two days Otho killed himself.

---

[340] Josephus, Wars. 4.9.2. Page 688.
[341] Josephus, Wars. 4.9.8-9. Page 690.

Vespasian, having been encamped this whole time at Caesarea, decided to move forward with his campaign in Judea, marching against those places that had not yet been overthrown. We mentioned this in chapter 14 above when discussing the treading of the winepress. This renewal of his campaign began on the fifth of the month Daesius[342], which is the same as June 13, 69 CE.

In and around Jerusalem itself the sedition continued. John of Gischala, one of the leaders of the other two factions that formed in the city, was subject to a mutiny. His own army decided to form a sedition against him. In so doing, however, one of the decisions they made was to foolishly allow the tyrant Simon with open arms into the city. Upon entering and being lauded by the people therein as their savior and protector, Simon had successfully gained possession of most Jerusalem in the month Xanthicus [Nisan][343].

Rome was at that time still in a state of flux and great chaos. After Vespasian had overthrown all the cities and towns around Jerusalem, he returned to Caesarea. Upon hearing of the troubles in the Empire and the transfer of power thereof to Vitellius, he became enraged. Vespasian's soldiers counseled among themselves and, after meeting with the general himself, declared him openly their emperor. Vespasian's crown was not officially secured until he was recognized by the Senate at the end of the year, late December 69 CE. After his confirmation, Vespasian once again turned his thoughts towards Judea and what yet remained unsubdued. Thus, he sent his son Titus with a select party of his army to destroy Jerusalem.[344] Here, having traced much of the period of history we already have in previous chapters, we have now arrived at the point where the seven angel's judgment bowls are poured out in the heavenly realm, soon to result in their earthly realities.

As we read above, the very first of the attacks of the Romans against

---

[342] Daesius is the Macedonian equivalent to the Hebrew month Sivan.
[343] Josephus, Wars. 4.9.9-11. Pages 690-691.
[344] Josephus, Wars. 4.10-4.11. Pages 692-696.

the city were talent-sized stones. When these stones were cast towards the city the watchmen cried aloud, "The Son is Coming!" Similar to what we read in Isaiah 19 quoted above, Yeshua, instead of Yahweh, was riding on the clouds of judgment and vengeance inflicting the first death blows upon the harlot city. The cries of the people at the sight of the "Son" coming showed that their hearts had melted within them and their spirits had failed. In returning once again to the accounts of Matthew, Mark, and Luke above, we see that after the great tribulation against the true assembly of Yeshua had ended and the conquering of Judea was completed, the siege of Jerusalem started, and the Son of man came on the clouds of heaven.

When everything above is taken together, we can see that John is confirming that Yeshua did indeed come with the clouds in vengeance and judgment at this very time, at the casting of that first great hail stone by the war engine of the Roman tenth legion, in a siege that began on the day of Passover in 70 CE. No eye was spared the sight of the Roman war machine which surrounded the city and no heart was free from melting in fear of the great destruction and doom that had come upon them.

CHAPTER SEVENTEEN

The Great Harlot

(1) And there came one of the seven angels that had the seven bowls, and spoke with me, saying, Come here, I will show you the judgment of the great harlot that sits upon many waters; (2) with whom the kings of the earth committed fornication, and they that dwell in the earth were made drunken with the wine of her fornication.

Chapters 17 and 18 are very clearly parenthetical breaks in the normal flow of the Apocalypse. John's focus moves from statements regarding absolute and complete destructions and judgments into a chapter describing the nature, character, and ultimate identity of Babylon. As we read and study the scriptures we will see that this break is in every way merited. John ends his previous statements with a qualification – a "and Babylon the great was remembered in the sight of Elohim, to give unto her the cup of the wine of the fierceness of his wrath." This statement should give every student of the scriptures pause. After all, didn't we just read in chapter 15 verse 1 that the bowls of the seven angels are "the last, for in them is finished the wrath of Elohim?" Yet, here we see that Yahweh's wrath is apparently still incomplete as it still has to be poured upon Babylon the great. How can we reconcile these apparently contradictory statements?

They are reconciled by the concept we have repeated several times above. The trumpet and bowl judgments are poured out in the heavens before any effect resulting from them takes place on the earth. John is seeing the angels blow their trumpets and pouring out their bowls in a vision in the heavens. There is no mention of John shifting his gaze from heaven to earth between each trumpet or bowl. It isn't until after the trumpets are blown and after the bowls are poured out that the effects of them take place upon the earth. In chapter 16 verses 19-21 we see the very beginning of the earthly effects of these heavenly judgments taking place. John, after announcing how the beginning of these judgments is to take place, pauses to give clarity and certainty to his audience regarding the identity and outcome of Babylon, the great city.

As we enter these two parenthetical chapters of the Apocalypse we'll open with a very poignant quote from James Stuart Russell[345].

> "We now approach a part of our investigation in which we are about to make great demands upon the candour and impartiality of the reader, and must ask for a patient and unbiased weighing of the evidence that shall be brought before him. Possibly we may run counter to many prepossessions, but if the seat of judgment be occupied by an impartial love of the truth, we do not fear an adverse decision."

Well said. The view presented by Mr. Russell and others[346] is contrary to the many different theories that have been espoused throughout the last nineteen generations. Beliefs on the identity of this mysterious figure abound. Some believe it speaks of the Roman Empire. Others believe it speaks of the Papacy. Still others believe it speaks of a revived Roman or Babylonian empire in the future. But is this what the context of both the scriptures and history tell us? Is there an alternative option? We believe that when the context of the scriptures is properly exegeted and the historical record is properly referenced her identity becomes clear and undeniable. Babylon the great harlot is

---

[345] Russell. Page 482.
[346] Chilton, Desperez, et al.

none other than earthly Jerusalem in the time of Yeshua.

Dissecting this chapter verse by verse is essential to ascertain her identity as Jerusalem, especially given the doctrinal biases that have been perpetuated for generations. First, we see that this character is labeled a harlot. Keeping afresh in our minds the fact that John is using prophetic imagery to convey the message to his audience, we must search the scriptures to see which ones John is referencing here.

Isaiah 1:21
How is the faithful city **become a harlot**! she that was full of justice! righteousness lodged in her, but now murderers.

Isaiah 57:7-8
(7) Upon a high and lofty mountain have you set your bed; thither also went you up to offer sacrifice.
(8) And behind the doors and the posts have you set up your memorial: for you have uncovered *yourself* to another than me, and are gone up; you have enlarged your bed, and made you a covenant with them: you loved their bed where you saw it.

Jeremiah 2:2, 22
(2) Go, and cry in the ears of Jerusalem, saying, Thus says Yahweh, I remember for you the kindness of your youth, the love of your espousals; how you went after me in the wilderness, in a land that was not sown.
(20) For of old time I have broken your yoke, and burst your bonds; and you said, I will not serve; for upon every high hill and under every green tree you did bow yourself, **playing the harlot**.

Jeremiah 3:1-3, 6, 14, 20
(1) They say, If a man put away his wife, and she go from him, and become another man's, will he return unto her again? will not that land be greatly polluted? But you have **played the harlot with many lovers**; yet return again to me, says Yahweh.
(2) Lift up your eyes unto the bare heights, and see; where have you not been lain with? By the ways have you sat for them, as an Arabian in the wilderness; and **you have polluted the land with your whoredoms** and with your wickedness.

(3) Therefore the showers have been withheld, and there has been no latter rain; yet **you have a harlot's forehead**, you refused to be ashamed.
(6) Moreover Yahweh said unto me in the days of Josiah the king, Hast you seen that which backsliding Israel has done? she is gone up upon every high mountain and under every green tree, and there has **played the harlot**.
(14) Return, O backsliding children, says Yahweh; for **I am a husband unto you**: and I will take you one of a city, and two of a family, and I will bring you to Zion.
(20) Surely as **a wife treacherously departs from her husband, so have you dealt treacherously with me**, O house of Israel, says Yahweh.

Jeremiah 4:30
(30) And you, when you are made desolate, what will you do? Though you clothe yourself with scarlet, though you deck yourself with ornaments of gold, though you enlarge your eyes with paint, in vain do you make yourself fair; *your* **lovers** despise you, they seek your life.

Jeremiah 13:27
(27) I have seen your abominations, even **your adulteries**, and your neighing, the lewdness of **your whoredom**, on the hills in the field. Woe unto you, O **Jerusalem**! you will not be made clean; how long shall it yet be?

In Ezekiel 16 Yahweh describes in detail how he found, cleaned, and married his bride. We then read what happened after He had done so:

Ezekiel 16:15-18, 25-26, 28-29, 32-35
(15) But you did trust in your beauty, and **played the harlot** because of your renown, and **poured out your whoredoms** on every one that passed by; his it was.
(16) And you did take of your garments, and made for you high places decked with diverse colors, and **played the harlot** upon them: *the like things* shall not come, neither shall it be *so*.
(17) You did also take your fair jewels of my gold and of my silver, which I had given you, and made for you images of men,

and did **play the harlot** with them;

(18) and you took your broidered garments, and covered them, and did set my oil and my incense before them.

(25) You have built your lofty place at the head of every way, and have made your beauty an abomination, and have opened your feet to everyone that passed by, and **multiplied your whoredom.**

(26) You have also **committed fornication** with the Egyptians, your neighbors, great of flesh; and have **multiplied your whoredom,** to provoke me to anger.

(28) You have **played the harlot** also with the Assyrians, because you were insatiable; yea, you have **played the harlot** with them, and yet you were not satisfied.

(29) You have moreover **multiplied your whoredom** unto the land of traffic, unto Chaldea; and yet you were not satisfied herewith.

(32) A **wife that commits adultery!** that takes strangers instead of her husband!

(33) They give gifts to all harlots; but you give your gifts to all your lovers, and bribe them, that they may come unto you on every side for **your whoredoms.**

(34) And you are different from *other* women in your whoredoms, in that none follows you to **play the harlot**; and whereas you give hire, and no hire is given unto you, therefore you are different.

(35) Wherefore, **O harlot**, hear the word of Yahweh.

The account goes on and on. Need we any more scriptural evidence to prove that Jerusalem can be, and indeed had been labeled a "harlot" by the Almighty? Yeshua himself specifically labeled the people of his generations "evil and adulterous."

Matthew 12:39
(39) But he answered and said unto them, An **evil and adulterous generation** seeks after a sign; and there shall no sign be given to it but the sign of Jonah the prophet.

Mark 8:38
(38) For whosoever shall be ashamed of me and of my words in

this **adulterous and sinful generation**, the Son of man also shall be ashamed of him, when he comes in the glory of his Father with the holy angels.

The identification of Jerusalem as an adulterous harlot shouldn't come as a surprise given that she has already been equated to Sodom and Egypt[347]. The harlotry spoken of throughout the prophets, which John is no doubt referencing here in identifying Babylon, refers unquestionably to spiritual adultery. One cannot commit adultery unless they are first married. Likewise, Babylon's label as the "great harlot" means that she was at one point in a covenant, marital relationship with Yahweh. No other nation has been in a covenant bond of marriage with Yahweh except Israel. This fact alone goes a long way in proving that Babylon, the great city, is none other than Jerusalem. Rome, for instance, cannot be a spiritual adulteress since she had never been in a covenant relationship with Yahweh. John's audience would have known this since the appellation of "harlot" was so common for Jerusalem in the scriptures.

We also read that the harlot is she who sits upon many waters. Under certain circumstances the phrase "many waters" might be one that comes with a greater degree of explanation required given the prophetic and apocalyptic language used throughout the Apocalypse. However, the text in verse 15 leaves us without any question as to its meaning here. The "many waters" are one and the same with "peoples, multitudes, nations, and tongues."

Some will contest that this could ever apply to Jerusalem, especially when contrasted with pagan Rome. But, Josephus clarifies exactly how widespread the influence of Jerusalem was over the world.

> "And from king David, who was the first of the Jews who reigned therein, to this destruction under Titus, were one thousand one hundred and seventy-nine years; but from its first building, till this last destruction, were two thousand one hundred and seventy-seven

---

[347] Revelation 11:8.

years; yet has not its great antiquity, nor its vast riches, nor **the diffusion of its nation over all the habitable earth,** nor the greatness of the veneration paid to it on a religious account, been sufficient to preserve it from being destroyed. And thus ended the siege of **Jerusalem.**"[348]

"For as **the Jewish nation is widely dispersed over all the habitable earth among its inhabitants.**"[349]

From the time of Solomon, when the riches of nations across the known world were brought into its gates, until its destruction in 70 CE, Jerusalem had an enormous influence over the world. Josephus' use of the word "diffusion" is quite poignant given the context of the Apocalypse and its identification of Babylon. Whatever adulterous actions were taking place in Jerusalem would have easily found their way to the ends of the known world.

Going back up to verse 2 we get further clarification on what is intended by her sitting upon many waters. The kings and rulers of the earth committed fornication with her and were made drunk with the wine of that fornication. She "slept around" with many nations, spiritually speaking, and the people in those many nations were consumed with the results of that harlotry.

The Adorned Woman

(3) And he carried me away in the spirit into a wilderness: and I saw a woman sitting upon a scarlet-colored beast, full of names of blasphemy, having seven heads and ten horns.
(4) And the woman was arrayed in purple and scarlet, and decked with gold and precious stone and pearls, having in her hand a golden cup full of abominations, even the unclean things of her fornication,
(5) and upon her forehead a name written, Mystery, Babylon

---

[348] Josephus, Wars. 6.10.1. Page 750.
[349] Josephus, Wars. 7.3.3. Page 753.

the Great, the mother of the harlots and of the abominations of the earth.

(6) And I saw the woman drunken with the blood of the saints, and with the blood of the martyrs of Yeshua. And when I saw her, I wondered with a great wonder.

Here we see that this woman rides a scarlet-colored Beast. The identity and description of this Beast were detailed previously in chapter thirteen above. However, it is worth noting briefly the characteristics of this scarlet beast that allows us to equate it to the one described in chapter 13 of the Apocalypse. This Beast also has seven heads and ten horns. The horns of this Beast represent kings or rulers, signified by diadems in chapter 13 and by explicit mention later in this chapter in verse 12. Commentators such as John Gill, Adam Clarke, and Albert Barnes agree, pointing their readers back to chapter 13 for more detailed descriptions of the same.

There are some that would say Babylon cannot be Jerusalem because she never had control over the Roman Empire. However, nowhere in this passage do we see that the woman riding the Beast is in control of it. In fact, the only thing we are told is that the Beast "carries" the woman. The Beasts of the Apocalypse are clearly not domesticated animals. They are wild, unpredictable, and uncontrolled. Babylon had just about as much control over the Beast she was being carried by as a bull rider has over the animal attempting to buck him off. Jerusalem may be a spur in the Beast's side prompting it to move in certain instances, but the Beast is still in control.

The woman is also described as being clothed with purple and scarlet robes and decked with gold and precious stones. Seeing that the apocalyptic symbol of Babylon is clearly referring to a city[350], not an individual, we need not look for people who adorned themselves with articles similar to those described above. Quotes from the historical record in chapter 18 below will present an overabundance of information that should allow any honest inquirer of the truth to see

---

[350] Revelation 17:18.

how Jerusalem was indeed "adorned" with the beauties of purple and scarlet robes, gold, precious stones, and the like. However, even if we were to point to specific individuals we need not go any further than the descriptions of the garments of the high priests[351]. There we find that cloths of blue, purple, scarlet and white, along with gold and precious stones such as onyx, sapphire, emerald, diamond, topaz and more. If any individuals were guiltier of spiritual adultery than others in Israel it would be the Roman-installed high priests of Jerusalem, so easily bought by their lust for riches.

John starts the name of this woman with "Mystery," which would appear to be another way he is telling his audience, "Here is wisdom." The Apocalypse, after all, is to be a revealing of the truth, not a shrouding of it in mysticism. As usual, though, John supplies us with plenty of information to solve this "mystery."

Jerusalem, being the religious center of the Jewish commonwealth, was the place from where false doctrine and wicked, idolatrous practices would have disseminated from. In this way, she is the "mother" of all harlots. Every institution or synagogue established by her throughout the world propagated her same lies. Referring to Ezekiel's prophecy we read the following:

Ezekiel 16:44
Behold, every one that uses proverbs shall use *this* proverb against you, saying, **As is the mother, so is her daughter.**

That this generation was so engulfed in sin is evidenced by the testimony of Josephus.

"It is therefore impossible to go distinctly over every instance of these men's iniquity. I shall therefore speak my mind here at once briefly: That neither did any other city ever suffer such miseries,

---

[351] Exodus 39.

nor did any age ever breed a generation more fruitful in wickedness than this was, from the beginning of the world."[352]

"I suppose, that had the Romans made any longer delay in coming against these villains, the city would either have been swallowed up by the ground opening upon them, or been overflowed by water, or else been destroyed by such thunder as the country of Sodom perished by, **for it had brought forth a generation of men much more atheistical than were those that suffered such punishments;** for by their madness it was that all the people came to be destroyed."[353]

This woman was also drunk with the blood of the saints and the martyrs of Yeshua. It is true that Rome, as well as the other nations surrounding Israel, were guilty of the murder of multitudes of believers. However, is that evidence supporting that she be identified as someone other than Jerusalem?

Matthew 23:34-38
(34) Therefore, behold, I send unto you prophets, and wise men, and scribes: some of them shall you kill and crucify; and some of them shall you scourge in your synagogues, and persecute from city to city:
(35) **that upon you may come all the righteous blood shed on the earth,** from the blood of Abel the righteous unto the blood of Zachariah son of Barachiah, whom you slew between the sanctuary and the altar.
(36) Truly I say unto you, **All these things shall come upon this generation.**
(37) O **Jerusalem, Jerusalem, that kills the prophets,** and **stones them that are sent unto her!** how often would I have gathered your children together, even as a hen gathers her chickens under her wings, and you would not!
(38) Behold, your house is left unto you desolate.

---

[352] Josephus, Wars. 5.10.5. Page 720.
[353] Josephus, Wars. 5.13.6. Page 726.

Luke 11:47-51

(47) Woe unto you! for you build the tombs of the prophets, and your fathers killed them.

(48) So you are witnesses and consent unto the works of your fathers: for they killed them, and you build *their tombs*.

(49) Therefore also said the wisdom of Elohim, I will send unto them **prophets and apostles**; and *some* of them they shall kill and persecute;

(50) that **the blood of all the prophets, which was shed from the foundation of the world**, may be required of **this generation**;

(51) from the blood of Abel unto the blood of Zachariah, who perished between the altar and the sanctuary: yea, I say unto you, it shall be required of this generation.

Luke 13:33

Nevertheless I must go on my way to-day and to-morrow and the *day* following: for **it cannot be that a prophet perish out of Jerusalem**.

Yeshua knew very well that there were prophets that had died outside of Jerusalem. After all, he named Abel among the prophets, and Jerusalem didn't even exist at that time. Many prophets lived and died before Jerusalem was a city, Moses being among them. Yeshua made it clear in the other passages that the bloodguilt for the deaths of all the prophets and apostles would be accounted against the generation of his day. The time of reckoning for the unjust slaughter of Yahweh's servants was upon them.

We have also already seen how the two witnesses themselves were slain in the "great city."[354] Is it really too difficult to conceive that a city so drenched in the blood of the prophets of old would not be an eligible candidate for Babylon the Great? The general hatred for Yeshua and his apostles first arose not out of Rome, but from out of

---

[354] Revelation 11:8.

Jerusalem. We know the first trials, persecutions, and executions of the apostles and disciples occurred in Jerusalem[355]. We also know that orders were sent from Jerusalem via the hands of messengers to capture disciples of Yeshua and return them[356], wherever they may have been. Where Nero and other pagan leaders began hating and persecuting the disciples decades later, the Jews' hands were already stained by their blood.

The Seven Heads of the Scarlet Beast

(7) And the angel said unto me, Wherefore did you wonder? I will tell you the mystery of the woman, and of the beast that carries her, which has the seven heads and the ten horns.
(8) The beast that you saw was, and is not; and is about to come up out of the abyss, and to go into perdition. And they that dwell on the earth shall wonder, *they* whose name has not been written in the book of life from the foundation of the world, when they behold the beast, how that he was, and is not, and shall come.
(9) Here is the mind that has wisdom. The seven heads are seven mountains, on which the woman sits:
(10) and they are seven kings; the five are fallen, the one is, the other is not yet come; and when he comes, he must continue a little while.

For the sake of brevity, we will not unnecessarily repeat here what has already been expounded in detail in chapter 13 above. Something intriguing happens in this passage though, and almost paradoxical if not examined further. The Beast in this passage refers at one point as a single being, such as in verse 8, yet as in verse 11 we see he is a multiple, consisting of seven then eight. This apparent conundrum is once again solved if we look to the pages of history.

At this point in the continuous timeline of the Apocalypse the siege of

---

[355] Acts 5:17-42, 7:54-60, 12:1-19.
[356] Acts 9:1-2.

Jerusalem had just begun. The Empire was still in a place of darkness after the chaos resulting from the "Year of the Four Emperors" we discussed in chapter 16 above. The Empire as a whole is the Beast symbolized in verse 8. It *was* in a strong state prior to Nero's suicide; it *was not* in John's time because it had been shrouded in darkness, descending into the abyss; and it *was about to come up out of the abyss* because the restoration of the Empire was about to begin after Vespasian took the reigns as emperor. According to Josephus, Vespasian's glorious reception in Rome didn't happen until after the siege of Jerusalem had been completed[357]. He tells us the following about Rome after this reception.

> "The multitude did also betake themselves to feasting; which feasts and drink-offerings they celebrated by their tribes, and their families, and their neighborhoods, and still prayed God to grant that Vespasian, his sons, and all their posterity, might continue in the Roman government for a very long time, and that his dominion might be preserved from all opposition. And this was the manner in which **Rome** so joyfully received Vespasian, and **thence grew immediately into a state of great prosperity.**"[358]

The Roman Empire was, was not, and was about to rise out of the abyss[359]. The phrase "to go into perdition" is in the present tense, active voice, and infinitive mood in the Greek. As we discussed briefly in chapter 12 above, the present tense in Greek is used to describe an ongoing action. Thus, we need not look for the destruction of the Roman Empire to occur in any short period of time after its resurrection to see that phrase fulfilled in history.

The representation of the seven heads as both seven hills and seven kings was detailed in chapter 13 above. In short, the seven heads upon which the woman sits are the seven hills upon which Rome, representing the Empire proper, is built. The Empire represented as a

---

[357] Josephus, Wars. 7.3.1. Page 752.
[358] Josephus, Wars. 7.4.1. Page 754.
[359] *I.e.* Become peaceful and prosperous after the darkness of the fifth plague.

wild, non-domesticated beast, "carries" the woman, taking her wherever it desires to. She is not in control, but is rather controlled by the Beast she rides upon. The seven kings are the first seven emperors of Rome – Julius, Augustus, Tiberius, Gaius, Claudius, Nero, and Galba. The five that had fallen at the time of John's writing of the Apocalypse were Julius, Augustus, Tiberius, Gaius, and Claudius. The one who was at that time was Nero, and the one who was to come and remain for a short time was Galba, who reigned for only seven months and seven days.

The Eighth King

(11) And the beast that was, and is not, is himself also an eighth, and is of the seven; and he goes into perdition.

We now arrive at what normally seems to be one of the most paradoxical verses in the Apocalypse. The seven-headed Beast that was about to be resurrected from the abyss somehow mysteriously has eight heads at the same time. How can this be possible? To answer this question, we must again go back to the prophecies of Daniel.

Daniel 7:16-27
(16) I came near unto one of them that stood by, and asked him the truth concerning all this. So he told me, and made me know the interpretation of the things.
(17) These great beasts, which are four, are four kings, that shall arise out of the earth.
(18) But the saints of the Most High shall receive the kingdom, and possess the kingdom forever, even forever and ever.
(19) Then I desired to know the truth concerning the fourth beast, which was diverse from all of them, exceeding terrible, whose teeth were of iron, and its nails of brass; which devoured, brake in pieces, and stamped the residue with its feet;
(20) and concerning the ten horns that were on its head, and the other *horn* which came up, and before which three fell, even that horn that had eyes, and a mouth that spoke great things, whose look was more stout than its fellows.
(21) I beheld, and the same horn made war with the saints, and

prevailed against them;

(22) until the ancient of days came, and judgment was given to the saints of the Most High, and the time came that the saints possessed the kingdom.

(23) Thus he said, The fourth beast shall be a fourth kingdom upon earth, which shall be diverse from all the kingdoms, and shall devour the whole earth, and shall tread it down, and break it in pieces.

(24) And as for the ten horns, out of this kingdom shall ten kings arise: and another shall arise after them; and he shall be diverse from the former, and he shall humble three kings.

(25) And he shall speak words against the Most High, and shall wear out the saints of the Most High; and he shall think to change the times and the law; and they shall be given into his hand until a time and times and half a time.

(26) But the judgment shall be set, and they shall take away his dominion, to consume and to destroy it unto the end.

(27) And the kingdom and the dominion, and the greatness of the kingdoms under the whole heaven, shall be given to the people of the saints of the Most High: his kingdom is an everlasting kingdom, and all dominions shall serve and obey him.

This passage is the interpretation of the dream that Daniel had recorded earlier in that chapter, specifically focused on the identity of the fourth beast. Without going into much detail about the identity of the first three beasts, history tells us that they are Babylon, Medo-Persia, and Greece, identical to the order found in Daniel's vision of the statue in chapter 2.

The fourth beast is the Roman Empire. It is diverse from all the other Beasts in that it was not originally a strict monarchy. Rome's government went through several stages. At the time, just prior to the second emperor, Augustus, Rome was a republic. Even after it became a monarchy the Senate still had great power in officially recognizing a person as the emperor.

The ten horns are officially kings, unlike the ten horns in Revelation 17 which, though labeled as kings, had as of yet no kingdom. These ten horns are, as one would expect, the first ten emperors of Rome. The first seven are listed above, the ones subsequent being Otho, Vitellius, and Vespasian. Logic would obviously tell us that Titus was then the eleventh horn. Titus was unique in his position in that he and Vespasian were both given the title of Caesar at the same time[360]. Though Vespasian was the emperor, both were given the highest ranking consular positions, Vespasian over Egypt, and Titus over Palestine. In this manner, Titus was a "little" horn. He was still a supreme ruler over Rome, but not in the same way as his father at that time.

Since Titus was declared Caesar at the same time as his father it can rightfully be said that three kings fell, or were humbled before him. Galba, Otho, and Vitellius all perished prior to the exaltation of Vespasian and Titus. Titus is also the one who meets the remaining criteria for the eleventh horn perfectly.

> "Vespasian sent Titus who said, 'Where is their God, the rock in whom they trusted?' This was the wicked Titus who blasphemed and insulted Heaven."[361]

The Jews themselves admitted in the Talmud that Titus was a blasphemer. As if Titus' destruction of the temple wasn't enough for him to "think to change the times and law," he slaughtered the last of the priests who remained in Jerusalem immediately after[362]. In addition, per church historian Sulpitius Severus, he made it his aim to utterly purge the religions of Judaism and Christianity.

> "But on the opposite side, others and Titus himself thought that the temple ought specially to be overthrown, in order that the religion

---

[360] Dio. Book 66, Chapter 1.
[361] Gittin. Folio 56b.
[362] Josephus, Wars. 6.6.1. Pages 743-744.

of the Jews and of the Christians might more thoroughly be subverted; for that these religions, although contrary to each other, had nevertheless proceeded from the same authors; that the Christians had sprung up from the Jews; and that, if the rooter were extirpated, the offshoot would speedily perish."[363]

Rashi, the eleventh century Jewish commentator, acknowledged with no hesitancy, as if it were the accepted historical tradition still in his day, that Titus was the eleventh horn. Twice in his commentary on Daniel chapter 7 he states this[364].

The people of Israel were given into the hands of Titus for time, times, and half a time as well. Vespasian's and Titus' campaign started in early Spring of 67 CE (late February, early March)[365] and the destruction of the temple and Jerusalem ended in late Summer of 70 CE (early September)[366]. The time between these is almost, if not exactly 1,260 days, 42 months, or "a time, times, and half a time."

The question of how Titus is the eighth king in Revelation 17:11 can now be answered. As usual John is referring his audience back to the prophets, in this case Daniel. Titus is obviously "of the seven" in that he was a Roman emperor like the rest. However, he was also the eighth because the three kings were humbled before him. The math is pretty simple and his audience would have picked up on it immediately. Of the initial ten horns three were humbled, leaving us with seven. Titus, being the little horn that grew up among them was "another" horn, therefore becoming the eighth. Just as the Roman Empire proper, symbolized by the Beast who was, was not, and was to come, Titus was destined to "go into perdition" at his destined time in the future.

---

[363] Severus. Book 2, Chapter 30.
[364] Commentaries on verses 8 and 24. See http://www.chabad.org/library/bible_cdo/aid/16490#showrashi=true. Last accessed 07/28/2017.
[365] Josephus, Wars. 3.4.2. Page 642.
[366] Josephus, Wars. 6.10.1. Page 750.

The Kingdom of Heaven

We must briefly note that the end of Daniel's vision in chapter 7 is again very telling as to when the kingdom was to be setup. During the lifetime of that little horn to whom was given power over the holy ones we read what was to happen.

Daniel 7:9-12
(9) I beheld till thrones were placed, and one that was ancient of days did sit: his raiment was white as snow, and the hair of his head like pure wool; his throne was fiery flames, *and* the wheels thereof burning fire.
(10) A fiery stream issued and came forth from before him: thousands of thousands ministered unto him, and ten thousand times ten thousand stood before him: the judgment was set, and the books were opened.
(11) I beheld at that time because of the voice of the great words which the horn spoke; I beheld even till the beast was slain, and its body destroyed, and it was given to be burned with fire.
(12) And as for the rest of the beasts, their dominion was taken away: yet their lives were prolonged for a season and a time.

This will once again be detailed more in chapter 20 below. But we see a scene here that is virtually a parallel to what we know as the "great white throne judgment" in Revelation 20:11-15. A throne is seen, one clothed in bright white raiment is seated thereon, judgment is about to ensue, and books are opened. It was at that time that the dominion of the beast was stripped and given to the holy ones of Yahweh. If this were not compelling enough, Rashi, the commentator mentioned previously, says that the one "that came with the clouds of heaven" and was "like unto a son of man" was "the King Messiah."[367]

---

[367] Commentary on verse 13. See http://www.chabad.org/library/bible_cdo/aid/16490#showrashi=true. Last accessed 07/28/2017.

The Ten Kings

(12) And the ten horns that you saw are ten kings, who have received no kingdom as yet; but they receive authority as kings, with the beast, for one hour.
(13) These have one mind, and they give their power and authority unto the beast.

As specified in chapter 13 above, these ten horns represent the ten praetorial provinces of Rome. These provinces, being under the ultimate power of Caesar, would have had their forces conscripted to aid in fighting the wars of Rome, including the one in Judea. The "one hour" here is no more literal than it is in John's first epistle.

1 John 2:18
Little children, it is the **last hour**: and as you heard that anti-messiah comes, even now have there arisen many anti-messiahs; whereby we know that it is the **last hour**.

The War Against the Lamb

(14) These shall war against the Lamb, and the Lamb shall overcome them, for he is Master of masters, and King of kings; and they *also shall overcome* that are with him, called and chosen and faithful.

Some Futurists hold that this verse is proof that the Apocalypse could not be symbolizing something that took place in the first century because there is no record of them waging war with Yeshua. However, this is once again missing the entire point of the Apocalypse. We cannot justly look at this passage as being any more literal in description than the rest. After all, if we did that, we'd expect to see in history, or at some point in the future, an actual lamb waging war. This is obviously absurd.

As this entire chapter is in the end devoted to identifying the harlot, Babylon, to his audience, John relates some of the things in this chapter as what he has already described. He starts with a description giving her spiritual name. Moves on to describing the Beast with additional details. Then here recapitulates how the Beast and his allies wage war against the Lamb. In chapter 13 above, verse 7, we read how the Beast was given the authority to wage war against the saints and overcome them. However, we know that in the end the Lamb and the resurrected saints are victorious, which is what is prefigured in this verse.

We can learn from Yeshua's teachings themselves how the Beast and the ten kings could be waging war against the Lamb, while Yeshua is not physically on the earth.

> Matthew 12:30
> **He that is not with me is against me**, and he that gathers not with me scatters.

To wage war against the apostles or disciples of Yeshua is tantamount to waging war with the Lamb himself. If we stand in opposition to those that are with him, those who gather with him, we stand against him. In torturing and killing Yeshua's followers, the Beast and his confederates declared open war on the Son of Elohim himself. Having been given authority over everything in heaven and on earth Yeshua will overcome each of them.

The Beast's Defeat of Babylon

(15) And he says unto me, The waters which you saw, where the harlot sits, are peoples, and multitudes, and nations, and tongues.
(16) And the ten horns which you saw, and the beast, these shall hate the harlot, and shall make her desolate and naked, and shall eat her flesh, and shall burn her utterly with fire.
(17) For Elohim did put in their hearts to do his mind, and to come to one mind, and to give their kingdom unto the beast, until the words of Elohim should be accomplished.

If we were to identify Babylon in the Apocalypse as Papal Rome, as some Futurist commentators do, aspects of this passage make absolutely no sense. Why would Rome, the city upon which the woman sits, rebel against the Papacy when, as we know from history, it succeeded in bringing excessive power, wealth, and wide-spread authority to it? Historically speaking this is an amazing passage that proves the identity of Babylon with apostate Jerusalem in the first century.

As we have clearly shown, the Beast represents the Roman Empire. The proofs of that are abundant and, in our opinion, undeniable. If, as we have shown, Babylon the great represents Jerusalem, this passage becomes completely clear. The Beast and its ten praetorial confederate provinces hate Jerusalem. She has rebelled and turned against his authority. He systematically dismantles and strips Babylon of all that made her who she was, leaving her desolate and naked. The people in Babylon are devoured, destroyed by pestilence, famine, and the sword. All that is left is to utterly burn her with fire. We read of these exact same things being prophesied by Yeshua.

Matthew 23:37-38
(37) O Jerusalem, Jerusalem, that kills the prophets, and stones them that are sent unto her! how often would I have gathered your children together, even as a hen gathers her chickens under her wings, and you would not!
(38) Behold, **your house is left unto you desolate**.

Luke 19:41-44
(41) And when he drew near, he saw the city and wept over it,
(42) saying, If you had known in this day, even you, the things which belong unto peace! but now they are hid from your eyes.
(43) For the days shall come upon you, when your enemies shall cast up a bank about you, and compass you round, and keep you in on every side,
(44) and shall dash you to the ground, and your children within you; and they shall not leave in you one stone upon another; because you knew not the time of your visitation.

Matthew 22:7
But the king was enraged; and he sent his armies, and destroyed those murderers, and **burned their city**.

Jerusalem once again fits all the descriptions of Babylon perfectly.

The Great City

(18) And the woman whom you saw is the great city, which reigns over the kings of the earth.

We must address the final phrase in this passage first. How can it be said that Jerusalem, which we are identifying as Babylon the great harlot, reigns over the kings of the earth? Interpretation and translation are factors in the proper exegesis of this passage. This phrase, contextually speaking, refers specifically to the land of Israel. Jerusalem was the chief city, from which all authority was divvied out and who which all authorities of the land reported. Josephus also tells us this.

> "The city Jerusalem is situated in the very middle; on which account some have, with sagacity enough, called that city the Navel of the country...it was parted into eleven portions, of which **the royal city Jerusalem** was the supreme, and **presided over all the neighboring country, as the head does over the body**. As to the other cities that were inferior to it, they presided over their several toparchies; Gophna was the second of those cities, and next to that Acrabatta, after them Thamna, and Lydda, and Emmaus, and Pella, and Idumea, and Engaddi, and Herodium, and Jericho; and after them came Jamnia and Joppa, as presiding over the neighboring people; and besides these there was the region of Gamala, and Gaulonitis, and Batanea, and Trachonitis, which are also parts of the kingdom of Agrippa."[368]

> "For he saw there would be occasion for great pains about **Jerusalem**, which was not yet taken, because it was **the royal city**, and the principal city of the whole nation."[369]

---

[368] Josephus, Wars. 3.3.5. Pages 641-642.
[369] Josephus, Wars. 4.2.1. Page 668.

Jerusalem is twice called the royal city by Josephus. In the first quote, it is said to rule over smaller cities, which themselves ruled over toparchies and kingdoms. Having established that Jerusalem is indeed a city which reigns over the kings of the land, we must now examine a phrase so commonly used in the Apocalypse, each time referring to the same place – "the great city." That phrase is found eight times in the Apocalypse. Five of them are in chapter 18, which we will address then. The three we have seen thus far are:

Revelation 11:8
And their dead bodies *lie* in the street of **the great city**, which spiritually is called Sodom and Egypt, where also their Master was crucified.

Revelation 16:19
And **the great city** was divided into three parts, and the cities of the nations fell: and Babylon the great was remembered in the sight of Elohim, to give unto her the cup of the wine of the fierceness of his wrath.

Revelation 17:18
And the woman whom you saw is **the great city**, which reigns over the kings of the earth.

There are no hermeneutical or exegetical reasons why the phrase "the great city" would refer to different cities in different verses. On the contrary, when they are all seen as referring to the same city the historical record and the scriptures once again come in to perfect alignment. The clearest of all the passages above, which leaves no room for interpretive error, is Revelation 11:8. The city where "also their Master was crucified" can be none other than Jerusalem. To question this is to question the veracity of not only the entirety of the New Testament, but every historical record that bears witness to it.

If the "great city" is undisputedly Jerusalem in 11:8, how can we not use the simplest of verses to explain those which require a greater level of research? To do so would be intellectually disingenuous. We will sum up all the points relating to the identity of the "great city" in chapter

18. We believe that there will be no room left for questioning after all the information, scriptural and historical, is considered.

CHAPTER EIGHTEEN

The Judgment of Babylon the Great

(1) After these things I saw another angel coming down out of heaven, having great authority; and the earth was lightened with his glory.

(2) And he cried with a mighty voice, saying, Fallen, fallen is Babylon the great, and is become a habitation of demons, and a hold of every unclean spirit, and a hold of every unclean and hateful bird.

(3) For by the wine of the wrath of her fornication all the nations are fallen; and the kings of the earth committed fornication with her, and the merchants of the earth waxed rich by the power of her wantonness.

(4) And I heard another voice from heaven, saying, Come forth, my people, out of her, that you have no fellowship with her sins, and that you receive not of her plagues:

(5) for her sins have reached even unto heaven, and Elohim has remembered her iniquities.

(6) Render unto her even as she rendered, and double *unto her* the double according to her works: in the cup which she mingled, mingle unto her double.

(7) However much she glorified herself, and waxed wanton, so much give her of torment and mourning: for she said in her heart, *I sit a queen, and am no widow,* and shall in no wise see mourning.

(8) Therefore in one day shall her plagues come, death, and mourning, and famine; and she shall be utterly burned with fire; for strong is Yahweh Elohim who judged her.
(9) And the kings of the earth, who committed fornication and lived wantonly with her, shall weep and wail over her, when they look upon the smoke of her burning,
(10) standing afar off for the fear of her torment, saying, Woe, woe, the great city, Babylon, the strong city! for in one hour is your judgment come.

In Jeremiah 51 the prophecy of the destruction of the kingdom of Babylon is described in vivid detail. There are several direct parallels between that prophecy and the episode we read here. Here are a couple of the verses in that chapter that are the most impactful:

Jeremiah 51:6-7
(6) **Flee out of the midst of Babylon**, and save every man his life; be not cut off in her iniquity: for it is the time of Yahweh's vengeance; he will render unto her a recompense.
(7) Babylon has been a golden cup in Yahweh's hand, that made all the earth drunken: **the nations have drunk of her wine**; therefore the nations are mad.

The entire chapter goes on to describe Babylon's destruction by the hand of the Medes. John's use of this symbolism isn't to declare that there will one day be a revived Babylonian empire. But, rather, that the same degree of destruction that was brought against that Babylon in the past will be brought against the Babylon described in the Apocalypse, the identity of which is found in chapter 17 above.

This entire chapter must be taken as a whole to understand how great this pivotal event in history was. The historical record is by no means silent on the specifics of this fall, as we shall see. The angel's proclamation of "Fallen, fallen is Babylon the great!," is familiar. It was announced prophetically in chapter 14. Her being a habitation of demons and of every unclean thing is evident.

"It is therefore impossible to go distinctly over every instance of these men's iniquity. I shall therefore speak my mind here at once briefly: That neither did any other city ever suffer such miseries, **nor did any age ever breed a generation more fruitful in wickedness than this was, from the beginning of the world.**"[370]

"So Caesar went his rounds through the legions, and hastened on the works, and showed the robbers that they were now in his hands. But these men, and these only, were incapable of repenting of the wickednesses they had been guilty of; and **separating their souls from their bodies,** they used them both as if they belonged to other folks, and not to themselves. For no gentle affection could touch their souls, nor could any pain affect their bodies, since they could still **tear the dead bodies of the people as dogs do**, and fill the prisons with those that were sick."[371]

"Now this was in reality no better than a pretense and a cloak for the barbarity which was made use of by them, and to color over their own avarice, which they afterwards made evident by their own actions; for those that were partners with them in their rebellion joined also with them in the war against the Romans, and went further lengths with them in their impudent undertakings against them; and when they were again convicted of dissembling in such their pretenses, they still more abused those that justly reproached them for their wickedness. And indeed **that was a time most fertile in all manner of wicked practices**, insomuch that **no kind of evil deeds were then left undone; nor could anyone so much as devise any bad thing that was new**, so deeply were they all infected, and strove with one another in their single capacity, and in their communities, who should run **the greatest lengths in impiety towards God**...Accordingly, they all met with such ends as God deservedly brought upon them in way of punishment; for all such miseries have been sent upon them as man's nature is capable of

---

[370] Josephus, Wars. 5.10.5. Page 720.
[371] Josephus, Wars. 5.12.4. Page 724.

undergoing, till the utmost period of their lives, and till death came upon them in various ways of torment; yet might one say justly that they suffered less than they had done, **because it was impossible they could be punished according to their deserving.**"[372]

We already showed in chapter 17 how widespread Jerusalem's influence was and therefore how the kings of the earth could very easily drink of the wine of her fornication. We also already showed in chapter 12 how the call to the people of Yahweh to come out of her was heeded by the Hebrews in Jerusalem as they fled to Pella in obedience to Yeshua's command. How can it be said that her plagues came in a day, though? After all, one day without food is hardly a famine. We must remember that the phrase "the day of Yahweh" is very common in the Old Testament[373]. It does not refer to a strict twenty-four-hour period. Prophetically and apocalyptically speaking, a specific "day" refers to a specific time when judgment is rendered. Thus, Babylon can fall in a single day because that was the Day of Yahweh, the time period appointed for the judgment to fall upon her.

The Spoils of War

(11) And the merchants of the earth weep and mourn over her, for no man buys their merchandise anymore;
(12) merchandise of gold, and silver, and precious stone, and pearls, and fine linen, and purple, and silk, and scarlet; and all thyine wood, and every vessel of ivory, and every vessel made of most precious wood, and of brass, and iron, and marble;
(13) and cinnamon, and spice, and incense, and ointment, and frankincense, and wine, and oil, and fine flour, and wheat, and cattle, and sheep; and *merchandise* of horses and chariots and slaves; and souls of men.
(14) And the fruits which your soul lusted after are gone from you, and all things that were dainty and sumptuous are perished

---

[372] Josephus, Wars. 7.8.1. Pages 762-763.
[373] Isaiah 2:12, 13:6; Lamentations 2:22; Ezekiel 13:5, 30:3; Joel 1:15, 2:1; Amos 5:18; Obadiah 1:15; Zechariah 14:1; Malachi 4:5; et al.

from you, and *men* shall find them no more at all.

(15) The merchants of these things, who were made rich by her, shall stand afar off for the fear of her torment, weeping and mourning;

(16) saying, Woe, woe, the great city, she that was arrayed in fine linen and purple and scarlet, and decked with gold and precious stone and pearl!

(17) for in one hour so great riches is made desolate. And every shipmaster, and every one that sails anywhere, and mariners, and as many as gain their living by sea, stood afar off,

(18) and cried out as they looked upon the smoke of her burning, saying, What *city* is like the great city?

(19) And they cast dust on their heads, and cried, weeping and mourning, saying, Woe, woe, the great city, wherein all that had their ships in the sea were made rich by reason of her costliness! for in one hour is she made desolate.

Verses 9 through 19 are dedicated to the mourning of Babylon's destruction by those who profited from her in some way. James Stuart Russell again supplies us with a great synopsis and introduction to this portion of the chapter[374]:

After this follows a solemn and pathetic dirge, if it may be so called, over the fallen city, whose last hour is now come. The kings or rulers of the land, the merchant-traders and the seamen who knew her in the plentitude of her power and glory, now lament over her fall. The royal city, the mart of trade and wealth, is wrapt in flames, and the mariners and merchants who were enriched by her traffic stand afar off, beholding the smoke of her burning, and crying, ' What city is like unto this great city?' The description given in this chapter of the wealth and luxury of the mystic Babylon might seem scarcely appropriate to Jerusalem were it not that we have in Josephus ample evidence that there is no exaggeration even in this highly-wrought representation.

---

[374] Russell. Page 507.

As Russell intimates, some question whether these passages could possibly relate to Jerusalem, especially one such as verse 19 that speaks of sea merchants also mourning. However, history once again sheds light on how perfectly these verses describe the fall of Jerusalem. Josephus tells us how far the smoke from the burning of just the temple was visible.

"**The flame was also carried a long way**, and made an echo, together with the groans of those that were slain; and **because this hill was high, and the works at the temple were very great, one would have thought the whole city had been on fire.** Nor can one imagine anything either greater or more terrible than this noise; for there was at once a shout of the Roman legions, who were marching all together, and a sad clamor of the seditious, who were now surrounded with fire and sword. The people also that were left above were beaten back upon the enemy, and under a great consternation, and made sad moans at the calamity they were under; the multitude also that was in the city joined in this outcry with those that were upon the hill. And besides, many of those that were worn away by the famine, and their mouths almost closed, when they saw the fire of the holy house, they exerted their utmost strength, and brake out into groans and outcries again: **Perea did also return the echo, as well as the mountains round about [the city,]** and augmented the force of the entire noise."[375]

Not only was the literal smoke of Jerusalem's burning visible for quite some distance, but the prophetic meaning of "smoke" also applies. As mentioned in the table of apocalyptic terminology in the Introduction, the smoke rising from a kingdom or city is representative of its utter destruction. Jerusalem was a booming metropolis, a thoroughfare through which the nations streamed from north to south dropping their wealth therein. Merchants from across the known world would have been affected financially by the destruction of Jerusalem because of how famous it was and how lucrative for business. These merchants all mourned and bewailed at the apocalyptic "sight" of Jerusalem's

---

[375] Josephus, Wars. 6.5.1. Page 741.

ascending smoke, but, as Russell briefly alludes to above, what about the great degree of effort that John took to detail specific items that were destroyed in Babylon's fall? Josephus provides us with an amazing account of the spoils taken from Jerusalem's destruction, which were paraded through Rome.

"The treasurer of the temple also, whose name was Phineas, was seized on, and showed Titus the **coats and girdles** of the priests, with a **great quantity of purple and scarlet**, which were there reposited for the uses of the veil, as also a great deal of **cinnamon** and **cassia**, with a large quantity of **other sweet spices**, which used to be mixed together, and offered as incense to God every day. A great many other treasures were also delivered to him, with sacred ornaments of the temple not a few; which things thus delivered to Titus obtained of him for this man the same pardon that he had allowed to such as deserted of their own accord."[376]

"Yet was there no small quantity of the riches that had been in that city still found among its ruins, a great deal of which the Romans dug up; but the greatest part was discovered by those who were captives, and so they carried it away; I mean the **gold** and the **silver**, and the rest of that most **precious furniture** which the Jews had, and which the owners had treasured up underground, against the uncertain fortunes of war."[377]

"Now it is impossible to describe the multitude of the shows as they deserve, and the magnificence of them all; such indeed as a man could not easily think of as performed, either by the labor of workmen, or the variety of riches, or the rarities of nature; for almost all such curiosities as the most happy men ever get by piece-meal were here one heaped on another, and those both admirable and costly in their nature; and all brought together on that day demonstrated the vastness of the dominions of the Romans; for there was here to be seen a mighty quantity of **silver**, and **gold**, and

[376] Josephus, Wars. 6.8.3. Page 747.
[377] Josephus, Wars. 7.5.2. Page 756.

ivory, contrived into all sorts of things, and did not appear as carried along in pompous show only, but, as a man may say, running along like a river. Some parts were composed of the **rarest purple hangings**, and so carried along; and others accurately represented to the life what was embroidered by the arts of the Babylonians. There were also **precious stones** that were transparent, some set in **crowns of gold**, and some in other ouches, as the workmen pleased; and of these such a vast number were brought, that we could not but thence learn how vainly we imagined any of them to be rarities. The images of the gods were also carried, being as well wonderful for their largeness, as made very artificially, and with great skill of the workmen; nor were any of these images of any other than very costly materials; and **many species of animals were brought,** everyone in their own natural ornaments. **The men** also who brought every one of these shows were great multitudes, and adorned with **purple garments,** all over **interwoven with gold**; those that were chosen for carrying these pompous shows having also about them such magnificent ornaments as were both extraordinary and surprising. Besides these, one might see that even the **great number of the captives** was not unadorned, while the variety that was in their garments, and their fine texture, concealed from the sight the deformity of their bodies. But what afforded the greatest surprise of all was the structure of the pageants that were borne along; for indeed he that met them could not but be afraid that the bearers would not be able firmly enough to support them, such was their magnitude; for many of them were so made, that they were on three or even four stories, one above another. The magnificence also of their structure afforded one both pleasure and surprise; for upon many of them were laid **carpets of gold.** On the top of every one of these pageants was placed the commander of the city that was taken, and the manner wherein he was taken. Moreover, there followed those pageants a **great number of ships**; and for the **other spoils,** they were carried in great plenty. But for those that were taken in the temple of Jerusalem, they made the greatest figure of them all; that is, **the golden table,** of the weight of many talents; **the candlestick** also, that was made of gold, though its construction were now changed from that which we made use of; for its middle shaft was fixed upon a basis, and the small branches were produced out of it to a great length, having the likeness of a trident in their position, and had every one a socket made of **brass** for a lamp at the tops of them. These lamps were in number seven, and represented the dignity of the number seven among the Jews; and the last of all the spoils, was carried the Law of the Jews."[378]

The following table shows exactly how precise the items carried away from the siege were to those detailed in Revelation 18:11-13 and 16.

[378] Josephus, Wars. 7.5.5. Page 757.

Item	Apocalypse	Josephus
Gold	√	√
Silver	√	√
Precious Stones	√	√
Pearls	√	
Fine Linen	√	√
Purple	√	√
Silk	√	
Scarlet	√	√
Precious Woods	√	
Ivory	√	√
Brass, Iron	√	√
Marble	√	
Cinnamon	√	√
Spices	√	√
Incense/Frankincense	√	√
Wine	√	
Oil	√	
Fine Flour	√	
Wheat	√	
Cattle	√	√
Sheep	√	√
Horses	√	√
Chariots	√	
Slaves	√	√

The image below is taken from the Arch of Titus in Rome. It shows the same parade that Josephus mentioned.

Things not specified by Josephus may very well have been a part of a general category. For instance, if any rooms in the temple that items for the sacrifices remained, prior to the complete destruction after the fire, surely they would have included wine, oil, fine flour, and wheat. Pearls, though not called out specifically, may be a part of his generalized "precious stones." As mentioned in chapter 11 regarding the resurrection of the two witnesses, *the absence of evidence isn't the evidence of absence.* The sheer degree of specificity to which these accounts agree is astounding, and in our opinion, any honest inquirer of the truth would be hard pressed to show that there is not some viable and solid link between the scriptures and history here.

Verse 17 is often questioned by Futurists as they think that shipmasters would have had nothing to mourn over because Jerusalem wasn't a port city. However, this question is easily answered when one considers the lucrative nature of business in Jerusalem, the desire for merchants to setup there because of that, and what we have stated in the historical record.

> "The city Jerusalem is situated in the very middle; on which account some have, with sagacity enough, called that city the Navel of the country. **Nor indeed is Judea destitute of such delights as come from the sea, since its maritime places extend as far as Ptolemais.**"[379]

Ptolemais should be a very familiar city to the reader at this point given how frequently it was used by Vespasian in his military campaign. The reason for this was because of the size of its port. Merchants and shipmasters of the sea would have unloaded their goods there for export to and sale within Jerusalem. Those merchants and shipmasters would have been just as injured financially as those who carried wealth into Jerusalem via land.

The Fall of Babylon

(20) Rejoice over her, you heaven, and you saints, and you apostles, and you prophets; for Elohim has judged your judgment on her.

(21) And a strong angel took up a stone as it were a great millstone and cast it into the sea, saying, Thus with a mighty fall shall Babylon, the great city, be cast down, and shall be found no more at all.

(22) And the voice of harpers and minstrels and flute-players and trumpeters shall be heard no more at all in you; and no craftsman, of whatsoever craft, shall be found any more at all in you; and the voice of a mill shall be heard no more at all in you;

(23) and the light of a lamp shall shine no more at all in you; and the voice of the bridegroom and of the bride shall be heard no more at all in you: for your merchants were the princes of the earth; for with your sorcery were all the nations deceived.

(24) And in her was found the blood of prophets and of saints,

---

[379] Josephus, Wars. 3.3.5. Page 641.

and of all that have been slain upon the earth.

Verse 21 is the final occurrence of the phrase "the great city" in the Apocalypse. As mentioned in chapter 17 above, we can now tie all the uses of it together to form one undeniable conclusion. The only city "where their Master was crucified" was Jerusalem. The only city which was the royal city, ruling over the kings of the land was Jerusalem. The only city that was raped, plundered, burned to the ground, and mourned over by merchants of land and sea was Jerusalem. The only city whose inhabitants were in a covenant, marriage relationship with the Almighty was Jerusalem. Babylon, the mother of harlots, the great city, was Jerusalem.

As if we needed more proof than that, John yet again points his readers back to the teachings of Yeshua to give them yet another clue as to the identity of Babylon, the great city. He tells them in Babylon was found the blood of prophets and saints and all those slain upon the earth.

Matthew 23:34-35
(34) Therefore, behold, I send unto you prophets, and wise men, and scribes: some of them shall you kill and crucify; and some of them shall you scourge in your synagogues, and persecute from city to city:
(35) **that upon you may come all the righteous blood shed on the earth**, from the blood of Abel the righteous unto the blood of Zachariah son of Barachiah, whom you slew between the sanctuary and the altar.

Luke 11:49-51
(49) Therefore also said the wisdom of Elohim, I will send unto them prophets and apostles; and *some* of them they shall kill and persecute;
(50) that the **blood of all the prophets**, which was shed from the foundation of the world, **may be required of this generation**;
(51) from the blood of Abel unto the blood of Zachariah, who perished between the altar and the sanctuary: yea, I say unto you, **it shall be required of this generation.**

In helping his audience to recall Yeshua's prophecy he once again told them, "Babylon is Jerusalem."

Futurists will make the claim that Babylon cannot be Jerusalem of the first century because there is a Jerusalem that exists today. They say that since there are flute-players, craftsman, lights, bridegrooms, and so forth, that this prophecy obviously doesn't apply. Yet, the smoke of the Jerusalem of old, to which the nations flooded due to its beauty, wealth, and "the greatness of the veneration paid to it on a religious account,"[380] continues to rise even to this day. In the words of Reverend P.S. Desperez:

> "Jerusalem fell so completely, so helplessly, was so 'torn up to its foundations, that they who came to see it after the Romans had finished their work of destruction, could not believe that it had ever been inhabited'...At the present day, nearly 2000 years since this desolation took place, it is only the wreck, the shadow of departed greatness. *As the city of God* it is found no more at all. The Jew exists there on sufferance; contending sects of Christians squabble about petty differences; and the Turk, the haughty master of the spot, worships Mahomet on the very altar of Yahweh."[381]

I would add to Desperez's statements that Jerusalem has never, to this day, seen a time of absolute peace that would be expected of one overseen and protected by the Almighty. War after war, crusade after crusade, Jerusalem, and Israel as a whole, remains a crumbled heap of smoking ash compared to its former glory. The beacon of light for truth, justice, and righteousness it once was is now shrouded in idolatry, bloodshed, and all forms of uncleanness and licentiousness. Jerusalem, the city once commissioned, blessed, and inhabited by the Creator of the universe, has been destroyed and its smoke rises up forever and ever. Josephus tells us of the magnitude of Jerusalem's destruction.

---

[380] Josephus, Wars. 6.10.1. Page 750.
[381] Desperez. Pages 387-388.

"Now as soon as the army had no more people to slay or to plunder, because there remained none to be the objects of their fury, (for they would not have spared any, had there remained any other work to be done,) Caesar gave orders that they should now **demolish the entire city and temple**, but should leave as many of the towers standing as were of the greatest eminency; that is, Phasaelus, and Hippicus, and Mariamne; and so much of the wall as enclosed the city on the west side. This wall was spared, in order to afford a camp for such as were to lie in garrison, as were the towers also spared, in order to demonstrate to posterity what kind of city it was, and how well fortified, which the Roman valor had subdued; but for all the rest of the wall, it was so thoroughly laid even with the ground by those that dug it up to the foundation, that **there was left nothing to make those that came thither believe it had ever been inhabited.** This was the end which Jerusalem came to by the madness of those that were for innovations; a city otherwise of great magnificence, and of mighty fame among all mankind."[382]

Thus, was Jerusalem destroyed on the eighth of the month of Gorpieus, or September 1, 70 CE[383]. John's illustration here isn't intended to be read as one that says there will never be a city called Jerusalem again, or even that a city might be rebuilt on Jerusalem's ruins having in it the voice of the bridegroom, etc. His intent is to convey to his audience the absolute and complete destruction and ruin they should expect to see in Jerusalem after its judgment is complete.

---

[382] Josephus, Wars. 7.7.1. Pages 750-751.
[383] The most commonly held date is September 8, 70 CE. That date is, however, not based on the timing of the visibility of the crescent moon, which places the first of Gorpieus on August 24, 70 CE. See Parker & Dubberstein. Page 47.

CHAPTER NINETEEN

Praise for Babylon's Fall

(1) After these things I heard as it were a great voice of a great multitude in heaven, saying, Hallelujah; Salvation, and glory, and power, belong to our Elohim:

(2) *for true and righteous are his judgments;* for he has judged the great harlot, her that corrupted the earth with her fornication, and *he has avenged the blood of his servants at her hand.*

(3) And a second time they say, Hallelujah. *And her smoke goes up forever and ever.*

(4) And the four and twenty elders and the four living creatures fell down and worshipped Elohim that sits on the throne, saying, Amein; Hallelujah.

(5) And a voice came forth from the throne, saying, Give praise to our Elohim, all you his servants, you that fear him, the small and the great.

Babylon the great, the apostate and adulterous city of Jerusalem, had been utterly destroyed. The martyrs of Yeshua who patiently waited under the heavenly altar for the consummation of her judgment were vindicated. Praise for the righteous and perfect judgments of Yahweh was lifted by the great multitude of resurrected believers, angels, and creatures in the heavenly realm. The time that was so prophesied about and anticipated had come and been accomplished.

As noted in the table of apocalyptic terminology in the Introduction, smoke arising from something forever and ever is representative of the continuation of a conquered people under the misery of subjection and slavery. Not only was the once holy and divinely protected city of Jerusalem now lying in an unrecognizable heap of crushed stone and ash, but Jerusalem of the present day is still not spiritually free. Today the holy places of Jerusalem, like many places in the world, are ruled over by an unholy and idolatrous people. Israel as a whole is engulfed in the sins of the world such as homosexuality and idolatry, amongst many other abominations. The apocalyptic smoke of her burning continues to rise. The old Jerusalem is never to be resurrected again. Instead, a New Jerusalem has been created. More details on this topic will be covered in chapter 21 below.

The Marriage Supper of the Lamb

(6) And I heard as it were the voice of a great multitude, and as the voice of many waters, and as the voice of mighty thunders, saying, Hallelujah: for Yahweh our Elohim, the Almighty, reigns.
(7) Let us rejoice and be exceeding glad, and let us give the glory unto him: for the marriage of the Lamb is come, and his wife has made herself ready.
(8) And it was given unto her that she should array herself in fine linen, bright *and* pure: for the fine linen is the righteous acts of the saints.
(9) And he said unto me, Write, Blessed are they that are bidden to the marriage supper of the Lamb. And he said unto me, These are true words of Elohim.
(10) And I fell down before his feet to worship him. And he said unto me, See you do it not: I am a fellow-servant with you and with your brethren that hold the testimony of Yeshua: worship Elohim: for the testimony of Yeshua is the spirit of prophecy.

In keeping with his apocalyptic theme John immediately brings yet another teaching of Yeshua back to the forefront of his audience's minds.

Matthew 22:1-14

(1) And Yeshua answered and spoke again in parables unto them, saying,

(2) The kingdom of heaven is likened unto a certain king, who made a marriage feast for his son,

(3) and sent forth his servants to call them that were bidden to the marriage feast: and they would not come.

(4) Again he sent forth other servants, saying, Tell them that are bidden, Behold, I have made ready my dinner; my oxen and my fatlings are killed, and all things are ready: come to the marriage feast.

(5) But they made light of it, and went their ways, one to his own farm, another to his merchandise;

(6) and the rest laid hold on his servants, and treated them shamefully, and killed them.

(7) But the king was enraged; and he sent his armies, and destroyed those murderers, and burned their city.

(8) Then said he to his servants, The wedding is ready, but they that were bidden were not worthy.

(9) Go you therefore unto the partings of the highways, and as many as you shall find, bid to the marriage feast.

(10) And those servants went out into the highways, and gathered together all as many as they found, both bad and good: and the wedding was filled with guests.

(11) But when the king came in to behold the guests, he saw there a man who had not on a wedding-garment:

(12) and he said unto him, Friend, how did you come in here not having a wedding-garment? And he was speechless.

(13) Then the king said to the servants, Bind him hand and foot, and cast him out into the outer darkness; there shall be the weeping and the gnashing of teeth.

(14) For many are called, but few chosen.

The parallels between these two accounts are undeniable. Think about the timeline. In Yeshua's parable we are told that the king, in that case Yahweh, invited his servants, the Jewish people, to the wedding feast of His son, Yeshua. Yeshua went, as he said, to the lost sheep of the house of Israel[384]. His message was, "Repent, for the kingdom of heaven is at hand!" In the words of the parable, "All things are ready: come to the marriage feast." But the people made light of him and he was rejected by them and brutally murdered. Yahweh sent His first group of servants, the twelve apostles, to all the land of Judea[385]. Though some likely accepted the message of Yeshua and the coming kingdom, many did not, and their fate was to be worse than that of Sodom and Gomorrah. Yahweh then sent other servants, the seventy-two disciples and other converts to the faith[386], and they likewise treated them with contempt, some being tortured and even killed.

This rejection of Yahweh's servants filled the cup of His wrath to the brim and it was poured out upon the Jews. His armies, in this case the powerful hordes of Roman soldiers, came to those people, destroyed those who rejected and murdered His servants, and burned their city, Jerusalem, to the ground. The servants of Yahweh that remained after the burning of the city, those who had fled across the Jordan or who were already in other cities outside of Israel, were commissioned to invite all that they saw to the wedding feast of His son Yeshua, the righteous and the unrighteous. The wedding clothes of the guests of the groom, Yeshua, were no different than those required of the bride. If you were invited as one who is righteous, you must continue in that righteousness doing righteous works. If you were invited as one who is unrighteous, you must turn from your unrighteous works and do the works of righteousness. Those who do not do this will be removed from the wedding supper and cast out to be destroyed.

In the passage in the Apocalypse we see that the bride has made herself ready, but, she has yet to come out of her chamber. We do not see this happen until chapter 21 below. The bride, as that chapter clearly states, is the New Jerusalem. Her coming out of her chamber was the descent of the New Jerusalem from heaven to earth. The ones outside of the city, who are removed from the feast, are those who are unclean,

---

[384] Matthew 10:5-6, 15:24.
[385] Matthew 10:5-15; Luke 9:1-6.
[386] Luke 10:1-12.

abominable and in any other regards unrepentant sinners not doing the works of righteousness. Only those who are invited and have adorned themselves with their wedding garments, whose names were written in the guest list known as the Lamb's book of life, are allowed in the new city.

Needless to say, there is more to this story of the wedding feast, the bride, and the groom than first meets the eye. This will all be discussed in more detail in chapter 21 below, but the reader should begin pondering some of the more complex imagery used here in preparation. How can a bride simultaneously be spoken of as an individual and then later as a city? How can our Messiah, who was most assuredly a man, marry a city? If he taught that there is no marrying or giving in marriage in the kingdom[387], why is he somehow exempt? How can the righteous acts be used as a bridal gown? Each of these apparent "mysteries" are solved when the proper identity of the bride of the Lamb is detailed later. What we can conclude for now is that the apocalyptic imagery John uses here is a sort of foreshadowing of the wedding itself that is to take place not long after.

The Demise of the Beasts and Their Armies

(11) And I saw the heaven opened; and behold, a white horse, and he that sat thereon called Faithful and True; and in righteousness he does judge and make war.
(12) And his eyes *are* a flame of fire, and upon his head *are* many diadems; and he has a name written which no one knows but he himself.
(13) And he *is* arrayed in a garment sprinkled with blood: and his name is called The Word of Elohim.
(14) And the armies which are in heaven followed him upon white horses, clothed in fine linen, white *and* pure.
(15) And out of his mouth proceeds a sharp sword, that with it he should smite the nations: and he shall rule them with a rod of iron: and he treads the winepress of the fierceness of the wrath

---

[387] Luke 20:27-40.

of Elohim, the Almighty.

(16) And he has on his garment and on his thigh a name written, King of kings, and Master of masters.

(17) And I saw an angel standing in the sun; and he cried with a loud voice, saying to all the birds that fly in mid heaven, Come *and* be gathered together unto the great supper of Elohim;

(18) that you may eat the flesh of kings, and the flesh of captains, and the flesh of mighty men, and the flesh of horses and of them that sit thereon, and the flesh of all men, both free and bond, and small and great.

(19) And I saw the beast, and the kings of the earth and their armies, gathered together to make war against him that sat upon the horse, and against his army.

(20) And the beast was taken, and with him the false prophet that wrought the signs in his sight, wherewith he deceived them that had received the mark of the beast and them that worshipped his image: they two were cast alive into the lake of fire that burns with brimstone:

(21) and the rest were killed with the sword of him that sat upon the horse, *even the sword* which came forth out of his mouth: and all the birds were filled with their flesh.

As stated above, Babylon the great harlot, Jerusalem and her inhabitants, had been completely destroyed. Yeshua had returned with the clouds of heaven in vengeance and judgment just as Yahweh had done to Egypt and Israel in the past. Yet, enemies of Yeshua that remained throughout Israel, those who rejected him and his message through his servants, had not yet been completely dealt with. In addition, the wicked antagonists in the Apocalypse, and their hosts, used by Yahweh and Yeshua as instruments of judgment, still remained. The kingdom of heaven that had begun while Yeshua was on the earth had yet to be officially brought down and established over all creation. This triumphant march of Yeshua from heaven was the one that was to bring about the final demise and judgment of the spiritual forces of darkness in addition to setting up the final and eternal kingdom.

It goes without saying that this passage is highly symbolic. Even the staunchest of Futurists would agree that they don't expect to see Yeshua coming with an actual sword protruding from his mouth. They don't expect to see literal flames gleaming forth from his eyeballs. They don't expect to see him come down to tread an actual winepress. That this episode of the appearing of the righteous king is one that takes place in the heavenly, or spirit realm is beyond question. John is speaking to them once again in images they were all too familiar with.

The apocalyptic language of the first three verses of this passage are given so that the identity of the one on the horse could not be questioned. He was the faithful and true one.

John 14:6
Yeshua said unto him, I am the way, and the **truth**, and the life: no one comes unto the Father, but by me.

He was the one crowned with many crowns. He had perfect and complete authority to rule over all, including death and the grave.

Matthew 28:18
And Yeshua came to them and spoke unto them, saying, **All authority has been given unto me in heaven and on earth**.

Hebrews 2:9
But we behold him who has been made a little lower than the angels, *even* Yeshua, because of the suffering of death **crowned with glory and honor**, that by the grace of Elohim he should taste of death for every *man*.

Revelation 1:17-18
(17) And when I saw him, I fell at his feet as one dead. And he laid his right hand upon me, saying, Fear not; I am the first and the last,
(18) and the Living one; and I was dead, and behold, I am alive for evermore, and **I have the keys of death and of Hades**.

As the high priest of heaven, his garment is represented as being sprinkled with blood, having entered the holy of holies with his own blood.

Hebrews 9:11-12
(11) But Messiah having come a high priest of the good things
to come, through the greater and more perfect tabernacle, not
made with hands, that is to say, not of this creation,
(12) nor yet through the blood of goats and calves, but **through
his own blood**, entered in once for all into the holy place, having
obtained eternal redemption.

After having been manifested in the flesh he was called the "word [*of
Elohim*] made flesh."

John 1:14
And the **word became flesh**, and dwelt among us and we beheld
his glory, glory as of the only begotten from the Father, full of
grace and truth.

1 John 1:1-4
(1) That which was from the beginning, that which we have
heard, that which we have seen with our eyes, that which we
beheld, and our hands handled, concerning the **word of life**
(2) and the life was manifested, and we have seen, and bear
witness, and declare unto you the life, the eternal *life*, which was
with the Father, and **was manifested unto us**;
(3) that which we have seen and heard declare we unto you
also, that you also may have fellowship with us: yea, and our
fellowship is with the Father, and with his son **Yeshua Messiah**:
(4) and these things we write, that our joy may be made full.

If it wasn't clear enough from the various allusions to this person and
event in the previous chapters, it is here. The one riding on this white
horse was none other than Yeshua the Messiah.

In this passage in Revelation, regarding the coming of Yeshua in his
kingdom, we also see him pictured as riding in front of the army of
resurrected saints, each one clothed with the fine linen of their
righteous acts. The weapon with which he is armed is spiritual in

nature, namely the word of Elohim. This same two-edged sword is mentioned in Revelation 1:16 above and the author of Hebrews:

Hebrews 4:12
For the word of Elohim is living, and active, and sharper than any two-edged sword, and piercing even to the dividing of soul and spirit, of both joints and marrow, and quick to discern the thoughts and intents of the heart.

A prophecy of Isaiah hundreds of years earlier that spoke of the coming Messiah was thereby fulfilled:

Isaiah 11:1-4
(1) And there shall come forth a shoot out of the stock of Jesse, and a branch out of his roots shall bear fruit.
(2) And the spirit of Yahweh shall rest upon him, the spirit of wisdom and understanding, the spirit of counsel and might, the spirit of knowledge and of the fear of Yahweh.
(3) And his delight shall be in the fear of Yahweh; and he shall not judge after the sight of his eyes, neither decide after the hearing of his ears;
(4) but with righteousness shall he judge the poor, and decide with equity for the meek of the earth; and **he shall smite the earth with the rod of his mouth**; and **with the breath of his lips shall he slay the wicked**.

This prophecy of Isaiah continues by discussing the kingdom of Yahweh, its rule over the earth, and the gathering of Yahweh's dispersed children to it, each of which are discussed below.

Yeshua doesn't come with only a sword, but also with a rod of iron. These two instruments must be taken together to understand their meaning. The sword represents the authority he was given in judgment, vengeance and war, while the rod represents his authority in leading and guiding the nations. Together they tell us that Yeshua's dominion and power are complete. He told his apostles the same:

Matthew 28:18
And Jesus came to them and spoke unto them, saying, **All authority has been given unto me in heaven and on earth.**

The message is clear. Yeshua was coming with his saints, who had been promised co-rule with him through their overcoming[388], to establish his rule and kingdom on the earth. As his kingdom is not of the earth we need not expect it to have been one visible to the fleshly eye, especially given the highly apocalyptic nature of the text in this passage. Yet his authority was then established over all.

The image of the birds coming to feast on the flesh of the already slain peoples within Jerusalem, those from all societal positions, is John again reminding his audience that the curses spoken in Deuteronomy 28 were fulfilled in that wicked generation:

Deuteronomy 28:26
And your dead body **shall be food unto all birds of the heavens,** and unto the beasts of the earth; and there shall be none to frighten them away.

Apocalyptically speaking, the flesh of these rebellious people were food for the ravenous birds of the heavenly realm. From a historical perspective, the scene described here in Revelation 19:17-18 couldn't have been any more literal than that which was in the destroyed city. As we read above in the descriptions of the seven angels' bowl judgments, the bodies and blood of priests and lay-people, the rich and the poor, men and women, and the elderly and the infant filled the city and the temple.

Verses 19-21 describe the demise of two of the three great spiritual antagonists in the Apocalypse, the Beast of the sea and the Beast of the land, also known as the False Prophet. These two spiritual beings had their purpose and mission. The Beast of the sea, realized as the Roman Empire, was mustered and sent as the weapon of judgment and

---

[388] Revelation 2:26-27, 12:5, 20:4-6.

vengeance from Yahweh against his apostate and wicked children. As we've detailed above in several places, this is not the first time that we see Yahweh using a foreign nation and its military force to decimate Israel. If anyone doubts that the Roman army could be used by Yahweh for this purpose he or she need only read His words through Jeremiah, Isaiah and Amos:

Jeremiah 25:8-11
(8) Therefore thus says Yahweh of hosts: Because you have not heard my words,
(9) behold, I will send and take all the families of the north, says Yahweh, and *I will send* unto **Nebuchadnezzar the king of Babylon, my servant,** and will bring them against this land, and against the inhabitants thereof, and against all these nations round about; and I will utterly destroy them, and make them an astonishment, and a hissing, and perpetual desolations.
(10) Moreover I will take from them the voice of mirth and the voice of gladness, the voice of the bridegroom and the voice of the bride, the sound of the millstones, and the light of the lamp.
(11) And this whole land shall be a desolation, and an astonishment; and these nations shall serve the king of Babylon seventy years.

Isaiah 10:5-6, 12
(5) Ho Assyrian, **the rod of my anger,** the staff in whose hand is my indignation!
(6) I will send him against a profane nation, and against the people of my wrath will I give him a charge, to take the spoil, and to take the prey, and to tread them down like the mire of the streets.
(12) Wherefore it shall come to pass, that, **when the Master has performed his whole work upon mount Zion and on Jerusalem,** I will punish the fruit of the stout heart of the king of Assyria, and the glory of his high looks.

Amos 2:4-5
(4) Thus says Yahweh: For three transgressions of Judah, yea, for four, I will not turn away the punishment thereof; because they have rejected the Torah of Yahweh, and have not kept his

statutes, and their lies have caused them to err, after which their fathers did walk.
(5) But **I will send a fire upon Judah**, and it shall devour the palaces of Jerusalem.

Nebuchadnezzar and the king of Assyria are two examples of how Yahweh used pagan and profane nations to render his judgments upon his disobedient children. King Cyrus of Persia is actually called by the title "anointed one,"[389] transliterated from Hebrew as "messiah." Amos prophesied of fire coming upon Judah. This wasn't a fire from heaven to earth. This fire was the one brought by Nebuchadnezzar when he pillaged, burnt, and destroyed Jerusalem and the temple.

However, nations that come against Israel, if even directed by the Almighty to do so, do not go unpunished. In Isaiah 10:12 above we see that Yahweh said he would punish the king of Assyria. In Jeremiah 51 we see a very detailed prophecy describing the destruction of Babylon by the Medes. Yahweh used these foreign nations as swords in His anthropomorphic hands to render judgment upon His disobedient children. But after their mission and purpose was fulfilled, they too were punished for the wicked actions they performed. Behind each of these was a spiritual force. The description of the king of Tyre and his prophesied fall found in Ezekiel 28:11-19 is the clearest example. This punishment of nations that come against Israel, and the spiritual influences behind them, is exactly what we see in Revelation 19:19-21.

Though the destruction of the spiritual Beast and the False Prophet was near, their lives had not yet run their course. After the fall of Babylon the great harlot there were still cities and strongholds in Israel that remained rebellious and wicked. Yahweh's use of the Beast would continue until these final strongholds were destroyed and the fullness of the holy people was either destroyed or captured. We read the following after the capture of the final stronghold, Masada, was completed on April 1, 74 CE:

---

[389] Isaiah 45:1.

"When Masada was thus taken, the general left a garrison in the fortress to keep it, and he himself went away to Cesarea; **for there were now no enemies left in the country, but it was all overthrown by so long a war.**"[390]

The entirety of the land of Israel had now been overthrown by the Romans with no one left to oppose them. That very day, which was also discussed in chapter 12 above, was the 1,335th day from the setting up of the abomination of desolation in the temple.

Daniel tells us that those who waited and came to the 1,335th day were blessed, and now we know why. The time had now come for the spiritual Beasts to be judged and destroyed. Their mission as the great destroyers and deceivers of both the obedient and apostate people of Israel had been accomplished. The Beast from the sea, representing the Roman Empire, who brought great destruction from Yahweh upon Israel, was on his heels in retreat from the rider on the white horse. Likewise, the last day of the spiritual Beast from the land, the source of the great deceptions promulgated by apostate and rebellious Israelites, had come. Whatever had remained of their spiritual kingdoms was leveled as the new kingdom had been brought down and established.

We read that those two wicked creatures were cast *alive* into the lake of fire. John is telling his audience that the *spiritual* creatures that were aligned against them and their people were to be utterly and permanently destroyed. Spiritually speaking, this may involve an eternity of torture. From the earthly and historical perspective, however, the two Beasts' representations were also destined for complete and endless destruction, though not necessarily immediately. We read the same thing above from Daniel's prophecy:

Daniel 7:11-12
(11) I beheld at that time because of the voice of the great words which the horn spoke; I beheld even till the beast was slain, and its body destroyed, and it was given to be burned with fire.

---

[390] Josephus, Wars. 7.10.1. Page 769.

(12) And as for the rest of the beasts, their dominion was taken away: **yet their lives were prolonged for a season and a time**.

The fourth beast of Daniel's vision and its dominion were to be utterly destroyed. This beast is obviously a *spiritual* representation of a *spiritual* dominion. The dominion given to the Roman Empire, which that fourth beast represents, was taken away never to be given back again. Likewise the earthly Roman Empire was to fall and never again arise. The dominions of the other beasts were also taken away, but the beasts themselves were allowed to live on for an undefined period of time. Rashi's commentary[391] on this verse is not only very interesting, but shows that there was a Jewish tradition in his time tying the lives of the other three beasts to a war with Gog and Magog in the future. Is it possible that the beast that is the Roman Empire is forever destroyed but the kingdoms of the other beasts will be allowed to rise once again in the future? Is it possible that it is these kingdoms that the Dragon will gather against the holy city after the thousand-year period? We cannot know for sure, but the prophecies in scripture would seem to tell us it is a possibility.

After the fire of the apocalyptic lake had consumed the Beast and the False Prophet of Revelation 19 their smoke would ascend forever and ever. They would never rise again. Historically speaking, the Roman Empire saw its final demise towards the end of the fifth century with the takeover by Odoacer, who became the first king of Italy. At that point the Roman Empire had already been shredded into two parts. The Eastern part had been conquered and ruled by the Byzantine empire since the time of Constantine the Great. Odoacer's conquest marked the end of the Western part of the empire. The Roman Empire is to this day no more. The earthly and historical representation of the False Prophet met its final demise when the destruction of Jerusalem, the temple, and the Jewish Commonwealth was complete, which we just detailed. The false, adulterous, and idolatrous religious system of the Jews had fallen with the rest of its nation. Its throne was gone, its place of rule in ruins, its organized attack against the followers of

---

[391] See http://www.chabad.org/library/bible_cdo/aid/16490#showrashi=true.

Yeshua destroyed. As we will see in the next section the destruction of the False Prophet allowed for the once hindered and exceedingly persecuted message of the gospel in the land to now flow much more freely and powerfully to the ends of the earth.

As always, we must remember that just as the binding of the Dragon in chapter 20 below is *spiritual* in its core intent, so is the capture of the Beast and False Prophet here. While their earthly representations were indeed destroyed, or to be destroyed in the future, their destruction here in chapter 19 is one in the heavenly realm. In verse 19 we also read of the "kings of the earth, and their armies" as being among those gathered against Yeshua and his army in this final battle. Where verse 19 gives the identity of all those who were standing against Yeshua, verses 20-21 give us the order and cause of their destructions. The destruction of the Beast and the False Prophet was just detailed. In the case of the kings of the earth and their armies, however, the cause of their destruction is different. They are destroyed by the sword that came forth from the mouth of Yeshua, which we already established was the word of Elohim. How true this is! Repeatedly we read the writings of the prophets and the teachings of Yeshua and see that the destruction of the people and their city was declared by the word of Elohim:

> Isaiah 55:10-11
> (10) For as the rain comes down and the snow from heaven, and returns not there, but waters the earth, and makes it bring forth and bud, and gives seed to the sower and bread to the eater;
> (11) so shall **my word be that goes forth out of my mouth: it shall not return unto me void**, but it shall accomplish that which I please, and it shall prosper in the thing whereto I sent it.

This distinction between the causes of destruction is very telling. John is telling his audience that the *spiritual* creatures that were aligned against them and their people were to be utterly and permanently destroyed. However, the remaining *earthly* enemies were to be destroyed by the word of Yahweh. Yahweh proclaimed it through His prophets and through His Son and it was as good as done; it did not return to him void. We've already outlined the historical accounts behind the apocalyptic imagery of Chapter 18 describing the fall of Babylon. Those accounts tell us in vivid detail what happened because of the outpouring of the seventh angel's bowl judgment. The people were slain mercilessly. Their bodies were trampled upon and thrown away like trash. The blood flowed like rivers in the holiest places. Their beloved temple was in flames. Those who remained alive were taken away in chains and given to the beasts in the Roman games.[392] The final verses of Deuteronomy 28, which details the visiting of numerable curses upon disobedient Israel, states:

Deuteronomy 28:62-68

(62) And you shall be left few in number, whereas you were as the stars of the heavens for multitude, because you would not obey the voice of Yahweh your Elohim.

(63) And it shall be, as Yahweh rejoiced over you to do you good, and to multiply you, so **Yahweh shall rejoice over you to destroy you, and to lay you waste. And you shall be plucked from the land you are going to possess.**

(64) And **Yahweh shall scatter you among all people,** from *one* end of the earth even to the *other*, and you shall serve other gods there, wood and stone, which you have not known, nor your fathers.

(65) And among these nations you shall find no ease, nor shall the sole of your foot have rest. But Yahweh shall give you there a trembling heart and failing of eyes, and sorrow of mind.

(66) And your life shall hang in doubt before you, and you shall fear day and night, and shall have no assurance of your life.

(67) In the morning you shall say, Oh that it were evening! And in the evening you shall say, Oh that it were morning! For the fear of your heart with which you fear, and for the sight of your eyes which you shall see.

(68) And Yahweh shall bring you into Egypt again with ships, by the way of which I said to you, You shall never see it again. And you shall be sold to your enemies there, for male slaves and slave-girls; and there shall be no buyer.

---

[392] Josephus, Wars. 7.3.1. Page 752.

The ultimate finality of the prophetic utterances regarding the destruction of Israel had come at the time the last standing enemies of Yeshua were slain and/or exiled. Now that the final enemies of Yeshua had been destroyed his kingdom could be firmly and finally established.

The Messengers Sent

The last verses in the passages quoted above from Matthew and Mark both speak of "angels" being sent forth to gather the elect of the Son of Man from the ends of the earth. We would venture to say that most followers of Yeshua today unknowingly read those verses through the lens of doctrinal bias and preprogramming. Unfortunately, without being presented with alternative ways of viewing certain verses or passages this is often unavoidable. We believe that these two verses must be reexamined by all believers today to determine whether the traditionally and almost globally accepted understanding of them is accurate.

Matthew 24:31
And he shall send forth his angels with *a great sound of a trumpet,* and *they shall gather together* his elect from the four winds, from one end of heaven to the other.

Mark 13:27
And then shall he send forth the angels, and shall gather together his elect from the four winds, from the uttermost part of the earth to the uttermost part of heaven.

Most who read those verses will immediately think, "That's speaking of the resurrection of the dead." If you are one who did not think that you are among the minority. The Greek text underlying parts of these passages needs to be examined for a proper understanding of these verses. The phrase "send forth his/the angels" in both verses is identical in the Greek text - ἀποστελεῖ τοὺς ἀγγέλους, *apostelei tous angelous.* The first thing to be clarified is the word ἀγγέλους, *angelous,* which is a derivative of the word ἄγγελος, *angelos,* typically translated in these verses as "angels." However, the proper translation of this verse is largely based on context. Where most today want to see this verse as discussing the resurrection of the dead, they typically translated it as "angels" because the angels are the ones said to reap the harvest of souls. However, what if this passage isn't talking about the resurrection at all?

The word ἄγγελος is defined as "a *messenger, envoy, one who is sent.*"[393] Robert Young's Literal Translation (YLT) provides us with a more literal and accurate rendering of these verses.

Matthew 24:31 (YLT)
And he shall send his **messengers** with a great sound of a trumpet, and they shall gather together his chosen from the four winds, from the ends of the heavens unto the ends thereof.

Mark 13:27 (YLT)
And then he shall send his **messengers**, and gather together his chosen from the four winds, from the end of the earth unto the end of heaven.

The entire message and timeline from the punishment and binding of Satan, the dragon, to the destruction of the Beast and the False Prophet, to the blowing of the great trumpet above is foreshadowed in another of Isaiah's prophecies. Given its importance we find it prudent to quote the entire passage here.

Isaiah 27:1-13
(1) In that day Yahweh with his hard and great and strong sword will punish **leviathan the swift serpent**, and **leviathan the crooked serpent**; and **he will slay the monster that is in the sea**.
(2) In that day: A vineyard of wine, sing you unto it.
(3) I Yahweh am its keeper; I will water it every moment: lest any hurt it, I will keep it night and day.
(4) Wrath is not in me: would that the briers and thorns were against me in battle! I would march upon them, I would burn them together.

---

[393] Thayer. Entry for ἄγγελος. Page 5.

(5) Or else let him take hold of my strength, that he may make peace with me; *yea*, let him make peace with me.

(6) **In days to come** shall Jacob take root; Israel shall blossom and bud; and **they shall fill the face of the world with fruit**.

(7) Has he smitten them as he smote those that smote them? or are they slain according to the slaughter of them that were slain by them?

(8) In measure, when you send them away, you contend with them; he has removed *them* with his rough blast in the day of the east wind.

(9) Therefore by this shall the iniquity of Jacob be forgiven, and this is all the fruit of taking away his sin: **that he makes all the stones of the altar as chalkstones that are beaten in sunder**, *so that* the Asherim and the sun-images shall rise no more.

(10) **For the fortified city is solitary, a habitation deserted and forsaken, like the wilderness**: there shall the calf feed, and there shall he lie down, and consume the branches thereof.

(11) When the boughs thereof are withered, they shall be broken off; the women shall come, and set them on fire; for it is a people of no understanding: therefore he that made them will not have compassion upon them, and he that formed them will show them no favor.

(12) And it shall come to pass in that day, that Yahweh will beat off *his fruit* from the flood of the River unto the brook of Egypt; and you shall be gathered one by one, O you children of Israel.

(13) **And it shall come to pass in that day, that a great trumpet shall be blown; and they shall come that were ready to perish in the land of Assyria, and they that were outcasts in the land of Egypt; and they shall worship Yahweh in the holy mountain at Jerusalem.**

Isaiah's prophecy states that there was to be a day in his future where the great serpent (*i.e.* dragon) was to be punished, the beast from the sea slain, and the ones perishing throughout the world[394] were to be called to the holy mountain at the sound of a great trumpet. The

---

[394] Egypt and Assyria being representative of the "four corners" of the earth in that they surrounded Israel.

events in his prophecy parallel those in the Apocalypse with great accuracy. The great trumpet to blown announces the time for the message of the gospel to go forth to all the earth.

As we mentioned briefly above, the destruction of Jerusalem, the temple, and the Jewish Commonwealth removed in large degree many hindrances that the gospel message was experiencing. The destruction of the spiritual Beast and False Prophet also did this. After the coming of the Son of Man on the clouds of heaven in the verses just prior to the above, freedom and power like never before was granted to the deliverers of the good news, the *messengers* of the covenant. This was not to a promise that messengers of the covenant would never again face persecution for their faith or message. In a very real sense the announcement sounded by this great trumpet was saying, "The great enemies of true Zion, the Beast and the False Prophet, have been slain! Go forth now in power and preach the message of the gospel to the places far beyond Israel!"

The verses about sending the messengers aren't saying that Yeshua was going to send out heavenly beings to resurrect the dead from around the world. The spectacles of doctrinal bias are telling us that. Yeshua was saying that after the judgment had been passed and the sentence of wrath completed his prophecy was going to be fulfilled and the Father's command obeyed:

Matthew 22:7-10
(7) But the king was enraged; and he sent his armies, and destroyed those murderers, and burned their city.
(8) Then said he to his servants, The wedding is ready, but they that were bidden were not worthy.
(9) **Go you therefore unto the partings of the highways, and as many as you shall find, bid to the marriage feast**.
(10) And those servants went out into the highways, and gathered together all as many as they found, both bad and good: and the wedding was filled with guests.

The burning of the city had taken place and the time to go to the rest of the peoples of the world, wherever they may be, had come. Each person was to be invited to come to the wedding supper of the Lamb. Each person was to believe upon Yeshua as their Messiah and be taught to humbly follow his perfect example of Torah-observance. Each of those was then to teach the same to others they were led to. Those who were elected and chosen to be guests of the Lamb's wedding would gratefully accept the invitation with the utmost praise to Yahweh. Many trusted commentators agree with our conclusion[395].

We detailed in chapter 1 above how trumpets were used to announce and declare various things. Likewise, the announcement that the time for the message to go forth to the ends of heaven and earth had been sounded. These invitations are still being sent out today. Guests are continually being invited into the wedding supper of the Lamb. Each time a follower of Yeshua spreads his message of salvation, obedience and righteousness to another, and the recipient accepts the invitation, they have succeeded in fulfilling the Messiah's command to gather his chosen ones. HalleluYah!

---

[395] See Clarke; John Gill's "Exposition of the Entire Bible"; Robert Hawker's "Poor Man's Commentary."

CHAPTER TWENTY

A Tale of Two Judgments

This chapter contains two separate visions that are directly related to one another – the judgment of Satan and the judgment of the resurrected dead. Each vision is divided into two portions in the chapter. However, when the passages of scripture that John is referencing and referring his audience to are recalled the individual visions are easy to distinguish. Before delving any deeper into the scriptures in this chapter, though, we need to discuss the apocalyptic nature of the thousand years.

The Thousand Years

The concept of the thousand-year period as found in this chapter is by far one of the most hotly debated topics in the Apocalypse. This is because it is the determining chapter as it relates to one's belief about the "millennium." First, this chapter is the sole one in scripture that speaks directly of a thousand-year period. Second, the symbolic use of the number "thousand" immediately tells us that the end of this period is intended to extend beyond the limits of the "things which must shortly come to pass." The beginning of the thousand years most definitely began at that time, but the end, described by the apocalyptically indefinite number "one thousand," is by nature outside of those limits.

It is important to point out that the word "millennium" is found nowhere in the entire corpus of scripture. It is a misnomer that has been the cause of much confusion on this topic. The phrase that is in the scriptures is "a/the thousand years." This fact is significant for a few reasons. First, "millennium" is clearly a mistranslation of the actual text. The words in Greek that are translated "thousand years" are χίλια ἔτη, *chilia ete*. In Ancient Greek it can also be found combined as a single word, χιλιέτης, *chilietes*. Either version one chooses it takes two words to bring across the meaning. The first word is χίλιοι, *chilioi*, and literally means "*a thousand*."[396] The second word is ἔτος, *etos*, and literally means "*a year*."[397] Put them together and the phrase is simple, "a thousand years."

The second reason it is significant is because calling it a "millennium" removes what is supposed to be an apocalyptic number, one thousand. As we've detailed numerous times, John's message is apocalyptic in nature. His intent is to communicate to his audience in a way that only they can understand, a way that would cause them to go deep into the recesses of their minds to discern his meaning. Calling the period a "millennium" removes any ability we have in understanding John's apocalyptic message here.

The third reason is because it gives rise to phrases such as "premillennialism," "postmillennialism," "amillennialism," and the like. Each of these phrases are used to squeeze various commentators, scholars, or lay persons into distinct and comfortable doctrinal "boxes." "Amillennialism" is really a misnomer of sorts itself. By definition an amillennialist believes that the thousand-year period is symbolic, not literal. So, as unorthodox or incomprehensible as it may sound, a better term for "amillennialist" would be "symbolic-thousand-year-ist."

In chapter 7 above we provided several pieces of conclusive information that shows how the number one thousand need not be

---

[396] Thayer. Entry for χίλιοι. Page 669.
[397] Thayer. Entry for ἔτος. Page 255.

understood literally. For ease, the same information is presented here again.

Exodus 20:4-6
(4) You shall not make unto you a graven image, nor any likeness *of anything* that is in heaven above, or that is in the earth beneath, or that is in the water under the earth:
(5) you shall not bow down yourself unto them, nor serve them; for I Yahweh your Elohim am a jealous Elohim, visiting the iniquity of the fathers upon the children, upon the third and upon the fourth generation of them that hate me,
(6) and showing lovingkindness unto **thousands** of them that love me and keep my commandments.

The word "thousands" here isn't intended to place a limit on the scope Yahweh's mercy and lovingkindness.

Deuteronomy 1:11
Yahweh, the Elohim of your fathers, make you **a thousand times** as many as you are, and bless you, as he has promised you!

Moses' blessing wasn't intended to be a limit to a thousand times, as if that was a maximum to the number of Israelites were permitted.

Deuteronomy 7:9-10
(9) Know therefore that Yahweh your Elohim, he is Elohim, the faithful Elohim, who keeps covenant and lovingkindness with them that love him and keep his commandments to **a thousand generations**,
(10) and repays them that hate him to their face, to destroy them: he will not be slack to him that hates him, he will repay him to his face.

This does not mean that Yahweh doesn't keep his covenant with the thousand and first generation.

Psalms 50:10
For every beast of the forest is my, And the cattle upon **a thousand hills.**

Just as he did in chapter 7, John is telling his audience that the thousand-year period of Messiah's reign, and the reign of those with him, will be a perfect, yet indefinite period. Having now laid the foundations about the thousand-year period we can move on to the scriptures in this chapter of the Apocalypse.

The Binding of Satan

(1) And I saw an angel coming down out of heaven, having the key of the abyss and a great chain in his hand.
(2) And he laid hold on the dragon, the old serpent, which is the Devil and Satan, and bound him for a thousand years,
(3) and cast him into the abyss, and shut *it*, and sealed *it* over him, that he should deceive the nations no more, until the thousand years should be finished: after this he must be loosed for a little time.

The first vision John sees is that of the judgment of Satan. It, like the second vision of the judgment of the resurrected dead, is divided into two portions. The fullness of the vision will become more apparent once viewed properly in context.

John's continued use of apocalyptic terminology here is very apparent. This antagonistic character visualized as the Dragon throughout the Apocalypse was now to be bound. Let us examine a teaching of Yeshua that is recalled upon reading of the binding of Satan.

Matthew 12:24-29
(24) But when the Pharisees heard it, they said, This man does not cast out demons, but by Beelzebub the prince of the demons.
(25) And knowing their thoughts he said unto them, Every kingdom divided against itself is brought to desolation; and every city or house divided against itself shall not stand:
(26) and if Satan casts out Satan, he is divided against himself; how then shall his kingdom stand?
(27) And if I by Beelzebub cast out demons, by whom do your sons cast them out? therefore shall they be your judges.
(28) But if I by the spirit of Elohim cast out demons, then is the

kingdom of Elohim come upon you.
(29) Or how can one enter into the house of the strong *man*, and spoil his goods, **except he first bind the strong** *man*? and then he will spoil his house.

Luke 11:20-22
(20) But if I by the finger of Elohim cast out demons, then is the kingdom of Elohim come upon you.
(21) When the strong *man* fully armed guards his own court, his goods are in peace:
(22) but when a stronger than he shall come upon him, and overcome him, he takes from him his whole armor wherein he trusted, and divides his spoils.

Yeshua is specifically addressing the Pharisees' accusations regarding him being used by Satan to cast out the servants of Satan. The "spoils" of Satan, to use the term John used, are deceived people. The more he successfully deceives, the richer he becomes. The reason for the binding of Satan is so that "he should deceive the nations no more." Satan, represented by the "strong *man*" in the passages above, was bound so that those who had been so deceived as to follow and serve him could be taken back. Those who would have been deceived by him in the future could be prevented from doing so.

Yeshua sending his messengers to the four winds of heaven to gather his elect, as discussed at the end of chapter 19 above, is a plundering of the enemy's spoils. Chronologically speaking, however, the strong man had to be bound *before* his goods could be spoiled. Satan had fallen like lightning from heaven[398] and the kingdoms of the world, once in his possession[399], were no longer his[400]. His power, authority, and property were now bound and spoiled. He will, however, have a time in the future where he will once again be permitted to propagate his lies.

As will be seen with the second vision detailed below, this first portion

---

[398] Luke 10:18.
[399] Matthew 4:8-9.
[400] Revelation 11:15, 12:10.

of the vision concerning the judgment of Satan ends rather abruptly and with no conclusion. It leaves one asking, "Okay, then what? What happens after the Dragon is loosed? Does the world have to go through the same cycles of life and death, obedience and idolatry, and righteousness and unrighteousness that it has been subjected to until now?" Thankfully, the conclusion drawn from and answers to these questions are answered for us later in this chapter.

The Current Presence of Evil

Some may very well ask, "If the Dragon, Satan, the ruler of evil has been bound, why is there still evil in the earth?" James gives us some excellent insight into this very topic.

James 1:12-15
(12) Blessed is the man that endures temptation; for when he has been approved, he shall receive the crown of life, which *the Master* promised to them that love him.
(13) Let no man say when he is tempted, I am tempted of Elohim; for Elohim cannot be tempted with evil, and he himself tempts no man:
(14) **but each man is tempted, when he is drawn away by his own lust**, and enticed.
(15) Then the lust, when it has conceived, bears sin: and the sin, when it is fully grown, brings forth death.

Simply put, the adage "the devil made me do it" isn't an excuse to Elohim. Every time we sin we cannot say that it is because Satan or some demon was driving us to do it. Was it Satan's goal from the beginning to deceive Yahweh's children and cause them to rebel against Him? Of course! But the choice to rebel or not is still in our hands. Our own lusts, whether of the eyes, the flesh, or otherwise, are what drive us to sin. Temptations arise because we allow them to arise. Even Cain, the first murderer, was told he could overcome sin.

Genesis 4:7
If you do well, shall it not be lifted up? and if you do not well, sin crouches at the door; and unto you shall be its desire; **but you do**

rule over it.

How much more do we have the power and ability to avoid temptations and overcome sin now that Yahweh's holy spirit is dwelling within us?

In addition to the temptations we bring upon ourselves we must also remember that scripture nowhere states that every wicked spirit was bound in the abyss as Satan was. The binding of their king undoubtedly resulted in a much lower level of organization as a wicked army. They are now, in a sense, sheep without a shepherd, or more correctly, wolves without a pack-leader. However, though these spirits know that there will be a day of reckoning for them as well[401], they are still here to wreak havoc wherever they can. There is no doubt that legitimate demonic possessions still occur around the world. There is no doubt that wicked and unjust rulers of nations have been strongly influenced by demonic powers. However, their dominion and authority is subject to Yeshua's. They have been put under his feet, in subjection to him. If they do certain things or move in certain ways it is only because the true king allows them to do so, like he did when they requested to be cast into pigs[402]. Likewise, those who serve and obey Yeshua had and continue to have the same authority given by our Messiah.

One final point needs to be addressed regarding Yeshua's teachings as recorded by Matthew and Luke above. In both accounts, he stated with no uncertainty that if he indeed cast out evil spirits by the spirit of Elohim, the kingdom of Elohim had come upon them. No true follower of Yeshua would say that he cast out demons by anything else other than the spirit of Yahweh. By admitting that he did cast out spirits by the spirit of Elohim, we must also openly admit that the kingdom of Elohim had come upon those standing there.

---

[401] Matthew 8:28-29.
[402] Matthew 8:30-32.

The Resurrections – Part II

(4) And I saw thrones, and they sat upon them, and judgment was given unto them: and *I saw* the souls of them that had been beheaded for the testimony of Yeshua, and for the word of Elohim, and such as worshipped not the beast, neither his image, and received not the mark upon their forehead and upon their hand; and they lived, and reigned with Messiah a thousand years.
(5) (The rest of the dead lived not until the thousand years should be finished.) This is the first resurrection.
(6) Blessed and holy is he that has part in the first resurrection: over these the second death has no power; but they shall be priests of Elohim and of Messiah, and shall reign with him a thousand years.

The second vision John sees is that which concerns the judgment of the resurrected dead. One of the first things we see in this passage is that there is a certain group of people that are seated on thrones and given the powers of judgment. However, the abrupt ending to this portion of the vision leaves us with several questions. Who were those people? Who or what were they given judgment over? Was there a "second resurrection?" If there was, what happened to them? Just as with the first vision, the answers are provided within the text and later down in this chapter. Prior to addressing those questions, though, we need to examine the text itself a little more carefully.

The Spurious Interjection

Revelation 5a surrounded by parentheses above is one that is greatly debated. The reason is multi-faceted. It forms a very strange parenthesis in the text that seems very out of place when read in context. Verse 4 tells us of the ones who were to rule and reign with Messiah. Then 5a tells us of the "rest of the dead" (i.e. those not a part of the ruling ones) who were to come to life *after* the thousand-year period. Then after we are told that "*This* is the first resurrection." A question should immediately come to one's mind – "Which is the first resurrection?" Is it the one that consisted of those ruling and reigning with Yeshua? Or is it the one referring to the nearest textual antecedent, that consisting of "the rest of the dead?" From a strictly textual standpoint John is saying that the first resurrection consisted of the "rest of the dead" who come to life after the thousand years. However, this defies all logic. After all, how could a resurrection that comes *after* a thousand-year period be considered "first" if there were others resurrected *before* that period?

Though our conclusion has been disputed and disagrees with that of some textual critics, there are several pieces of evidence that support the belief that verse 5a was a scribal addition. Several reliable manuscripts do not contain that portion of verse 5 at all. This includes the Codex Sinaiticus, the Majority Text, the Syriac text, and several other minuscules of both Alexandrian and Byzantine text-types. An image of the text from the actual manuscript of the Codex Sinaiticus[403] is shown on the following page:

---

[403] See http://www.codexsinaiticus.org/en/manuscript.aspx?book=59&chapter=20&lid=en&side=r&verse=5&zoomSlider=0.

Top

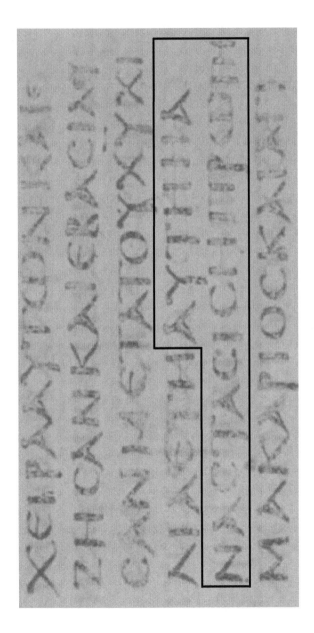

The Sinaiticus manuscript is written in what are known as "uncials" where each letter is capitalized. The entirety of verse 5 is outlined in yellow and reads AYTH H ANACTACIC H ΠΡΩΤΗ, *aute e anastasis e prote*. The portion just prior to this text is obviously the end of verse 4. In addition to the various manuscripts, it is omitted from Victorinus of Poetovio, an early "church father" of the mid-third century, who excluded it in his commentary on the Apocalypse. Jerome, almost a century later, made changes to Victorinus' original commentary, especially chapters 20 and 21. But we still have the original to reference today. On chapter 20 we have this portion of his commentary extant as it relates to verse 5 and his quoting of it:

> "*And the scarlet devil is imprisoned* and all his fugitive angels *in the Tartarus of Gehenna* at the coming of the Lord; no one is ignorant of this. And after the thousand years he is released, because of the nations which will have served Antichrist: so that they alone might perish, as they deserved. Then is the general judgment. Therefore he says: *And they lived*, he says, *the dead* who were written in the book of life, and *they reigned with Christ a thousand years. This is the first resurrection. Blessed and holy is he who has a part in the first resurrection: toward this one the second death has no power.* Of this resurrection, he says: *And I saw the Lamb standing, and with him 144 thousands*, that is, standing with Christ, namely those of the Jews in the last time who become believers through the preaching of Elijah, those who, the Spirit bears witness, are virgins not only in body, but also in language. Therefore, as he reminds above, the 24 elder-aged said: *Grace we bring to You, O Lord God who has reigned; and the nations are angry.*"[404]

The portions of the quote above that are italicized is Victorinus' quotes of the Apocalypse. Notice how his quote of verses 4 and 5 are identical to those in the Sinaiticus. The phrase "The rest of the dead lived not until the thousand years should be finished" is completely absent. An eighth century Spanish theologian, Beatus of Liébana (*ca.* 730-785 CE)

---

[404] Victorinus. Page 18.

also didn't include 20:5a in his *Commentaria in Apocalypsin* (Commentary on the Apocalypse)[405]. James Parkinson gives us a great summary of the textual issues related to verse 5a:

"Revelation 20:5 – 'This *is* the first resurrection.' should probably be the whole verse. However, many ancient manuscripts have an extra sentence to read (beginning in the latter part of verse 4), '...they lived, and reigned with Christ a thousand years. The rest of the dead lived not until were finished the thousand years. This is the first resurrection.' A problem becomes immediately evident: The extra sentence says that the first resurrection is really the absence of a resurrection! So, we should look at the ancient manuscripts.

It is reasonable to suspect that the extra sentence was accidentally omitted when a scribe's eye skipped from 'thousand years' at the end of verse 4 to 'thousand years' at the end of the extra sentence, as most text critics do. Yet, there are five observations that point to omission as being the earlier reading:

1. There are no pre-Constantine manuscripts covering Revelation 20 discovered yet. The only pre-Constantine evidence we have is Victorinus' commentary (ca. 300 A.D.). The manuscripts of Victorinus of Pettau omit the extra sentence, while Jerome a century later says Victorinus included it. [Victorinus was a chiliast (believer in a literal thousand-year kingdom of Christ on earth); so it is less credible that the manuscripts he saw would have contained the sentence.]

2. The oldest manuscript we possess of Revelation 20 is the Sinaitic of the mid-fourth century, and it omits the sentence, while the next oldest is the Alexandrian of the early-fifth century, which adds it. [Not strong evidence, based on just one manuscript, as even the best manuscript contains some mistakes.]

---

[405] Beatus. Pages 533-536.

3. There are two 'Majority Texts' ($\mathfrak{M}$) in Revelation, the 'Koine text," $\mathfrak{M}^K$, of the fourth or possibly early fifth century, and the 'Andreas-commentary text', $\mathfrak{M}^A$, which is unlikely to precede Andreas himself, ca. A.D. 600. The Koine omits, while the Andreas adds, the sentence.

4. The Aecumenius-commentary text is found in two forms. The earlier (represented by manuscripts 2053 and 2062), originating with Aecumenius near A.D. 540, omits the sentence in the Revelation text but includes it in his commentary. The later text (represented by a family of manuscripts, f^{1678}, including manuscripts 1678, 2080, 1778, and 052), apparently partially re-edited to conform more to the commentary, includes the sentence in both text and commentary.

5. From the fourth to thirteenth century, about equal numbers of manuscripts omit and add the disputed sentence. In the fourteenth century the fraction adding it jumps to about 69%, and it rises thereafter to 100% in the seventeenth century.

All five observations reveal a trend towards adding the disputed sentence, not deleting it. Such a change would be in keeping with the new political situation when Constantine released Christians from persecution: Now that this is Christ's kingdom, were we wrong in expecting the resurrection to begin? or, Are Christ's Kingdom and its resurrection still future? Thus, there was a perceived need to add a comment in the margin, 'The rest of the dead lived not until the thousand years were finished.' After the sentence was incorporated into the text, and seen to read roughly, some scribes prefixed 'And', while others prefixed 'But.' Centuries later other scribes inserted 'again' after 'lived not.' Thus this sentence is found in five different forms among the manuscripts which do add it."[406]

Considering all the information presented above we conclude that the

---

[406] http://www.heraldmag.org/2009/09so_6.htm. Last Accessed 8 August 2017. See also Parkinson. Pages 22-23.

best translation of verses 4-6 would read as follows:

(4) And I saw thrones, and they sat upon them, and judgment was given unto them: and *I saw* the souls of them that had been beheaded for the testimony of Yeshua, and for the word of Elohim, and such as worshipped not the beast, neither his image, and received not the mark upon their forehead and upon their hand; and they lived, and reigned with Messiah a thousand years.
(5) This is the first resurrection.
(6) Blessed and holy is he that has part in the first resurrection: over these the second death has no power; but they shall be priests of Elohim and of Messiah, and shall reign with him a thousand years.

When rendered as above, the message is clear and consistent. We agree with Parkinson's conclusion that 5a should be omitted from our printed versions. Inserting the highly spurious passage confuses the entire flow of the message. It mysteriously defines the first resurrection as "the rest of the dead" who "lived not until the thousand years should be finished." It unnecessarily and incorrectly places the thousand-year period between the resurrections, which has caused many false doctrines to arise throughout the generations regarding the true timing of the resurrection of the dead. Reading the passage as it is above allows the context of the Apocalypse and the remainder of this chapter to establish the timing of the resurrections, not the manmade doctrines of generations past, present and future. We can now begin to examine some of the questions raised earlier in this section.

The Thrones Are Set

The scene illustrated in Revelation 20:4-6, which is completed in verses 11-15 below, is a mirror of what Daniel prophesied about in Daniel chapter 7.

Daniel 7:9-10
(9) I beheld till thrones were placed, and one that was ancient of days did sit: his raiment was white as snow, and the hair of his

head like pure wool; his throne was fiery flames, *and* the wheels thereof burning fire.

(10) A fiery stream issued and came forth from before him: thousands of thousands ministered unto him, and ten thousand times ten thousand stood before him: the judgment was set, and the books were opened.

Just how closely this prophecy mirrors the judgment scene in Revelation 20 will be clearer after 11-15 is evaluated below. For now, however, we see in both visions that thrones were set in place and that the purpose was for judgment.

In 20:4-6 John tells us of a group of people who would be ruling and reigning with Yeshua during the thousand years. He has already provided us with enough information in the previous chapters of the Apocalypse to allow us to identify exactly who they are. The description of them is found in chapters 6, 7, 12, 14 and 15. The fullness of the martyred saints of Yeshua, as well as those who had been tried by and overcame the Beast and his name, who patiently endured holding to the testimony of Yeshua and keeping the commandments of Elohim, are those pictured here reigning with Messiah – the 144,000 first fruits. Those were what is known as the "first resurrection." It is to these that the power of judgment was given.

This concept is different than what most eschatological doctrines teach, including those endorsed or taught by Futurists. Typically, those teach that the ones ruling and reigning with Messiah are *all* who would be a part of his kingdom regardless of what age they lived and died in. This is not, however, what the plain language of the text tells us. It tells us that those who were martyred for their faith and those that had the opportunity to serve the Beast, or accept his mark, and avoided doing so, were the ones who were to judge and rule.

There have obviously been many thousands of others who have entered the kingdom through death since that time, just as Revelation 14:13 tells us there would be. Those people are, of course, not precluded from having positions in the kingdom. However, those who were faced with the trials of the great tribulation in the days of the apostles were deemed worthy of greater positions. We need not be surprised or disheartened by this scriptural and historical truth. Rather, let us always remember that being a foot washer in the kingdom of heaven is immeasurably better than tasting of the second death. What's more, we have an amazing promise from our Master and Messiah that the obedient will be granted much more:

Matthew 5:17-19
(17) Think not that I came to destroy the Torah or the Prophets: I came not to destroy, but to fulfil.
(18) For verily I say unto you, Till heaven and earth pass away, one jot or one tittle shall in no wise pass away from the Torah, till all things be accomplished.
(19) Whosoever therefore shall break one of these least commandments, and shall teach men so, shall be called least in the kingdom of heaven: but **whosoever shall do and teach them, he shall be called great in the kingdom of heaven.**

Our example is Yeshua. Our Master is Yeshua. We must serve our Master with our whole hearts. His instruction to his apostles and disciples then is no different than the one for those who follow him today. We are to keep, do, and teach the commandments of Yahweh contained in the Torah and the Prophets, *just as he did.* The apostle John's message was consistent as well. Let us never forget these words:

1 John 2:5-6
(5) ...Hereby we know that we are in him:
(6) he that says he abides in him **ought himself also to walk even as he walked.**

The question of who or what those of the first resurrection were given judgment over won't be answered until verses 11-15 below are addressed.

The "Second" Resurrection

The phrase "second resurrection" is not found explicitly in the scriptures. However, the sheer use of the phrase "first resurrection" implies at least one more. Having already detailed the spurious interjection of 5a above we have no need to project another resurrection event into some unknown time in the future. In fact, given all that has been shown in the previous chapters above, especially 12 and 14, the identity of those in the "second resurrection" has already been revealed. The scriptures are consistent in their description of the makeup of that resurrection:

Daniel 12:1-2
(1) And at that time shall Michael stand up, the great prince who stands for the children of your people; and there shall be a time of trouble, such as never was since there was a nation even to that same time: and at that time your people shall be delivered, **every one that shall be found written in the book**.
(2) And many of them that sleep in the dust of the earth shall awake, **some to everlasting life, and some to shame and everlasting contempt**.

Matthew 13:24-30
(24) Another parable set he before them, saying, The kingdom of heaven is likened unto a man that sowed good seed in his field:
(25) but while men slept, his enemy came and sowed tares also among the wheat, and went away.
(26) But when the blade sprang up and brought forth fruit, then appeared the tares also.
(27) And the servants of the householder came and said unto him, Sir, did you not sow good seed in your field? why then does it have tares?
(28) And he said unto them, An enemy has done this. And the servants say unto him, Will you then that we go and gather them up?
(29) But he said, Nay; lest haply while you gather up the tares, you root up the wheat with them.
(30) **Let both grow together until the harvest**: and in the time of the harvest I will say to the reapers, **Gather up first the tares**, and bind them in bundles to burn them; but **gather the wheat into my barn**.

Matthew 13:47-50
(47) Again, the kingdom of heaven is like unto a net, that was

cast into the sea, and gathered of every kind:

(48) which, when it was filled, they drew up on the beach; and they sat down, and **gathered the good into vessels**, but **the bad they cast away**.

(49) So shall it be in the end of the age: **the angels shall come forth**, and **sever the wicked from among the righteous**,

(50) and shall cast them into the furnace of fire: there shall be the weeping and the gnashing of teeth.

Matthew 25:31-34, 41, 46

(31) But when the Son of man shall come in his glory, and all the angels with him, then shall he sit on the throne of his glory:

(32) and before him shall be gathered all the nations: and he shall separate them one from another, as the shepherd separates **the sheep** from **the goats;**

(33) and he shall set **the sheep on his right hand**, but **the goats on the left**.

(34) Then shall the King say unto **them on his right hand**, Come, you blessed of my Father, inherit the kingdom prepared for you from the foundation of the world...

(41) Then shall he say also unto **them on the left hand**, Depart from me, you cursed, into the eternal fire which is prepared for the devil and his angels...

(46) And **these shall go away into eternal punishment**: but **the righteous into eternal life**.

John 5:24-29

(24) Verily, verily, I say unto you, He that hears my word, and believes him that sent me, has eternal life, and comes not into judgment, but has passed out of death into life.

(25) Verily, verily, I say unto you, The hour comes, and now is, when the dead shall hear the voice of the Son of Elohim; and they that hear shall live.

(26) For as the Father has life in himself, even so gave he to the Son also to have life in himself:

(27) and he gave him authority to execute judgment, because he is a son of man.

(28) Marvel not at this: for the hour comes, in which all that are in the tombs shall hear his voice,

(29) and shall come forth; they that have done good, unto **the resurrection of life**; and they that have done evil, unto **the resurrection of judgment**.

Acts 24:14-15

(14) But this I confess unto you, that after the Way which they call a sect, so serve I the Elohim of our fathers, believing all things which are according to the Torah, and which are written in the prophets;

(15) having hope toward Elohim, which these also themselves look for, that there shall be **a resurrection both of the just and unjust**.

The passages in the scriptures that most clearly detail this final resurrection event each speak of resurrection that was divided into two different groups. We've already detailed in chapter 12 above how amazingly the chronology of Daniel 12:1-2 lines up with that of Revelation 12:7-11. That chapter in Daniel clearly says the resurrection was to consist of righteous and unrighteous dead. Yeshua's explicit teaching in John 5:29 above confirms the same. Yeshua's parables also quoted above show representations of the resurrection of the dead. Each of them have their own parallels showing how the resurrection consisted of both the righteous and the unrighteous. The tares were sons of the evil one and the wheat were the sons of kingdom[407]. Both were reaped as a part of the wheat harvest, detailed in chapter 14 above, but one is separated from the other, the righteous from the unrighteous. The good fish captured in the drag-net were gathered into vessels while the bad were discarded. The righteous sheep who served "the least of these"[408] were welcomed into the kingdom of their Master. The goats, the unrighteous, were cast into the fire and thereby punished eternally.

The 144,000 first fruits were the first resurrection. The "second" resurrection was that of the remainder of the dead, righteous and

---

[407] Matthew 13:38.
[408] Matthew 25:35-40.

unrighteous. This was none other than the remainder of the wheat harvest reaped in Revelation 14:14-16 above. That resurrection occurred on the "last day" of the forty-year period of repentance that the Israelites were granted.

Though there is a clear chronological sequence to the resurrections, the lack of the phrase "the second resurrection" could be explained in a different way. *"First, in a series which is so complete, either in fact or in thought, that other members are conceived of as following the first in regular order,"*[409] is one accepted and accurate translation of the Greek πρῶτος, *protos.* Thayer provides several scriptural examples of this definition, each of which have an established sequence.

Acts 1:1
The **former** treatise I made, O Theophilus, concerning all that Yeshua began both to do and to teach.

The author of Acts had previously composed the work known as the Gospel of Luke[410]. Thus, we can see an established sequence of a first and second treatise written to Theophilus.

Mark 14:12
And on the **first** day of unleavened bread, when they sacrificed the passover, his disciples say unto him, Where wilt you that we go and make ready that you may eat the passover?

The feast of unleavened bread was a seven-day feast[411]. Thus, we know that this use of "first" is one of sequence.

Revelation 4:1
After these things I saw, and behold, a door opened in heaven, and the **first** voice that I heard, *a voice* as of a trumpet speaking with me, one saying, Come up here, and I will show you the things which must come to pass hereafter.

---

[409] Thayer. Entry for πρῶτος. Specifically 1.b.β. Page 555.
[410] Luke 1:1-4.
[411] Leviticus 23:4-8.

This first voice, defined as Yeshua's in Revelation chapter 1, was not the only voice John heard in the Apocalypse. An example of another voice he heard can be found in 5:2. Once again "first" here is one of sequence.

Hebrews 8:7
For if that **first** *covenant* had been faultless, then would no place have been sought for a second.

We know that there was the covenant made at Sinai[412] then the new covenant established through Yeshua[413].

The examples could go on, but we think the point has been made. The word πρῶτος can mean the first in a sequence of events or things. However, as in each of the examples above, one must be able to establish the existence of a second to confirm that this definition of πρῶτος is what is intended in Revelation 20:5.

Thayer provides us with another definition of πρῶτος that does not require a sequence of events, which we feel may explain the explicit absence of the phrase "second resurrection." Πρῶτος can also mean *"first in rank, influence, honor; chief, principal."*[414] Examples of this usage of πρῶτος are found in the following passages:

Luke 15:22
But the father said to his servants, Bring forth quickly the **best** robe, and put it on him; and put a ring on his hand, and shoes on his feet.

The Greek behind this word is πρῶτος. In this context, there is no "second" robe in view, therefore the meaning is the best robe.

Acts 17:4
And some of them were persuaded, and consorted with Paul and

---

[412] Exodus 24:7.
[413] Matthew 26:26-29.
[414] Thayer. Entry for πρῶτος. Specifically 2. Page 555.

Silas, and of the devout Greeks a great multitude, and of the **chief** women not a few.

The women referred to here were those who were leaders in the community. Again, no sequence is found in the context. Therefore "first," translated as "chief," again carries with it the meaning of those of highest position or honor.

> Luke 19:47
> And he was teaching daily in the temple. But the chief priests and the scribes and the **principal** men of the people sought to destroy him.

Similar to the previous passage, these men were those of the highest honor among the peoples. These were likely elders of the community looked up to as pious and holy men.

More examples could be provided, but again, the use of πρῶτος in the context of these verses is clear. There is nothing there that alludes to a "second" event or thing within an established sequence. The Septuagint (LXX), the Greek version of the Old Testament compiled in the mid-third century BCE, provides several other examples of where πρῶτος is used to describe something first in rank or honor instead of sequence[415].

We believe that the second definition of πρῶτος may be why John excluded the specific phrase "second resurrection." It wasn't that there wasn't a second resurrection event from a chronological perspective, but the first resurrection was "better" in that "the second death has no power" over them and they were to be "priests of Elohim and of Messiah" reigning with him for the thousand-year period. He was encouraging his audience that their rewards for perseverance and obedience in the face of the worst trials would be "chief," the best.

---

[415] Genesis 32:17; 1 Samuel 15:12; Esther 1:14; Daniel 10:13.

Satan's Demise

(7) And when the thousand years are finished, Satan shall be loosed out of his prison,
(8) and shall come forth to deceive the nations which are in the four corners of the earth, Gog and Magog, to gather them together to the war: the number of whom is as the sand of the sea.
(9) And they went up over the breadth of the earth, and compassed the camp of the saints about, and the beloved city: and fire came down out of heaven, and devoured them.
(10) And the devil that deceived them was cast into the lake of fire and brimstone, where are also the beast and the false prophet; and they shall be tormented day and night forever and ever.

The second portion of the vision of the judgment of Satan is found in this passage. Where we were left with a multitude of questions based on the abrupt ending to the first portion we now see the answers. The entirety of this vision has one single message. Its intent is to convey the absolute, final, and eternal binding and destruction of the archenemy of Yahweh, His Son, and His children. The first portion of the vision tells us of the binding of Satan and the fact that he will be loosed once more for a short time. It doesn't, however, answer the questions relating to the final demise of the enemy.

The binding of Satan, the stripping of his authority and weakening of his power, is to last for the entire apocalyptic, indefinite period of a thousand years. After that time, he is to be freed to once again work his great deceptions and assemble his wicked armies from the four corners of the earth. There is no guarantee that his deceptions will take hold of each person on the earth at that time. His release may not be unlike the sending of false prophets by Yahweh found in Deuteronomy 12:32-13:5. Yahweh intends to try the faith of those who have believed upon and followed His Son to see if they will cling to Him. Those who have been elected will overcome Satan's deceptions.

Gog and Magog

The only passage in scripture that can truly give us any insight into this battle with Gog and Magog is in Ezekiel chapters 38 and 39. We are not going to quote both chapters here for brevity's sake. However, as the reader studies the chapters in question while comparing the account in verses 7-10 above some striking similarities will be seen. The following table illustrates these.

Event/Attribute	Ezekiel	Revelation
Innumerable Host	38:4-9	20:8
Surround Israel/Jerusalem	38:10-17	20:9
Devouring Fire	38:18-23; 39:4-6	20:9

John's message here is simple. The final battle waged against the holy city and people of Yahweh after the thousand years is representative of the battle of Gog and Magog that Ezekiel prophesied of. Just as Gog was to gather his armies from around the world in Ezekiel, so does Satan gather his armies from around the world. Just as Gog marches against Israel, the chosen people, so Satan will march against the saints in the beloved city. Most importantly, just as Gog is utterly destroyed by Yahweh, with no intervention of His people being necessary, so it will be with Satan's final siege. Yahweh will fight for His people and destroy His archenemy without them having to lift a finger.

Similar to what he has done repeatedly in the Apocalypse, John is encouraging his audience by telling them that the enemy of the people, the one who has deceived and destroyed them since the beginning, will be gone, never to return. John's message is clear. Persevere and you will overcome. Overcome and you will have eternal life. Have eternal life and you will be able to witness the final destruction of the adversary and partake in the everlasting joy of the presence of Yahweh and Yeshua.

One final point should be made here. The reader should take notice that there is no "second coming" of Messiah mentioned at the end of the thousand years. There is no textual evidence to suggest that the insertion of a second coming here is correct or merited. This is yet another bias passed down to us through traditionally accepted doctrine.

Thus is the vision of the judgment of Satan complete.

Judgment of the Dead

(11) And I saw a great white throne, and him that sat upon it, from whose face the earth and the heaven fled away; and there was found no place for them.
(12) And I saw the dead, the great and the small, standing before the throne; and books were opened: and another book was opened, which is *the book* of life: and the dead were judged out of the things which were written in the books, according to their works.
(13) And the sea gave up the dead that were in it; and death and Hades gave up the dead that were in them: and they were judged every man according to their works.
(14) And death and Hades were cast into the lake of fire. This is the second death, *even* the lake of fire.
(15) And if any was not found written in the book of life, he was cast into the lake of fire.

The second portion of the vision of the judgment of the resurrected dead is found in this passage. Since this is a continuation of verses 4-6, and those verses are themselves mirrors of portions of Daniel's prophecy, we will now demonstrate how the two accounts are speaking of the same event. The passages in the Apocalypse can been seen above. The relevant passages in Daniel's prophecy are quoted again here:

Daniel 7:9-10
(9) I beheld till **thrones were placed**, and one that was ancient of days did sit: **his raiment was white as snow**, and **the hair of his head like pure wool**; his throne was fiery flames, *and* the wheels thereof burning fire.

(10) A fiery stream issued and came forth from before him: thousands of thousands ministered unto him, and ten thousand times ten thousand stood before him: **the judgment was set**, and **the books were opened**.

The similarities between the two accounts couldn't be clearer.

Daniel 7:9 – "**thrones** were placed"
Revelation 20:4 – "and I saw **thrones**"

Daniel 7:9 – "**ancient of days did sit**: his **raiment**...white...the hair of his head...pure wool**
Revelation 20:11 – "and I saw a great **white** throne, and **him that sat** upon it"

Daniel 7:10 – "the **judgment was set**"
Revelation 20:4,12 – "and **judgment was given unto them**...and the dead were **judged**"

Daniel 7:10 – "**books were opened**"
Revelation 20:12 – "**books were opened**"

The context, chronology, and content of these two accounts demand that they be speaking of the same event. The judgment scene in the Apocalypse shows all the resurrected dead, great and small, righteous and unrighteous, standing before the throne. The exceptions obviously being those of the 144,000 who were raised as the first fruits and given the power of judgment. In this judgment scene, we see that books are opened, one of which is the book of life. The righteous dead, who were among those harvested as a part of the spiritual wheat harvest detailed in chapter 14 above, are judged accordingly. Their resurrection was one resulting in life. Therefore, they were granted the blessing of eternal life, just as Yeshua promised. The unrighteous dead – the tares, the bad fish, the goats – were also judged according to their works. Their resurrection was one unto shame and everlasting contempt, resulting in eternal death.

John, in his giving of the first portion of this judgment vision, tells us of the setting up of the thrones for the judgment of the dead. However, as we mentioned above, that vision ends abruptly. Every student of the scriptures knows that both the righteous and the unrighteous are to come to judgment. It is in these last five verses of chapter 20 that we finally learn of the judgment of both. The righteous are given eternal life, and the unrighteous are cast into the lake of fire.

We also see in this chapter that death and the grave themselves, being the middle places between temporal life and eternal life, are cast into the lake of fire. We briefly mentioned this in the section entitled "A Blessed Death" in chapter 14 above. This destruction of death and the grave allows for those who die in the Master after to immediately rest from their labors and enter the kingdom prepared for them from the foundation of the world. There is no more need to sleep in the grave or to await a future resurrection.

Why Is There Still Death?

After reading the above, some may ask, "Why, then, do we still see people dying around us?" The answer lies in the *type* of death that was destroyed at that time. Consider the event that originally brought death into this world – the eating of the forbidden fruit in Eden. The commandment of Yahweh to Adam was clear:

> Genesis 2:16-17
> (16) And Yahweh Elohim commanded the man, saying, Of every tree of the garden you may freely eat:
> (17) but of the tree of the knowledge of good and evil, you shall not eat of it: for **in the day that you eat thereof you shall surely die.**

In the underlying Hebrew text the phrase "you shall surely die" is מוֹת תָּמוּת, *mot tamut*. These are two tenses of the same Hebrew verb, the first being the infinitive and the last being the imperative. Literally it would be more correctly translated as "dying, you shall die!" Simply put, Yahweh was emphasizing that *true* death would come upon them if they disobeyed. However, as we know from the infamous story in the garden, Adam and Eve did *not* die...physically, that is. Was Yahweh's judgment not meted out? Did He neglect to carry out the punishment He made so very clear to them? No.

The truth is that the death Yahweh spoke of was not physical death, but the death that really matters, spiritual death. That this is the case is also confirmed by the fact that Yeshua's teachings on the kingdom of heaven (or Elohim) were referring to spiritual life, not fleshly life. His kingdom is not of this world[416]. Eternal life is not to be spent in the flesh as flesh and blood cannot inherit the kingdom[417]. Our heavenly bodies won't be flesh[418]. Our war, while in this world, isn't a fleshly one[419] and the weapons of our warfare aren't fleshly[420]. Yahweh's "end game" has always been about a restoration of eternal, spiritual life, not fleshly life.

Spiritual death is an eternity of separation from Yahweh. For Adam and Eve, their forceful removal from Eden, the place wherein eternal life was forever promised, was the start of their spiritual death, as well as all those who succeeded them. Without the promise of eternal life through repentance and obedience by Yeshua's sacrifice, none would have ever risen from their graves. The death that was cast into the lake of fire, never to be seen again for those in the Master, was spiritual death, not physical death. Yeshua gave the following promise, which we also quoted in chapter 14 above:

John 11:25-26
(25) Yeshua said unto her, I am the resurrection, and the life: he that believes on me, though he die, yet shall he live;
(26) and whosoever lives and believes on me **shall never die**.

Those who live their lives after that resurrection of the dead took place,

---

[416] John 18:36.
[417] 1 Corinthians 15:50.
[418] 1 Corinthians 15:42-49.
[419] Ephesians 6:12.
[420] 2 Corinthians 10:3-6; Ephesians 6:10-17.

who are "in the Master" through faith and obedience, shall *never* die, unlike those who died and needed a resurrection. We go from life to life. As we will detail in chapter 21 below, the absence of death is something only found in the New Jerusalem. Nowhere else do we see that death is non-existent. Yeshua promised us eternal life through our obedient faith, but that life was to be a spiritual and heavenly one, like unto angels[421], who are obviously heavenly creatures. It is not to be an earthly, fleshly life.

The Second Death

Unlike the phrase "second resurrection," which is not found in the scriptures, we do find the phrase "the second death." This chapter and chapter 14 above tells us what happens to those who die "in the Master" after the resurrection of the dead. However, we aren't told about the fate of those who would die as disobedient unbelievers. Verse 14 in this chapter is interesting in that it tells us that death is thrown into the lake of fire (i.e. destroyed), yet death, this time in the form of the lake of fire, still exists. This second death is different than the first death in that it is not a temporary holding place where those who were sleeping awaited their judgment. The second death is a permanent one with no subsequent judgments to follow. While those who die in the Master immediately enter into the kingdom of heaven to live spiritually forever, those who are not in the Master at their death are immediately thrown into the lake of fire never be seen or heard from again.

Thus is the vision of the judgment of the resurrected dead complete and the tale of the two judgments concluded.

---

[421] Luke 20:36.

CHAPTER TWENTY-ONE

We come now to the chapter containing the descriptions of the utmost blessings for those who persevere in their faith, overcome their sin, and place their trust in Yeshua as their Messiah. John's illustrations in this chapter have parallels throughout the writings of the prophets of old concerning the promises of Elohim to those who love and serve Him. John's intent in this chapter is two-fold. First, he wants to tell his audience that the blessings promised for hundreds of years through the prophets were soon to come. Second, he wants to tell his audience exactly who or what the bride is, which was first mentioned in chapter 19 above.

A New Heaven and Earth

(1) And I saw a new heaven and a new earth: for the first heaven and the first earth are passed away; and the sea is no more.

(2) And I saw the holy city, New Jerusalem, coming down out of heaven from Elohim, made ready as a bride adorned for her husband.

(3) And I heard a great voice out of the throne saying, Behold, the tabernacle of Elohim is with men, and he shall dwell with them, and they shall be his peoples, and Elohim himself shall be with them, *and be* their Elohim:

(4) and he shall wipe away every tear from their eyes; and death

shall be no more; neither shall there be mourning, nor crying, nor pain, any more: the first things are passed away.
(5) And he that sits on the throne said, Behold, I make all things new. And he says, Write: for these words are faithful and true.
(6) And he said unto me, They are come to pass. I am the Alpha and the Omega, the beginning and the end. I will give unto him that is thirsty of the fountain of the water of life freely.
(7) He that overcomes shall inherit these things; and I will be his Elohim, and he shall be my son.
(8) But for the fearful, and unbelieving, and abominable, and murderers, and fornicators, and sorcerers, and idolaters, and all liars, their part shall be in the lake that burns with fire and brimstone; which is the second death.

One cannot read these verses without being brought immediately to Isaiah's prophecy. John is clearly referring his audience to that passage as the phrase "new heaven and new earth" and other aspects are exactly paralleled.

Isaiah 65:17-25
(17) For, behold, I create **new heavens and a new earth**; and the **former things shall not be remembered**, nor come into mind.
(18) But be you glad and rejoice forever in that which I create; for, behold, I create Jerusalem a rejoicing, and her people a joy.
(19) And I will rejoice in Jerusalem, and joy in my people; and **there shall be heard in her no more the voice of weeping and the voice of crying**.
(20) There shall be no more there an infant of days, nor an old man that has not filled his days; for the child shall die a hundred years old, and the sinner being a hundred years old shall be accursed.
(21) And they shall build houses, and inhabit them; and they shall plant vineyards, and eat the fruit of them.
(22) They shall not build, and another inhabit; they shall not plant, and another eat: for as the days of a tree shall be the days of my people, and my chosen shall long enjoy the work of their hands.
(23) They shall not labor in vain, nor bring forth for calamity; for they are the seed of the blessed of Yahweh, and their offspring

with them.

(24) And it shall come to pass that, before they call, I will answer; and while they are yet speaking, I will hear.

(25) The wolf and the lamb shall feed together, and the lion shall eat straw like the ox; and dust shall be the serpent's food. They shall not hurt nor destroy in all my holy mountain, says Yahweh.

As we've mentioned above and as is shown in the table of apocalyptic terminology in the Introduction, "heavens and earth" in prophetic or apocalyptic passages refer to governmental and/or religious systems. Unlike Isaiah 65:17 above, John specifies that the former, or old heavens and earth were passed away. We've already shown how the governmental and false religious system of the Jews in the first century were utterly laid waste and purged. With the wicked of the land having now been either slain or brought captive to Rome, and the temple and city having been destroyed, there were none left to perpetuate the system represented by the "first heaven and first earth." A new and perfect order, one in the heavenly realm, had now been established and is the one that is to remain forever.

Several things need to be addressed regarding Isaiah's prophecy above. First, notice how Isaiah's and John's structures are virtually identical. Both quickly mention the creation of a new heavens and new earth first. Then the context and focus immediately shifts to Jerusalem. This tells us that John truly had Isaiah's prophecy in mind when writing this portion of the Apocalypse. Second, most, if not all traditional Christian commentators understand much of Isaiah's prophecy to be literal. However, there are several aspects of it that show this to be an impossibility, which will be detailed below. Others believe that the passage in Isaiah 65 refers to the condition of the earth *outside* of the New Jerusalem. However, Isaiah tells us that each of the profound blessings mentioned are all to be realized *within* Jerusalem by saying "in her." "There shall be heard *in her* no more the voice..." "There shall be no more *there* an infant of days..." John's and Isaiah's messages are clear and consistent.

Several aspects of the passage in Isaiah prevent it from being read literally. First, if read literally, there is a glaringly obvious contradiction between the new heavens and earth of the Apocalypse and the new heavens and earth of Isaiah's prophecy. Isaiah's account would, at first glance, seem to say that literal death will still exist. The account in the Apocalypse, on the other hand, specifically says, "and death shall be no more." How this apparent contradiction is dissolved will be addressed shortly. Second, verse 20 specifies that the "child" will die a hundred years old. It can hardly be said that someone who is one hundred years old is a "child." Third, it would be a gross assumption to think that the physical structure and genetic make-up of a lion would change such that it would eat straw. We're talking about a change in skeletal structures, such as their teeth, and their digestive functionality, etc. To assume this is to also assume that their physical structures changed after the fall in the garden, a change which is nowhere documented. Fourth, it says that the serpent's food will be dust. Are we really to expect a serpent to suddenly be able to survive on dry soil? These are all symbolic representations.

Death in the New Jerusalem?

Prior to going over all the representations in general we need to address verse 20 specifically, which supposedly mentions the presence of death in the New Jerusalem. In addition to his allusion to Isaiah 65, John also points his audience to the promises of Yahweh in Isaiah 25.

Isaiah 25:6-9
(6) And in this mountain will Yahweh of hosts make unto all peoples a feast of fat things, a feast of wines on the lees, of fat things full of marrow, of wines on the lees well refined.
(7) And he will destroy in this mountain the face of the covering that covers all peoples, and the veil that is spread over all nations.
(8) **He has swallowed up death forever**; and the Master Yahweh **will wipe away tears from off all faces**; and the reproach of his people will he take away from off all the earth: for Yahweh has spoken it.
(9) And it shall be said in that day, Lo, this is our Elohim; we have waited for him, and he will save us: this is Yahweh; we have waited for him, we will be glad and rejoice in his salvation.

John is clearly pulling together the aspects of these prophecies of Isaiah to convey one concise message to his audience. As a part of his descriptions he states that in the New Jerusalem Elohim "shall wipe away every tear from their eyes." We just read the same thing in Isaiah 25. John is once again drawing the minds of his audience to the prophecies they were all familiar with.

In the case of Isaiah's prophecy in chapter 25, he specifically says that death will be swallowed up. If the death mentioned in Isaiah 65 is taken literally these are irreconcilable contradictions. After all, wherever death is there *will* be mourning and crying, both of which are said to be absent in the New Jerusalem. If any were to doubt that all three chapters are referring to the same place they must only look at the commonalities between them. Each of them mention the absence of weeping or crying[422]. Each of them are spoken of as being present on the mountain of Yahweh, where Jerusalem was[423].

If we see the removal of death in Isaiah 25 and Revelation 21, yet the presence of death in Isaiah 65, some other explanation must exist. Proper biblical hermeneutics requires that we interpret the more difficult passages in light of the simpler ones. John's and Isaiah's explicit statements about the abolition of death in Revelation 21 and Isaiah 25, respectively, make it clear that the statements about death in Isaiah 65 must be understood differently. Indeed, when the scriptures are studied properly this understanding reveals itself.

Isaiah 65:22 must also be read as a part of the context of verse 20 and the concept of death in the New Jerusalem. Most English translations have the phrase "for as the days of **a** tree shall be the days of my people," or something very similar. Notice the emphasis placed on the letter "a." We must examine the Hebrew text of this passage to understand how the translation of that phrase is, in a very essential and important way, incorrect.

---

[422] Isaiah 25:8, 65:19; Revelation 21:4.
[423] Isaiah 25:6, 65:25; Revelation 21:10.

לֹא יִבְנוּ וְאַחֵר יֵשֵׁב לֹא יִטְּעוּ וְאַחֵר יֹאכֵל כִּי־כִימֵי הָעֵץ יְמֵי עַמִּי
וּמַעֲשֵׂה יְדֵיהֶם יְבַלּוּ בְחִירָי:

A word-for-word translation of this text, as unintelligible as it is in that form, would read as follows:

> Not they-shall-build and-another he-shall-dwell not they-shall-plant and-another he-shall-eat for as-days-of **the-tree** days-of my-people and-deed-of hands-of-them they-shall-use-full chosen-ones-of-me.

Or, more simply rendered:

> They shall not build and another dwell, nor plant and another eat; for as the days of **the tree** *are* the days of my people, and my chosen ones shall use the works of their hands to the full.

Notice that the Hebrew text uses the definite article הַ in the phrase כִּי־כִימֵי הָעֵץ. The word before it, כִימֵי, is in the construct form, which means it conveys possession, hence "of the" in the phrase "days *of the* tree." However, as we can see the phrase is not "of *a* tree" but "of *the* tree." This raises the question, "What tree?" The Septuagint provides us with insight into this question.

> καὶ οὐ μὴ οἰκοδομήσουσιν καὶ ἄλλοι ἐνοικήσουσιν, καὶ οὐ μὴ φυτεύσουσιν καὶ ἄλλοι φάγονται· κατὰ γὰρ **τὰς ἡμέρας τοῦ ξύλου τῆς ζωῆς** ἔσονται αἱ ἡμέραι τοῦ λαοῦ μου, τὰ ἔργα τῶν πόνων αὐτῶν παλαιώσουσιν.

Here is Sir Lancelot Brenton's translation of that verse:

> Isaiah 65:22 (Brenton's Translation of the LXX)
> They shall by no means build, and others inhabit; and they shall by no means plant, and others eat: for as **the days of the tree of life** shall be the days of my people, they shall long enjoy the fruits of their labours.

What other tree better matches the description of "*the* tree" than the

Tree of Life? Contextually this makes perfect sense given that Isaiah is discussing the life of His people in the new heavens, new earth, and New Jerusalem that He is creating. The truth here isn't that the days of the people will be like "a" tree, which are numbered, but the days of "the" tree, the Tree of Life, which are innumerable. Isaiah 65:20 must be read in the context of this verse, as well as those of Isaiah 25 and Revelation 21. The conclusion is then clear. Death will be non-existent in the New Jerusalem.

What the Symbols Are Telling Us

In chapters 8, 9, and 16 of the Apocalypse above, et al, we have shown how the punishments inflicted upon apostate Israel were the exact ones listed in Deuteronomy 28. All the plagues of Egypt and those not inflicted upon Egypt came upon the wicked Israelites, amongst many other horrible things. These were all brought upon them because of their disobedience to and breaking of His Torah, His perfect law and teaching[424]. However, in Isaiah 65 we see Yahweh telling us that those curses were to be no more.

The blessings in Isaiah's prophecy must be taken together as a whole to be properly understood. Removing or isolating one of them from the others is to do something to the text that was never intended. Taken as a whole, we can see the opposites of the curses in Deuteronomy 28. Isaiah 65:21 is the blessing opposite the curse in Deuteronomy 28:30. Verse 23 is the opposite of the curse in Deuteronomy 28:41, 48-49 and 53. Verse 24 is tied directly to Zechariah 8:7-8 and Revelation 21:3 wherein Yahweh is dwelling amongst His children able to communicate with them real-time. Wolves, lions and other wild beasts are used to represent fierce, cruel, or wicked men or nations throughout the scriptures[425]. The wolf lying with the lamb in verse 25, and the lion eating straw as the ox, don't represent a changing of the temperament

---

[424] Psalms 19:7, 119:1.
[425] Psalms 57:4, 58:6; Proverbs 28:15; Isaiah 11:6-9.

or nature of both of those animals. In this and other prophetic passages[426] it represents that the fierce, cruel, and wicked will not be present in the New Jerusalem. All who are a part of the kingdom will be made peaceable and everything that destroyed or harmed others will no longer do so. The serpent's food being dust is representative of the fact that the curse upon the serpent[427], the great deceiver, will never be lifted. Its punishment is eternal, which is exactly what we see of the Dragon's demise in chapter 20 above.

When taken in context and Isaiah's message is clear. All those things that were curses, all those things that were painful and caused mourning, and all those things that were destructive or wicked wouldn't be a part of the promised blessings of life in the New Jerusalem. Chapter 66 carries the same message but also shows how those things considered as defiant against the Torah, such as eating unclean animals and the breaking of the Sabbath also won't be present. This brings us back to Revelation 21:5 where Yahweh says, "Behold, I make all things new."

The New Jerusalem

(9) And there came one of the seven angels who had the seven bowls, who were laden with the seven last plagues; and he spoke with me, saying, Come here, I will show you the bride, the wife of the Lamb.

(10) And he carried me away in the spirit to a mountain great and high, and showed me the holy city Jerusalem, coming down out of heaven from Elohim,

(11) having the glory of Elohim: her light was like unto a stone most precious, as it were a jasper stone, clear as crystal:

(12) having a wall great and high; having twelve gates, and at the gates twelve angels; and names written thereon, which are *the names* of the twelve tribes of the children of Israel:

(13) on the east were three gates; and on the north three gates;

---

[426] Isaiah 11:6-9.
[427] Genesis 3:14-15.

and on the south three gates; and on the west three gates.

(14) And the wall of the city had twelve foundations, and on them twelve names of the twelve apostles of the Lamb.

(15) And he that spoke with me had for a measure a golden reed to measure the city, and the gates thereof, and the wall thereof.

(16) And the city lies foursquare, and the length thereof is as great as the breadth: and he measured the city with the reed, twelve thousand furlongs: the length and the breadth and the height thereof are equal.

(17) And he measured the wall thereof, a hundred and forty and four cubits, *according to* the measure of a man, that is, of an angel.

(18) And the building of the wall thereof was jasper: and the city was pure gold, like unto pure glass.

(19) The foundations of the wall of the city were adorned with all manner of precious stones. The first foundation was jasper; the second, sapphire; the third, chalcedony; the fourth, emerald;

(20) the fifth, sardonyx; the sixth, sardius; the seventh, chrysolite; the eighth, beryl; the ninth, topaz; the tenth, chrysoprase; the eleventh, jacinth; the twelfth, amethyst.

(21) And the twelve gates were twelve pearls; each one of the several gates was of one pearl: and the street of the city was pure gold, as it were transparent glass.

(22) And I saw no temple therein: for the Yahweh Elohim the Almighty, and the Lamb, are the temple thereof.

(23) And the city has no need of the sun, neither of the moon, to shine upon it: for the glory of Elohim did lighten it, and the lamp thereof *is* the Lamb.

(24) And the nations shall walk amidst the light thereof: and the kings of the earth bring their glory into it.

(25) And the gates thereof shall in no wise be shut by day (for there shall be no night there):

(26) and they shall bring the glory and the honor of the nations into it:

(27) and there shall in no wise enter into it anything unclean, or he that makes an abomination and a lie: but only they that are written in the Lamb's book of life.

John continues his use of apocalyptic symbolism in this last section of chapter 21 to again relate to his audience exactly what he is talking about. First, let's remember what we read earlier in chapter 19 about the bride of the Lamb.

Revelation 19:7-8
(7) Let us rejoice and be exceeding glad, and let us give the glory unto him: for the marriage of the Lamb is come, and his wife has made herself ready.
(8) And it was given unto her that she should array herself in fine linen, bright *and* pure: for the fine linen is **the righteous acts of the saints**.

Verses 9 and 10 of chapter 21 would make it seem that the Lamb, who we've already established is Yeshua, is to marry a city. Are we to believe that Yeshua is marrying an actual city? Just above we read that the clothing of the woman is the righteous acts of the saints. Can a city be clothed at all? There is more here than first meets the eye. Let's examine the symbolism more closely to see what John is saying.

We first read that the New Jerusalem has a wall great and high. Why would a heavenly city where the Almighty Creator of all and His Messiah dwell need a wall at all? The short answer is that it doesn't. That is one reason we need to see this as a symbol and search for what it is trying to convey. We read that the wall was one hundred forty-four cubits tall, or approximately two hundred sixteen feet. That is about as high as a twenty-story building. Needless to say, such a wall would be unscalable. Even if someone were to attempt such an astounding feat they would make it nowhere near the top without having first been found and captured by the guardians and watchmen of the city. This description is given to remind us of Yeshua's parable.

John 10:1-2
(1) Verily, verily, I say unto you, He that enters not by the door into the fold of the sheep, but **climbs up some other way**, the same is a thief and a robber.
(2) But he that enters in by the door is the shepherd of the sheep.

John is telling his audience that the New Jerusalem is not some city that you can enter uninvited. You must enter through the gates because the wall is not something you can attempt to gain access by. The number one hundred forty-four was discussed in chapter 7 above when discussing the 144,000. It is also symbolic. The height of the wall is perfect and complete in all ways. The protective structure of the holy city is complete and impenetrable.

Next, we read that the city has twelve gates, each of which has the name of one of the twelve tribes of Israel written thereon. Each gate was a solid pearl. What could this represent?

> Jeremiah 31:31-34
> (31) Behold, the days come, says Yahweh, that I will make a new covenant **with the house of Israel, and with the house of Judah**:
> (32) not according to the covenant that I made with their fathers in the day that I took them by the hand to bring them out of the land of Egypt; which my covenant they broke, although I was a husband unto them, says Yahweh.
> (33) But this is the covenant that I will make with the house of Israel after those days, says Yahweh: I will put my Torah in their inward parts, and in their heart will I write it; and I will be their Elohim, and they shall be my people.
> (34) And they shall teach no more every man his neighbor, and every man his brother, saying, Know Yahweh; for they shall all know me, from the least of them unto the greatest of them, says Yahweh: for I will forgive their iniquity, and their sin will I remember no more.

We can see in this passage about the new covenant exactly who that covenant was to be made with – the houses of Israel and Judah. This is a very important concept to understand. Each of us must enter the New Jerusalem, access to which is given only to those who are in the new covenant through Yeshua, through one of the gates of the twelve tribes. We must be united to true Israel to gain entry into the holy city. Paul says the same:

Romans 9:6-8
(6) But *it is* not as though the word of Elohim has come to nothing. **For they are not all Israel, that are of Israel:**
(7) neither, because they are Abraham's seed, are they all children: but, *In Isaac shall your seed be called.*
(8) That is, **it is not the children of the flesh that are children of Elohim; but the children of the promise** are reckoned for a seed.

Romans 11:17-24
(17) But if some of the branches were broken off, and **you, being a wild olive, were grafted in among them, and did become partaker with them of the root of the fatness of the olive tree;**
(18) glory not over the branches: but if you glory, it is not you that bear the root, but the root you.
(19) You wilt say then, Branches were broken off, that I might be grafted in.
(20) Well; by their unbelief they were broken off, and you stand by your faith. Be not high-minded, but fear:
(21) for if Elohim spared not the natural branches, neither will he spare you.
(22) Behold then the goodness and severity of Elohim: toward them that fell, severity; but toward you, Elohim's goodness, if you continue in his goodness: otherwise you also shall be cut off.
(23) And they also, if they continue not in their unbelief, shall be grafted in: for Elohim is able to graft them in again.
(24) For if you were cut out of that which is by nature a wild olive tree, and were grafted contrary to nature into a good olive tree; how much more shall these, which are the natural *branches*, be grafted into their own olive tree?

Gentiles, even though they are not of the direct lineage of one of the twelve tribes of Israel, are nonetheless joined to Israel, grafted into the true vine, through Yeshua. It is our opinion that all Gentiles who are joined to Israel through Yeshua will enter in through the gate of Judah, being grafted into the Messiah's tribe.

The gates being made of pearl also help us to recall another one of Yeshua' parables about the kingdom of heaven.

CHAPTER TWENTY-ONE

Matthew 13:45-46
(45) Again, the kingdom of heaven is like unto a man that is a merchant seeking **goodly pearls**:
(46) and **having found one pearl of great price**, he went and sold all that he had, and bought it.

Seeking entry into the gates of the New Jerusalem is one and the same with seeking after that pearl of great price. John is reminding his audience of this parable and its relation to the kingdom of heaven through the imagery of the "pearly gates."

The city is said to have been built on twelve foundations, each of which has the name of one of the twelve apostles of Yeshua written thereon. We are reminded of scriptures that refer to Yeshua as being the chief cornerstone of the new temple[428]. We are also told that Cephas, or Simon Peter was to be a foundation of the assemblies of Yeshua[429]. The same was said of the other apostles[430].

The measurements of the city were twelve thousand stadia in height, width, and breadth. We are not to interpret this size as literal any more than the twelve thousand of each tribe in Revelation 7 is to be interpreted literally. We should not expect to see a city fourteen hundred miles cubed come down out of heaven to earth, as the common Futurist claim would assert. Just like in that chapter the meaning here is one of indefinite completeness. The size of this spiritual New Jerusalem, the true identity of which is soon to be revealed, is complete, perfect, and not lacking in any way.

The foundations of the wall were also twelve in number, each made up of a different kind of precious stone. When contrasted with the stones in the high priest's breastplate as shown in the table below the similarities are undeniable.

---

[428] Psalms 118:22; Isaiah 28:16; Matthew 21:42.
[429] Matthew 16:18.
[430] Ephesians 2:19-22.

English Translation	Revelation 21:19-20	English Translation	Exodus 28:17-20 (LXX)
Topaz	τοπάζιον	Topaz	τοπάζιον
Sardius	σάρδιον	Sardius	σάρδιον
Chrysolite	χρυσόλιθος	Chrysolite	χρυσόλιθος
Beryl	βήρυλλος	Beryl	βηρύλλιον
Amethyst	ἀμέθυστος	Amethyst	ἀμέθυστος
Emerald	σμάραγδος	Emerald	σμάραγδος
Jasper	ἴασπις	Jasper	ἴασπις
Sapphire	σάπφιρος	Sapphire	σάπφειρος
Chalcedony	χαλκηδών	Chalcedony	ἀχάτης
Jacinth	ὑάκινθος	Jacinth	λιγύριον
Sardonyx	σαρδόνυξ	Onyx	ὀνύχιον
Chrysoprase	χρυσόπρασος	Carbuncle	ἄνθραξ

The first eight stones in the table above are identical between both accounts. The ninth and tenth are different words in the Greek text but are often equated to one another by lexicographers. The eleventh stones are different shades of the same stone – Onyx – the first a reddish hue and the second black. John is telling his audience through the imagery of these stones that the New Jerusalem is to be one filled with priests. We read the same in other places in the scriptures.

1 Peter 2:1-9
(1) Putting away therefore all wickedness, and all guile, and hypocrisies, and envies, and all evil speaking,
(2) as newborn babes, long for the spiritual milk which is without guile, that you may grow thereby unto salvation;
(3) if you have tasted that the Master is gracious:
(4) unto whom coming, a living stone, rejected indeed of men, but with Elohim elect, precious,
(5) you also, as living stones, are built up a spiritual house, to be **a holy priesthood**, to offer up spiritual sacrifices, acceptable to Elohim through Yeshua Messiah.
(6) Because it is contained in scripture, *Behold, I lay in Zion a chief corner stone, elect, precious: And he that believeth on him shall not be put to shame.*

(7) For you therefore that believe is the preciousness: but for such as disbelieve, *The stone which the builders rejected, The same was made the head of the corner,*

(8) and, *A stone of stumbling, and a rock of offence,* for they stumble at the word, being disobedient: whereunto also they were appointed.

(9) But you are an elect race, **a royal priesthood**, a holy nation, a people for *Elohim's* own possession, that you may show forth the excellencies of him who called you out of darkness into his marvelous light.

Peter not only calls the assembly a holy and royal priesthood, but he places it in the context of the foundation, specifically the chief cornerstone, Yeshua. We have already read in Revelation 1:6, 5:10, and 20:6 above how people that are a part of the kingdom of heaven are to be priests.

John is using the imagery in Revelation 21:22-27 to help them recall yet another prophecy of Isaiah. Those verses tell us of the glory and wealth of nations being brought into New Jerusalem, how the light of the sun and moon will no longer be necessary, how it will be the place of His sanctuary, and more.

Isaiah 60:3, 11-22

(3) And **nations shall come to your light**, and kings to the brightness of your rising...

(11) **Your gates also shall be open continually; they shall not be shut day nor night; that men may bring unto you the wealth of the nations,** and their kings led captive.

(12) For that nation and kingdom that will not serve you shall perish; yea, those nations shall be utterly wasted.

(13) The glory of Lebanon shall come unto you, the fir-tree, the pine, and the box-tree together, to beautify the place of my sanctuary; and I will make the place of my feet glorious.

(14) And the sons of them that afflicted you shall come bending unto you; and all they that despised you shall bow themselves down at the soles of your feet; and they shall call you **The city of Yahweh, The Zion of the Holy One of Israel.**

(15) Whereas you have been forsaken and hated, so that no man passed through you, I will make you an eternal excellency, a joy of many generations.

(16) You shall also suck the milk of the nations, and shall suck the breast of kings; and you shall know that I, Yahweh, am your Savior, and your Redeemer, the Mighty One of Jacob.

(17) For brass I will bring gold, and for iron I will bring silver, and for wood brass, and for stones iron. I will also make your officers peace, and your exactors righteousness.

(18) Violence shall no more be heard in your land, desolation nor destruction within your borders; but you shall call your walls Salvation, and your gates Praise.

(19) **The sun shall be no more your light by day; neither for brightness shall the moon give light unto you: but Yahweh will be unto you an everlasting light,** and your Elohim your glory.

(20) **Your sun shall no more go down, neither shall your moon withdraw itself; for Yahweh will be your everlasting light,** and the days of your mourning shall be ended.

(21) Your people also shall be all righteous; they shall inherit the land forever, the branch of my planting, the work of my hands, that I may be glorified.

(22) The little one shall become a thousand, and the small one a strong nation; I, Yahweh, will hasten it in its time.

All the information above tells us the identity of the New Jerusalem. It is representative of *the assembly of Yeshua*. As stated previously, Yeshua didn't marry a city. He married a people. The assembly is clothed in white because of her righteous, Torah-observant acts. To enter the assembly means to unite one's self with Israel spiritually under the new covenant, being then allowed in through one of the gates of the twelve tribes. In her are found kings and priests and she was founded upon the faith and teachings of the twelve apostles, her chief cornerstone being Yeshua. The light shining upon the assembly is Yeshua[431]. His light of truth, righteousness, and salvation shines through his bride that the nations may see and desire it[432]. Her gates are never shut

---

[431] John 8:12, 9:5, 12:46.
[432] Matthew 5:14-16.

because any are welcome into her regardless of when they come. Those outside of the New Jerusalem, those not a part of the assembly, are those who remain impenitent and unrepentant regarding the things that are unclean, abominable, defiant, lawless[433] and in any other way infractions against Yahweh's Torah in their lives.

Though the descriptions John gives of the New Jerusalem mirror the attributes of the assembly of Yeshua, this in no way precludes the existence of a literal city in the heavenly realm wherein Yahweh, Yeshua, and the saints dwell. John, Peter, the author of Hebrews, and others provide some details about the city in which the bride of the Lamb will reside. No temple is found in her because Yeshua is its temple[434]. This fact would have been an amazing encouragement to the first century followers of Messiah because they loved their city and temple. Peter and the author of Hebrews tell us that the sacrifices made in the New Jerusalem are spiritual, not physical[435]. Bloody sacrifices were never desired by Yahweh[436], and when His Son made that perpetual sacrifice the need for them, especially in the assembly of Yeshua, became wholly unnecessary. The New Jerusalem is also set upon the true mount Zion and populated with innumerable hosts of angels and the spirits of just men made perfect[437].

When one joins themselves to Yeshua through faith and obedience, they enter the assembly, the spiritual New Jerusalem. They simultaneously acquire their citizenship[438] to the literal New Jerusalem in the heavenly realm[439], which is in the better and perfect country that is not of this world. Their entrance into the new heavenly country and the literal New Jerusalem happens immediately after their earthly death. Knowing these truths, we can easily understand how John's words in these last chapters of the Apocalypse would have been a great

---

[433] Matthew 7:21-23.
[434] John 2:13-22.
[435] 1 Peter 2:5; Hebrews 13:7-16.
[436] Proverbs 21:3; Jeremiah 7:22; Hosea 6:6; Micah 6:6-8.
[437] Hebrews 12:18-24.
[438] Philippians 3:20.
[439] Hebrews 11:10, 16.

encouragement to his audience. It would also have provided them with the motivation they needed to patiently endure any hardships they were to see in their near future. This passage is also an encouragement to all those in Yeshua who would read it from then until the thousand years are complete. We are blessed enough to partake of the heavenly kingdom he has prepared for us. HalleluYah!

CHAPTER TWENTY-TWO

The Waters of Life

(1) And he showed me a river of water of life, bright as crystal, proceeding out of the throne of Elohim and of the Lamb,
(2) in the midst of the street thereof. And on this side of the river and on that was the tree of life, bearing twelve *manner of* fruits, yielding its fruit every month: and the leaves of the tree were for the healing of the nations.
(3) And there shall be no curse any more: and the throne of Elohim and of the Lamb shall be therein: and his servants shall serve him;
(4) and they shall see his face; and his name *shall be* on their foreheads.
(5) And there shall be night no more; and they need no light of lamp, neither light of sun; for Yahweh Elohim shall give them light: and they shall reign forever and ever.

John's illustrations here bring together a few different topics. First, we see the teaching of Yeshua regarding the waters of life.

John 4:7-14
(7) There came a woman of Samaria to draw water: Yeshua said unto her, Give me to drink.
(8) For his disciples were gone away into the city to buy food.
(9) The Samaritan woman therefore said unto him, How is it

that you, being a Jew, asks drink of me, who am a Samaritan woman? (For Jews have no dealings with Samaritans.)
(10) Yeshua answered and said unto her, If you knew the gift of Elohim, and who it is that said to you, Give me to drink; you would have asked of him, and he would have given you living water.
(11) The woman said unto him, Sir, you have nothing to draw with, and the well is deep: where then do you have that living water?
(12) Are you greater than our father Jacob, who gave us the well, and drank thereof himself, and his sons, and his cattle?
(13) Yeshua answered and said unto her, Every one that drinks of this water shall thirst again:
(14) but whosoever drinks of the water that I shall give him shall never thirst; but the water that I shall give him shall become in him a well of water springing up unto eternal life.

The river of life in verse 1 is something that flows in the New Jerusalem from the Lamb. As we have shown above, the New Jerusalem is the assembly of Yeshua. Just as Yeshua said he would, our faith in and obedience to him allows wells of living water to spring forth from us. This water results in eternal life to those who would drink of it. The water is the word of faith spoken to someone leading them to repentance and faith in Yeshua. That faith in him then results in eternal life, just as he promised.

The trees of life are also indicative of the attributes of the members of the assembly of Yeshua.

Matthew 7:17-18
(17) Even so **every good tree brings forth good fruit**; but the corrupt tree brings forth evil fruit.
(18) A good tree cannot bring forth evil fruit, neither can a corrupt tree bring forth good fruit.

Matthew 13:23
(23) And he that was sown upon the good ground, this is he that hears the word, and understands it; **who verily bears fruit**, and

brings forth, some a hundredfold, some sixty, some thirty.

John 15:1-8
(1) I am the true vine, and my Father is the husbandman.
(2) Every branch in me that bears not fruit, he takes it away: and every *branch* that bears fruit, he cleanses it, that it may bear more fruit.
(3) Already you are clean because of the word which I have spoken unto you.
(4) Abide in me, and I in you. As the branch cannot bear fruit of itself, except it abide in the vine; so neither can you, except you abide in me.
(5) I am the vine, you are the branches: He that abides in me, and I in him, the same bears much fruit: for apart from me you can do nothing.
(6) If a man abide not in me, he is cast forth as a branch, and is withered; and they gather them, and cast them into the fire, and they are burned.
(7) If you abide in me, and my words abide in you, ask whatsoever you will, and it shall be done unto you.
(8) Herein is my Father glorified, **that you bear much fruit**; and *so* shall you be my disciples.

Hebrews 12:11
(11) All chastening seems for the present to be not joyous but grievous; yet afterward it yields **peaceable fruit unto them that have been exercised thereby**, *even the fruit* of **righteousness**.

James 3:18
(18) And the **fruit of righteousness is sown in peace for them that make peace**.

The fruits of righteousness borne by the followers of Yeshua are once again to be things that provide life to those around them. Those fruits are found all year round and are never lacking. They are to be so attractive that the people in the world around us want to grasp hold of them, eat of them, and thereby acquire eternal life.

We have gone over the removal of the curse from the New Jerusalem and its inhabitants in detail above. However, the throne of Elohim and the Lamb being in the New Jerusalem hasn't yet been addressed. Yeshua taught us the following:

John 14:1-14

(1) Let not your heart be troubled: believe in Elohim, believe also in me.

(2) In my Father's house are many mansions; if it were not so, I would have told you; for I go to prepare a place for you.

(3) And if I go and prepare a place for you, I come again, and will receive you unto myself; that where I am, *there* you may be also.

(4) And whither I go, you know the way.

(5) Thomas said unto him, Master, we know not where go; how know we the way?

(6) Yeshua said unto him, I am the way, and the truth, and the life: no one comes unto the Father, but by me.

(7) If you had known me, you would have known my Father also: from henceforth you know him, **and have seen him**.

(8) Philip said unto him, Master, **show us the Father**, and it suffice us.

(9) Yeshua said unto him, Have I been so long time with you, and you do not know me, Philip? **he that hath seen me hath seen the Father**; how say you, Show us the Father?

(10) Do you not believe that I am in the Father, and the Father in me? the words that I say unto you I speak not from myself: but the Father abiding in me does his works.

(11) Believe me that I am in the Father, and the Father in me: or else believe me for the very works' sake.

(12) Verily, verily, I say unto you, He that believeth on me, the works that I do shall he do also; and greater *works* than these shall he do; because I go unto the Father.

(13) And whatsoever you shall ask in my name, that will I do, that the Father may be glorified in the Son.

(14) If you shall ask anything in my name, that will I do.

(15) If you love me, you will keep my commandments.

(16) And I will pray the Father, and he shall give you another Comforter, that **he may be with you** forever,

(17) *even* the spirit of truth: whom the world cannot receive; for it beholds him not, neither knows him: you know him; for he abides with you, and shall be in you.

(18) I will not leave you desolate: I come unto you.

(19) Yet a little while, and the world beholds me no more; **but you behold me: because I live, you shall live also.**

(20) **In that day you shall know that I am in my Father, and you in me, and I in you.**

(21) He that has my commandments, and keeps them, he it is that loves me: and he that loves me shall be loved of my Father, and I will love him, and will manifest myself unto him.

(22) Judas (not Iscariot) says unto him, Master, what is come to pass that you wilt manifest thyself unto us, and not unto the world?

(23) Yeshua answered and said unto him, **If a man love me, he will keep my word: and my Father will love him, and we will come unto him, and make our abode with him.**

Therein we have yet more parallels to Yeshua's teachings being used by John. A promise we have throughout the scriptures is that we will once again see the face of Yahweh, something that had been stripped since the exile from the garden. The Father, however, is spirit[440]. No one has seen the Father, but He has instead been revealed by the Son[441]. Yahweh and Yeshua come and make their abode, set their thrones, in the hearts and spirits of those who choose to follow and obey them. He does so by His spirit in us. We can see the "face" of the Father because we are able to look upon the pure perfection of Yeshua, who is the image of the invisible Elohim[442]. A promise made over eunuchs, foreigners, and the native-born Israelites is that they will be given an everlasting name for their obedience in keeping Yahweh's Sabbaths and holding fast to His covenant[443].

The first five verses in Revelation 22 tell us of the amazing blessings we

---

[440] John 4:24.

[441] John 1:18, 6:46; 1 Timothy 1:17, 6:13-16; Hebrews 11:27.

[442] Colossians 1:15; Hebrews 1:3.

[443] Isaiah 56:1-8.

receive from the Father due to our faith in His Son and our humble obedience to his Sabbaths and other commandments. Eternal life, no more curse, dwelling in the presence of Yahweh and Yeshua, receiving a name greater than that of sons and daughters, and reigning forever and ever are all gifts from Him.

Behold, I Come Quickly

(6) And he said unto me, These words are faithful and true: and Yahweh, the Elohim of the spirits of the prophets, sent his angel to show unto his servants the things which must shortly come to pass.

(7) And behold, I come quickly. Blessed is he that keeps the words of the prophecy of this book.

(8) And I John am he that heard and saw these things. And when I heard and saw, I fell down to worship before the feet of the angel that showed me these things.

(9) And he said unto me, See you do it not: I am a fellow-servant with you and with your brethren the prophets, and with them that keep the words of this book: worship Elohim.

(10) And he said unto me, Seal not up the words of the prophecy of this book; for the time is at hand.

(11) He that is unrighteous, let him do unrighteousness still: and he that is filthy, let him be made filthy still: and he that is righteous, let him do righteousness still: and he that is holy, let him be made holy still.

(12) Behold, I come quickly; and my reward is with me, to render to each man according as his work is.

(13) I am the Alpha and the Omega, the first and the last, the beginning and the end.

(14) Blessed are they that wash their robes, that they may have the right to come to the tree of life, and may enter in by the gates into the city.

(15) Without are the dogs, and the sorcerers, and the fornicators, and the murderers, and the idolaters, and every one that loves and makes a lie.

(16) I Yeshua have sent mine angel to testify unto you these things for the churches. I am the root and the offspring of David,

the bright, the morning star.
(17) And the spirit and the bride say, Come. And he that hears, let him say, Come. And he that is athirst, let him come: he that will, let him take the water of life freely.
(18) I testify unto every man that hears the words of the prophecy of this book, If any man shall add unto them, Elohim shall add unto him the plagues which are written in this book:
(19) and if any man shall take away from the words of the book of this prophecy, Elohim shall take away his part from the tree of life, and out of the holy city, which are written in this book.
(20) He who testifies these things says, Yea: I come quickly. Amein: come, Master Yeshua.
(21) The grace of the Master Yeshua be with the saints. Amein.

In this epilogue of the grand Apocalypse there is one point that is emphasize more than any other. Yahweh and Yeshua are coming *quickly*. The "Time Indicators" section in the Introduction details each of the phrases used in the Apocalypse that emphasize the nearness of the events prophesied therein. There are five occurrences of those phrases in just these final sixteen verses alone. The content of the Apocalypse is bookended by these types of phrases. John's message couldn't be clearer. The events he wrote about, which Yeshua signified to him to deliver to his fellow servants, were to take place very shortly. Regardless of whether one assumes the early or late date of the Apocalypse's authorship, almost two millennia can hardly be regarded as "at hand," or something that was to "shortly come to pass." There is no viable exegetical or hermeneutical reason to sever or skew these extremely clear statements about the timing of the events found in the Apocalypse. The simplest and least ambiguous rendering of the text is that the events surrounding the second appearing of Yeshua were to come to pass in the very near future to John's audience.

Another point of emphasis that John brings out in these final verses is the great importance of obedient faith, which is evidenced by righteous works. Verses 12, 14, and 15 state that each person will be given based on their works. Those who work lawlessness will not be allowed in the city. The cleansing of one's robes, to make them white in righteous acts just as the bride's gown, was and continues to be essential. The

works of righteousness have been the same since the beginning and will continue to be the same – obedience to Yahweh's perfect laws and commandments.

Continued Torah Observance

To gain entrance into the blessed and holy city we must mimic our Master and Messiah, Yeshua. He told us, "A disciple is not above his teacher, nor a servant above his master. It is enough for the disciple that he be as his teacher, and the servant as his master."[444] Thinking that we are exempt from the requirement of obedience to the Torah simply because Yeshua died, or Jerusalem and the temple were destroyed, is to place ourselves above our Master. We are not greater than he is. It is enough for us to strive to be just like him.

1 John 2:6
(6) He that says he abides in him ought himself also to walk **even as he walked**.

We would ask our reader this: Do you claim to abide in Yeshua? If so, are you walking *even as he walked*? We must ask ourselves: How did Yeshua walk? Did he keep the weekly seventh-day Sabbath[445]? Yes; so should we! Did he keep the annual festivals that were commanded to be kept forever[446]? Yes; so should we! Did he abstain from eating all things unclean[447]? Yes; so should we! The reader would do well to remember that fulfillment doesn't equate to abolition, nor does fulfillment cause an inherent change in everything. Yeshua's perfect obedience to the Sabbath doesn't nullify the commands for those who claim to serve Yahweh to do the same. Yeshua's perfect abstinence from eating unclean foods doesn't change the nature of a pig, vulture,

---

[444] Matthew 10:24-25a.
[445] Exodus 20:8-11, 31:12-17; Deuteronomy 5:12-15; Hebrews 3:7-4:12.
[446] Exodus 12:1-20; Leviticus 23:21, 26-44; et al.
[447] Leviticus 11; Isaiah 66:17.

squid, or human to make them lawfully edible. Yeshua's perfect sacrifice doesn't suddenly render homosexuality, bestiality, incest, or any other sexual sin lawful.

Fulfillment and abolition must be properly understood in order to grasp these concepts. For instance, the need to offer animals as sacrifices for sin has been fulfilled, not abolished. The commandment still exists as the Torah is forever and ever[448]. But, the sacrifice that is now accepted by the Father for our atonement is that of Yeshua. Our perfect sacrifice that is found in him never goes away as he lives forever. Therefore, we no longer offer animals to cleanse us from sin. Other examples can be provided from the Torah; however, we must address something that we believe is often overlooked. Before doing so let's look once again at the passage that is so often used by the dispensationalists to prove Torah-observance, called the "Mosaic dispensation" by them, is no longer required:

> Matthew 5:17-19
> (17) Think not that I came to destroy the Torah or the prophets: I came not to destroy, but to fulfil.
> (18) For verily I say unto you, Till heaven and earth pass away, one jot or one tittle shall in no wise pass away from the Torah, till all things be accomplished.
> (19) Whosoever therefore shall break one of these least commandments, and shall teach men so, shall be called least in the kingdom of heaven: but whosoever shall do and teach them, he shall be called great in the kingdom of heaven.

Verse 18 specifically is what is typically used to show the abolition of Torah-observance. The dispensationalists would say that "heaven and earth" in this instance refer to the governmental and religious systems in existence in Yeshua's day. Thus, since those systems were destroyed in 70 CE, all the Torah commands had then been fulfilled. However, we must remember that the symbolism of "heaven and earth" being representative of governmental and/or religious systems only applies

---

[448] Psalms 119:44.

when it is found in *prophetic* or *apocalyptic* context. To say that each occurrence of the words "heaven" and "earth" are symbolic is ludicrous. In the case of Yeshua's discourse in Matthew chapters 5-7, we see no reason to interpret this phrase apocalyptically any more than we would see the phrase "You shall not commit adultery" as such. One reason an incorrect understanding of this passage may arise is due to a faulty translation of the word "accomplished." Here is a more literal translation of that passage:

> Matthew 5:17-19 (J. P. Green's Literal Version)
> (17) Do not think that I came to annul the Law or the Prophets; I did not come to annul, but to fulfill.
> (18) Truly I say to you, Until the heaven and the earth pass away, in no way shall one iota or one point pass away from the Law until all **comes to pass**.
> (19) Therefore, whoever relaxes one of these commandments, the least, and shall teach men so, he shall be called least in the kingdom of Heaven. But whoever does and teaches *them*, this one shall be called great in the kingdom of Heaven.

The dispensationalist would have us believe that everything in the Torah is fulfilled or "accomplished." Yeshua, however, is only referring to those things in the Torah that have the *ability* to "come to pass." Think about it, did the law of bestiality "come to pass" in a fulfillment sense? What about the law against adultery? What about the law against moving your neighbor's property marker[449]? How did that "come to pass?" Are we now permitted to lawfully take over any property we want to?

The truth is that the only things that can "come to pass" in the Torah are prophecies or types, which is why Yeshua grouped both the Torah and the Prophets together in verse 17. One example would be the prophecy in Deuteronomy 18:15-22 concerning the prophet to come

---

[449] Deuteronomy 19:14.

after Moses. Another would be the prophecy in Genesis 3:15 where the seed of the woman was to crush the head of the serpent. More examples include the one coming from Judah to rule and the star coming forth from Jacob[450]. Those examples don't even include various "types" of Yeshua such as the Passover lamb, the willing sacrifice, Joseph, the goats offered on the Day of Atonements, the red heifer, et al[451]. *Those* are the kinds of things that can "come to pass" in the Torah. Thus, even if one were to say a particular commandment or law was abolished, it could only be seen as such through the lens of fulfillment. To use the example of animal sacrifices again, the commandments themselves weren't stricken out or abolished. However, through the lens of fulfillment they appear abolished due to the lack of necessity for us to offer them any longer.

Certain things mentioned above, like abstaining from eating unclean things, cannot "come to pass" in a fulfillment sense. If that were the case, we would stop nowhere short of complete lawlessness. Even if "types" such as the Passover lamb, the weekly Sabbath, and the annual festivals are fulfilled, we are still told that they are laws and commandments to be kept *forever*. If even they be only done as remembrances, the commands still stand true. Let us again remind the reader, we strive to mimic our Master and Messiah, Yeshua. If he was the only one that did everything perfectly, completing his earthly life without sinning, and that lack of sin was a result of perfect Torah-observance, why would we even want to do anything different?

As will be detailed in Appendix I below, the earliest assemblies of Yeshua after the destruction of Jerusalem, the temple, and the entire Jewish commonwealth were monotheistic, Torah-observant believers, who "obeyed the commandments of Elohim and held to the testimony of Yeshua."

---

[450] Genesis 49:10; Numbers 24:17.
[451] Exodus 12:1-51; Genesis 22:1-18; Genesis 37-47; et al.

SUMMARY & CONCLUSION

The Apocalypse is unlike any other work. It is an artful masterpiece of prophetic and apocalyptic literature throughout which is woven a plethora of truths from the scriptures and the historical record. Where some are likely to reject the conclusions drawn above, surely their spirits and hearts will be pricked into doing further research to determine whether their own stances are scripturally defensible and founded upon the truth. In our opinion, the fulfillment of the vast majority of the Apocalypse isn't something that diminishes our hope in eternal life, as Futurists may fear. On the contrary, its fulfillment solidifies even more our faith in, obedience to, and love of Yahweh our Heavenly Father and His Son Yeshua the Messiah. The undeniable fulfillments both scriptural and historical that are found in the Apocalypse confirm, beyond a shadow of a doubt, its divine origin. That confirmation then proves to confirm itself the divine origin of the prophecies of Isaiah, Jeremiah, Daniel, Ezekiel, Zechariah, and so many others who all spoke of the same "Day of Yahweh." It is because of these fulfillments and our ever-growing faith in and love of Yahweh and Yeshua that we can boldly and joyously proclaim:

John's Elohim, Yahweh Almighty, is our Elohim!

John's Messiah, Yeshua of Nazareth, is our Messiah!

CHRONOLOGICAL TIMELINE

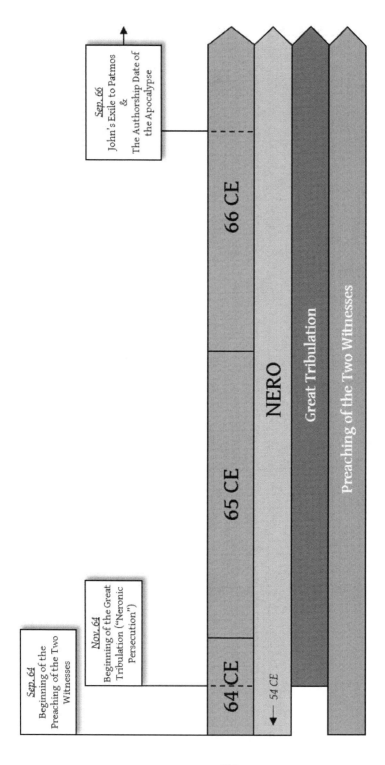

Sep. 64
Beginning of the Preaching of the Two Witnesses

Nov. 64
Beginning of the Great Tribulation ("Neronic Persecution")

Sep. 66
John's Exile to Patmos & The Authorship Date of the Apocalypse

64 CE

65 CE

66 CE

54 CE

NERO

Great Tribulation

Preaching of the Two Witnesses

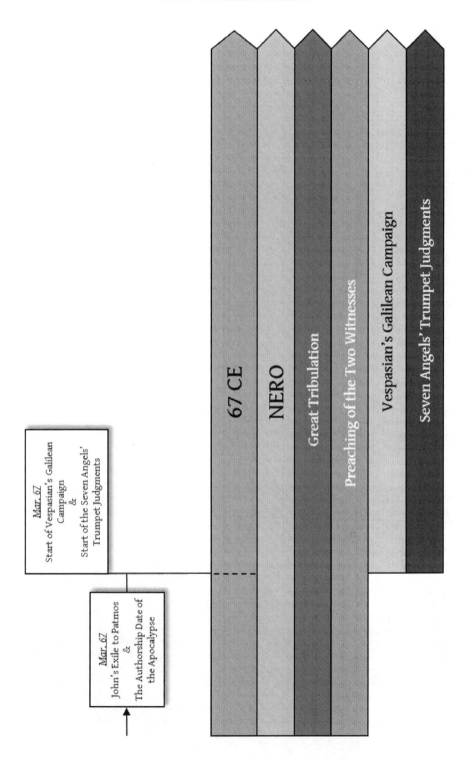

Mar. 67
Start of Vespasian's Galilean
Campaign
&
Start of the Seven Angels'
Trumpet Judgments

Mar. 67
John's Exile to Patmos
&
The Authorship Date of
the Apocalypse

67 CE

NERO

Great Tribulation

Preaching of the Two Witnesses

Vespasian's Galilean Campaign

Seven Angels' Trumpet Judgments

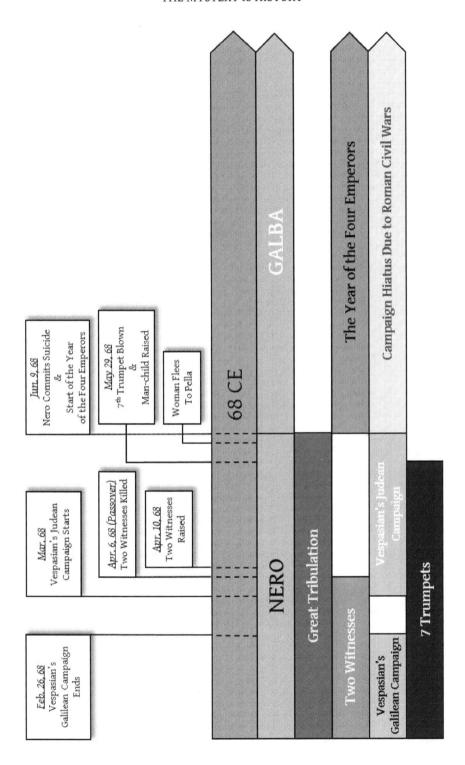

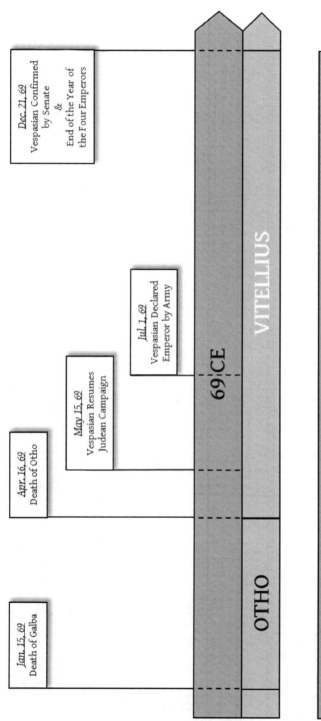

Jan. 15, 69
Death of Galba

Apr. 16, 69
Death of Otho

May 15, 69
Vespasian Resumes
Judean Campaign

Jul. 1, 69
Vespasian Declared
Emperor by Army

Dec. 21, 69
Vespasian Confirmed
by Senate
&
End of the Year of
the Four Emperors

69 CE

OTHO

VITELLIUS

The Year of the Four Emperors

Campaign Hiatus

Judean
Campaign

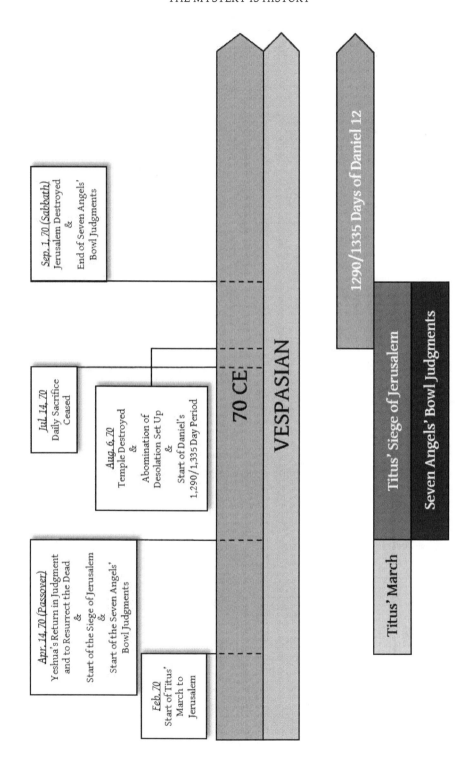

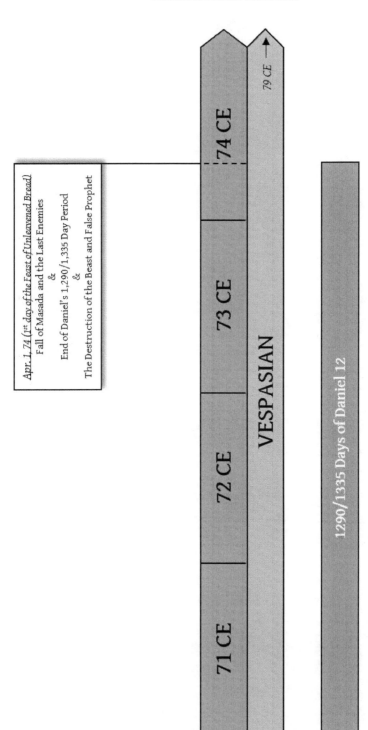

Apr. 1, 74 (1st day of the Feast of Unleavened Bread)
Fall of Masada and the Last Enemies
&
End of Daniel's 1,290/1,335 Day Period
&
The Destruction of the Beast and False Prophet

74 CE

73 CE

72 CE

71 CE

VESPASIAN

79 CE

1290/1335 Days of Daniel 12

APPENDIX I

*Proof of the Continuance of the Hebrew, Torah-Observant
Assembly After the Resurrection of the Dead*

It is unfortunate in several regards that the accounts we have of the Hebrew assembly of Yeshua after the destruction of Jerusalem and the Jewish commonwealth are few. The ones we do have are found within the accounts of people who, at the time of their writing, considered those "sects" to be heretical. We know, however, that the opinions of people hundreds of years after the existence of the "sects" they condemn must be studied with extreme caution. The purpose of this Appendix isn't to seek out every dark corner of history to present all information that may exist regarding the existence and propagation of the Hebrew assemblies. We will, however, provide information below that goes a long way to show that the existence of Torah-observant, Hebrew assemblies after the war is far more than a coincidental one.

As was shown in detail in chapter 12 above, the destination of Zion upon her flight from Jerusalem as it was being encompassed by armies was Pella, a city on the eastern side of the Jordan river in an area known as the Decapolis. The testimonies quoted below will not only supply abundant proof of that fact, but also give us some very interesting information as to what was found in and originated from that very city and area.

All three gospel accounts are one in their testimony of Yeshua's instruction to his apostles and disciples regarding their flight. He said, "Let them that are in Judaea flee unto the mountains."[452] We showed how their flight was indeed to the mountains, to the east of Jerusalem. Testimonies of the historians of the third and fourth centuries CE provide us with the evidence showing that the destination of their flight was Pella.

The Testimony of Eusebius

Eusebius of Caesarea (ca. 260-340 CE), also known as Eusebius Pamphili, was a Greek historian of Christianity and is thought to be one of the "church fathers." He testifies of the location to which the Hebrew assembly of Jerusalem and Judea fled.

---

[452] Matthew 24:16; Mark 13:14; Luke 21:21.

"The whole body, however, of the church at Jerusalem, having been commanded by a divine revelation given to men of approved piety there before the war, removed from the city, and dwelt at a certain town beyond the Jordan, called **Pella**."[453]

The Testimony of Epiphanius

Epiphanius of Salamis (*ca.* 310-403 CE) is yet another Christian who has been considered a "church father." On the location of the flight of Zion he tells us:

"Their origin came after the fall of Jerusalem. For since practically all who had come to faith in Christ had settled in Peraea then, in **Pella**, a town in the 'Decapolis' the Gospel mentions, which is near Batanaea and Bashanitis."[454]

"For they were such as had come back from the city of **Pella** to Jerusalem and were living there and teaching. For when the city was about to be taken and destroyed by the Romans, it was revealed in advance to all the disciples by an angel of God that they should remove from the city, as it was going to be completely destroyed. They sojourned as emigrants in **Pella**, the city above mentioned, in Transjordania. And this city is said to be of the Decapolis."[455]

"This sect of Nazoreans is to be found in Beroea near Coelesyria, in the Decapolis near **Pella**, and in Bashanitis at the place called Cocabe —Khokhabe in Hebrew. For that was its place of origin, since all the disciples had settled in **Pella** after their remove from Jerusalem— Christ having told them to abandon Jerusalem and withdraw from it because of the siege it was about to undergo. And they settled in Peraea for this reason and, as I said, lived their lives there. It was

---

[453] Eusebius. Book 3, Chapter 5, Section 3.
[454] Epiphanius, Panarion. Book 1, Section 2, Part 30, 2:7.
[455] Epiphanius, On Weights and Measures. Chapter 15.

from this that the Nazoraean sect had its origin."[456]

Some may question whether Pella was a likely location for the believers to flee to given that it was destroyed by Jews in retaliation for the slaughter of twenty thousand of their countrymen in Caesarea[457]. However, the destruction of Pella took place over a year and a half before Zion's flight from Jerusalem and Judea. The testimonies above and the fact that a year and a half is more than enough time to rebuild an ancient city the size of Pella, confirm that the believers would indeed have had a place to dwell there. Even if the reconstructed portions didn't support the entirety of the Hebrew assembly they could have very well stayed in nomadic tents just as their ancestors did for centuries.

The destination of Zion's flight must come together with what the historians say originated there for the full picture to become clear. The context of the passages above need to be examined to attain the identity and beliefs of the early Hebrew settlers in Pella, as "heretical" as they may have seemed to the third and fourth century historians.

"Thus Christ's holy disciples too called themselves 'disciples of Jesus' then, as indeed they were. But when others called them **Nazoraeans** they did not reject it, being aware of the intent of those who were calling them that. They were calling them **Nazoraeans** because of Christ, since our Lord Jesus was called 'the **Nazoraean**' himself—as the Gospels and the Acts of the Apostles say— because of his upbringing in the city of Nazareth (now a village) in Joseph's home, after having been born in the flesh at Bethlehem, of the ever-virgin Mary, Joseph's betrothed. For Joseph had settled in Nazareth after leaving Bethlehem and taking up residence in Galilee. But these same sectarians[458] whom I am discussing here disregarded the name of Jesus, and neither called themselves Jessaeans, kept the name of Jews, nor termed themselves Christians—but '**Nazoraeans**'

---

[456] Epiphanius, Panarion. Book 1, Section 2, Part 29, 7:7-8.
[457] Josephus, Wars. 2.18.1. Page 627.
[458] *I.e.* Those who settled in Pella, specified later in the quote.

supposedly from the name of the place 'Nazareth.' But they are Jews in every way and nothing else. **They use not only the New Testament but the Old Testament as well,** as the Jews do. For **they do not repudiate the law, the prophets, and the books which are called Writings** by the Jews and by themselves. They have no different views but **confess everything in full accord with the doctrine of the Law** and like the Jews, **except that they are supposedly believers in Christ.** For **they acknowledge both the resurrection of the dead** and that **all things have been created by God,** and **they declare that God is one, and that his Son is Jesus Christ. They are perfectly versed in the Hebrew language,** for the entire Law, the prophets, and the so-called Writings—I mean the poetic books, Kings, Chronicles, Esther and all the rest—are read in Hebrew among them, as of course they are among the Jews. They are different from Jews, and different from Christians, only in the following ways. **They disagree with Jews because of their belief in Christ;** but they are not in accord with Christians because **they are still fettered by the Law—circumcision, the Sabbath,** and **the rest.** As to Christ, I cannot say whether they too are misled by the wickedness of Cerinthus and Merinthus, and regard him as a mere man—or whether, as the truth is, they affirm that he was born of Mary by the Holy Spirit."[459] [*the quote then finishes with the passage quoted above from the same chapter*]

As he continues his discussion on these Nazoraeans, Epiphanius denounces them as heretics for continuing to observe the commands and precepts contained in the Torah. At the end of his discourse on the Nazoraeans he believes he did so with such sufficiency that he says he "squashed it [*the sect*] with the words of truth." However, as is to be expected of one who had been raised up in the doctrines that arose greatly from the integration of the Romans, the Greeks, and their respective cultures and practices into the assembly, his "scriptural" arguments aren't founded in a proper contextual exegesis or one based in an actual knowledge of the Torah. No one who lovingly and humbly obeys the commandments and statutes of Elohim as contained in the Torah think they are in fetters to it. They know they are doing exactly

---

[459] Epiphanius, Panarion. Book 1, Section 2, Part 29, 6:7-7:6.

what Yeshua did and taught.

Regardless of whether one agrees with Epiphanius' beliefs on and condemnation of the Nazoraean sect, what cannot be denied is that this group arose directly from the same city Zion fled to, immediately after they fled to it, and maintained the same beliefs that the Hebrew followers of Yeshua held so dearly to. Epiphanius provides us with information on yet another group that arose out of Pella:

"Following these [*the Nazoraeans*] and holding views like theirs, Ebion, the founder of the **Ebionites**, arose in the world in his turn as a monstrosity with many forms, and practically represented in himself the snake-like form of the mythical many-headed hydra. He was of the Nazoraeans' school, but preached and taught other things than they...For this Ebion was contemporary with the Jews, and since he was with them, he was derived from them. In the first place, he said that Christ was conceived by sexual intercourse and the seed of a man, Joseph—I have already said that he agreed with the others in everything, with this one difference, **his adherence to Judaism's Law of the Sabbath, circumcision**, and all the other Jewish and Samaritan observances. But like the Samaritans he goes still further than the Jews. He added the rule about taking care not to touch a gentile; and that every day, if a man has been with a woman and has left her, he must immerse himself in water[460]—any water he can find, the sea or any other. Moreover, if he should meet anyone while returning from his immersion and bath in the water, he runs back again for another immersion, often even with his clothes on! This sect now forbids celibacy and continence altogether, as do the other sects which are like it. For at one time they prided themselves on virginity, presumably because of James the Lord's brother, and so address their treatises to 'elders and virgins.' **Their origin came after the fall of Jerusalem.** For since practically all who had come to faith in Christ had settled in Peraea then, in **Pella**, a town in the 'Decapolis' the Gospel mentions, which is near Batanaea and Bashanitis—as they had moved there then and

---

[460] Leviticus 15:16-18.

were living there, this provided an opportunity for Ebion. And as far as I know, he first lived in a village called Cocabe in the district of Qarnaim—also called Ashtaroth—in Bashanitis. There he began his evil teaching—the place, if you please, **where the Nazoraeans I have spoken of came from.** For since Ebion was connected with them and they with him, each party shared its own wickedness with the other. Each also differed from the other to some extent, but they emulated each other in malice. But I have already spoken at length, both in other works and in the other Sects, about the locations of Cocabe and Arabia."[461]

Here again Epiphanius tells us of another Torah-observant group of believers who settled in Pella after the fall of Jerusalem. He has specific judgments and condemnations towards them, of course, but again, the point isn't to try to determine exactly what Epiphanius' motives were in his descriptions of these people. It is to point out that there was yet another group of believers in Yeshua that arose from Pella, immediately after the fall of Jerusalem, who were also Torah-observant.

Eusebius tells us more about these Ebionites that can aid us in our understanding.

"The spirit of wickedness, however, being unable to shake some in their love of Christ, and yet finding them susceptible of his impressions in other respects, brought them over to his purposes. These are properly called Ebionites by the ancients, as those who cherished low and mean opinions of Christ. For they considered him a plain and common man, and justified only by his advances in virtue, and that he was born of the Virgin Mary, by natural generation. With them **the observance of the law was altogether necessary,** as if they could not be saved, only by faith in Christ and a corresponding life. Others, however, besides these, but of the same name, indeed avoided the absurdity of the opinions maintained by the former, not denying that the Lord was born of the Virgin by the Holy Ghost, and yet in like manner, not acknowledging his

---

[461] Epiphanius, Panarion. Book 1, Section 2, Part 30, 1:1, 2:1-9.

preexistence, though he was God, the word and wisdom, they turned aside into the same irreligion, as with the former **they evinced great zeal to observe the ritual service of the law.** These, indeed, thought on the one hand that all the epistles of the apostle [*Paul, specifically*] ought to be rejected, calling him an apostate from the law, but on the other, only using the gospel according to the Hebrews, they esteem the others as of but little value. They also observe the Sabbath and other discipline of the Jews, just like them, but on the other hand, they also celebrate the Lord's days very much like us, in commemoration of his resurrection. Whence, in consequence of such a course, they have also received their epithet, the name of Ebionites, exhibiting the poverty of their intellect. For it is thus that the Hebrews call a poor man."[462]

Eusebius' condemnation of the Ebionites, though not quite as scathing as Epiphanius' entire discourse on them, is still very revealing. Both of these "church fathers" considered the Ebionites as heretics whose faith was a great deviation from what they believed was the true one. Eusebius claims that the Ebionites rejected Paul of Tarsus as an apostle because they saw him as an apostate from the Torah. Establishing whether this is indeed true is far beyond the scope of this book. Either way, when you strip away Epiphanius' and Eusebius' preconceived biases and inherited vehemence against obedience to the Torah you have two clear testimonies of the fact that Torah-observant followers of Yeshua flourished in the first century CE, in and around Pella, immediately after the siege and destruction of Jerusalem. Coincidence? We think not! Yet, there's more information to present.

In his Dialogue With Trypho, a Jew of the late first-early second century CE, Justin Martyr (*ca.* 100-165 CE), when asked whether those who observe the Torah *after* believing in Yeshua as the Messiah will be saved, responds by saying:

"There are, Trypho, was my reply, and persons who are bold enough not even to join with such in conversation or meals; with whom I

---

[462] Eusebius. Book 3, Chapter 27.

myself do not agree. But, if they, because of the weakness of their mind, desire to keep such of the sayings of Moses as are now possible – which we perceive were appointed because of the hardness of the people's heart – while they still hope on Christ, and also desire to keep those ordinances of the practice of righteousness and of piety which are everlasting and in accordance with nature, and deliberately choose to live with Christians and believers, as I said before, without persuading them either to receive circumcision like themselves, or to keep Sabbath, or to observe other things of the same kind – I declare that we must fully receive such, and have communion with them in all respects as being of one family and as brothers. But if, Trypho, I said, they who are of your race say that they believe on this Christ of ours, and in every way compel those who are of Gentile birth and believe on this Christ to live in accordance with the law appointed by Moses, or choose not to have communion with them that have such a life in common, these also in like manner I do not accept. Now they that follower their advice, and live under the law, as well as keep their profession in the Christ of God, will, I suppose, perhaps be saved."[463]

Justin goes on to say that anyone who doesn't believe in Yeshua as the Messiah, including righteous men of the stock of Abraham, cannot be saved. What we can conclude from this account of Justin Martyr, written almost two centuries prior to Eusebius', is that the opposition to Torah-observant followers of Yeshua was a progressive one. It isn't what one would expect if Yeshua indeed taught that the Torah was to be abrogated upon or immediately after his death and resurrection. Were the apostles, those who sat at the feet and leaned upon the very breast of Messiah, or the seventy disciples who he sent out two-by-two, so mistaken as to his teachings that they just neglected to obey them or make it clear to their own disciples? Surely we must have faith enough to believe that our Messiah's hand-picked apostles would have been taught and maintained the true faith, and taught the same to their own disciples.

---

[463] Justin, Dialogue. Chapter 47.

One of two conclusions can be drawn at this point. One, if Torah-abrogation was indeed the message of Yeshua we must conclude that the apostles were inept imbeciles who utterly failed, even after a span of forty years, to obey this message or convey it clearly to their hearers, and that while being filled with the very spirit of Elohim! Their disciples were so hopelessly and irreversibly brainwashed that even the spirit-led preaching of the Messiah's apostles couldn't purge Torah-observance from them. Or, two, if continued Torah-observance was Yeshua's message, his apostles and disciples succeeded in preaching that message and it was carried on well after his death and resurrection. Even after the death and resurrection of the twelve apostles his loyal followers believed the true faith was the one repeated twice-over in the Apocalypse. It is made up of those who "keep the commandments of Elohim *and* their faith in Yeshua." They maintained their faith and devotion to Yeshua, humbly and lovingly keeping all that he taught them, which included continued observance to those things in the Torah.

We can read yet another quote from Epiphanius that tells us just how devoted the first generations of disciples were.

"So Aquila, while he was in Jerusalem, also saw **the disciples of the disciples of the apostles flourishing in the faith and working great signs, healings, and other miracles.** For they were such as had come back **from the city of Pella to Jerusalem** and were living there and teaching. For when the city was about to be taken and destroyed by the Romans, it was revealed in advance to all the disciples by an angel of God that they should remove from the city, as it was going to be completely destroyed. They sojourned as emigrants in **Pella,** the city above mentioned, in Transjordania. And this city is said to be of the Decapolis. But after the destruction of Jerusalem, when **they had returned to Jerusalem**, as I have said, **they wrought great signs**, as I have already said."[464]

He tells here that the disciples of the disciples of the apostles were still

---

[464] Epiphanius, On Weights and Measures. Chapter 15.

obedient and faithful, and that to the point of miracle-working. As an example, if Clement were indeed a disciple of Peter, as the Clementines most definitively prove, it means that a disciple of Clement was said to have still held to the apostles' original faith, and therefore that of Yeshua's. Interestingly enough, though Epiphanius goes on to condemn Aquila, he doesn't condemn the above mentioned third generation disciples of Yeshua. Given what we've already read of his above how can we not see a contradictory issue here? The disciples of the apostles (*i.e.* Clement) would have very likely been the ones who fled to and taught within Pella. It would then be their disciples that left Pella after a certain period of time to return to Jerusalem and minister therein. Are we to believe that the disciples of the apostles, who we can assume were thriving and working miracles within Pella while they were there just as their disciples did in Jerusalem after them, weren't aware of the Nazoraean and Ebionite "heresies" that were sprouting? Are we really to believe that these true and faithful followers, filled with the spirit of Yahweh, wouldn't have confronted and put a stop to the madness of those "heretical" sects while they were in Pella? We find it exceedingly difficult to believe that the zealous, miracle-working disciples after the apostles wouldn't have done all they could do to purge the poison of false doctrine while in Pella *and* been successful in doing so.

We must return to the sect of the Nazoraeans briefly to provide a full-circle evaluation of them. The scriptures themselves label the earliest believers in and followers of Yeshua by this term[465]. Based on Epiphanius' description of the Nazoraeans above we can safely conclude their core doctrines are as follows. They:

- Used the Old and New Testaments (whatever existed of them in their day)
- Adhered to the Torah, Prophets, and Writings (The Tanakh - Hebrew Bible)
- Confessed everything in full accord with the Torah
- Believed that Yeshua is the Messiah

---

[465] Acts 24:5.

- Believed in the resurrection of the dead
- Believed there is only one creator, Elohim
- Believed that there is only one Elohim, and that He has a Son, Yeshua the Messiah
- Were perfectly versed in the Hebrew language, obviously knowing the value of understanding it
- Observed important facets of the Torah such as circumcision, observance of the Sabbath, and the rest

These beliefs are identical with those of the early assembly of Yeshua. Even the Jews in the time of the writing of the book of Acts saw Yeshua's followers as a "sect" of Judaism[466], not a new religion as traditional Christianity is today. The earliest believers are confirmed as those who believed in Yeshua and were at the same time zealous for the Torah[467]. Where many dispensationalists would assert that the "purging" of the remnants of "Judaism" and the "law" was a progressive act in the early assembly of Yeshua, we believe they made no efforts to do so at all. It wasn't the original apostles, disciples, or the disciples of the apostles that desired or strove to do that. On the contrary, the understanding of who Yeshua was and how they were to mirror their lives after his was rooted in the Torah. Their obedience to him was inseparable from the obedience to the commandments of Yahweh. It wasn't until the pagan, lawless, unclean and idolatrous ways of the Gentile converts were introduced into and allowed to take hold of the true assembly of Yeshua that disobedience to the Torah was not only permitted, but praised. From the historical records we've just quoted above, we can see that this drastic shift in the early assembly's practices didn't take hold until several generations of disciples had come and gone. Some may ask, "Why?" The simple answer is that the apostles and disciples couldn't be everywhere at one time. An account of Hegesippus on this very topic is quoted within the pages of Eusebius' writings that sheds some light on how and when the new doctrines were introduced:

---

[466] Acts 24:5, 14, 28:22.
[467] Acts 21:20.

"'Of these heretics,' says he, 'some reported Simeon the son of Cleophas, as a descendant of David, and a Christian; and thus he suffered as a martyr, when he was a hundred and twenty years old, in the reign of the emperor Trajan, and the presidency of the consular Atticus...There are, also, those that take the lead of the whole church as martyrs, even the kindred of our Lord. And when profound peace was established throughout the church, they continued to the days of the emperor Trajan, until the time that the above-mentioned Simeon, the relative of our Lord, being the son of Cleophas, was waylaid by the heretics, and also himself accused for the same cause, under Atticus, who was of similar dignity. After he was tormented many days, he died a martyr, with such firmness, that all were amazed, even the president himself, that a man of a hundred and twenty years should bear such tortures. He was at last ordered to be crucified.' **The same author, relating the events of the times, also says, that the church continued until then as a pure and uncorrupt virgin; whilst if there were any at all, that attempted to pervert the sound doctrine of the saving gospel, they were yet skulking in dark retreats; but when the sacred choir of apostles became extinct, and the generation of those that had been privileged to hear their inspired wisdom had passed away,** then also the combinations of impious error arose by the fraud and delusions of false teachers. These also, as there were none of the apostles left, henceforth attempted, without shame, to preach their false doctrine against the gospel of truth."[468]

Eusebius provides us with information about when the "generation of those that had been privileged to hear their inspired wisdom had passed away":

"We have not ascertained in any way, that the times of the bishops in Jerusalem have been regularly preserved on record, for tradition says that they all lived but a very short time. So much, however, have I learned from writers, that down to the invasion of the Jews under Adrian, there were fifteen successions of bishops in that

---

[468] Eusebius. Book 3, Chapter 32.

church, **all which, they say, were Hebrews from the first, and received the knowledge of Christ pure and unadulterated** ; so that, in the estimation of those who were able to judge, they were well approved, and worthy of the episcopal office. For at that time **the whole church under them consisted of faithful Hebrews, who continued from the time of the apostles, until the siege that then took place.** The Jews then again revolting from the Romans, were subdued and captured, after very severe conflicts. In the meantime, as the bishops from the circumcision failed, it may be necessary now to recount them in order, from the first. The first, then, was James called the brother of our Lord ; after whom, the second was Simeon, the third Justus, the fourth Zaecheus, the fifth Tobias, the sixth Benjamin, the seventh John, the eighth Matthew, the ninth Philip, the tenth Seneca, the eleventh Justus, the twelfth Levi, the thirteenth Ephres, the fourteenth Joseph, and finally, the fifteenth Judas. These are all the bishops of Jerusalem that filled up the time from the apostles until the above-mentioned time, all of the circumcision."[469]

The first through fifteenth leaders of the assembly of Yeshua after his death were Hebrews. All the way through the death of the last one, Judas [elsewhere Judah], Eusebius tells us that they received the knowledge of Messiah *pure* and *unadulterated*. Epiphanius' supplies us with this list of these first fifteen Hebrew leaders:

"James, who was martyred in Jerusalem by beating with a cudgel. [He lived] until the time of Nero. Symeon, was crucified under Trajan. Judah; Zachariah; Tobiah; Benjamin; John, bringing us to the ninth [or] tenth year of Trajan; Matthias; Philip; Seneca; Justus, bringing us to Hadrian; Levi; Vaphres; Jose; **Judah, bringing us to the eleventh year of Antonius.** The above were the circumcised bishops of Jerusalem."[470]

The eleventh year of Caesar Antonius Pius was 148 CE, which is

---

[469] Eusebius. Book 4, Chapter 5.
[470] Epiphanius, Panarion. Book 2, Section 5, Part 20, 1.

presumably when Judah, the last Hebrew leader of the assembly of Yeshua, died. We find it amazing that the historians quoted above couldn't put the pieces of their own records together to ascertain the truth of the first followers of Yeshua. We can draw the following conclusions from their different accounts when read together:

- Torah-observant followers of Yeshua originated from and flourished in Pella, the location to which the true Zion fled in obedience to Yeshua's warning
- The apostles, their disciples, and the disciples of their disciples preached the truth in power from Pella through Jerusalem after its destruction
- The leaders of the assembly after Yeshua, through 148 CE, were all circumcised, Torah-observant Hebrews
- The truth, knowledge, and wisdom of Yeshua the Messiah that was lived and taught by those leaders during those generations of believers was that of the pure, unadulterated, and uncorrupted version of the faith
- It wasn't until after that generation of Hebrew leaders, when Gentile converts began leading the assembly, that false teachers crawled out of their hiding places and began to lead the assembly into lawless doctrines, eventually resulting in a faith wholly amalgamated with the pagan culture and practices of the world around them

The true Hebrew faith, consisting of obedience to Yahweh's Torah and faith in Yeshua as the Messiah, was the one taught by the apostles and subsequently maintained by several generations of believers beyond them. Though we can see disputes over obedience to the commands in the Torah within the pages of the New Testament itself, we learn from history that those disputes always resulted with Torah-observance being the final judgment. Those closest to the teachings of Yeshua, the apostles, led and taught their disciples accordingly. As long as there was a Hebrew in charge, one who was familiar with the Torah and its proper and righteous application, the assembly of Yeshua remained wholly pure in doctrine. The rise and installment of Gentile believers as leaders, those who were too far separated from Yeshua and his apostles, unlearned in the teachings of the Torah, led to the eventual corruption of the true faith. However, as we will show below, the true Hebrew faith was far from gone even centuries after the destruction of Jerusalem and the Jewish commonwealth.

British Library Additional Manuscript 12150 (BL Add. 12150) contains the text of the Recognitions and Homilies of Clement of Alexandria in Syriac. That manuscript is the oldest dated manuscript in the world, having a date equivalent to 411/412 CE. The contents and message of this manuscript are Hebraic through and through. The following are some select passages that clearly show this. In addition, they show a distinct unity between the doctrines of the people spoken of in the manuscript and those of the Nazoraean/Ebionite believers of the first century CE.

> "**Elohim is one, the world His work**, and because He is just He will thence recompense everything and every person **according to his deeds.**"[471]

> "Then in the fifteenth generation, human beings first did homage to fire and made idols. Until then one language was held, **Hebrew, the beloved of Elohim.**"[472]

> "However, the justice of truth prevailed, for because we were few their lying about us did not protect them. Moreover, exceedingly, as if by the zeal of Elohim, we were all the time growing greater than them so that now even their priests feared lest, by the providence of Elohim to their own confusion, all the people should come over to our faith. And frequently they were sending out and requesting us to talk with them about Yeshua, if he be that prophet formerly declared by Moses, who is the eternal Messiah – **for regarding only this is there a division between us believers in Yeshua and the**

---

[471] Recognitions, Syriac. 1.25.
[472] Recognitions, Syriac. 1.30.

unbelievers from our people."[473]

"When therefore we twelve Apostles had **assembled during the days of Passover** with the multitude of the assembly at Jerusalem, in order to be gathered together with our brethren **at the festival.**"[474]

"The Jews are thus mistaken regarding the first coming of our Master, and **they have a disagreement with us concerning Yeshua alone**, for even they know that the Messiah comes and they wait for him. However, they did not recognize the one who came in humility who was called 'Yeshua.'"[475]

"But concerning the rest of the things that thence happen, it is impossible for them to be told – neither to angels nor to human beings – but they should only know that Elohim sits before the good for the sake of blessings, and **for eternity without end He delights those who have kept and observed his Law.**"[476]

"And thus in **the resurrection of the dead**, their souls will clothe themselves with their body that was cleansed with dissolution, and on account of the achievements of their good works they shall inherit eternal life. Wherefore those who encounter and receive the Kingdom of the Messiah are happy, for they shall escape from the punishment of Sheol, go free, and continue without corruption, as they also longed to escape from the awfulness of the Judgment."[477]

"Or did you not know that the end of the justice of the Law is peace? For from sins come contentions, to which correspond wars, and **thus by listening to the Law peace occurs** on account of not sinning."[478]

---

[473] Recognitions, Syriac. 1.43.
[474] Recognitions, Syriac. 1.44.
[475] Recognitions, Syriac. 1.50.
[476] Recognitions, Syriac. 1.51.
[477] Recognitions, Syriac. 1.52.
[478] Recognitions, Syriac. 2.36.

"Do not fear, O Simon [*Magus*], for we are neither stopping up our ears nor fleeing. For it is ours first to show this against your false case: **One alone is Elohim, Who is the creator of the heavens and the earth**, and of all those who are called 'elohim' **He is the only Elohim.**"[479]

Virtually all the tenets of the Nazoraeans are repeated in this text. Repeatedly in the manuscript, Peter quotes from, argues from, and lauds the Torah. He teaches that obedience to Yahweh and His Perfect Law is how followers of Yeshua are to walk. Whether one accepts this manuscript as a copy descending from an original written by Clement as he followed Peter on his travels, or as one written by a fifth-generation follower of Yeshua, one fact remains the same. A true believer and follower is described as one who honors Yahweh as the only Elohim and creator, strives to keep His Torah, and serves His Son Yeshua as Master and Messiah. This manuscript is either further evidence that the true faith of and taught by Yeshua and his apostles was a Torah-observant one, or evidence that such a faith, attributed to the earliest followers of Yeshua after Jerusalem's fall, was yet in existence in the fifth century CE.

There is an interesting passage in this manuscript that does point to the fact that this is a descendant from a much more ancient work, compiled prior to the destruction of Jerusalem:

"Thus indeed we know that He is increasingly angry on account of your sacrificing after the completion of the time of sacrifices. Wherefore even **this Temple shall be broken down and they shall set up the Abomination of Desolation in the Holy Place**. Thereupon the gospel shall be established for the Gentiles as a testimony, for the sake of healing the divisions that exist, so that it shall even be your sundering."[480]

---

[479] Recognitions, Syriac. 2.40.
[480] Recognitions, Syriac. 1.64.

The quote places the authorship of the manuscript prior to the destruction of the temple and Jerusalem. If this is indeed accurate, this manuscript provides us with sufficient proof that the teaching of Yeshua to the apostles, then from the apostles to their disciples, was one of Torah-observance, not Torah-abrogation.

The fulfillment of the Apocalypse and/or certain prophecies of Yeshua or the prophets of old doesn't mean that Torah-observance suddenly became unnecessary. It doesn't mean Yeshua's death and resurrection suddenly transformed what were once abominable sins into acceptable practices, so long as they are done "in faith." It didn't suddenly become lawful to have sexual relations with an animal, move your neighbor's property marker, drink blood, sacrifice to idols, be a homosexual, eat human or other unclean flesh, neglect observance of the seventh-day Sabbath or annual festivals, or do any other thing strictly forbidden in the Torah.

Torah-observance, though spoken of slanderously and proclaimed "heretical" by Christians hundreds of years removed from the original apostles, was and continues to be the way of life of the true followers of Yeshua. History tells us that the continuance of the Hebraic faith arose from Pella, where Zion fled to prior to Jerusalem's destruction. We do not believe this is a matter of mere historical coincidence. It is one of divine providence. The disciples of the apostles weren't "fettered" by the Torah, as though being led captive to a foreign, pagan land against their will. They were bound to it as a servant who loves his master is bound by oath and covenant to him. Where historians and theologians centuries later saw their continued obedience to Torah as a slow and progressive purging of the "Judaization" of the faith, the disciples knew it to be the faith taught to them by their Master and Messiah, Yeshua. May we strive to and attain that pure and unadulterated faith of the early assembly who sat at the very feet of our glorified King!

APPENDIX II

What Now?

"Okay, so the Apocalypse is fulfilled, along with many of Yeshua's prophecies and the prophecies of the Old Testament prophets...now what do we do?" Such is the question that many current or former Futurists ask themselves after they realize the truth about the Apocalypse, and rightfully so. After all, prior to that their lives were spent watching for and awaiting the visible return of Yeshua from the clouds of heaven to resurrect the dead and destroy anything and everything evil on the planet. The answer, as we should expect, lies in the teachings of Yeshua and the prophets.

> Matthew 19:28-30
> (28) And Yeshua said unto them, Verily I say unto you, that you who have followed me, in **the regeneration** when the Son of man shall sit on the throne of his glory, you also shall sit upon twelve thrones, judging the twelve tribes of Israel.
> (29) And every one that has left houses, or brethren, or sisters, or father, or mother, or children, or lands, for my name's sake, shall receive a hundredfold, and shall inherit eternal life.
> (30) But many shall be last *that are* first; and first *that are* last.

The Greek word rendered "generation" here is παλιγγενεσία, *palingenesia*, and is defined as "*new birth, reproduction, renewal, re-creation, regeneration.*" Read the passage carefully. Yeshua says that the twelve apostles will be sitting on twelve thrones *in* the regeneration, not *after* it. Again, most, if not all Futurists understand the coming of the kingdom of heaven to be hand-in-hand with an instantaneous and universal restoration of all things to an Eden-like state. If the phrase read "after the regeneration" instead of "in the regeneration" there might be a foundation for such an argument. However, that is not what the text says. The regeneration is spoken of as something that is to last for an indefinite period of time. We addressed this topic more in chapter 11 above under the section entitled "Immediate Outcome or Progressive Regeneration?"

Isaiah tells us the same about the regeneration:

> Isaiah 65:17
> For, behold, I create new heavens and a new earth; and the former things shall not be remembered, nor come into mind.

The word "create" is in the Hebrew Qal stem, Active Participle aspect. Once again Young's Literal Translation gives us a more accurate rendering:

Isaiah 65:17
For, lo, **I am creating** new heavens, and a new earth, And the former things are not remembered, Nor do they ascend on the heart.

Yahweh is telling His people through Isaiah that He is *creating* a new heavens and earth, not that they were *created* in the past. John confirms that was still the case in his day by his use of a specific Greek tense, voice, and mood in Revelation 21:5 when speaking about the new heavens and new earth:

Revelation 21:5
And he that sits on the throne said, Behold, I make all things new. And he says, Write: for these words are faithful and true.

The verb "make" is in the Present tense, Active voice, and Indicative mood. In Greek, this indicates an action that is continual, on-going. More accurately it would read, "Behold, I *am making* all things new."[481] It was never intended or prophesied to be an instantaneous restoration or regeneration. We weren't to see a restored or regenerated world, but one that requires restoration and regeneration, things that require action on the part of Yahweh's people.

So, what do we do now? Simply put, act like you are a representative of Yeshua to this world. You are an ambassador, a citizen of a nation and city *not* of this world, sent to bring a message of salvation and obedience to *this* broken and damaged world. You are a messenger sent to invite more guests to the wedding feast of the King's Son. You are a warrior armed with spiritual weapons that this world knows nothing

---

[481] So the translation in the New American Standard Bible, World English Bible, International Standard Version, New Revised Standard Version, and Lexham English Bible. Also the Hebrew text of Franz Delitzsch's Hebrew New Testament translated from the Greek manuscripts.

about, but are stronger than anything they can muster. You are a witness to the change that Yahweh can do in any person's life. Walk through this life with the utmost faith that the holy spirit of Yahweh inside of you, your token of citizenship in the new heavens and earth, your gateway of communication directly through the veil to the Father, will work wondrous things through you. Speak life. Pray as though things you request according to His will shall indeed come to pass. Fulfill Yeshua's great commission to his apostles, which they passed on to their own disciples:

Matthew 28:19-20
(19) Go you therefore, and make disciples of all the nations, baptizing them in the authority of the Father, Son, and holy spirit[482]:

---

[482] Although there is patristic evidence of the phrase "my name" as opposed to the "Father, Son, and holy spirit," it lies almost exclusively with Eusebius, who is known to abbreviate passages in his works. In addition, Eusebius, in his Letter on the Council of Nicaea, quotes the full phrase. There has not yet been any manuscript evidence unearthed or revealed that contains the shorter phrase. Some would present Shem-Tov's Hebrew Matthew (ca. 1380-1385 CE) as evidence of the lack of the longer phrase. However, given that the content in Shem-Tov's version is significantly different in many other respects, it is hardly a strong comparison. The two other well-known Hebrew Matthew editions, those of Sebastian Münster and Jean du Tillet, contain the longer phrase.

We know from the book of Acts and various epistles in the New Testament, however, that the phrase "in the name of Yeshua," or something very similar, is what is found. It is our understanding that the issue lies not with the tripartite phrase, but with the word commonly translated as "name." The Greek ὄνομα, onoma, though most often carrying with it the meaning of a "name," as in an appellation, can also mean "that which is used for everything which the name covers, everything the thought or feeling of which is aroused in the mind by mentioning, hearing, remembering, the name, i.e. for one's rank, authority, interests, pleasure, command, excellences, deeds etc." Such would be the meaning of one coming "in the name" of another. If one comes "in the name of" a king as

(20) teaching them to observe all things whatsoever I commanded you: and lo, I am with you always, even unto the end of the age. Amein.

To "make disciples" of all the nations isn't merely to introduce them to Yeshua as their Messiah. It means to train them up diligently in "all the things whatsoever" he commanded, which we can discern from both the scriptures and history is obedience to the Torah coupled with a humble and obedient faith in him. What we do now is work and fight the good fight for the kingdom to which we were so graciously invited into. May we do so with all our heart, soul, and strength, to the glory of Yahweh Elohim our Father and Yeshua the Messiah His Son!

---

an ambassador, he comes with the authority of the king. Yeshua says the same, "I am come *in my Father's name*, and you receive me not: if another shall come in his own name, him you will receive." (John 5:43; *cf.* John 10:25) He also says, "And I am no more in the world, and these are in the world, and I come to you. Holy Father, keep them *in your name which you have given me*, that they may be one, even as we *are*." (John 17:11) Yeshua wasn't given the appellation "Yahweh." He was given the authority of Yahweh and desires that his apostles remain in that authority. Many other passages from the Old Testament can be studied where one came "in the name of Yahweh," the contextual meaning being "in the authority of Yahweh." From an ancient manuscript perspective the Didache (*ca.* 50-100 CE) and the Syriac Recognitions quoted in Appendix I above, which very likely reflect a much earlier edition of the Clementines, both contain the tripartite phrase.

It is in light of this information that we believe the tripartite phrase is indeed the most accurate one, at least based on what we have available to us today. However, the traditional rendering of "in the *name* of the Father, Son, and holy spirit" has become so adulterated from its original, historical context, that its meaning is all but lost. From the aspect of a Hebrew, which Yeshua was, to come "in the name" of his Father was to come with all the authority and power of Yahweh, similar to how Joseph was granted all authority over Egypt by Pharaoh, witnessed by the signet ring placed on his hand. (Genesis 41:37-44). Thus, in an attempt to forcefully overcome this cultural and linguistic gap, while yet maintaining an accurate meaning of ὄνομα, we have translated the phrase as "in the *authority* of the Father, Son, and holy spirit," which authority he was granted in the verse prior (Matthew 28:18).

APPENDIX III

Psalm 119:
Proof that Obedience to the Torah is
Love and Freedom, not Bondage

א

(1) Blessed are they that are perfect in the way, who **walk in the Torah of Yahweh.**
(2) Blessed are they that **keep his testimonies,** that seek him with the whole heart.
(3) Yea, they do no unrighteousness; they walk in his ways.
(4) You have commanded *us* your precepts, that we should observe them diligently.
(5) Oh that my ways were established **to observe your statutes!**
(6) Then shall I not be put to shame, when I have respect unto all your commandments.
(7) I will give thanks unto you with uprightness of heart, **when I learn your righteous judgments.**
(8) **I will observe your statutes:** Oh forsake me not utterly.

ב

(9) Wherewith shall a young man cleanse his way? By taking heed *thereto* according to your word.
(10) With my whole heart have I sought you: **oh let me not wander from your commandments.**
(11) Your word have I laid up in my heart, that I might not sin against you.
(12) Blessed art you, O Yahweh: **Teach me your statutes.**
(13) **With my lips have I declared All the ordinances of your mouth.**
(14) **I have rejoiced in the way of your testimonies,** as much as in all riches.
(15) I will meditate on your precepts, and have respect unto your ways.
(16) **I will delight myself in your statutes:** I will not forget your word.

ג

(17) Deal bountifully with your servant, that I may live; so will I observe your word.
(18) **Open my eyes, that I may behold wondrous things out of your Torah.**
(19) I am a sojourner in the earth: hide not your commandments from me.
(20) **My soul breaks for the longing that it hath unto your ordinances at all times.**
(21) You have rebuked the proud that are cursed, that do wander from your commandments.
(22) Take away from me reproach and contempt; for I have kept your testimonies.
(23) Princes also sat and talked against me; *but* **your servant did meditate on your statutes.**
(24) **Your testimonies also are my delight** *and* **my counsellors.**

ד

(25) My soul cleaves unto the dust: quicken you me according to your word.
(26) I declared my ways, and you answered me: **teach me your statutes.**
(27) **Make me to understand the way of your precepts:** so shall I meditate on your wondrous works.
(28) My soul melts for heaviness: strengthen you me according unto your word.
(29) Remove from me the way of falsehood; and **grant me your Torah graciously.**
(30) I have chosen the way of faithfulness: **your ordinances have I set** *before me.*

(31) I cleave unto your testimonies: O Yahweh, put me not to shame.

(32) I will run the way of your commandments, when you shall enlarge my heart.

ה

(33) Teach me, O Yahweh, the way of your statutes; and I shall keep it unto the end.

(34) Give me understanding, and I shall keep your Torah; yea, I shall observe it with my whole heart.

(35) Make me to go in the path of your commandments; for therein do I delight.

(36) Incline my heart unto your testimonies, and not to covetousness.

(37) Turn away my eyes from beholding vanity, and quicken me in your ways.

(38) Confirm unto your servant your word, which *is in order* unto the fear of you.

(39) Turn away my reproach whereof I am afraid; for your ordinances are good.

(40) Behold, I have longed after your precepts: quicken me in your righteousness.

ו

(41) Let your lovingkindnesses also come unto me, O Yahweh, even your salvation, according to your word.

(42) So shall I have an answer for him that reproaches me; for I trust in your word.

(43) And take not the word of truth utterly out of my mouth; for I have hoped in your ordinances.

(44) So shall I observe your Torah continually For ever and ever.

(45) And I shall walk at liberty; for I have sought your precepts.

(46) I will also speak of your testimonies before kings, And shall not be put to shame.

(47) And I will delight myself in your commandments, which I have loved.

(48) I will lift up my hands also unto your commandments, which I have loved; And I will meditate on your statutes.

ז

(49) Remember the word unto your servant, because you have made me to hope.

(50) This is my comfort in my affliction; for your word hath quickened me.

(51) The proud have had me greatly in derision: yet have I not swerved from your Torah.

(52) I have remembered your ordinances of old, O Yahweh, and have comforted myself.

(53) Hot indignation hath taken hold upon me, because of the wicked that forsake your Torah.

(54) Your statutes have been my songs in the house of my pilgrimage.

(55) I have remembered your name, O Yahweh, in the night, and have observed your Torah.

(56) This I have had, because I have kept your precepts.

ח

(57) Yahweh is my portion: I have said that I would observe your words.

(58) I entreated your favor with my whole heart: be merciful unto me according to your word.

(59) I thought on my ways, and turned my feet unto your testimonies.

(60) **I made haste, and delayed not, to observe your commandments.**

(61) The cords of the wicked have wrapped me round; *but* I have not forgotten your Torah.

(62) **At midnight I will rise to give thanks unto you because of your righteous ordinances.**

(63) I am a companion of all them that fear you, and of them that observe your precepts.

(64) The earth, O Yahweh, is full of your lovingkindness: **teach me your statutes.**

ט

(65) You have dealt well with your servant, O Yahweh, according unto your word.

(66) Teach me good judgment and knowledge; For I have believed in your commandments.

(67) Before I was afflicted I went astray; But now I observe your word.

(68) You are good, and do good; **teach me your statutes.**

(69) The proud have forged a lie against me: **with my whole heart will I keep your precepts.**

(70) Their heart is as fat as grease; but **I delight in your Torah.**

(71) It is good for me that I have been afflicted; **that I may learn your statutes.**

(72) **The Torah of your mouth is better unto me than thousands of gold and silver.**

י

(73) Your hands have made me and fashioned me: **give me understanding, that I may learn your commandments.**

(74) They that fear you shall see me and be glad, Because I have hoped in your word.

(75) I know, O Yahweh, that your judgments are righteous, and that in faithfulness you have afflicted me.

(76) Let, I pray you, your lovingkindness be for my comfort, according to your word unto your servant.

(77) Let your tender mercies come unto me, that I may live; **for your Torah is my delight.**

(78) Let the proud be put to shame; for they have overthrown me wrongfully: *but* I **will meditate on your precepts.**

(79) Let those that fear you turn unto me; and they shall know your testimonies.

(80) **Let my heart be perfect in your statutes,** that I be not put to shame.

כ

(81) My soul faints for your salvation; *But* I hope in your word.

(82) My eyes fail for your word, while I say, When will you comfort me?

(83) For I am become like a wine-skin in the smoke; Yet do I not forget your statutes.

(84) How many are the days of your servant? When will you execute judgment on them that persecute me?

(85) **The proud** have dug pits for me, who **are not according to your Torah.**

(86) **All your commandments are faithful**: they persecute me wrongfully; help you me.

(87) They had almost consumed me upon earth; but I forsook not your precepts.

(88) Quicken me after your lovingkindness; so shall I observe the testimony of your mouth.

ל

(89) Forever, O Yahweh, Your word is settled in heaven.

(90) Your faithfulness is unto all generations: You have established the earth, and it abides.

(91) They abide this day according to your ordinances; for all things are your servants.

(92) **Unless your Torah had been my delight, I should then have perished in my affliction.**

(93) **I will never forget your precepts; for with them you have quickened me.**

(94) I am yours, save me; for I have sought your precepts.

(95) The wicked have waited for me, to destroy me; *but* I will consider your testimonies.

(96) I have seen an end of all perfection; *but* your commandment is exceeding broad.

מ

(97) **Oh how love I your Torah! It is my meditation all the day.**

(98) **Your commandments make me wiser than my enemies**; for they are ever with me.

(99) **I have more understanding than all my teachers; for your testimonies are my meditation.**

(100) **I understand more than the aged, because I have kept your precepts.**

(101) I have refrained my feet from every evil way, that I might observe your word.

(102) **I have not turned aside from your ordinances**; for you have taught me.

(103) How sweet are your words unto my taste! *Yea, sweeter* than honey to my mouth!

(104) **Through your precepts I get understanding**: therefore I hate every false way.

נ

(105) Your word is a lamp unto my feet, and light unto my path.

(106) I have sworn, and have confirmed it, **That I will observe your righteous ordinances.**

(107) I am afflicted very much: Quicken me, O Yahweh, according unto your word.

(108) Accept, I beseech you, the freewill-offerings of my mouth, O Yahweh, and teach me your ordinances.

(109) My soul is continually in my hand; yet do **I not forget your Torah.**

(110) The wicked have laid a snare for me; yet have I not gone astray from your precepts.

(111) **Your testimonies have I taken as a heritage forever; for they are the**

rejoicing of my heart.

(112) **I have inclined my heart to perform your statutes forever, even unto the end.**

ס

(113) I hate them that are of a double mind; but **your Torah do I love.**

(114) You are my hiding-place and my shield: I hope in your word.

(115) Depart from me, you evil-doers, **that I may keep the commandments of my Elohim.**

(116) Uphold me according unto your word, that I may live; and let me not be ashamed of my hope.

(117) Hold you me up, and I shall be safe, and shall have respect unto your statutes continually.

(118) You have set at nought all them that err from your statutes; for their deceit is falsehood.

(119) You put away all the wicked of the earth like dross: **therefore I love your testimonies.**

(120) My flesh trembles for fear of you; and I am afraid of your judgments.

ע

(121) I have done justice and righteousness: Leave me not to my oppressors.

(122) Be surety for your servant for good: let not the proud oppress me.

(123) My eyes fail for your salvation, and for your righteous word.

(124) Deal with your servant according unto your lovingkindness, and **teach me your statutes.**

(125) I am your servant; give me understanding, **that I may know your testimonies.**

(126) It is time for Yahweh to work; for they have made void your Torah.

(127) **Therefore I love your commandments above gold, yea, above fine gold.**

(128) **Therefore I esteem all** *your* **precepts concerning all** *things* **to be right**; *and* I hate every false way.

פ

(129) **Your testimonies are wonderful**; therefore does my soul keep them.

(130) The opening of your words gives light; it gives understanding unto the simple.

(131) I opened wide my mouth, and panted; **for I longed for your commandments.**

(132) Turn you unto me, and have mercy upon me, as you used to do unto those that love your name.

(133) Establish my footsteps in your word; and let not any iniquity have dominion over me.

(134) Redeem me from the oppression of man: **so will I observe your precepts.**

(135) Make your face to shine upon your servant; and **teach me your statutes.**

(136) **Streams of water run down mine eyes, because they observe not your Torah.**

צ

(137) Righteous are you, O Yahweh, and upright are your judgments.

(138) **You have commanded your testimonies in righteousness and very faithfulness.**

(139) My zeal has consumed me, because my adversaries have forgotten your words.

(140) Your word is very pure; therefore your servant loves it.

(141) I am small and despised; *yet* **do I not forget your precepts.**

(142) **Your righteousness is an everlasting righteousness, and your Torah is truth.**

(143) Trouble and anguish have taken hold on me; *yet* **your commandments are my delight.**

(144) **Your testimonies are righteous forever: give me understanding, and I shall live.**

ק

(145) I have called with my whole heart; answer me, O Yahweh: **I will keep your statutes.**

(146) **I have called unto you; save me, and I shall observe your testimonies.**

(147) I anticipated the dawning of the morning, and cried: I hoped in your words.

(148) My eyes anticipated the night-watches, that I might meditate on your word.

(149) Hear my voice according unto your lovingkindness: **quicken me, O Yahweh, according to your ordinances.**

(150) **They draw near that follow after wickedness; they are far from your Torah.**

(151) You are near, O Yahweh; and **all your commandments are truth.**

(152) **Of old have I known from Your testimonies, that you have founded them forever.**

ר

(153) Consider my affliction, and deliver me; for **I do not forget your Torah.**

(154) Plead you my cause, and redeem me: quicken me according to your word.

(155) **Salvation is far from the wicked; for they seek not your statutes.**

(156) Great are your tender mercies, O Yahweh: **quicken me according to your ordinances.**

(157) Many are my persecutors and my adversaries; *yet* **have I not swerved from your testimonies.**

(158) I beheld the treacherous, and was grieved, because they observe not your word.

(159) **Consider how I love your precepts: quicken me, O Yahweh, according to your lovingkindness.**

(160) **The sum of your word is truth; and every one of your righteous ordinances** *endures* **forever.**

ש

(161) Princes have persecuted me without a cause; but my heart stands in awe of your words.

(162) I rejoice at your word, as one that finds great spoil.

(163) I hate and abhor falsehood; *But* your Torah do I love.

(164) Seven times a day do I praise you, because of your righteous ordinances.

(165) Great peace have they that love your Torah; and they have no occasion of stumbling.

(166) I have hoped for your salvation, O Yahweh, and have done your commandments.

(167) My soul hath observed your testimonies; and I love them exceedingly.

(168) I have observed your precepts and your testimonies; for all my ways are before you.

ת

(169) Let my cry come near before you, O Yahweh: give me understanding according to your word.

(170) Let my supplication come before you: deliver me according to your word.

(171) Let my lips utter praise; for you teach me your statutes.

(172) Let my tongue sing of your word; for all your commandments are righteousness.

(173) Let your hand be ready to help me; for I have chosen your precepts.

(174) I have longed for your salvation, O Yahweh; and your Torah is my delight.

(175) Let my soul live, and it shall praise you; and let your ordinances help me.

(176) I have gone astray like a lost sheep; seek your servant; for I do not forget your commandments.

INDEX OF SCRIPTURES

Made in the USA
Columbia, SC
27 June 2024